Microsoft® Small Business Kit

Joanna L. Krotz
John Pierce
Ben Ryan

PUBLISHED BY
Microsoft Press
A Division of Microsoft Corporation
One Microsoft Way
Redmond, Washington 98052-6399

Library of Congress Cataloging-in-Publication Data
Krotz, Joanna L.
    Microsoft Small Business Kit / Joanna L. Krotz, John Pierce, Ben Ryan.
       p. cm.
    Includes index.
    ISBN 0-7356-2054-7
    1. New business enterprises I. Pierce, John, 1954- II. Ryan, Ben, 1950- III. Title.

  HD62.5.K76 2004
  658.1'1'0285--dc22   2004054269

Printed and bound in the United States of America.

1 2 3 4 5 6 7 8 9   QWT   9 8 7 6 5 4

Distributed in Canada by H.B. Fenn and Company Ltd.

A CIP catalogue record for this book is available from the British Library.

Microsoft Press books are available through booksellers and distributors worldwide. For further information about international editions, contact your local Microsoft Corporation office or contact Microsoft Press International directly at fax (425) 936-7329. Visit our Web site at www.microsoft.com/learning/. Send comments to *mspinput@microsoft.com*.

Microsoft, ActiveSync, bCentral, Encarta, FrontPage, Hotmail, Microsoft Press, MSN, Outlook, PivotChart, PivotTable, PowerPoint, SharePoint, Tahoma, Verdana, Windows, and Windows Server are either registered trademarks or trademarks of Microsoft Corporation in the United States and/or other countries. Other product and company names mentioned herein may be the trademarks of their respective owners.

The example companies, organizations, products, domain names, e-mail addresses, logos, people, places, and events depicted herein are fictitious. No association with any real company, organization, product, domain name, e-mail address, logo, person, place, or event is intended or should be inferred.

This book expresses the author's views and opinions. The information contained in this book is provided without any express, statutory, or implied warranties. Neither the authors, Microsoft Corporation, nor its resellers or distributors will be held liable for any damages caused or alleged to be caused either directly or indirectly by this book.

Acquisitions Editor: Juliana Aldous Atkinson
Developmental and Project Editor: Sandra Haynes
Technical Editor: Jim Johnson
Copy Editor: Jennifer Harris
Indexer: Julie Hatley

Body Part No. X10-80197

Table of Contents

Acknowledgments xiii

About the CD. xv

Introduction. xvii

Part One **Fun & Fundamentals: Control What You Can**

Chapter One **Thinking It Through** **2**

How to Begin. 4

Small Biz Profile 5

Some Ideas for Start-Ups 6

Learning from Experience 9

Meeting Tomorrow's Customer. 11

What It Takes: A Woman Who Can't Hear "No" 15

Ready, Set, Go 18

For More Information. 18

Chapter Two **Developing a Business Plan** **20**

Who Needs a Plan?. 22

Getting a Reality Check 22

Planning Affordable Market Research 24

How to Find Your Best Customer 25

Consider Your Product Price Tag 27

Choosing a Business Structure 29

Sole Proprietorship 30

DBA, or Doing Business As 31

C Corporation 32

Subchapter S Corporation. 33

General Partnerships 34

Limited Liability Corporation (LLC) 36

Guidelines for Creating Your Plan. 36

Tone Will Tell. 40

Doing It with Office: Online Business Plan Templates. 41

Basic Training 42

Doing Your Homework in Word 44

Doing It with Styles. 45

A Few Extras: More Tips for Your Professional Documents. 48

For More Information. 49

Chapter Three	**How to Find Backing**	**52**
	Financing Basics	54
	Growing in Stages	54
	Preparing for the Unexpected	56
	Savings and Credit Cards	58
	Tapping Family, Friends, and Generous Relatives	60
	Bootstrapping—Lean and Mean Financing	62
	Angels Who Help You Fly	64
	Approaching an Angel	66
	Loans and Venture Capitalists	67
	Working with a Commercial Bank	67
	Factoring or Commercial Finance Companies	70
	Government Loans and Programs	70
	Accessing Venture Capital	73
	For More Information	74
Chapter Four	**Self-Preservation**	**76**
	Investigating Licenses and Permits	78
	Applying for a Federal Taxpayer ID	80
	Finding Insurance and Reassurance	81
	Why Insurance Matters	81
	What Is Business Insurance?	82
	Choosing Coverage	83
	Reviewing Life Insurance Needs	84
	Protecting Your Home Business	85
	Renting Space and Signing Leases	86
	Signing a Lease	87
	Tackling Contract Concerns	88
	Recordkeeping Counts	89
	Paying Yourself	91
	Creating the Right Impression	93
	Forming an Advisory Board	95
	For More Information	97

Part Two   Profit and Loss: Getting the Facts on Figures

Chapter Five **Follow the Money** **100**

Accounting Essentials.. 103

    Choosing the Cash Method or the Accrual Method 103

    Double-Entry Accounting 105

Preparing Financial Statements: The Balance Sheet
and the Income Statement 106

Using a Chart of Accounts................................... 108

    Accounts Receivable 109

    Inventory.. 110

    Fixed Assets 111

    Liabilities.. 112

    Net Worth... 114

Cutting Paychecks.. 114

Preparing and Managing a Budget 116

Managing Cash Flow 121

List of Resources 123

For More Information.. 124

Chapter Six **Tax Tactics** **126**

Tax Strategies for Major Business Expenses.................... 128

    Exceptions to the Rules 129

How to Interview a Tax Pro 131

Secrets Tax Pros Never Share................................ 134

Frequent Tax and Bookkeeping Mistakes 136

Travel Expense Deduction Strategies 138

When a PC at Home Isn't a Home PC 140

For More Information.. 143

Chapter Seven **By the Numbers: Analyzing Your
Business with Excel** **144**

Excel Training and Assistance 146

What Data Should I Collect?.................................. 147

"What If I...?": Tools for Analyzing Common
Business Questions 148

Knowing What You Need to Meet Your Goals:
Using the Goal Seek Command............................149

A Little Change Can Make a Difference:
Sensitivity Analysis with Data Tables 154

Managing Business Scenarios 161

Spotting Trends: Sorting, Filtering, and
Charting Information.. **165**

Sorting to See Groups and Patterns 166

Filtering Information to View Selected Records 167

Charting Data..171

Slicing and Dicing Your Business Data: Why You
Should Use a PivotTable **173**

Two Important Excel Functions **178**

For More Information **180**

Part Three

Makes and Models: How to Stand Out in a Crowd

Chapter Eight

Branding Basics **182**

Developing Brand Personality 184

Image Counts 184

What Is the Mission of Your Business? 186

Focusing on Your Point of Difference (POD) 188

Finding the Right Image: Logos and Icons..................... 190

Mastering Your Domains: Two Steps for
Building a Presence on the Web 192

Domain name registration scams 194

Free Web site hosting....................................196

Web site forwarding 196

Building Credibility.. 198

Protecting Your Intellectual Property: Trademarks,
Copyrights, and Patents...................................... 199

Search and protect 201

The limits of protection..................................204

Hire an experienced pro.................................205

List of Resources 206

For More Information 206

Chapter Nine   **Crafting Your Message** **208**

Disciplined Messaging and the Seamless Sell. 210

    Marketing mandate 211

Developing a Marketing Strategy. 212

Selling Benefits, Not Features 213

Making Messages Work Across Channels 216

Marketing Return on Investment (ROI) 217

    Calculate the NPV of your marketing. 218

Low-Cost, High-Impact Marketing Ideas. 220

    Consider marketing with a cause 224

    Keyword power 234

Generating Sales Leads. 236

For More Information. 242

Chapter Ten   **Go to Market with Publisher,**
Make a Pitch with PowerPoint. **244**

Business Communications and Microsoft Publisher 246

    A personal touch 247

    Don't forget your Web host 254

    Publisher doesn't provide a shopping cart. 257

    Stay on message 264

    Saving Publisher 2003 files for earlier
    versions of Publisher 265

    Page preparedness 269

The Pitch and the Presentation: Using
Microsoft PowerPoint 2003 269

    Room for disagreement. 270

    The PowerPoint task pane. 273

For More Information. 284

Part Four   **Connect and Conquer: Building the Company**

Chapter Eleven   **The Customer Comes First** **286**

Identifying Your Best Customers: The 80/20 Rule 288

    Creating a Customer Database. 289

    Leveraging Customer Intelligence 291

Rewarding Return Customers 294
    Timing Your Marketing Message 296
    When Good Customers Go Bad 298
Protecting Customer Trust and Privacy 299
Understanding When to Expand 301
    Planning for Growing Pains 302
Forging Strategic Alliances 303
For More Information 305

Chapter 12   **Managing Customer Contacts: Business Contact Manager 306**

Understanding What Business Contact
Manager (BCM) Can Do 309
    BCM doesn't work with Exchange 310
    More assistance for using BCM 312
Installing and Running BCM 313
    BCM installation locations 314
Working with Business Contacts 317
    Importing contact data 317
Creating and Using Accounts 321
    The useful Account History list 322
Creating and Using Opportunities 324
    Importing a product list 326
Tracking Item History 327
    View the history of an item 329
Attaching Items 329
Creating Reports 330
    Use AND and OR logic 334
Importing and Exporting Information 336
    What's the Default Quantity field? 339
Managing Your BCM Data 341
    Keep your backup copies in a safe place 342
    Remove a database associated
    with the current profile 343
For More Information 344

Part Five **Gurus, Guides, and Staff: Employment Dos and Don'ts**

Chapter Thirteen **Hiring and Firing** **346**

When to Hire. 348

    Your Very First Employee. 348

    Hiring for Next-Level Growth 350

Where to Find Talent 351

Conducting Interviews and Background Checks 353

    Find Out Who You're Really Hiring 355

    Consider Professional Screening. 356

Recruiting the 21st-Century Team 357

    Be Careful About Hiring Friends 360

    Why Drafting a Company Handbook Is a
    Smart Use of Precious Time 361

Figuring Out How Much to Pay 367

Providing Benefits You Can Afford. 370

    Healthcare Innovations 373

Deciding When to Call It Quits. 374

For More Information. 376

Chapter Fourteen **Managing Like a Coach**. **378**

The Bossing Thing. 380

Delegating: Dos and Don'ts. 381

Making Employees Feel Valued 384

    Saying Thanks with Low-Cost Rewards 385

Measuring Performance. 386

    Reviewing the Review 387

    Tough Love and Accountability. 389

Training Staff Pays Off. 390

    E-Learning Options 392

Managing the New Work Force 395

    Getting Return on Investment (ROI) from
    On-Staff Telecommuters 395

    Harnessing the Power of Free Agents 397

For More Information. 399

Part Six   The Electronic Desk, The Digital Business

Chapter Fifteen   **The Outlook Is Bright:
E-Mail and Your Business** **404**

E-mail facts and figures 406

   E-Mail Decisions: What Do You
and Your Business Need? 407

Web hosting options 407

E-mail signatures as a simple marketing tool 410

Separate personal and business e-mail 411

Implementing Small Business Server 412

   Online Training and Assistance for Outlook 412

   E-Mail Security and Protecting E-Mail Data 413

Beware the messenger 418

   Taking Care of the Messages You Need
and Those You Don't 421

Flags in Outlook Express 424

Retaining records 434

   Simple E-Mail Marketing: Adding a Signature 435

   Scheduling Appointments and Tasks 438

Synchronizing Outlook and a PocketPC 439

   For More Information 440

Chapter Sixteen   **Small Business Networks and Servers** **442**

Determining Needs and Available Choices 444

   Assessing Your Location 444

   Determining Service Types and Availability 445

   Planning Your Local Area Network (LAN) 447

Selecting Network Types 449

   Wired Networks: Ethernet 449

   Wireless Networks: Wi-Fi 450

   Mixed Network Types 451

   Other Networking Methods 451

Choosing Networking Equipment 451

   Routers and Hubs and Servers, Oh My! 452

Enabling Mobile Computing. 456

Securing Your Network. 457

For More Information. 457

Chapter Seventeen **Computer Security Basics. 458**

Considering Access Requirements 460

    Planning to Share Data 460

    Controlling Data. 461

Planning Physical Security 467

    Avoiding Hardware Theft. 468

    Guarding Against Data Loss 468

Backing Up Your Data. 469

    Developing a Backup Strategy 469

    Implementing a Backup Plan. 470

Protecting Against Viruses. 472

    Choosing an Antivirus Program 473

    Maintaining Virus Protection. 474

Choosing and Using Firewalls 474

Dealing with Spyware and Adware. 475

For More Information. 476

Index. 478

Acknowledgments

My thanks go to Bevolyn Williams-Harold for her research support.

--Joanna L. Krotz

My thanks and appreciation to Juliana Aldous, Josh Barnhill, Jennifer Harris, Sandra Haynes, Jim Johnson, Joanna Krotz, Lucinda Rowley, and Ben Ryan for our work together on this book.

--John Pierce

About the CD

On the CD enclosed in the back of this book, you will find an electronic version of this book, dozens of templates and sample files, hundreds of links to resources on the World Wide Web, and much more.

These resources have been selected to give you a broad overview of the wide variety of information available to you as you plan, launch, and succeed with your new business. The resources are organized chapter by chapter; in some cases, there are subsections that reflect the organization of this book.

Most of the Web sites referenced are rich sources of further ideas and links. All of these Web sites are accurate at the time of this writing, but—as you very likely already know—Web pages have a way of moving around much faster than a printed reference can be updated. When information has disappeared, going back to the "root" site (www.microsoft.com, for example) will often lead you to new links that you can follow to the same data. Also try searching for the page with MSN Search, Google, Teoma, or another tool.

Always bear in mind that no one guarantees the accuracy of information on the Web: if it sounds too good to be true, it probably is. Many searches for business resources will point you to pay sites, consultants, or software. Some of these are great and worth every penny, but there's also a vast amount of free information available to you. As you will find out in a few chapters, managing your money is a critical task in business. Don't be misled by anyone who tells you, "It's a deductible business expense"—that might be true, but it is still money out of your pocket!

CD Requirements

There are no special requirements for using the enclosed CD. You will need a Web browser (Internet Explorer is recommended) and a CD drive, of course, but the links and files will be accessible to you on a PC or a Macintosh. The template files assume that you have access to Microsoft Office; we have used Microsoft Office 2003, but most of the files can be used with older versions of Office and with various other compatible software programs. If you do not already have Adobe Reader (or its antecedent, Acrobat Reader), you might want to download that standard software, which is used by the Internal Revenue Service (IRS) and the Small Business Administration (SBA), as well as by many other organizations. There's a link on the CD to the free download site.

Introduction: Are You the Entrepreneurial Type?

People often say to me, "When you built the system, you must have known that making it self-sustainable was the only way eBay could grow to serve 40 million users a day." Well...nope. I made the system self-sustaining for one reason: Back when I launched eBay on Labor Day 1995, eBay wasn't my business—it was my hobby. I had to build a system that was self-sustaining... So I guess what I'm trying to tell you is: Whatever future you're building,...don't try to program everything...Build a platform— prepare for the unexpected.

— Pierre Omidyar, founder of eBay, May 2002 commencement speech, Tufts University

Once upon a time, the American Dream was built on working 40 years at some monolithic organization and then walking away with a gold watch, a company pension (remember those?), and a house with requisite white picket fence—or was it a palm tree? Those days are gone, of course. The renovated American Dream, believe it or not, is the one you're now contemplating: becoming an entrepreneur, someone who charts his or her own course, a calculated risk-taker who thrives on personal independence and innovation. Every entrepreneur takes the heat for his or her own destiny. Come what may, you're in charge. In the vividly updated and contemporary American Dream, you get to boss yourself. It's your show to produce. Your ball to run with. Your screen to write on. Your game. Your strategy. Your rules. Breathtaking, isn't it?

The business of creating a business is a fabulous adventure. While it's true that only a fraction of start-ups hit the big time, it's equally true that there's no definitive way to predict which businesses will rocket up and which will fall by the wayside. The next icon of entrepreneurial derring-do, the face gracing national magazine covers, could turn out to be you. Only one thing is for sure. If you don't make the attempt, you won't have the opportunity to find out.

In their eye-opening 1996 bestseller *The Millionaire Next Door*, which documents how America's elite get rich and stay rich, authors Thomas Stanley and William Danko found that a staggering two-thirds of the nation's 3.5

million millionaires are self-employed. These hard-working and surprisingly frugal business owners bossed themselves into the ranks of the rich and successful. Maybe you can, too. Certainly, this book is here to help you do just that, step by step, tip by tip, chapter by chapter—from business concept to business plan, company launch, up-and-running operation, and then next-stage growth.

Choosing to launch a business is hardly ever a snap decision. It's also a different process and timeline for every entrepreneur. (See the section "How to Begin" on page 4 for tips about getting started, and see "Small Biz Profile" on page 5 for a snapshot of the American small business owner.) One typical scenario? A skilled professional begins taking jobs or projects on the side of a full-time company position. Buzz builds; customers call. Slowly, the pro eases into full-time, full-blown launch as the culmination of a long-envisioned evolution.

Another profile? Months or perhaps years earlier, an idea or an event or an experience fueled a spark of commercial excitement. That bit of brainstorm refuses to calm or fade. After several weeks, or maybe a decade, the spark generates a full-scale energy field that keeps throwing off heat. The business is born of meticulous plans, inventions, and long-simmering desire. (See the section "What It Takes: A Woman Who Can't Hear 'No'" on page 15 to learn about revving up a business model.)

Just as often, fully employed people who are feeling smothered in corporate silos realize, in their hearts, that they can produce such a better, smarter mousetrap that only a fool or a coward would keep hanging around corporate precincts. Then there are the restless, the downsized, the creative change agents or misfits, and the underestimated and underutilized employees—many of whom stumble into entrepreneurship "accidentally on purpose." These budding owners don't consciously decide, "Now I will set up a business." They simply begin supplying a service or producing a product. They discover, to their delight, that they can make some money doing it. Then they realize that they love what they're doing. In truth and in time, the venture starts the owner, rather than the other way around. Such "freelancers" ultimately stop marking time and put their feet on a path. They found their own company. (See the section "Preparing for the Unexpected," on page 56 to feel this magic.)

Those are only a few instances of the fever known as "starting a business." There are dozens. Yet each one shares recognizable qualities. Most often mentioned is the need for entrepreneurs to have "passion." But there's a much better way to define this necessary quality. Think of it as Reason + Feeling.

Controlled fire. You do need passion to start your own business, but it's passion soldered to ambition, determination, and discipline. Intense feelings alone don't get the job done. You must also have patience, grit, and drive.

If you have never felt that surge—an electric jolt of "I'm going to do it my way and I can't wait"—then perhaps you should keep turning over your idea or holding on to that "freelance" mindset for a while longer before leaping into the entrepreneurial fray. Because, truthfully, launching a business is a towering, life-changing decision. Make no mistake.

Driving a start-up is not a nifty way to avoid getting up for work in the morning. It's not an entertaining interlude of playing "boss." Hardly. Starting a business is flat-out commitment and challenge. Day in. Day out. Weekends. Nights. Years. All the time. The organization you start and shape will be a moving, breathing, daunting, hungry organism that eats at least as much in time, energy, and resources as it returns in profit and pride—if, that is, you're one of the lucky ones.

Before conceiving any semblance of a business plan, before hitting up friends or relatives for funding, before shopping for gear and technology, before setting up accounting systems, and long before a first sale or customer (all of which are discussed in the chapters that follow), you need a smart commercial idea. You must decide how your business will meet a market or consumer need that no one else can or will do as fast or as cost-effectively or as exquisitely as you can. And be prepared for change. As likely as not, you'll go through several iterations and refinements of that idea before settling on your business model. Be honest about your strengths and weaknesses. If you lack skills or experience, hire them, or take the time to get yourself up to speed. Make sure you're a self-starter. No one will be checking your work or telling you what to do. You must also be comfortable selling your idea and your products and your company, so you might need to brush up on presentation skills—whether or not you hire a salesperson. You should be the business's most effective advocate. (See the section "Creating the Right Impression" on page 93 to learn more about honing presentations.)

Despite those challenges, the rewards of running your own business are unlike any other enterprise. Entrepreneurs come in all sizes and shapes, but they all seem to exude a sense of purpose and pride. As you begin your business, remember to be your own best fan. Communicate the confidence that you're the ideal architect to shape this business. You will get it right. And this guidebook will help you to do it.

Part One

Fun & Fundamentals: Control What You Can

In this part

Chapter One   Thinking It Through 2
Chapter Two   Developing a Business Plan 20
Chapter Three   How to Find Backing 52
Chapter Four   Self-Preservation 76

"The Way I see it, if you want the rainbow, you gotta put up with the rain."

— *Dolly Parton*

Chapter One

Thinking It Through

The high-wire act of starting a business can fly only when it's built on clear-eyed evaluations of your idea and your expectations for timing and resources. Here is top-line advice and inspiration to help you see clearly before your big leap. Here too are insights into the current climate for small business.

Chapters that follow offer step-by-step guides to the decisions and the details of ramping up and running a business you can proudly call your own.

Chapter One: **Thinking It Through**

Part One:
Fun &
Fundamentals:
Control What
You Can

What you'll find:

- ❏ How to begin
- ❏ Small biz profile
- ❏ Some ideas for start-ups
- ❏ Learning from experience
- ❏ Meeting tomorrow's customer
- ❏ What it takes: A woman who can't hear "No"
- ❏ Ready, set, go

Part One:
Fun &
Fundamentals:
Control What
You Can

Microsoft Small Business Kit

How to Begin

Are you ready to run your own show? The dream of starting a business means moving into reality. You must cross a serious bridge between wishing and doing. Dreams are achieved by planning and by work. As a would-be entrepreneur, you need to figure out how to get from daydream to up-and-going, how to make progress despite trials and errors (and these will occur), and how to remain focused on creating a profitable business.

Soon enough, you will also need to think about a business plan, which typically takes several months to draft and polish. (See Chapter 2, "Developing a Business Plan.") You will need keen-eyed financial projections. (See Part Two, "Profit and Loss: Getting the Facts on Figures.") You will want to develop mission-controlled marketing, branding, and promotions. (See Part Three, "Makes and Models: How to Stand Out from the Crowd.") You will also want to develop all the other elements of launching and running a business, as described in the following sections.

All of that excitement lies ahead. But first things first. Before you dive into decisions and details, and before you kick up energy and engage the support of friends, family, partners, and potential backers, take a step back. Think.

Define what it is you plan to offer. Analyze how you will get money, how you will spend money, and how you will nourish your idea into operation. To begin, get some hardheaded answers to these burning and basic questions:

1. What is your product? Is it viable? Can you sell it? Will customers want it and pay enough to make it worth your while?

2. What's your team? Do you have the skills you need? Who must you recruit or persuade to work with you?

3. Can you achieve the financial results you expect? How much debt can you carry? Do you have enough cash to carry you until breakeven and profitability?

4. Are you self-directed, organized, and efficient? Can you manage your time and resources to accomplish what must get done?

5. Do you have the perseverance to keep going despite setbacks and challenges?

Chapter One: **Thinking It Through**

Part One:
Fun &
Fundamentals:
Control What
You Can

Small Biz Profile

What is a small business, really? Actually, there is no official definition. Some authorities say small businesses are defined by annual revenues—say, $5 million or less. Others base their definition on how many employees the company has. The closest thing to a formal definition comes from the U.S. Small Business Administration (SBA), and even that varies depending on which industry you're talking about. According to the SBA, you're a small business if you meet one of the following criteria:

Small Business Snapshot

According to the Small Business Administration (SBA):

- There are nearly 23 million small businesses in the United States

- 18 million business owners are sole proprietors

- The top industries for business owners are services, retail, construction, manufacturing, and financial services, including insurance and real estate

- 57 percent of small firms use the Internet

- For most manufacturing and mining industries, you have 500 employees, or less

- For wholesale trade industries, you have 100 employees, or less

- For most retail and service industries, your annual revenues are $6 million, or less

- For most general and heavy construction industries, your annual revenues are $28.5 million, or less

- For all special trade contractors, your annual revenues are $12 million, or less

- For most agricultural industries, your annual revenues are $1 million, or less

Wherever you draw the lines, it's clear that small business increasingly drives the U.S. economy. Smaller enterprises now employ about half of the nation's workforce. For all sorts of reasons, it's a great time to start your own enterprise. Over the past few years, a wealth of resources and funding has arisen to support the growing ranks of small business wannabes. It's easier for all kinds of people to get a business up and going. Banks and other institutional lenders are much more friendly to the needs of start-up owners than they were even 10 years ago. Moreover, a slew of facilities across the country now offer affordable courses, both in traditional classrooms and online, to help you fill in any gaps you might have in knowledge or skills. (See the section "Training Staff Pays Off," on page 390.)

Part One:
Fun &
Fundamentals:
Control What
You Can

Microsoft Small Business Kit

Entrepreneurs used to be young, white, and male. No longer. Fueled by the country's increasing diversity; an aging workforce; cheap, networked technology; and growing desires to match avocations to occupations, entrepreneurs of every age, race, sex, and national origin are busy setting up shop.

Entrepreneurs Look More and More Like America

Across the United States, entrepreneurs of every race, sex, age, and ethnic origin. Are starting and running their own businesses.

- Women-owned firms, defined as a 50 percent or greater share of ownership, are growing at close to twice the rate of all privately held firms (17 percent vs. 9 percent). The women leading these companies spend an estimated $546 billion annually on payroll and benefits, according to the Center for Women's Business Research. (Visit www.womensbusinessresearch.org.)

- Minorities owned only 7 percent of U.S. firms in 1982, but that more than doubled, to about 15 percent, by 1997, according to the SBA. By 2001, minority-owned businesses generated revenues of $591 billion, created 4.5 million jobs, and provided about $96 billion in payroll.

- The average age of entrepreneurs is 39 years old.

As of 2004, there were nearly 11 million privately held firms in the United States that were 50 percent or more women-owned, accounting for nearly half (48 percent) of all privately held firms in the country. These firms generate a whopping $2.5 trillion in sales and employ a staggering 19 million people nationwide, according to the Center for Women's Business Research, a nonprofit organization based in Washington, D.C. Businesses owned by Asian-American, Hispanic, and African-American entrepreneurs also are on the rise. For instance, the ING Gazelle Index, an annual survey conducted by the U.S financial services company, solicits input from 350 CEOs of the nation's fastest-growing African-American–owned businesses with 10 to 100 employees. The Index found that these Gazelles experienced an average employment growth over the past five years of a blistering 212 percent. More than half of the Gazelles (51 percent) anticipated increased hiring in 2004.

Some Ideas for Start-Ups

Nobody can tell you what kind of business to start. Naturally, you're the one who must decide what you will sell and how to create a viable business model and then (likely as not) how to refine the business model so that it actually turns a profit. Even so, just by way of potential inspiration, here's a rundown of some long-term market trends that might fuel businesses. These ideas are meant only as background, a way of getting entrepreneurial juices going rather than a real blueprint to build. Scroll through these notions and consider: What meaningful consumer or business-to-business (B2B) services or products can you produce?

Chapter One: **Thinking It Through**

Part One:
Fun &
Fundamentals:
Control What
You Can

Feather upscale nests   The top end of the real estate market has been booming in recent years. Irresistibly low mortgage rates during 2000
through 2003 motivated thousands of homeowners to leverage equity
and trade up. That translates into opportunities for high-quality services for childcare, household help, interior and landscape design or
maintenance, and home alarms or security. Also consider that home
service companies require support systems, like recruiters, accountants, marketers, product suppliers, and private investigators for background checks and other evaluations.

Make hay with fur or fins   Treating pets like family is a fast-growing trend,
according to consumer researcher Packaged Facts. In 2002, pet product sales racked up a staggering $7.5 billion. This "humanization of
pets" suggests many business ideas, including (yes, really) luxury pet
resorts and spas, grooming services, gourmet pet food and delivery
services, pet sitting, daycare, and walking services. Pet toy design and
manufacture is also blossoming. Hasbro recently debuted Tonka-
brand toys for dogs (see the section "Financing Basics," on page 54 to
learn about a pet business that went from making $5,000 to $10 million). To tap into the market, imagine human or childcare needs that
can migrate. Pet obesity, for instance, is a growing problem, but only
about 1 percent of pet dogs and cats carry owner-purchased health
and life insurance. That market has been growing at a rocketing 45
percent annually and is valued at about $88 million.

Bet on boomers   As you've surely heard, Americans are living longer and
enjoying active retirements. During the 1990s, seniors over age 85
increased by a dramatic 37 percent, compared to only a 13 percent
increase for the overall population, according to the U.S. Census. So
senior-care businesses are burgeoning, whether these are products or
services and whether for in-home or facility use. Bigger opportunities
are yet to come. In 2011, the first wave of 80 million baby boomers
will turn 65. By 2030, one in every five people is likely to be 65 or
older. There are dozens of businesses that can serve this dominant
generation that intends to stay forever young. Try investigating cos-
metic maintenance or makeover services, from dentistry and plastic
surgery to chiropractics and physical therapy, massage and spa services, skincare services and products, makeup, and fashion as well as
senior educational, recreational, or travel agencies. Also consider long-
term-care insurance, medical supplies, home design products or s
vices that help the aging and disabled, and in-home food and
services.

Part One:
Fun &
Fundamentals:
Control What
You Can

Microsoft Small Business Kit

Profit on the cutting edge   Technology, information, and life sciences services, research, and products are providing increasing opportunities for start-ups. The biotech industry is particularly hot. Ever more frequently, nimble biotech companies announce breakthroughs that are helping to develop diagnostics and therapies to cure major diseases, such as cancer and autoimmune diseases like diabetes and multiple sclerosis. To get ahead of this curve, consider training and staffing agencies that specialize in life sciences technicians or bioinformatics, as well as management, sales, and marketing services for science-based businesses; legal and paralegal services; and bioengineering products, such as medical devices, robotic instruments, and software.

The Competitive Landscape

Small business owners see the climate as increasingly competitive. According to a National Federation of Independent Business (NFIB) poll in 2004:

- 81 percent of small business owners say today's economic climate is highly competitive

- More than half (57 percent) of small businesses typically compete against a mix of large and small companies

- Nearly half (49 percent) of small business owners say their primary competition is located within ten miles of their business

- One in five small business owners (21 percent) think that a major competitor is competing against his or her company using illegal or unethical means. To remain competitive, small businesses deliver the highest possible quality (87 percent) and offer better service (83 percent).

Go for green   Escalating fears about the safety of the food chain because of mad cow disease and other outbreaks are changing public perceptions. Increasingly, consumers are paying a premium for the safety or reassurance of organic and locally grown or produced foods and products.

Become weight conscious   In the U.S, millions of people are desperately seeking to lose weight and become healthier. Low-calorie and health-conscious foods as well as diet and fitness services are going gangbusters. Sales of diet candy, as just one example, rose 51 percent in twelve months, according to Packaged Facts. Just look at how fast copies of The South Beach Diet are jumping off bookstore shelves. Businesses poised for takeoff include health food products or online (brick-and-click) retail shops, carryout food services, meal preparation and delivery services, and exercise products or instruction.

Deliver Web-based training and services   As businesses of every size scramble to stay competitive, online learning tools and applications offer

Chapter One: **Thinking It Through**

Part One:
Fun &
Fundamentals:
Control What
You Can

breathtaking economies of scale and reach. Nationwide, training expenditures per employee jumped from $734 in 2001 to $826 in 2002, according to ASTD, the American Society for Training & Development. Training delivered via Web-based or telephone learning technologies climbed 15.4 percent in 2002, up from about 10 percent in 2001.

Produce memories or experiences   More and more consumers crave special adventures and experiences to mark occasions, rather than tangible gifts. Specialty catering businesses can market events from start to finish, whether a romantic anniversary dinner on the beach, or a waiter in livery to serve a celebration dinner, or a horse-drawn carriage ride.

It's definitely the time to put dreams into action.

Learning from Experience

The first year of a business charts a steep learning curve. No matter how careful or how knowledgeable you try to be, mistakes will happen. Get used to the idea. But if you keep an open mind and heed voices of experience, you can dodge many of the more common missteps. Here are seven mistakes and seven often painful lessons based on the most frequent missteps that newbies make as well as advice about how to jump the potholes.

Mistake 1: Driving a fire engine.   You often hear about how entrepreneurs need determination to succeed—the so-called fire in the belly. But you need more than high energy to fan start-up flames. You need a plan, as mentioned above in "How to Begin." Thoroughly investigate your market and target customers, the competition, and other basics, like what makes a sound business model. Focus on answering one deceptively simple question: How will you make money? As a case study in errors, Tim Berry, president of Palo Alto Software, points to the ubiquitous video store on the corner, the one we've all seen open and shutter in record time. Typically, some starry-eyed owner rents the space up front. Now he's got fixed monthly overhead well before opening. He then spends his capital on snazzy design, forgetting about the cost of cash registers, business software, and store signage. When it's time to stock the shop, the owner is tapped out. The video store opens with trendy decor and lousy inventory. There's not one penny for marketing. Before the year is out, the store is "picked up by a chain that knows what it's doing," says Berry.

Lesson: Don't quit your day job without a plan.

Part One:
Fun &
Fundamentals:
Control What
You Can

Microsoft Small Business Kit

Mistake 2: Selling way cheap.   Ask a child to choose between 12 rhinestones and 1 diamond, and she'll go for the rhinestones every time. Start-up owners are just like that. They fall for the fallacy of quantity over quality. They figure rock-bottom prices will fuel skyrocketing sales and they'll become millionaires. But it doesn't work that way. Don't price your goods below market value or below your margin for profit. If you do, no matter how much you sell, you'll keep losing money. Before pricing products, do the math. Calculate fixed and variable costs. Figure the margin you need to walk away with dollars in your pocket. (See the section "Consider Your Product Price Tag," on page 27, for more on how to set prices.)

Lesson: Don't sell diamonds for the price of rhinestones.

Mistake 3: Desperately seeking adrenaline.   Entrepreneurs tend to be big-picture types—visionaries, risk-takers, thrill seekers. The longer they must sweat the details, the jumpier they get. So they often engineer a crisis, just to get back in the game and feel the rush of adventure. The purpose of a business is to make money. If you come alive only by jumping off a cliff, take up bungee jumping.

Lesson: Don't start a business to find life on the edge.

Mistake 4: Being clueless about marketing.   Start-ups rarely plan or budget for marketing because new owners think marketing is an unnecessary expense. Or, compounding the error, they confuse marketing with sales. In a rough definition, think about marketing when you're trying to build sales for tomorrow. Sales are focused on closing deals today, immediately. Underlying this mistake is a lack of experience about the drawn-out process of a typical sales cycle. Entrepreneurs usually hire salespeople first. But the initial hire, whether contracted or project, should be a marketing expert to get out the word. Then it's time to send out the sales force.

Lesson: Don't try to close deals before getting out your message.

Mistake 5: Being a pal instead of a boss.   At launch, everyone works three or four jobs, seven days a week. There seems little reason to pull rank or worry over management procedures. Everything's done on a first-time basis. Problems are fixed ad hoc. But eventually, trial and error turn inefficient and wasteful, and systems need to be installed. You're the one in charge. It's up to you to set expectations and develop procedures or appoint someone to do it. Without defined policies for job performance, hiring and firing, vacations, sick leave, benefits, compensation, promotions, and the rest, your fledging company is vulner-

Chapter One: **Thinking It Through**

Part One:
Fun &
Fundamentals:
Control What
You Can

able to legal problems and low morale. (To learn more, see Part Five, "Gurus, Guides, and Staff: Employment Dos and Don'ts.") Ultimately, business will suffer. A company handbook can be as simple as a one-page memo.

Lesson: Don't abdicate authority.

Mistake 6: Blowing through capital. Most new business owners woefully underestimate financial needs. Typically, inexperienced owners overspend at the outset, buying more furniture, technology, and office supplies or hiring way too many executives or experts than they really need to get up and going. New owners also don't realize that few customers pay promptly. So even when sales are immediate, cash is often tight. After developing personal and business budgets that can sustain the company for the time you think it'll take to get to breakeven, add at least 50 percent as a buffer and to cover contingencies.

Lesson: Don't be rash with cash.

Mistake 7: Overlooking loved ones. Start-ups demand 80- to 100-hour workweeks and serious support systems. That can certainly put stress on relationships. The commitment isn't yours alone. You need ongoing buy-in from friends and family. Make sure your time and money is also spent on family or a significant other.

Lesson: Don't let a launch cause lifelong regrets.

In the end, many missteps occur because new owners insist on doing everything themselves. Instead, review what you do best, and try to delegate or outsource the expertise you lack. And when the inevitable errors do arise, remember the old adage: *Learn from your mistakes.*

Meeting Tomorrow's Customer

The job of identifying your target customer takes time, research, and thoughtful analysis. Every start-up must evolve its own profile of a "best customer," defining his or her characteristics, age, demographics, psychographics, location, and so on. (See Chapter 9, "Craft Your Message," to learn more.) Even so, you still need to make an educated bet that your target groups will remain a vital segment of the marketplace. Will these customers support your business 10 years from now? Or do you have a plan to refine your targets? What about growth and expansion? Can the customers you target support a business that's twice your size? Three times?

Part One:
Fun &
Fundamentals:
Control What
You Can

Microsoft Small Business Kit

You see the point. Before investing money and sweat in a business idea, consider the long-term demographic, social, and economic trends of your market. Global communications, technology, and satellite media mean that society changes must faster than it used to. Look ahead—a few years, even a decade. Can you see your customer?

Here are some market trends that might be worth your attention as you develop your business plan.

What Women Want: How to Market to 51 Percent of Americans

Even traditional male categories, like autos, financial services, and technology, are lately making obvious efforts to attract women customers. Yet such initiatives still tend to be small potatoes compared to marketers' mainstream marketing plans. Women might represent a majority of the population, but they remain an astoundingly untapped market. Consider the following:

- By 2010, women are expected to control $1 trillion, or 60 percent, of the country's wealth, according to research conducted by Business Week and Gallup.

- Women purchase or influence the purchase of 80 percent of all consumer goods, including stocks, computers, and autos.

- Studies indicate that women control 75 percent of the country's wealth and account for 43 percent of Americans with gross assets over $500,000—with a substantial portion of this wealth held by older women.

- Besides underestimating their financial clout, marketers often see women as just one homogenous group. Even companies focused on women customers, like cosmetics or baby care, seem to view women as a single target group. Overall, women are much better defined by their occupations, interests, and lifestyle identities than by gender.

Coming of Age in the United States: Meet the Market That Rules Your Brand

They're growing up on the wired alphabet: PC, CD, PDA, and DVD. They average $100 a week in disposable income, spending a stunning $150 billion or so a year. They influence another $50 billion in family purchases,

Chapter One: **Thinking It Through**

Part One:
Fun &
Fundamentals:
Control What
You Can

bumping their total spending to $200 billion. Say hello to Generation Y, also called *echo boomers* or *millennials*. For sheer spending power and cultural hegemony, this consumer group is unrivaled in American history. Born between roughly 1980 and 2000, they are the 70-million-plus offspring of boomer parents, or about a quarter of all Americans. Gen Y's leading edge is graduating college, while the youngest are busy multitasking to a Britney Spears soundtrack.

A recent study of teens, age 13 to 17, from Jupiter, a market researcher, found that the number of teens online between 2004 and 2008 will increase from 18 million to 22 million. It further found that 17 percent of teens are "teen influencers," a group that is highly active online, style conscious, popular, and that exerts strong sway over friends and family.

Every generation, of course, is shaped by cultural and political events of its time. This group, however, has been weaned on some rather nasty and transforming national traumas, as noted by American Demographics. That list includes the O.J. murder trial, a president's impeachment, the 1999 Columbine school shootings, and a presidential election that needed the Supreme Court to pick a winner. All *before* 9/11 and the wars in Afghanistan and Iraq.

If you haven't thought much about how your wares might attract this cohort of big spenders—who are savvy and wary in about equal parts—start thinking. It's where your future lies. Attracting a teen customer is like triple dipping: First you get the youngster, second you get that teen's parent, and third you get the loyal customer that teen grows up to be. When pitching to Gen Y, keep in mind that they've grown up on slick ads and commercial messages. Don't talk down to them, and don't try to be too cute.

The Hip Senior: Boomers Still Have the Bucks

Americans are getting older and living longer lives. (See the section "Some Ideas for Start-Ups," earlier in this chapter, for some eye-opening statistics.) People turning 50 today may have almost half their lives ahead of them. By 2050, more than a million Americans are expected to be 100—or older.

These folks can afford to spend. For starters, the net worth for Americans 50 and older rose a hefty 38 percent between 1983 and 1998. Various surveys show that they dine out four or five times a week; account for the lion's share of spending in leisure travel; purchase gobs of gifts, clothes, and financial services; are keen for online banking; and are generally acknowledged

Part One:
Fun &
Fundamentals:
Control What
You Can

Microsoft Small Business Kit

as the nation's most affluent consumer segment. This generation also defies received wisdom about old age interests and pursuits. One study from the American Society on Aging, headquartered in San Francisco, found that boomers—born between 1946 and 1964—believe that they will need more money than their parents' generation to live comfortably. Boomers also think that their generation is more self-indulgent than the one before.

Yet marketers continue to overlook them.

Multicultural Marketing: Target Diverse Customers

The 2000 U.S. Census confirms that Hispanic, African-American, and Asian-American markets are growing faster than the mainstream population in both numbers and purchasing power. Yet multicultural markets are typically underserved and overlooked. Need motivation? Check out the facts:

- Minority-owned businesses grew more than four times as fast as U.S. firms overall between 1992 and 1997.

- Between 1990 and 2001, African-American representation among women employed grew 43 percent, according to a recent study from the U.S. Equal Employment Opportunity Commission (EEOC). Earned income for African-American women was estimated to be $284 billion in 2002, according to Target Market News, a Chicago consumer research company.

- Asian-American households have a 30 percent higher median income than the general population: $53,553 vs. $41,400. Asian-Americans also have the highest education of all U.S. racial groups—including whites—with a 65 percent college graduation rate.

- The Hispanic population is now the fastest-growing minority group in the country, expanding an astonishing 61 percent from 1990 to 2003—from 22 million to 35 million—according to the U.S. Census Bureau. And Hispanics also represent a commercial powerhouse, according to the Selig Center for Economic Growth at the University of Georgia:

  - Hispanic consumers currently control about $653 billion in spending power

  - The Hispanic population skews younger. Median Latino age is almost 26, compared to 35 for the total U.S. population

Chapter One: **Thinking It Through**

Part One:
Fun &
Fundamentals:
Control What
You Can

❏ The average Hispanic teen spends $320 a month, outspending the non-Hispanic teen by 4 percent

To be effective in targeting multicultural customers, you must do your homework. Each ethnic group is not homogeneous. Within each group, you'll find cultural distinctions and segments that respond to varying images and messages. The Hispanic market, for instance, embraces several countries/regions of origin, including Mexico, Central and South American nations, Cuba, and Puerto Rico. Some individuals are foreign born; others were born in the United States. Some are bilingual, others speak only Spanish or English, and some speak Portuguese. Within each segment, there are varying levels of acculturation. The same wisdom holds true among African Americans and Asian Americans. The first rule, then, is not to lump people together. Analyze the market. Look for buying patterns. Find out who lives where and what they purchase. You'll need to set up formal or informal focus groups and online or phone surveys. Walk around and talk to community leaders and business owners. Get in touch with minority trade and professional associations and publications—in other words, use all the usual market research techniques.

Money Management

According to an SBA survey of more than 800 new businesses in 2003:

■ The average amount of money required by sole practitioners to start self-sustaining businesses is $6,000

■ Owners needed an average of $1,000 to meet the first 30 days of operating cash

■ Owners expected their firm to gross an average of $25,000 income for the first year

■ Owners anticipated an average of $90,000 of annual gross income for their business by their fifth year

What It Takes: A Woman Who Can't Hear "No"

There are dozens of stories of successful small business founders that can serve as models as you develop your evaluations and research. Here's one that might help and inspire you.

Carolyn Gable got her start by refusing to take no for an answer, a trait entrepreneurs will recognize. In the early 1980s, after dropping out of

Part One:
Fun &
Fundamentals:
Control What
You Can

Microsoft Small Business Kit

beautician school, Gable was working as a waitress at the revolving restaurant atop the Hyatt Hotel in Chicago's O'Hare Airport. She liked watching the women customers, who were getting into business big time back then. "They used to come in carrying briefcases and wearing those power suits with big shoulder pads," recalls Gable. "And I thought, 'I can do that.'" She was on the money.

Today, Gable owns the New Age Transportation, Distribution, and Warehousing Company, a multimillion-dollar freight brokerage business based in Lake Zurich, Illinois. New Age manages traffic and distribution for manufacturers and producers that are too busy creating products to also worry about moving their wares to market. On any given day, New Age has hundreds of contracts with air and trucking carriers around the country, working for clients that include Fortune 500 companies as well as small and midsize enterprises. "I didn't have any supporting family or education," says Gable. "If I can do it," she says, "anyone can."

When the Hyatt restaurant closed for repairs for a few months, she registered at an employment agency. A few days later, she lucked into an interview at a trucking company in Elk Grove, Illinois, that had trouble retaining employees because of the long commute from downtown Chicago. Gable got the job. She kept waiting tables at the Hyatt, just in case, working 70 hours a week. And she began asking her trucker boss for a chance to sell. When he gave in, she proved to be very good at it.

She decided she was meant for sales, despite a lack of experience and training. Characteristically, Gable's next moves were to take on more risky challenges. In the mid-1980s, the freight industry was roiled by consolidation. Gable jumped to a start-up, and then to a larger, regional carrier. By 1989, she began working out of the basement of her home as a commissioned rep. "The business just took off," she says. "It was unbelievable for me. I was making commissions of over $100,000 a month. I hired three employees, and they'd arrive at 7:30 in the morning. I'd still be in pajamas."

She rented an 800-square-foot office in nearby Schaumburg. "It was a beautiful corner office with many windows, full of light," she says. That turned out to be a smart move. In 1992, her largest client consolidated all its freight business. "Overnight," says Gable, "I lost 40 percent of my commissions." So she went to work on a new business model. "Most carriers had contracts with clients that charged a standard 5 percent to 7 percent of their revenues on all accounts," she says. Instead, Gable calculated that by brokering and customizing freight services, she could offer innovative discounts, taking a percentage of the fee while saving clients money. "I decided to become a broker and take over billing," she says. The handsome office turned out to be just the ticket to impress new clients. "I stopped working on commission and that beautiful office made me look legitimate. I got the pricing I asked for."

Nowadays, Gable credits her success to a passion for selling and to never taking any deal, any customer, or any account for granted. "You have to always be in position," she says. "You can't sit back or go golfing two days a week. I can go in Monday morning and find I lost all my big accounts. It might have nothing to do with me. You must have new accounts. You must focus on keeping that level of service you've always had."

Tips to Grow On

After a quarter-century of successful empire building, Gable offers these tips to newbie entrepreneurs as they grow their business:

- Never say anything bad about a competitor.
- Always follow through.
- Hire positive employees.
- Have a life.
- Take care of accounts.
- Be creative about rejections.
- Be personal.

"It's really about building relationships," sums up Gable. "Everyone with a big title is still a person. Whoever it is will enjoy when I ask about his [or her] daughter. Share your life. Get to know clients as people. Relationships put you over the top."

Part One:
Fun &
Fundamentals:
Control What
You Can

Microsoft Small Business Kit

Ready, Set, Go

Besides the online resources offered by the SBA, mentioned earlier in the chapter, there are some other topnotch resources on the Web that offer helpful overviews of small business issues and needs. These sources can help kick-start your startup:

Online Resources

Microsoft Small Business Center Resources (www.microsoft.com/smallbusiness/issues/primary.mspx): Expert advice on small business issues, including financing, marketing, management, tax strategies and, of course, technology and automating your business operations.

Small Business Innovative Research (SBIR; http://www.sba.gov/sbir/): A federal program that helps to fund and promote early-stage research and development at small technology companies.

Entre World (http://www.entreworld.org/): Designed for small businesses that don't have a lot of time for research. It includes online case studies, discussion groups, and a searchable library of articles from other Web sites on such topics as pricing, finance, recruitment, advertising, and other management issues.

SCORE (Senior Corps of Retired Executives; www.score.org): This nonprofit group, billed as "Counselors to America's Small Business," provides entrepreneurs with free, confidential face-to-face and email business counseling. You can find advice and workshops at nearly 400 local chapter offices across the country.

Armed with your passion, energy, and discipline, and supported by the smart thinking and planning you're about to do, you're ready to take the leap. Welcome to the ranks of small business.

For More Information

In addition to the resources mentioned in this chapter, you will find links and information on the companion CD. Some books, magazines, and Web sites particularly useful as you think about starting a business include:

Chapter One: **Thinking It Through**

Part One:
Fun &
Fundamentals:
Control What
You Can

Books

- Bernard B. Kamoroff, *Small-Time Operator* (Bell Springs Publishing, 2000)

- Peri Pakroo, *The Small Business Start-Up Kit: A Step-by-Step Legal Guide* (Nolo Press, 2004)

- Jan Norman, *What No One Ever Tells You About Starting Your Own Business: Real Life Start-Up Advice from 101 Successful Entrepreneurs,* (Dearborn Trade, 2004)

Magazines

- *Entrepreneur*

- *Home Business Opportunities*

- *American Venture*

- *Black Enterprise*

Web sites

- The small-business portal of the Small Business Administration: *www.sba.gov/starting_business/startup/basics.html*

- Advice, newsletters, and much more from SCORE: *www.score.org/*

- Business Owner's Toolkit: *www.toolkit.cch.com/*

- Entrepreneur magazine online: *www.entrepreneur.com/*

- Business Know-How: *www.businessknowhow.net/bkh/startup.htm*

- Business.gov, the United States government portal to business information: *www.business.gov/*

Part One:
Fun &
Fundamentals:
Control What
You Can

Microsoft Small Business Kit

Don't blame the people who burn the cookies when your oven is on the blink.

— *Wally Amos, founder, Famous Amos Cookies,* The Cookie Never Crumbles *(St. Martin's Press, 2001)*

Chapter Two

Developing a Business Plan

You may be a real mover and shaker, but how do you know if you're headed in the right direction? A strategic plan is a helpful roadmap that points the way when you reach a crossroads. It tells you where you've been and where you're going. Without plotting a path, it's not only hard to find your destination, but you also might not realize when you've arrived.

Chapter Two: Developing a Business Plan

Part One:
Fun &
Fundamentals:
Control What
You Can

What you'll find:

❑ Who needs a plan?

❑ Getting a reality check

❑ Planning affordable market research

❑ Choosing a business structure

❑ Guidelines for creating your plan

❑ Doing it with Office: Online business plan templates

Part One:
Fun &
Fundamentals:
Control What
You Can

Microsoft Small Business Kit

Who Needs a Plan?

The answer to that question is easy: you do. Anyone and everyone who wants a successful, growing business needs to plan for it. Starting a business doesn't begin with buying a desk or renting space. It begins with research and advance planning. There are several reasons to think through and write down your business plan, not the least of which is the focus such an exercise requires. To get where you want to go, you need to choose a pioneering, strategic route. You need to hone operational tactics. And you need to set the benchmarks or signs of growth that, when achieved, validate your moves.

Typically, business plans are created for two overriding reasons:

To inform and attract investors   If you're looking for financial backing from family and friends or from a financial institution or individual investors, you need a clearly defined, documented analysis of what your business is all about. Potential investors want the opportunity to assess your thinking and anticipated course of action on goals, risks, competitive threats, and financial projections. Whoever gives you money also wants to delve into your skills and background to verify that you're up to the challenges.

See Chapter 3, "How to Find Backing," for more about getting financial backing.

To educate and inspire the team   Your business plan serves not only bankers or investors but also your management team, significant consultants or experts, and anyone else who is fueling your launch. The plan offers guidelines for the team about how it should expend time, energy, and resources.

Without faking anything, the plan must work as a cheerleading document. It's meant to sell your idea and make a compelling argument for why—and how—you will succeed.

Getting a Reality Check

At this point, you've undoubtedly defined the basic outlines of your business idea, tested it with some industry and small business experts, scanned your resources, and, presumably, decided that the idea has enough merit to move ahead. Now it's time to fill in details and determine the viability of your business.

Chapter Two: **Developing a Business Plan**

Part One:
Fun &
Fundamentals:
Control What
You Can

See Chapter 1, "Thinking It Through," for more about testing start-up ideas.

To begin, set up some meetings with your *brain trust*, meaning the trusted professional and networked circle of advisors around you. These counselors might include your lawyer, accountant, mentors, former and present coworkers, high-school buddies, your CFO (chief financial officer) sister-in-law and computer whiz nephew, and so on. It's the group of associates and acquaintances, friends, and professionals who know something about both you and the business you plan to enter (and, of course, who are willing to help). Tapping the expertise of such associates and industry veterans is a smart and affordable way to examine your assumptions. You can get them together for dinner or meet one on one. Take notes or record the sessions via audio or video so that you have a record for future reference.

See Chapter 4, "Self-Preservation," for more about choosing an advisory board.

Ask for ideas and advice about such issues as:

- Objectives and goals of the business
- Market positioning and channels
- Distribution channels and costs
- Strategies for targeting market segments
- Sales expectations and strategies
- Handling competitors
- Evaluating necessary resources and how these will be allocated or supported
- Costs and expenses for the first year and beyond
- Processes for tracking and measuring performance

Consider SWOT

A useful way to organize these discussions is by asking everyone to come to the meeting prepared to offer a SWOT analysis. That means a focused evaluation of the following issues:

Strengths   What will support growth and recognition of your business?

Weaknesses   Where are you vulnerable? What challenges do you face?

Opportunities   What market conditions exist that can build business for you?

Threats   What are competitors doing or planning that could have an impact? How are they snapping at your heels?

Part One:
Fun &
Fundamentals:
Control What
You Can

Microsoft Small Business Kit

Don't make this meeting too casual in tone. You want the benefit of every-one's honest and high-level expertise. Also be sure that you're prepared to hear advice without becoming defensive or critical. These advisors are your chosen fan club. Listen and remain receptive and open-minded. Don't for-get that, when it's all over, you're in charge. You can always jettison whatever you don't like or trust.

Planning Affordable Market Research

Before you can make a strong case for your business in a written plan, you need to be up to speed on the market you're entering, the challenges you'll face, and the characteristics and needs of your customers. Who, after all, will be buying your products? You will, of course, need to invest some time and money in market research, although it can be low-cost and done in phases to save capital.

Most of all, you need to identify the customers who are your best targets and then listen to what they want or need, tracking reactions to your quality and price, service and delivery, image and brand—everything, in short, that influ-ences their purchasing decisions. Based on what you learn, you might want to rethink your concept or refine your choices before writing the plan.

Free Research Sources

To learn more about your customer demographics, check the U.S. Census Bureau Web site, at *www.census.gov/*. On the home page, click American FactFinder.

For an overview of U.S. government statistics and resources, check the FedStat search page, at *www.fedstats.gov/*, which scans information from more than 100 U.S. federal agencies.

Remember that your customers are seg-mented long before you show up. You might think that marketing generates the buyer, but the truth is, he or she is already out there. Your job is not to draw boundaries among market segments, it's to discover where the lines lie for your firm. Think like an explorer, not an archi-tect. You must reach people interested in benefits you deliver, not wares you sell.

See Chapter 9, "Craft Your Message," to learn more about marketing a product's features vs. its benefits.

First delve into your customer demographics. Demographics derived from census research turn up objective facts. The U.S. government census can help you with this information. More targeted and current data can be found in industry, university, or professional market research surveys. Check online or hard-copy trade and business publication sources. Or join a few industry or professional organizations that conduct proprietary surveys.

Chapter Two: Developing a Business Plan

Part One:
Fun &
Fundamentals:
Control What
You Can

This research reveals your potential customers' vital statistics, such as gender, household income, age, and marital status. Your target customer might have kids, own a late-model car, or pay a mortgage. But demographics tell you little about the kind of furnishings chosen for a living room or the model of car that customer *really* wants to drive. You don't learn about personality or aspirations. Two neighbors, for instance, with equivalent incomes and an average 2.2 children are clearly not the same people. One adores opera, and the other listens to hip-hop. Want to rely on a single message to sell your SuperService to both? We don't think so.

Next step: *psychographics*. Businesses have been relying on psychographic profiling of various sorts for 30 years. Early on, categorizing the customer's activities, interests, and opinions (AIO) summed it up. Nowadays, with technology that can slice-and-dice so accurately into so many more segments, psychographics is a lot more sophisticated. Still, the basic idea holds.

Psychographics is a process of grouping customers according to lifestyle choices, personal characteristics, hobbies and activities, beliefs, and values. This is where the real definitions are formed. Psychographic segmentation is typically built on targeted research, whether formal surveys, informal questionnaires, virtual or actual focus groups, or software that captures customer data and matches the information against consumer types and groups.

Indisputably, this kind of marketing puts you in touchy-feely land. But does it work? Yes, indeed. By learning about a consumer's taste and inclinations and passions, you discover how to fulfill needs and what will make him or her receptive to your messages and products.

How to Find Your Best Customer

While research and focus group facilitators can be enormously helpful, all you really need to do to discover what potential customers think is to ask them. You can buy direct-mail lists rather inexpensively. (Check in with the Direct Marketing Association at *www.the-dma.org/* to get some advice, although you might have to become a paying member for access to detailed, industry-specific information.)

You can ask the management of a nearby appropriate mall for permission to put up a desk or a kiosk—or find out how much it would cost to do so for a day or so. Then give away a discounted item or a free sample in exchange for consumer responses to an electronic or a written survey. You can mount an informal phone survey. Or you can send customer surveys via e-mail or

Part One:
Fun &
Fundamentals:
Control What
You Can

Microsoft Small Business Kit

prepaid postcards. Again, include an incentive to boost participation. For business-to-business marketers, offer a look at the data you collect or a research report.

See Chapter 11, "The Customer Comes First," to learn more about direct-mail marketing.

Customer Characteristics

The Small Business Administration's (SBA) Online Women's Business Center offers a guide to developing effective marketing strategies. Go to *www.onlinewbc.gov*, and click Business Basics.

Here is the SBA's list of the four essential characteristics of a customer:

They have a particular need.   People have all kinds of needs, including basic survival needs (food, shelter, health), rational needs (dependability, durability, economy), and emotional needs (love, sex appeal, status, security, acceptance, and power).

They have enough money to buy what you are selling.   Keep in mind that just because someone wants to own something you are selling does not mean they have enough money to buy it.

They have decision-making power.   The key here is to spend your time wisely. Find the person who has the actual authority to say "yes" or "no" to buying your product or service.

They have easy access to your product or service.   Accessibility is important. For example, if you want to sell baked goods to people in your neighborhood, you must either take your goods directly to your customers or have a small shop where they can come to you.

Many online and Web market research companies now offer affordable services for online questionnaires that test customer responses and satisfaction. Such services also request contact information and include that when they deliver survey results. You can find a reliable and appropriate service by asking for recommendations from your industry or professional association or from local small business resource centers. When conducted properly, an online survey can track the opinions and needs of preferred customers. The results can then be used to diagnose and improve your business model and targets.

To start building a customer databank, you need ongoing answers to these key questions:

- Who are your customers? Identify them by name, address, age, gender, geographic location, and economic level.

- Why do customers buy your product? Is it, for instance, because of price point or brand consciousness or convenience?

- What would these customers buy from you in the future?

Chapter Two: Developing a Business Plan

Part One:
Fun &
Fundamentals:
Control What
You Can

Consider Your Product Price Tag

Start-ups frequently overlook the issue of setting a price for the products or services the business will sell. Many business owners, even established ones, simply close their eyes and pick a number. In fact, small firms tend to underprice, assuming that if they offer lots of bargains, they will boost sales. Maybe. But is that a good thing? The volume of sales is not nearly as important as the profit you make on them. At best, underpricing leaves money on the table. At worst, it can put you out of business.

Calculating your product's price is worth some special attention. That price will certainly determine a host of other factors in your planning. For just one example: If your target customer would pay a high price for your service, you might not need as much funding as you think. Or you might need more because you'll need to rent and furnish an upscale office that matches your high-end marketing image. Think about pricing in relation to the success of Starbucks. It might seem obvious nowadays, but what about at the planning stage? What went into turning a 50-cent cup of coffee into a personalized experience for $3.50?

Before drafting your business plan, talk to experienced entrepreneurs about their pricing trials and errors. This is hard stuff to nail down. Pricing ought to be a long, thoughtful process—not a gut guess. The smart way to set a price is to define the value of what you're offering, whether product or service. The only way to do that is to discover what your customers call "value," which could be at odds with your original assumptions.

To figure pricing, many owners simply tally their variable product costs, their overhead or fixed costs, and then add some margin, sometimes calling that margin "profit." Costs and margins might be important information, but that's not the key. To a very large degree, the perceptions and pocketbooks of your customers determine the value—and therefore the price—of your offerings.

Here are some ways to define the value of what you sell:

Talk to your best prospects.   Whether you can afford formal focus groups or you simply do a lot of personal calling around, be sure to invest in detailed research of your ideal and best customers. Ask potential clients straightforward questions:

- What price makes this product so expensive that you won't buy it?

- What price makes it seem a good value to your target customer?

Part One:
Fun &
Fundamentals:
Control What
You Can

Microsoft Small Business Kit

- What makes it a good deal?

- What price would make you walk away without any consideration?

- What price makes it look cheap or makes you suspicious about quality?

- What added benefits or features would make you buy it?

- If those benefits or features were added, how much more would you pay?

> Marketing experts say you can generally charge about 20 percent higher than focus group indications. That gives you a pricing benchmark. Armed with such information, you can see whether the perceived market price will cover all your costs. You can also tell, of course, if you're on track to making money. If not, you might have to rejigger your business plan.

Get to know the competition.   You ought to research how much your competitors charge for similar goods and services. Then plan how you'll make your wares stand out. Typically, differentiating your product is the key to pricing. But competitive pricing only goes so far. Some owners consciously set prices way above the competition because the value of what they offer attracts customers who will pay the freight—for example, amazing service or more convenient hours. And some products don't have any direct competitors. In those cases, you should be able to show measurable benefits for the value you're selling.

Understand your operating numbers.   You must be clear about your breakeven point before you can raise or lower prices or margins. Likewise, an overview of your balance sheet gives you negotiating wiggle room. When the need arises, you'll be able to quickly quote a lower price that says, "I can lose a little but make out OK." In a negotiation, you'll also know how much you can discount and which price should make you head for the door.

Coordinate your marketing strategy.   Which comes first, branding or pricing? Probably pricing, although the pair tend to move in lockstep. You need to thoroughly understand the value of what you sell before you can market its benefits. That means pricing begins the process. Once you can expertly describe your product's benefits and, in turn, the profile of your best prospects, branding will be that much easier.

See Chapter 9, "Craft Your Message," for more about how to create a brand.

Chapter Two: Developing a Business Plan

Part One:
Fun &
Fundamentals:
Control What
You Can

Consider product life cycles.   Pricing must be sensitive to how long your product or service will have value. Is this a one-shot deal, or are you in it for the long term? Perhaps you can envision a suite of extended products in the future. Will your customers be buying several items in your line—say, in the case of hair-care products? That will certainly influence the value of what you offer and where you set the price.

Choosing a Business Structure

Part of starting a business and drafting your plan is figuring out what's called your *business formation*—in other words, deciding on the legal ownership structure of your company. There is no one right structure or answer. Each business has different needs, and there are definite advantages and disadvantages to each choice. The two simplest organizational structures are a sole proprietorship and a general partnership, neither of which are considered separate legal entities, but more like statements of operational fact. In either case, an individual or two or more people own and run the business. More complex structures include corporations or limited liability corporations (LLC).

Sole proprietorships and general partnerships are easier to manage. There are fewer tax considerations and also less legal or accounting compliance and oversight. So why doesn't everyone choose one of those options? Because they might expose you to risks. If, for example, you run a landscaping business as a sole proprietorship and someone gets hurt in the course of a project, you're personally on the hook. A client can take you to court, and if the suit is found to have merit, you could lose all your personal assets, including your home and car. Even the fact of a lawsuit could lead to costs that overwhelm the business—and that you don't want to be personally responsible for paying. If, however, the landscaping business has been formed as a legal entity, that client can be rewarded only with assets from the business, not with anything you own personally. That's one of the reasons why it's important to choose structures carefully.

Factors that influence which structure to choose include:

■ Size of your company

■ Revenues and profits

■ Tax requirements and accounting costs

■ Number of owners

Part One:
Fun &
Fundamentals:
Control What
You Can

Microsoft Small Business Kit

- Funding and investor profiles
- Possible liabilities or risks of doing business that are not covered by your insurance

See Chapter 4, "Self-Preservation," for more about insurance needs and Chapter 7, "By the Numbers: Analyzing Your Business with Excel," for more about tax advice.

Here's a description of the main business structures. Making the choice about which structure will work for you entails many individual details and tradeoffs. Check with your attorney and accountant before making a final decision. This list covers only the main federal tax filing needs—there might well be more and different requirements for your particular business. And be sure to investigate any state or local tax filing requirements.

See Chapter 6, "Tax Tactics," for more on tax filings and obligations.

Sole Proprietorship

A sole proprietorship—a business owned and run by one person—is the easiest way to start. Your name and your work is the business. Most small businesses start out this way, of course, and in fact, the vast majority of small businesses stay that way—single-owner operations.

Advantages

A sole proprietorship is the easiest structure to create and walk away from. As the owner, you have full control of debt or assets, operations, and decisions. There are no government papers to file, other than your personal income tax forms (federal, state, and in some cases, city). If you make a profit, it's yours. If you lose money, you can take that deduction as a personal tax filing. Likewise, you can apply for credit cards or open bank accounts in your name to do business.

Disadvantages

The good news is the bad news here. You are completely responsible for the debt and the company's liabilities. Should there be any legal action or business loss, the owner's business and personal assets are both at risk. Not only that, but if representatives of the company, whether independent agents or employees, encounter a problem that leads to negligence, you're also personally at risk. If you have insurance for such circumstances and the claim is greater than your coverage, you're personally liable over and above

Chapter Two: Developing a Business Plan

Part One:
Fun &
Fundamentals:
Control What
You Can

the insurance claim. In addition, the employee benefits you might pay, either to yourself or to others, are not necessarily deductible from the business (because it's a business simply in name, without any legal standing). And those benefits' costs might be only partially deductible as personal income taxes.

Federal Tax Filing

Typically, you'll need the following federal tax forms (although your individual circumstances might require others):

- Form 1040: Individual Income Tax Return

- Schedule C: Profit or Loss from Business (or Schedule C-EZ)

- Schedule SE: Self-Employment Tax

- Form 1040-ES: Estimated Tax for Individuals

- Form 4562: Depreciation and Amortization

- Form 8829: Expenses for Business

The same forms are used for a Doing Business As (DBA) and an LLC, described in the following sections.

DBA, or Doing Business As

Officially called a *Certificate of Doing Business Under an Assumed Name*, DBA standing allows you to operate the business under a different name than your own—say, Adventure Works rather than [*Your Given Name*] Agency. You can apply for and get a DBA certificate at your local government office, whether county or city, usually for a nominal fee. The legal standing means a search has been done and the certificate verifies that no other business is operating in that county or city with the same name.

Advantages

A DBA allows you to open a business under a name other than your own legal name. For example, Margie Shoop launches a business called Margie's Travel. Usually, you file that name and then receive a DBA certificate from your local county clerk's office. To find where to file a DBA in your area, call your state commerce office. The DBA alerts your customers, suppliers, and others that you are the owner of the company. It also permits you to open a business account at the bank, which might offer credit advantages.

Part One:
Fun &
Fundamentals:
Control What
You Can

Microsoft Small Business Kit

In some cases, local newspapers can help you to register your DBA and will also list your information in an edition of the paper.

Disadvantages

There is usually a nominal filing fee. When registering your DBA via a newspaper, make sure that the registration includes submission of your paperwork to the county clerk or county recorder's office. DBAs typically expire within five years and need to be reissued.

C Corporation

Generally, incorporating your business separates your personal obligations, assets, and liabilities from those of the business, whatever form of corporation you choose. A C Corp, however, has its own tax schedule, apart from your individual income or other tax requirements. A C Corp must first pay taxes before it can distribute profits to you or to shareholders.

Advantages

A corporation is considered a unique legal entity. It has legal life separate and apart from any owner or partners. When the business changes hands, there is simply a new owner. The business entity itself does not dissolve or change. Corporations are chartered by the state in which they are headquartered. If you do business across state lines, get legal and financial advice before setting up the corporation. A C Corp is empowered to sell stock in the business, which can raise funds for you. It also limits the liability of the shareholders. Once you have incorporated the business, the business community is more comfortable with your stability and standing. That means you might find it easier to apply for loans, find willing suppliers, and hire talent. Customers might also be reassured that you're serious and committed.

Disadvantages

Incorporating your business takes time and money. There are up-front legal and accounting fees to pay, usually at a time when new business owners can least afford it. You must maintain financial records and be scrupulous about keeping your personal assets independent from the business's operations and revenues. You're also expected to hold annual shareholder meetings and maintain various other corporate formalities or you could lose the corporation's separate identity. There are many small business services that can handle these details for you, but of course, that adds to your costs. In addition, a corporation pays higher taxes than an individual (or sole proprietor)

Chapter Two: **Developing a Business Plan**

Part One:
Fun &
Fundamentals:
Control What
You Can

does. You also end up with what's called *double taxation*, meaning that the corporation pays taxes on its income and profits and then, as a shareholder who has enjoyed the corporation's dividend or profit, you end up paying personal income tax on the money you've already paid corporate taxes on.

Federal Tax Filing

You'll need the following federal tax forms:

- Form 1120 or 1120-A: Corporation Income Tax Return

- Form 1120-W: Estimated Tax for Corporation

- Form 8109-B: Deposit Coupon

- Form 4625: Depreciation

- Various employment tax forms, such as Social Security, Medicare, unemployment rate, employee income tax withheld, and so on

- Forms, as needed, for capital gains, sale of assets, alternative minimum tax, and more

Subchapter S Corporation

Subchapter S Corporations offer the same benefits as C Corps of separating business from personal obligations, but Sub S Corps allow corporation profits to pass through.

Advantages

All the benefits of the C Corp hold in an S Corp, such as being a separate legal entity and limiting your liability. The S Corp is primarily a *tax election*—that is, the structure is chosen because it allows shareholders to avoid double taxation. The profits of the business are said to "pass through" the company, going straight to the shareholders, so you pay tax only once.

Disadvantages

Only certain businesses qualify for S Corp election (accomplished via IRS Form 2553). The company must have fewer than 35 shareholders, and the shareholders can't be other corporations or nonresident aliens. Plus, there are restrictions on the kind of stock the company can issue. There are also some restrictions on the amount you can pay yourself as an employee of the corporation, which are governed by what the IRS calls "reasonable compensation." Again, you're best off getting advice before deciding.

Part One:
Fun &
Fundamentals:
Control What
You Can

Microsoft Small Business Kit

Federal Tax Filing

You'll need the following federal tax forms:

- Form 1120S: Income Tax Return for S Corporation
- 1120S K-1: Shareholder's Share of Income, Credit, Deductions
- Form 4625: Depreciation
- Form 1040: Individual Income Tax Return
- Schedule E: Supplemental Income and Loss
- Schedule SE: Self-Employment Tax
- Form 1040-ES: Estimated Tax for Individuals
- Various employment tax forms, such as Social Security, Medicare, unemployment rate, employee income tax withheld, and so on
- Forms, as needed, for capital gains, sale of assets, alternative minimum tax, and more

General Partnerships

The majority of small business partnerships are set up as *general partnerships*, which means they share everything equally, including losses, work, ownership, profits—the lot. Do put everything in writing before creating a general partnership. And get the help of a lawyer to set that up. No matter how close to your partner you are, conflicts will arise. The written agreement is the best way to avoid trouble or grief.

Advantages

In a general partnership, owners share the management and profit or loss of the business. Profits from a partnership business flow directly through to the partners' personal tax returns, like an S Corp. A general partnership (as opposed to a limited partnership or a joint venture, described in a moment) requires no formal filing, paperwork, or costs. It exists as soon as there's an agreement between two or more people.

Here are two other types of partnership:

Limited partnership and partnership with limited liability   Most of the partners have limited liability (usually, to the amount of their investment) as well as limited input regarding management decisions. This struc-

Chapter Two: **Developing a Business Plan**

Part One:
Fun &
Fundamentals:
Control What
You Can

ture often encourages investors to get involved for short-term projects or for investing in capital assets. It tends to be a complicated structure and probably isn't a great idea for a start-up or small business.

Joint venture   This is similar to a general partnership but is in force for a limited period of time or for the duration of a single project. Should the partners keep doing business or continue their operations, they will then be recognized as an ongoing partnership and will have to file as such.

Disadvantages

Without any written agreement, the laws of the state govern the business partner relationship, which might not be what you or your partner prefers. You ought to draft a formal partnership agreement about terms and operating conditions that spells out what happens in the event of various scenarios, such as the death or divorce of a partner. Depending on which partnership structure is in place, the risk of liability can be great or small. General partnerships pose risks similar to those found in sole proprietorships—that is, your personal assets can be exposed if there is legal or financial trouble. Partners are liable both jointly and individually. Profits must be shared, and some employee benefits are not deductible from business income on tax returns. The partnership might have a limited life and dissolve upon the withdrawal or death of a partner.

Federal Tax Filing:

You'll need the following federal tax forms:

- Form 1065: Partnership Return of Income
- Form 1065 K-1: Partner's Share of Income, Credit, Deductions
- Form 4562: Depreciation
- Form 1040: Individual Income Tax Return
- Schedule E: Supplemental Income and Loss
- Schedule SE: Self-Employment Tax
- Form 1040-ES: Estimated Tax for Individuals
- Various employment tax forms, such as Social Security, Medicare, unemployment rate, employee income tax withheld, and so on

Part One:
Fun &
Fundamentals:
Control What
You Can

Microsoft Small Business Kit

Limited Liability Corporation (LLC)

Increasingly popular with small business owners, LLCs are less complicated to set up than corporations and typically require less paperwork and
accounting to maintain. Yet an LLC offers the same benefits as an S Corp's
pass-through advantage.

Advantages

A hybrid business structure, now permissible in most states, the LLC is a
very popular small business structure. It combines the limited liability features of a corporation and the tax efficiencies and operational flexibility of a
general partnership or sole proprietorship.

Disadvantages

LLCs can cost up to $1,000 or so to set up.

Guidelines for Creating Your Plan

Every business plan is a unique document because each plan details the
specifics of one business. Yet every plan also shares common themes and an
organizational format so that investors and other important readers can
quickly understand the business idea and turn to sections of interest to
them. You must cover all the elements of the business and its strategies for
growth and success. (See the section "Doing It with Office: Online Business
Plan Templates," later in this chapter, for information about using the Office
Online Business Plan templates in Microsoft Word.)

Business plans generally run 20 to 30 pages, but they range from 10 to 50
pages or more. The length depends on your preferences and the plan. Just
keep in mind that you're likely to be a more passionate reader than most.
Put yourself in the shoes of your readers. What do they need to know? What
can be left for a later discussion or report once you've engaged their interest?

This isn't a document you dash off, either. Most plans require two or three
months of researching, analyzing, and writing (and reviewing and refining
and rewriting). It can take up to 300 hours and, in some cases, up to a year
to get the plan right.

In addition to a cover page that lists your company name and contact information, here's a guide to what's generally included in a business plan:

Chapter Two: Developing a Business Plan

Part One:
Fun &
Fundamentals:
Control What
You Can

Table of contents   Each section in the plan should include a category heading with a few descriptive lines and a page number to allow readers to quickly flip to what they most want to learn. Your goal is to make this an easy, compelling read. If you've included charts or graphs, note those in the contents listing or individually at the back in the appendix pages.

Executive summary   This is probably the most important section of your plan. In two pages or less, it should sum up what your business will do, the market opportunities, and how you will make money—in other words, just what the headline promises, an "executive summary." Many investors will first read the summary and then, if they're interested, go on to other sections. Others might read the summary and jump to the financials. Some investors will read the summary and simply stop. You'd be smart to write this section last, after you've thought through and written everything else. It will be a lot easier then.

Company description   Step back and think about what first sparked your enthusiasm to start this business before writing this section. You must set it up so that someone who has no notion of your field or industry will understand why you've jumped in. Describe any significant trends or industry innovations or big players in the market. Summarize the current state of your industry and its future. This is a positioning overview that covers the market's driving forces as well as current and future opportunities. You're creating a map so that you can show where your idea fits in and why your company fills a gap or a need. You'll want to cover your business's target customers as well as your strengths in the marketplace. If you've crafted a company mission statement, this is the place to add it.

See Chapter 9, "Craft Your Message," for more about creating mission statements.

This section also covers the kind of legal business structure you anticipate or have already formed for the company. (See the section "Choosing a Business Structure," earlier in this chapter, for details.)

Products and services   Explain what you plan to sell. What is your product or service? What makes it special or desirable? Why will customers want it? What does it do that competitor products do not? Where in the market do you plan to position it—top, middle, or mass market? If your product requires training or legal oversight or compliance with regulations, be sure that you include your plan for that as well. Don't get too technical and fall into industry jargon. Remember, the entire plan should be written for someone outside your industry.

Part One:
Fun &
Fundamentals:
Control What
You Can

Microsoft Small Business Kit

Marketing plan   Your marketing strategy is the heart of a business. Sure, finances are important, including how you'll acquire backing and how you'll manage operating costs. But really, without a marketing strategy, finances fall by the wayside. How can you make money if you don't know how to sell your product? Who are your customers? How will you find them? How much will it cost to acquire and service them? In some ways, this section is a focused version of the overall plan. It should include the following:

- A summary of your market position and goals.

- The market objectives. Vague announcements are not as effective as specific targets: "We will sell 150 widgets by the fourth quarter," not "We will own the market in widgets."

- Your target markets.

- A strategy for each segment or market.

- Marketing expenses and resources—and how they will be allocated.

- The marketing channels you plan to use. This is where you choose e-mail marketing, radio ads, highway billboards, or more.

- Competitive scenarios. What are your moves if, say, a competitor lowers its price as soon as you launch?

- Communications strategy. Set up benchmarks to show when the marketing pays off. Connect the dots with the sales staff.

- The implementation or marketing calendar. Plans are great, but if you don't also designate responsibility, set deadlines, and hold people accountable, marketing efforts will fail.

This section should detail the results of the customer or market research you've done and explain what you foresee as difficulties in getting into the market, sometimes called *barriers to entry*. You want to answer some key questions for readers and investors, including the size of your market, what percentage (be realistic) of the market you intend to target, and what it will cost to do so. Do you have any special marketing advantages to offer, such as guarantees or distribution rights? Be sure that you cover those as well.

Operations plan   This is your tactical section. You need to provide details about your office or facility requirements, equipment needed or manufacturing capabilities, and human resources (staff and contracted or consultant), as well as your systems for getting from idea to up and running. Don't forget to include any inventory control or quality

Chapter Two: Developing a Business Plan

Part One:
Fun &
Fundamentals:
Control What
You Can

assurance processes. You should also offer a rundown of what kind of operation funds this will take, including rents, leases, licensing, registration, and production costs. If your business is a manufacturing or production model, it might help to include a floor plan of the space you've chosen.

See Chapter 4, "Self-Preservation," for more about licensing and insurance needs.

Management   Most of the time, investors care more about who's driving the business and the quality of his or her background and character than a shelf full of rosy financial projections. This is the place to toot your own horn and itemize the achievements and top-notch skills and experience of your launch team. Don't be shy or modest. List every bit of your bench strength, not simply the frontline players—that includes lawyers, accountants, advisors, mentors, bankers, and so forth. Include each one's bio and a description of what they bring to your launch party. Remember that brain trust you gathered? This is the time to leverage its power.

Finances   Each entrepreneur will have his or her own way of explaining the money side of the business idea. For that matter, each investor will have a slightly different question about finances as well. Some plans include detailed information about the owner's personal finances, the idea being that it's better to show that the entrepreneur won't be strapped for cash during the start-up dry spells. Other plans include a special section focused on start-up and capitalization costs because that phase includes one-time costs as a prelude to actual operation. Certainly, the financial section must have a detailed outline of your cash flow expectations, usually for a 12-month projection. You should also figure out the business's projected balance sheet—what it will take to get to breakeven and then profitability, including what kind of cash drain you anticipate until then. Your projections for sales, expenses, and margins of profit will inform those figures. Basically, this is your statement of what's coming in and what's going out. Don't try to complete it without the help of your accountant. If you don't have an accountant, hire a consultant to help. It'll make your life much easier in the long run.

Exit strategies   If your plan is designed to attract investors (rather than act as a map for yourself and your team), be sure to include an *exit strategy*. That means a chosen path from success to profit, sometimes called *harvesting*—whether that's selling your company, going public, or some other method of cashing out. One common exit strategy is a buy-sell

Part One:
Fun &
Fundamentals:
Control What
You Can

Microsoft Small Business Kit

10 Key Questions for Your Business Plan

In his recent book *You Need to Be a Little Crazy: The Truth About Starting and Growing Your Business* (Dearborn Trade Publishing, 2003), serial entrepreneur Barry Moltz suggests that business plans boil down to the following straightforward questions. Answer them, and you'll be on track to completing your plan.

- ■ What problem exists that your business is trying to solve? Where is the pain?

- ■ What does it cost to solve that problem now? How deep and compelling is the pain?

- ■ What solutions does your business have that solve this problem?

- ■ What will the customer pay you to solve this problem?

- ■ How will solving this problem make the company a lot of money?

- ■ What alliances can you leverage with other companies to help your company?

- ■ How big can this business get if given the right capital?

- ■ How much cash do you need to find a path to profitability?

- ■ How will the skills of your management team, their domain knowledge, and track record of execution make this happen?

- ■ What is the investors' exit strategy?

agreement. It can guarantee that there will be a buyer for the business if a partner leaves, provide a first right of refusal to the person remaining, and set out a sales formula to determine the price of the company in case part or all of it is sold.

See Chapter 3, "How to Find Backing," for more about exit strategies.

Appendixes This is the footnote/ research/value-added section that supports the assumptions and projections you make throughout the earlier pages. Include here any media articles, research documents or studies, advertising or marketing prototypes, and copies of leases or contracts—in short, anything that shows you're on solid ground and have painted a realistic picture in the plan.

Tone Will Tell

It's easy to get bogged down in an avalanche of facts and figures when drafting a business plan. Don't. Walk a judicious line between narrative and statistics. You're telling the story of your business. You're making an argument for success (and perhaps backing). Here are some tips to making your business plan more compelling:

Capture attention. Your executive summary must be both exciting and readable. Avoid all technical or industry terms or jargon. If you must invoke complicated terminology or concepts, be brief and define them.

Put yourself in the mind of the reader. The plan is about the market and how you will make money, not about how smart you've been to come up with a fabulous new product. Be sure that you stick to the goal of the plan, which is to convince readers that your business is viable.

Chapter Two: Developing a Business Plan

Part One:
Fun &
Fundamentals:
Control What
You Can

Be realistic.   Don't avoid weaknesses, and don't gloss over strong competitors. Everyone who reads a plan is an interested, astute professional. If you leapfrog over problems or difficulties, you lose credibility.

Showcase your ending.   Be sure that the last page is as dramatic as the first. Don't trail off into numbers or detailed explanations. Sum up with as much excitement as you began.

Doing It with Office: Online Business Plan Templates

One of the templates you can download from Microsoft Office Online is a framework of a business plan for a start-up company. To locate the template, open the home page for Microsoft Office Online (*www.microsoft.com/office*), click Templates, and then click Finance And Accounting in the Browse Templates section. On this page, you'll see a link to the business plan templates.

The start-up business plan template isn't a fill-in-the-blank form. The document includes a couple of tables that you can use as models for a competitive analysis, but in the main, the template offers guidance by indicating the topics you should include in a business plan and recommending the sort of information you should include about each topic. You need to know the basic features of Microsoft Word to effectively prepare the document, and you need to know all about your business to write an effective plan. If you know more than the basics, you can prepare your business plan that much more easily. You can spend time sharpening the quality of the information you provide about your business rather than formatting the document.

Here's the table of contents provided in the template, which gives you an idea of the topics you need to be prepared to write about when you develop your business plan.

Part One:
Fun &
Fundamentals:
Control What
You Can

Microsoft Small Business Kit

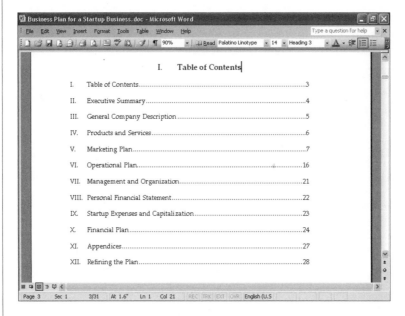

In general, to use the template, read through the advice and descriptions provided for each section of the document. You can then select the descriptive text and delete it before entering the information that's relevant to your business. You can, of course, print a copy of the model business plan for reference or start a new document in Word and refer to the template online.

Other business plan documents

Among the templates related to business plans that you can obtain from Microsoft Office Online are a Microsoft Excel spreadsheet named Start-up Expenses.xls and a Microsoft PowerPoint business plan presentation. Both of these templates come with directions for how you can use them in preparing a business plan. You'll learn more about how to use Excel for budgeting and tracking expenses in Chapter 5, "Follow the Money," and Chapter 7, "By the Numbers: Analyzing Your Business with Excel." You'll learn more about using PowerPoint presentations in Chapter 10, "Go to Market with Publisher and PowerPoint." Office Online also includes a business plan template in Word that's designed for established businesses.

Basic Training

If you're new to Word, Microsoft Office Online offers plenty of assistance and training. The online assistance provides instructions for the full range of tasks you perform in Word—everything from creating a document to mass mailings. Figure 2-1 shows you the extent of the offerings.

Chapter Two: Developing a Business Plan

Part One:
Fun &
Fundamentals:
Control What
You Can

Figure 2-1 You'll find lots of online assistance for Word through Microsoft Office Online.

Here are some of the specific training topics you might want to check out before using the business plan template. We'll touch on a couple of these topics in the sections that follow.

- "See What You Can Do with the Research Service"

- "Format Your Document with Styles"

- "Add Graphics and Keep Them Where You Want Them"

- "Headers and Footers, Simple to Elaborate"

For a full list of the available online training, go to office.microsoft.com/training, and then click the link that lets you browse the training courses available for Microsoft Word.

If your preference is to learn from a book, *Microsoft Office Word 2003 Step by Step* (Microsoft Press, 2003) offers hands-on examples and guided exercises that cover all the basic features. If you're a more experienced user of Word or want a comprehensive reference, check out *Microsoft Office Word 2003 Inside Out* (Microsoft Press, 2003).

Part One:
Fun &
Fundamentals:
Control What
You Can

Microsoft Small Business Kit

Doing Your Homework in Word

As part of putting together a business plan, you need to formulate a marketing plan. The background for a marketing plan is developed through research—whether that's knowing how many similar businesses are located in your city or reading about recent trends in the market segment you're targeting. As you'll see in the template's description of what makes for a solid marketing plan, market research is broken down into primary and secondary research. Primary research is the data you gather—the number of regional competitors, for example. Secondary research is gathered from printed sources such as census data, trade journals, and other periodical publications. You can conduct secondary research at your local library or over the Internet. You can consult numerous online sources right when you're working in Word by using the Research task pane, which is shown in Figure 2-2. To open the Research task pane, click Tools, Research, or press Alt and click either mouse button.

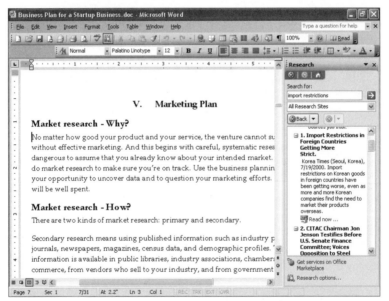

Figure 2-2   Online resources are available by using the Research task pane in Word.

After you've displayed the Research task pane, enter the item you need information about in the Search For box, and then select whether you want to search all the reference books the Research pane makes available (reference books such as the Microsoft Encarta Dictionary and the thesaurus), one or all of the available research sites (such as the Encarta Encyclopedia,

Chapter Two: Developing a Business Plan

Part One:
Fun &
Fundamentals:
Control What
You Can

the MSN search engine, or the Factiva News service), or a business and financial Web site. (To take full advantage of the Factiva News service, you need to set up a username and password.)

It's always wise to document your sources, of course, so be sure you correctly attribute any information you collect online and check whether permission is required to reproduce graphs, drawings, photographs, or similar types of content.

Doing It with Styles

Formatting a long Word document by hand can take hours of work and often results in a document's appearance being inconsistent. One paragraph might be indented five spaces, the next one three. If you come to page 38 of your business plan and then decide to change the font for all the section headings, you have to scroll back through the document and make each change by hand again. Because you'll share your business plan with people who will scrutinize it carefully, the plan's content as well as its appearance needs to be right. Noticeable variations in how the plan appears won't create the best impression about how carefully you prepared it.

Rather than format a Word document manually, use *styles*. Styles are a collection of formatting properties that you can apply and maintain all at once. The business plan template includes styles for headings, a regular paragraph, a list of bulleted items, a caption for tables, and others.

Seeing the Styles in a Document

For the most part, styles are applied to each paragraph in a document. An easy way to see which style is applied to a paragraph is to display the document in Normal view and then adjust the setting for the Style Area Width in Word's Options dialog box.

Display your document styles

1. With the template open, click Normal on the View menu.
2. On the Tools menu, click Options.
3. On the View tab of the Options dialog box, shown here, set Style Area Width to between .5 and 1 inch:

Part One:
Fun &
Fundamentals:
Control What
You Can

Microsoft Small Business Kit

As you can see here, the style names are listed along the left margin of the document:

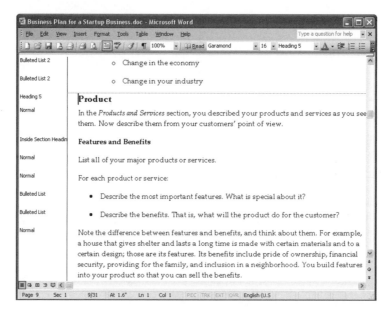

You can also view styles in the task pane by choosing Styles And Formatting from the Format menu or in the Style list that's displayed on the Formatting toolbar.

You use these same tools to apply a style to a paragraph. Start by selecting the paragraph, and then choose the style you need from the Style list on the toolbar or from the list of styles in the Style And Formatting task pane.

Chapter Two: Developing a Business Plan

Part One:
Fun &
Fundamentals:
Control What
You Can

Changing the Look of a Style

Let's say that you're working in the business plan template and want to change the formatting that defines the Normal paragraph style. For example, you'd like to use a different font, indent the first line of all paragraphs, and reduce the space between each line of text.

Quickly change your formatting

To start, be sure that the Styles And Formatting task pane is displayed. If it isn't, click Styles And Formatting on the Format menu. Move to a paragraph that has the Normal style applied to it, and then follow these steps:

1. In the Styles And Formatting task pane, right-click Normal in the drop-down list of styles, and then click Modify on the shortcut menu.

2. At the bottom of the Modify Style dialog box, click the Format button, and select Font. In the Font dialog box, select the font you want to use (say, Times New Roman), and then click OK.

3. Back in the Modify Style dialog box, click Format again, and select Paragraph.

4. In the Paragraph dialog box, under Indentation, select First Line from the Special list, and then set the By box to the amount of indentation you want.

5. In the Spacing area of the Paragraph dialog box, in the After box, change 12 pt to 6 pt.

6. Click OK in the Paragraph dialog box, and then click OK in the Modify Style dialog box. The new attributes of the style are now applied to each paragraph styled with Normal.

Taking these few steps is a lot less work than changing each paragraph one by one and keeps the look of the document consistent. You can follow steps similar to these to change other styles and other formatting properties that make up a style.

Defining your own style

If you want to create a style of your own to use in the business plan template (or in another Word document), open the Style And Formatting task pane, and then click New Style. In the New Style dialog box, enter a name for the style, and then define the properties of the style such as the font, the font size, the line spacing, and so on.

Part One:
Fun &
Fundamentals:
Control What
You Can

Microsoft Small Business Kit

A Few Extras: More Tips for Your Professional Documents

After working through the business plan template, be sure that you take care of a few mechanical matters before you distribute your business plan, either as a printed document or as an e-mail attachment.

Headers and Footers

The first task is to update the information for page headers and footers—the text that appears at the top or bottom of each page. The business plan template includes the page number (in the format *Page X of XX*) in the document header. You might want to change the format of the pagination, show the page number in the footer instead, or insert additional text—your company's name, for example, or the label *Confidential* if you're disclosing information that you want people to treat with discretion.

To work with document headers and footers, click Header And Footer on the View menu, and then use the Header And Footer toolbar to modify or insert the information you want to include.

Updating the Table of Contents

Another important task is to update the entries in the table of contents and the page number where each section begins. In the business plan template, each major section heading shown in the table of contents is formatted with the style named Heading 3. If you add a section to the template and want the section title included in the table of contents, be sure you use the Heading 3 style. Also, if you build a business plan by deleting the template's descriptive text and adding your own, the page numbers on which each section begins will change.

Update the table of contents

1. Right-click anywhere within the current table of contents.

2. On the shortcut menu, click Update Field.

3. In the Update Table Of Contents dialog box, select the option to update only page numbers or the option to update the entire table of contents (section titles and pagination).

Chapter Two: Developing a Business Plan

Part One:
Fun &
Fundamentals:
Control What
You Can

Table of contents options

If you want to modify which styles Word uses to identify the items it includes in a table of contents, click Insert, Reference, Index And Tables. In the Index And Tables dialog box, click the Table Of Contents tab, and then click Options. You can then choose which styles you want to use to build the table of contents. The Table of Contents tab also provides options for the format of the table of contents. For example, you can use the same formatting as in the document or choose one of the formats that comes with Word.

Controlling Page Breaks

Finally, you often want to start or end a page at a specific spot. You don't want to split a table across two pages unless you have to, for example, and you don't want the title of the next section to appear by itself at the bottom of a page.

You can use the Line And Page Breaks tab of the Paragraph dialog box to control how Word paginates your document. For example, you can prevent a page break from occurring within a paragraph. To set the ways in which Word will paginate your business plan document, click Paragraph on the Format menu, and then select the Line And Page Breaks tab. Here's a rundown of the options you have:

Widow/Orphan Control   If you choose this option, Word won't print the last line of a paragraph by itself at the top of a page (a widow) or the first line of a paragraph by itself at the bottom of a page (an orphan).

Keep Lines Together   This option keeps Word from inserting a page break within a paragraph.

Keep With Next   Select this option if you don't want a page break between a paragraph you've selected and the paragraph that follows it.

Page Break Before   If you choose this option, Word will insert a page break before the paragraph you've selected.

For More Information

In addition to the resources mentioned in this chapter, you will find links and information on the companion CD. Some books and Web sites particularly useful as you research your market opportunity include:

Part One:
Fun &
Fundamentals:
Control What
You Can

Microsoft Small Business Kit

Books

- Dan Hill, *Body of Truth: Leveraging What Consumers Can't or Won't Say* (Wiley)

- Gerald Zaltman, *How Customers Think: Essential Insights into the Mind of the Market* (Harvard Business School Press)

- Paco Underhill, *Why We Buy: The Science of Shopping* (Simon & Schuster)

Web Sites

- 2001 Statistical Abstract of the United States: *http://www.census.gov/prod/2002pubs/01statab/stat-ab01.html*

- About.com marketing portal: *http://marketing.about.com*

- Conducting Market Research, a brief how-to: *http://ohioline.osu.edu/cd-fact/1252.html*

- Economic Indicators from the National Bureau of Economic Research: *http://www.nber.org/releases/*

Having money is just the best thing in the world.

— *Madonna (b. 1958), quoted in* People *magazine, August 30, 1993*

Chapter Three

How to Find Backing

Money is critical to starting a business. But without a proven track record, it's tough to find capital. These funding sources and ideas can help you launch your business and support you through the early phases of its operation.

What you'll find:

- ❏ Financing basics
- ❏ Angels who help you fly
- ❏ Loans and venture capitalists

Part One:
Fun &
Fundamentals:
Control What
You Can

Microsoft Small Business Kit

Financing Basics

After the research, planning, refining, and tweaking, there comes that time when you must find money to finance your idea. Few entrepreneurs have the luxury of much money to start. Most start small and build incrementally.

In 2003, for example, the Small Business Administration (SBA) named Sharon E. Bennett and co-owner Evan C. Wooten National Small Business Persons of the Year for their Premier Pet Products, a Richmond, Virginia, company that produces and sells leashes and specialty pet products.

Bennett got the idea for her business in 1988, after her family adopted a greyhound racing dog whose competitive days at the track were over. She learned that most retired greyhounds are put to death. So Bennett founded the Richmond chapter of Greyhound Pets of America to promote adoptions. A year later, with a loan of only $5,000, she bought a couple of used sewing machines and some raw materials and began making unusual and less restrictive dog collars and leashes at home. Over the intervening years, Premier Pet Products grew, along with the help of an SBA-backed loan. In 1998, she brought in Wooten to help on the business side. The company now distributes its products to big pet specialty retail chains and about 10,000 independent pet supply retailers, veterinarians, and dog trainers. Sales hit a whopping $10 million in 2002.

Bennett, of course, tapped into a fast-growing market—early. Treating pets like one of the family has been an intensifying phenomenon across the country. To succeed, you will need a smart, thought-out idea that fills a need or a niche—like Bennett's. But you don't need a lot of dough at the outset to build a multimillion-dollar business.

For more information about winners of the Small Business Person of the Year award, visit the SBA Web site at www.sba.gov/50/winners.html.

See "Some Ideas for Start-Ups," page 6, to learn more about start-up ideas.

Growing in Stages

Throughout the life of a company, businesses alternately rely on two categories of financing to fund the traditional stages of growth. There's *debt financing*, which means money that's borrowed, whether from friends and family or, later on, from private or public institutions, banks, or credit lenders. The second is *equity financing*, which means money that's invested in the business, whether your own savings or savings from friends and family. Again,

Chapter Three: How to Find Backing

Part One:
Fun &
Fundamentals:
Control What
You Can

after the business has grown, more formal equity financing might come from private or public venture capitalists, strategic business partners, or ultimately, from a public offering that sells stock in the company.

At the start-up stage, you need what's called *seed capital* and *first-stage financing*. That's money that will put the finishing touches on your products or services to ready them for sale. These funds also cover the immediate costs of getting up and going, which can vary considerably. Imagine, for a moment, the needs of a consulting practice. That might begin with a shingle on the front lawn and a PC on the kitchen table. Then think what's needed for an international freight business. That might require three or more private aircraft, hangar and runway fees, and maintenance staff and pilots—not to mention licenses and government documents for trade in world capitals and major cities. Seed capital can add up to a little or quite a lot, depending on your business. First-stage money (which includes seed capital) must see you through to the time when you actually have some cash coming in.

Second-stage financing is typically for the growth phase, when the business has proven its mettle and you're looking for capital to expand. Sales are steady and building. Customers are numerous and growing. The business owns significant assets, both *tangible* (inventory and equipment) and *intangible* (your brand and reputation or customer loyalty).

Third-stage financing usually includes what's called an *exit strategy*. This is when you've decided to reap the profits of your hard work, either by selling to another owner or by agreeing to an acquisition by another company. Third-stage financing might also mean taking the company public with a first sale of stock to the public—that is, an *initial public offering* (IPO). (Sometimes IPOs are planned for the second stage, although not as often.) If you've been tapping venture capital—that is, money professionally managed by a company that invests in start-ups—this is the stage when the venture capitalists get their cash payoff and move on.

Financing Stages

Seed capital and first stage   Money to develop your concept, business plan, prototypes, products, or services. Funding that will support your personal and business operating expenses for the time it takes to develop a positive cash flow.

Second stage   The business is a going concern. Sales are growing and customers are buying. More sophisticated second-stage financing is needed to fund expansion plans.

Third stage   The business is a success. Marketing, distribution, sales, and management are all working. The company is being prepared for "harvest." Financing might be needed to improve the balance sheet or boost profit margins to prepare for a buyout or acquisition.

Part One:
Fun &
Fundamentals:
Control What
You Can

Microsoft Small Business Kit

Preparing for the Unexpected

For our purposes, and for your needs in getting a business off the ground, we're concentrating here on beginnings: seed capital and first-stage financing. What follows in this chapter is advice and ideas about getting from zero to launch and initial operation. There's also some explanation of what it takes to borrow money, including attracting venture capital, but because that kind of financing usually kicks in at second-stage growth, the explanations are brief outlines, just to give you an idea of what comes next.

Naturally, an analysis of your business's financial needs was calculated into your business plan. But real-time, down-to-earth, now-or-never launches have a way of forcing entrepreneurs to fill in details that big-picture plans might have overlooked. In addition, your thinking about the business might have changed since you drafted the plan and went looking for backers. Or conditions in the marketplace might have pushed you to reevaluate the business model. There are any number of reasons to pause and consider your needs. Raising money always takes longer and proves harder than most owners think it will. As you cast about for backing, you have an opportunity to rejigger your plans for financing and operating costs.

See "Guidelines for Creating Your Plan," page 36, to learn more about business plans.

While it's true that you don't need much to start, the flip side is equally the case. Would-be entrepreneurs tend to underestimate the amount of money they'll need to sustain themselves and the business before sales grow and cash starts flowing. It pays to be conservative. Typically, inexperienced owners overspend at the outset, buying more furniture, technology, and office supplies or hiring way too many executives or experts than they really need to get up and going. New owners also don't realize that few customers pay promptly. Even when sales are immediate, cash can remain very tight. The irony is that if you don't have adequate funds to see you through the drought between orders and cash flow, you can actually go under by attracting too many sales.

Consider, for example, Ruta Fox and her "Ah ring." A few years back, Fox began marketing the first diamond ring made for single women. *Ah* stands for "available" and "happy." Worn on the pinkie and priced competitively, the ring is a 14-karat white-gold band of small diamonds with *Ah* engraved inside. "Engaged women have their engagement rings, and married women have their wedding bands," says Fox. "But there was nothing on the market

Chapter Three: How to Find Backing

Part One:
Fun &
Fundamentals:
Control What
You Can

specifically designed for single women." There are about 43 million single women in the United States alone.

Fox meandered into being an entrepreneur, basically as her own best customer. In the summer of 2000, as dot-coms went bust, Fox, an advertising copywriter and creative director, left her job at a New York branding agency. In the fall, she bought herself a diamond pinkie ring. "I've always bought jewelry for myself, and I've always loved diamonds," she says. "This ring was fresh looking. I liked the look." A friend liked it too and asked Fox to get her one. Then a few more friends had to have one. "My friends are all single, happy, great women," says Fox, who grew up in Los Angeles and has lived in New York since 1994. "They all wanted the ring. I figured maybe I could write part-time and try this cottage industry. The ring was cute, and the quality and value was there. The price was right. Maybe it would build into something."

After years of working in the fashion industry, Fox knew people in the style biz all over town. She also had a connection in New York's wholesale jewelry district. She began adding a bit to the price of each ring to make it worth her while. Then she hand-delivered the bands, making sure of a perfect fit. After Fox had sold a half dozen or so, a friend reminded her that she was a branding pro. The ring needed an identity. "I sat down one day and cooked up the hook of the Ah ring," says Fox. "I knew it was a big idea right away." By November, Fox had cashed in $3,000 in savings to buy more rings. She created a press kit, with a folder and a press release. She began packaging the rings in velvet and suede pouches. Editor friends at fashion magazines invited her to their offices to present the rings for sale to their staffs. One of those was *O*, Oprah Winfrey's magazine.

The rest became Ah ring history. An editor sent off a ring to Oprah, who loved it and the concept of women celebrating being single and buying diamonds for themselves. Oprah included the Ah ring in her "O List"—a popular column that features Oprah's fave raves. "I got the call that said Oprah loves the ring and it would be in the March issue," says Fox. "The editor asked for my 800 number and my Web site, and I said, 'Oh, I have another call. Let me call you back.'"

Monthly magazines hit newsstands about three weeks before the cover date. Fox had roughly six weeks to put a business into place that could respond to who-knew-how-many orders. "I kept thinking this is my shot, the brass ring," says Fox. "*O* has a circulation of 2.2 million—and this was Oprah's own recommendation! I started dialing everyone I could think of to ask questions about merchant bank accounts and fulfillment houses. I kept a notebook by the phone and logged in everyone's advice."

Part One:
Fun &
Fundamentals:
Control What
You Can

Microsoft Small Business Kit

Then Fox went into action. She set up Divine Diamonds as an S Corporation, trademarked the Ah Ring name, hired a fulfillment house to maintain phone lines and take orders, created a Web site (just for information, not transactions), opened a UPS shipping account, ordered velvet pouches, and planned to process orders herself. When the issue of *O* appeared, she was ready. "My phone rang off the wall because of Oprah," says Fox. "I got hundreds of orders."

See "Choosing a Business Structure," page 29, to learn more about forming business structures.

There was just one problem. A month later, she hit the entrepreneurial wall. Fox had orders aplenty but no cash for inventory. She was about to go under with dozens of orders she couldn't afford to fulfill, when her accountant advised her to borrow the money. Reluctantly, Fox borrowed $30,000 from her mother. Some customers waited six weeks for delivery, but at the end of the rush, she honored every order. And she paid back her mom—with interest—after a month.

Fox had a lucky strike—built on well-honed marketing instincts, of course. But she faced decisions and obstacles encountered by all baby businesses. Among your other strategies, make sure you have some contingency plan in case your product takes off. After developing personal and business budgets that can sustain the company for the time you think it'll take to get to breakeven, add at least 50 percent, suggests John Reddish, whose management consultant firm, Advent Management International, specializes in growth strategies. "That's managing your risk."

Savings and Credit Cards

Until a business has a track record and is poised for second-stage expansion, it's almost impossible to convince backers to bet on your enterprise. These days, most entrepreneurs start by relying on a combination of savings (their own money or loans from friends and family) and revolving credit card debt.

If you plan to quit your day job and live off savings while funding your start-up, be careful. Be very careful. You don't want to risk eroding your own or your family's financial security or future options. Borrowing funds from a retirement savings account, such as an IRA or a 401(k), not only incurs heavy penalties but also eats away at the time and the amount that can compound—and compounding is the magic that fuels tax-deferred investments. Draining such accounts or cashing in investments might also impact your kids' college dreams. Instead of tapping into retirement or educational savings, many people leverage the equity accumulated in their homes by apply-

Chapter Three: How to Find Backing

Part One:
Fun &
Fundamentals:
Control What
You Can

ing for home equity loans or taking a second mortgage. These options too present risks. If your company goes under, you might be forced to sell your home to pay debts. Consider whether there's a life insurance policy that you don't really need. If so, you might cash in that policy to fund the business.

The lesson here is not to avoid all risk. That's impossible when starting a business. But do think through all the consequences of using any personal assets or savings beforehand—not when it's too late.

Part of running a business is getting used to the idea of being in debt—at least in a manageable way. In the past decade, as entrepreneurs have thrived, a host of banks and financial institutions have developed credit cards and lines of credit or revolving loan accounts that are specifically designed to serve the small business market. Credit cards have become an increasingly popular source of funding for small companies.

If you do rely on personal and business credit cards or a line of credit to float your operating expenses, perhaps bolstered by savings, you need to pay careful attention. Your agreement with the bank or financial institution gives you a specific amount, a limit of credit that you can tap. That way, you can pay expenses and have the financial resources to weather unexpected crises or big-ticket, one-time costs, such as office equipment or travel. But it also means that you must pay back what you've used within the month or pay interest on the outstanding amount. And interest rates offered by credit cards and lines of credit are usually the most expensive form of financing you'll find. If you let the outstanding balance mount, you could soon be overwhelmed by the interest payments.

When using credit cards, be sure to:

- Clean up your credit rating before applying for any cards. If you need to establish credit, try setting up charge accounts with retailers, like Office Depot, Kinko's, or Staples. Your track record with retailers will help your credit rating when you apply for bankcards.

Credit Cards Support Small Businesses

A 1998 study of sources of financing for small businesses from the SBA's Office of Advocacy surveyed 3,500 nationally representative companies with 1 to 499 employees. Here are their findings:

- Personal credit cards were the number one source of financing.

- More than 80 percent of small businesses used some kind of credit and had outstanding debt.

- More than seven out of 10 (71 percent) of small businesses had used credit cards and owner loans.

- Nearly half (46 percent) of small businesses used personal credit cards.

- 34 percent of small businesses used business credit cards.

Part One:
Fun &
Fundamentals:
Control What
You Can

Microsoft Small Business Kit

- Carefully track how much you're spending against your credit limit.

- Each month, pay off as much of the balance as possible. Ideally, pay it entirely.

- Keep records of what you charge on your personal card vs. business cards. Basically, charges on your personal cards are loans from yourself to the business. Check with your accountant about how to handle that.

- Assuming that you're conscientious about paying off the debt each month, the higher the credit limit the bank will extend, the better. When you're ready for expansion in a few years, you'll have developed a relationship and proven yourself as reliable.

Check your credit rating

Before applying for a credit card or a loan, check out your credit rating from one of the three major credit bureaus:

- Equifax: *www.equifax.com/*
- Experian: *www.experian.com/*
- TransUnion: *www.transunion.com/*

Note The cost is about $10 for a personal report or about $35 for an overview report consisting of a credit report from each of the three credit reporting agencies.

Tapping Family, Friends, and Generous Relatives

Sometimes called *love money*, for obvious reasons, capital that comes from relatives or friends is typically a doubled-edged blessing. On the one hand, the money is given with great faith and affection. Everyone knows the players. Everyone feels good about helping each other. On the other hand, make no mistake, the exchange of money injects tension into any relationship.

If you have well-off loved ones who agree to give you a portion of your start-up fund, here's advice that can avoid trouble down the line:

Separate the personal from the business.   Don't offer business updates at social get-togethers. If the relevant relatives want to hear details, or if you feel like reporting to them on your progress, send out a casual letter or e-mail message every quarter. Keep that report focused on business; don't use it to chat about the kids as well.

Chapter Three: How to Find Backing

Part One:
Fun &
Fundamentals:
Control What
You Can

Explain the risks up front.   The whole family is rooting for you. No one wants to even utter the words "What if...?" It's up to you to do so. Be sure that anyone giving you money—even your little sister—spends time with your business plan. Have an unembarrassed, unhurried conversation that clearly explains the potential downside. At that time, ask the lender if he or she is able and prepared to lose the money. Not that it will happen, of course. But it could.

Check about the strings attached.   Often, family and friends will simply hand over the money with expectations about which you're blissfully unaware. For example, they might expect that you'll do a lot more than simply reimburse them for the borrowed amount at some future date—you'll fork over a share of the profits. They might assume that they now own equity in the company. They might expect you to add interest to the term of the loan at whatever the going rate is for bank loans. Or they might wait to see how much bonus you plan to add by way of a thank-you and then tell you what they expected. You'd be surprised what people think when they lend money, even when it's your mom. Explore expectations before taking any cash. Make it clear that this is a loan, not equity (unless that's what you've decided to sell). Then be sure that you'll be comfortable running your business with whatever strings might get yanked. Or don't take the money.

Make a formal agreement.   Five years after receiving that very necessary $3,500 loan from Uncle Harry, it seems he's sure it was actually $4,500. Not only that, he's absolutely positive that he mentioned he wanted some kind of payback or interest on the loan. So now you own him $4,500 plus some kind of compounded bonus. It's not like you can argue with Uncle Harry or take him to court. You get the picture. For everyone's benefit, sign some sort of legal agreement at the outset. Spell out the details of the arrangement, including the amount, whether there's any interest expected, the term of the loan—every detail. Then make sure you get everyone's signature on it. Uncle Harry might keep waving off the piece of paper, saying he trusts you. Yes, everyone trusts everyone. Just get the agreement signed.

Plan how you will say no.   Somewhere along the line, without question, one of those loved ones who gave money will turn up to ask for something you can't or don't want to give. It might be hiring young Susan to be your marketing director—"she needs the experience." It might be letting poor Andrew hang out at your office—"just till he gets on his feet." Whatever the request, you'll need to steer clear. Once someone gives you money to run a business, a sense of ownership settles in. It's

Part One:
Fun &
Fundamentals:
Control What
You Can

Microsoft Small Business Kit

human nature. Your college roommate, who gladly handed over $10,000 when you needed it, has now been promoted to senior vice president in a Fortune 500 corporation. She's convinced that she knows what's right for your firm. Maybe so. Entrepreneurs are notorious for ignoring sage advice from trusted sources, but in the end, it's your company. When you have to, just say no.

See sections "Angels Who Help You Fly" and "Loans and Venture Capitalists," later in this chapter, and in Chapter 4, see "Forming an Advisory Board," page 95, and "Where to Find Advisors," page 97 to learn more about informal advisors.

Bootstrapping—Lean and Mean Financing

There are various definitions floating around about the financing strategy called *bootstrapping*. For some owners, bootstrapping means focusing on a smaller playing field or a less-expensive product that will offer immediate returns. When revenue starts flowing, the entrepreneur can move on to what he or she really wants to produce. For other owners, it's tight cost control, with step-by-step progress that avoids any serious financial risk until it's clear the business can take it. Sometimes, bootstrapping is a rigorous, narrow-focus mission shaped by a consultant or a venture capital firm to drive a start-up—typically, a service or technology business—toward second-stage growth and a public offering. During the dot-com heyday, that was a big favorite, as you can imagine. But in less exuberant times, bootstrapping is still a useful tool. It's a time-honored technique for growing the company that's neither rocket science nor hard to apply. When you're fresh out of funds, you always have bootstrapping to fall back on. In fact, savvy entrepreneurs rely on bootstrapping even with adequate money in the bank.

Some Like It Cheap

There are dozens of ways to be frugal while you bootstrap your way to success. You'll likely figure how your business can leverage such tactics as you go along.

What Is Bootstrapping?

Bootstrapping basically means you pinch pennies and cut corners to save money for when it counts. You use imagination, sweat, and know-how instead of money to stretch your time and resources. Lacking ready cash, you build the business by leveraging what you've got and by forging alliances with helpful partners. When you don't qualify for a bank loan or an SBA loan, and when you can't interest an angel or a venture capitalist (who rarely are interested in companies worth less than $5 million or so), you go with the limited means you have. (See the sections "Angels Who Help You Fly" and "Loans and Venture Capitalists," later in this chapter, for more about angels, loans, and venture capital funding.)

Chapter Three: How to Find Backing

Part One:
Fun &
Fundamentals:
Control What
You Can

In the meantime, steal these bootstrapping ideas:

Select the right customers.   Cash is key. You can get revenues flowing either by targeting customers who will pay right away or by focusing on big-ticket sales, so every pitch counts for a lot.

Create a high profile.   If you take on big-deal projects that clients thought were beyond your start-up resources, you project an image of confidence and size. Sooner, rather than later, it's actually true—you're bigger than you think. That goes for such tactics as call forwarding or pretending to be the receptionist when someone calls. Who's to know you're a sole proprietor?

Cut your salary.   The less the business must pay for, the better. Nurse your old car. Work holidays and weekends. Don't buy a new suit. Postpone, postpone, postpone.

Turn customers into sales staff.   Word-of-mouth and other customer-centric marketing is the cheapest and most effective way to boost sales.

See "Creating Word of Mouth or Word of Mouse" page 220, and "Rewarding Return Customers," page 294, to learn more about customer evangelists.

Go to Plan B.   When you draft your business plan, try to create *side-by-side alternatives*—strategies for thriving and strategies for surviving, as one small business consultant puts it. If your funds start shrinking, have a fallback plan.

Forget about status symbols.   No, you don't need a Mont Blanc pen, or the latest in cell phones, or dinners with clients at the hottest restaurant in town. The only exception to this advice is when you need to impress a big-deal client, as described in the earlier list item, "Create a high profile."

Track every dollar.   This is a serious skill to develop. If you know where the cash is going, you can adjust on a dime. Pay attention to your tax requirements. Find out which suppliers will let you float for a while. Speed up invoicing, if the customers won't howl. Don't offer preferential treatment or discounts to special customers—one price fits all. Delay payments to vendors (if it won't end up hurting you long-term).

See Chapter 6, "Tax Tactics," for more information on tax issues particular to small businesses.

Discover the power of partners.   This strategy is usually underutilized, and it can cover a lot of your needs. Find another business owner and share equipment, technology, office space, or supplies. You can leverage the cost of leasing cars and other gear with a partner. You can buy used equipment and share that too. If you coordinate your projects

Part One:
Fun &
Fundamentals:
Control What
You Can

Microsoft Small Business Kit

with another business, you might be able to share consultant or employee support as well, such as a marketing or an IT expert. You can swap services or equipment when each business needs it. You can also coordinate purchases so that you get volume discounts.

Pay in trade.   Bartering exchanges and organizations that help members trade services and products are everywhere these days, both online and offline. These groups allow participating members to exchange their own wares for goods or services they want in return. No money actually changes hands. The unit of currency is usually some kind of points or credits. These bartering groups keep track of all legal and tax responsibilities and usually send along the paperwork to members so that you don't have to. Whether this arrangement works often depends on what you're offering and what you're shopping for. You need to be careful about getting good value. Try checking out the offerings of a few exchanges (an online search will bring up dozens of options) to see whether they're for you.

Hire free agents.   Instead of paying full-time help, hire consultants, temps, or freelancers on a short-term basis.

See "Managing the New Work Force," page 395, to learn more about independent contractors.

Bootstrapping benefits

- ■ If you avoid heavy debt, the company will be worth more when you're ready to expand.

- ■ Backers will lend money more readily if your credit rating is good and you have a history of fiscal restraint.

- ■ It's easy to pull the plug if the business isn't clicking. No investors. No loans to replay. It's a great way to experiment with a start-up.

Angels Who Help You Fly

Typically, *angels* are wealthy private investors looking for a business opportunity, an active role, and high-risk, high-yield investments that have greater returns than conventional investments—that is, 25 percent or more. The term *angel* comes from the prosperous businessmen who invested their money in Broadway productions back in the early 1900s. Some very famous businesses, such as Ford Motor Company, The Body Shop, and Amazon.com, were all dusted with angel money before becoming the giants you know today.

Chapter Three: How to Find Backing

Part One:
Fun &
Fundamentals:
Control What
You Can

Often, angels have entrepreneurial experience or business success themselves, which is why they like to stay involved. They tend to focus on ventures with a basic business plan and strategy in the seed stage of growth.

Counting angels

In 2002, according to a study conducted by the University of New Hampshire's Center for Venture Research (*www.unh.edu/cvr*) on angels across the country, a profile of angel financing looks like this:

- About 200,000 angels in the United States invested about $15.7 billion in approximately 36,000 businesses (down from $30 billion in 2001).
- On average, five to six investors joined forces to fund a start-up.
- Approximately 1 in 10 start-up or early-stage companies in the United States receive equity capital from angel investors.

In fact, angel financing is the largest source of capital in the United States for seed money and start-ups, whether in the form of loans or actual equity in the company. This private investor financing bridges the gap between self-funding (including money from friends and family) and more formal financing, represented by financial institutions and venture capitalists, whether public or private. Unlike friends or family, however, a *business angel investor* is accredited and is legally empowered to invest under terms defined by the U.S. Securities and Exchange Commission (SEC). For most entrepreneurs, angels bring a lot more than money, however. They also offer hands-on experience, long-term expertise, industry and financial contacts, and a rich source of seasoned counsel.

There are dozens of groups, dinner clubs, networks, and other groups that embrace all kinds of angel investors. Angels come in all sizes, personalities, and levels of wealth; they can be individual investors or an informal group of people.

Various industry sources suggest that the profile of a typical angel investor runs something like this:

Age   40 to 60 years old

Education   Postgraduate degree with experience in management or building a company

Net worth $1 million or more

Amount invested $25,000 to $250,000 per deal

Part One:
Fun &
Fundamentals:
Control What
You Can

Microsoft Small Business Kit

Number of deals   One to four per year

Length of investment   Usually five to seven years

Approaching an Angel

Any Web search will turn up a dizzying array of potential angel investors. You can also ask your lawyer or accountant (or friends in that profession) to recommend local angels.

A good place to start is Access to Capital Electronic Network (ACE-Net, also known as the Angel Capital Electronic Network; available at *acenet.csusb.edu*), which is a program that grew out of the 1995 White House Conference on Small Business. ACE-Net was developed under the guidance of the SBA's Office of Advocacy for the express purpose of helping newbie entrepreneurs gain access to capital, especially because new businesses today demand so much more start-up money than they did even a few decades ago.

The organization acts as a facilitator as well as a training resource. Through an Internet database, ACE-Net helps individual accredited investors, venture capitalists, and public-private venture partnerships known as *Small Business Investment Companies* (SBICs) to find small businesses in need of capital. (See the section "Accessing Venture Capital," later in this chapter, for details about SBICs.) Today, local ACE-Net Network Operators can be found in just about every state, operating with the help of state government or university nonprofit development groups.

Note   Since its founding, ACE-Net is estimated to have helped 2,500 entrepreneurs gain access to more than $4 billion, for both start-up and expansion needs.

If you're trying to attract an angel investor or want to work with one, keep these tips in mind:

Be up-front about your business strengths and weaknesses.   Angels are "been there, done that" types, and the truth will always surface, sooner or later. You're much better off being candid about what you need and what you're confident about. You'll end up winning points for showing integrity.

Put your passion and your experience front and center.   Angels invest in people much more than in companies or business models. The first questions they ask are always about management and vision, domain, or industry expertise.

Chapter Three: How to Find Backing

Part One:
Fun &
Fundamentals:
Control What
You Can

Be sure that your product or service is ready for sale. Virtual businesses typically don't interest angels.

Be prepared for tough questions. Angels know how much time and money new businesses demand. Don't hustle an angel. And don't sugarcoat your situation. You should be clear about what it will take to grow your business, with specific details and a clear budget forecast. If you need to fine-tune the financials of your plan before meeting with an angel investor, get help from an accountant or a management consultant.

Don't be hasty. Check with your lawyer, accountant, and other appropriate experts before making any deal. You might want to talk to your significant other as well, assuming that he or she is going to be living the lifestyle you choose.

To find angel resources online, search the following Web sites: The ACE-Net database: acenet.csusb.edu/ and The Entrepreneur's Search Engine (supported by the Ewing Marion Kaufman Foundation): www.entreworld.org/.

Loans and Venture Capitalists

When you're ready to borrow money—and remember this usually means that you've reached the expansion phase, requiring second-stage, or mezzanine, financing—there are several sources to consider. These include commercial bank loans, loans backed by state or federal government small business programs, or venture capitalists, either public or private. Here's a quick rundown of the options.

Working with a Commercial Bank

Most of the time, banks will require some kind of guarantee for giving you money, called *collateral*. That could be your house, which might guarantee a home equity loan, or some other kind of tangible asset, such as investments, property, or the like. You can even back a loan by keeping cash in a savings account that can't be touched until you've paid off the loan. Banks often approve home equity loans more easily than other kinds of loans because the collateral of a house provides them with lower risks. In other words, there's something substantial they can take in case you default on your loan. Not a fun prospect. On the plus side, the interest on home equity loans is usually tax-deductible (as is most interest on loans).

When you're ready to apply for a loan, it's worthwhile to have already established a relationship with a bank. (See the section "Savings and Credit Cards," earlier in this chapter, for more information.) You'll have a history of credit-

Part One:
Fun &
Fundamentals:
Control What
You Can

Microsoft Small Business Kit

worthiness as well as a track record of being a good money manager. Call the bank you've been using for your line of credit or other financing needs, and set up an appointment to talk about the types of financing that might work for you. Most banks now have officers who specialize in the needs of small businesses. But any bank officer will be delighted to explain all the possibilities and nuances of the bank's lending policies and packages, no matter how small your business or how much financial education you might need. It pays for them to loan you money and grow along with you.

As a trusted customer with an existing relationship, you might be able to negotiate a lower interest rate on your loan. If you need to buy equipment, you can discuss the options of leasing vs. purchasing with your bank officer. Sometimes, your money needs might be satisfied by simply raising the ceiling on your current line of credit.

Before meeting with a banker, be prepared for serious financial discussion. Show up with all the business documents and projections that will bolster your credibility and success, and be prepared to answer question about the past and the future.

You'll need the following rationale and documents to make a good impression on a loan officer:

A cash-flow story   What's the money earmarked for? What will the cash do for your business? Why do you need more credit?

A revised business plan   Bring in the plan to show to the banker, but also include your refinements or changes based on your current needs or changing market conditions. This gives the banker a clear idea of where you've been and where you're going, as well as an overview of your industry, market size, and profit projections. If you need help with revisions, tap the expertise of a consultant. You can get free help from a local Service Corps of Retired Executives (SCORE) office.

Note   SCORE (*www.score.org/*) is a national nonprofit resource group that partners with the SBA. It has 10,500 volunteers who offer small business counseling and training via 389 chapters and 800 branches. SCORE also provides many of the business templates available on Microsoft Office Online. One of the templates they provide—described in the sidebar "Using the Bank Loan Request For Small Business Template," at the end of this section—is a sample cover letter for requesting a bank loan for a small business.

Chapter Three: How to Find Backing

Part One:
Fun &
Fundamentals:
Control What
You Can

A diversified customer base and supplier network   Bankers are uncomfortable when all your revenue is tied to one or two big customers. Having all the eggs in one or two baskets doesn't look like a safe bet.

A strategic accountant   Your financial professional should be able to help you package your financial story and set up a business picture with the best possible view.

Using the Bank Loan Request For Small Business Template

If you're planning to submit a loan request to a bank, a good place to start is the sample cover letter included among the Business Financial Planning templates (in the Finance and Accounting category) on Microsoft Office Online (*www.office.microsoft.com/templates*). The letter (a Microsoft Word document) lists the sort of business information a bank would expect—a description of your business (including a brief history and a list of the business's activities), financial information, a statement about the purpose of the loan—and some of the documentation you will likely need to provide, including a business plan, a balance sheet, and some market analysis.

The sample cover letter also comes with a writing guide, pointing out that written information you provide to people who don't know you will be judged in part by the quality of the writing. You'll find tips such as "Avoid slang and contractions" and "Write in the active voice and in short sentences." The advice is right on the mark.

As you compose your own version of a loan request cover letter in Microsoft Word, you can use a couple of Word's tools to help the quality of your written presentation. The Research task pane (choose Tools, Research) includes a thesaurus that you can use to find just the right word. And, of course, Word comes with a spelling and grammar checker. When you're checking the spelling of a document or letter, in addition to correcting mistakes that Word finds, be sure to add terms that are unique to your business—a product name, for example—to the dictionary so that you don't risk misspelling them in the future. You can also set up a list of stylistic qualities that you want Word to check in your writing, as shown here:

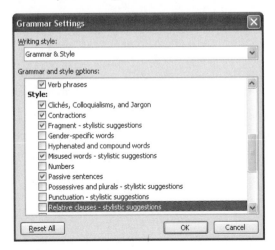

Banks typically make business loans based on the five Cs.

Think about how you will explain your ability to meet these five critieria:

- Capacity to repay
- Capital required
- Character of the lender
- Collateral security
- Condition of the lender's overall financial picture

Factoring or Commercial Finance Companies

Independent, private finance companies can also lend you money—at an extremely expensive interest rate. These loans raise cash fast and are based on the current assets of your company. That might include the value of your accounts receivable, your inventory, or other valuable equipment, such as autos or computers. If you default on the loan, the finance company moves in and liquidates those assets. This is not the safest financing choice. Factoring, or asset-based, lenders typically extend about 80 percent of the worth of your assets (for nondelinquent accounts) and will charge you a stiff 14 percent to a staggering 50 percent rate of interest. You have to need cash—bad—to select this financing.

Lending terms

Here's a quick review of the terms you're likely to encounter:

Capital   Money invested in a business to be used for buying fixed assets rather than to cover everyday operating expenses. Also known as *venture capital*.

Tangible assets   Any property owned by an individual or the business, such as land, equipment, investments, inventory, autos, or other valuables.

Current assets   Accounts receivable (usually limited to what income is expected within a year), cash on hand, and inventory. For more information about managing accounts receivable and other accounting categories, see Chapter 5, "Follow the Money."

Government Loans and Programs

There's an enduring myth that all you have to do to get government money to start a business is ask Uncle Sam. He'll gladly dip into his moneybag and

Chapter Three: How to Find Backing

Part One:
Fun &
Fundamentals:
Control What
You Can

hand out money to enterprising entrepreneurs. If you've been hot on the trail of this rich government source, forget it. There is no free launch!

What you will find in government support is a slew of amazing programs that offer low interest rates, long repayment terms, helpful loan guarantees (so you don't have to come up with crippling collateral), and a wide range of community, municipal, state, and federal programs. These initiatives are designed to serve entrepreneurs who would not otherwise qualify for loans from commercial sources. To find out about local options, check with your bank (that handy-dandy relationship with your bank officer kicks in here too) as well as the local chamber of commerce and your city and state commerce divisions.

For more information or to find your local chapter, visit the U.S. Chamber of Commerce Small Business Center: www.uschamber.com/sb/default.

The most well-known government programs, of course, are overseen by the SBA (*www.sba.gov*), which partners with other groups, both government and private. There are billions of dollars set aside to assist small businesses, and you can find various programs for loans that offer a few hundred to millions of dollars. Many SBA programs also provide free advice and training. The SBA has also set up programs specifically designed to aid businesses owned by minorities, special interests, and women.

SBA programs

Here are links where you can find information about several SBA programs:

- For women: *www.sba.gov/financing/special/women.html*
- For minorities: *www.sba.gov/financing/special/minorities.html*
- For veterans: *www.sba.gov/financing/special/veterans.html*
- For Native Americans: *www.sba.gov/financing/special/native.html*

An excellent resource to learn more about government funding and assistance is one of the Small Business Development Centers (SBDC). Overseen by the SBA, the SBDC program offers one-stop shopping in counseling, training, and technical assistance for small businesses. (Centers also provide assistance to small businesses applying for Small Business Innovation and Research [SBIR] grants from federal agencies.) The SBDC program is a joint effort of private support, educational facilities, and federal, state, and

Part One:
Fun &
Fundamentals:
Control What
You Can

Microsoft Small Business Kit

local governments. There are about 1,000 SBDC locations, with a center in every state. Most are located at colleges, universities, community colleges, vocational schools, chambers of commerce, and economic development corporations.

Call to make an appointment. (See the section "Working with a Commercial Bank," earlier in this chapter, for a list of materials you should bring to the meeting.) After getting financing advice, you might decide to apply for a loan backed by the SBA. You must qualify for these loans. There's a good bit of due diligence done by the banks before you get any SBA loan. Be prepared.

For more information, visit the SBDC: www.sba.gov/sbdc.

Across the country, SBA loans are available from lenders and banks that participate in the program, with the SBA acting as facilitator, or middleman, in the loan process. Each lender reviews your application according to its individual policies and credit qualifications. The bank or lender then submits your request to the SBA to see whether the application will be approved. It will take several weeks to go through the approval process. Take that wait into account when you apply for the loan.

For the application process, as with bank loans, you'll need the following information:

- Proof of your creditworthiness and money managing history. (See the section "Savings and Credit Cards," earlier in this chapter, for more about getting a credit report.)

- Financial statements, both personal and business, for at least the past three years, including tax returns, financial statements, and other documents that show you're a smart manager of money and a good prospect.

- A detailed cash-flow projection, probably prepared by your accountant, that sets out estimated revenues, expenditures, and so forth.

- A specific amount of money, with an explanation of what you will do with it.

There are also SBA loan options that offer smaller amounts and a streamlined approval processes. Here are some examples:

- The Low-Doc program for loans of under $100,000 has a one-page application form and a turnaround time of a few days.

- SBA Express loans have a $250,000 maximum and offer revolving loans for up to seven years and a turnaround time of 36 hours.

Chapter Three: How to Find Backing

Part One:
Fun &
Fundamentals:
Control What
You Can

Accessing Venture Capital

Venture capital investors developed something of a slick reputation during the dot-com bubble years, but such investment sources have been around for years. The difference between a private investor or an angel and a venture capitalist is that the venture capitalist is a professional manager or company that has control of a fund of money to be invested. Venture capitalists look for home runs—investments that return at least 30 percent and preferably much more. This is hardly a hobby for the venture capitalist, as it might be for the angel looking for some adventure. Venture capitalists might have no expertise in your field or industry, or they might have quite a lot of experience and expect to a play a very active role. It varies. They're always looking for *good numbers*—a reasonable, if risky, bet in fast -growing companies that show great potential for growth (which is how venture capitalists became so associated with technology start-ups).

Venture capital money can come from lots of sources, including public or private pension funds, private firms that make investments on behalf of clients, nonprofit foundations, government-private joint ventures, foreign investors or banks, or endowment or foundation capital. This is money looking for a high rate of return and willing to take the risk to find it.

As an example of venture capital money you might access, consider one of the most widely recognized venture capital programs, the public-private partnerships of Small Business Investment Companies (SBICs). The SBIC program acts as a pool of money, often called a "fund of funds," overseen by the SBA. All investment decisions and management remain the province of the for-profit companies that are partners in the program, so the government is never directly involved in distributing money or choosing the companies in which to invest. Only the for-profit partners do that. Typically, an SBIC private partner manages a fund of $30 million to $170 million, which is a combination of money from the government and money from private sources.

Small business owners can search for an SBIC that might be interested in investing in their companies by researching the following resources:

The SBIC Program

Founded in 1958, the SBIC program is part of the SBA and was set up to help small businesses find access to venture capital. The federal government is currently the largest single investor in the nation's private equity funds. By the end of 2003, the government had invested nearly $5.5 billion in about 450 funds and committed to an additional $3.7 billion. When combined with the $12 billion in private capital, the SBIC program adds up to a huge $21 billion in equity capital that's earmarked for entrepreneurs.

Part One:
Fun &
Fundamentals:
Control What
You Can

Microsoft Small Business Kit

- The SBIC online directory, at *www.sba.gov/inv*.

- A member listing of the National Association of Small Business Investment Companies (NASBIC), at *www.nasbic.org*.

- The National Association of Investment Companies (NAIC), at *www.naicvc.com*.

For More Information

In addition to the resources mentioned in this chapter, you will find links and information on the companion CD. Some books and Web sites particularly useful as you research how to finance your business include:

Books

- Brian E. Hill and Dee Power, *Inside Secrets to Venture Capital* (Wiley, 2001)

- Harold R. Lacy, *Financing Your Business Dreams with Other People's Money: How and Where to Find Money for Start-Up and Growing Businesses* (Rhodes and Easton, 1998)

- Mark Van Osnabrugge and Robert J. Robinson, *Angel Investing: Matching Startup Funds with Startup Companies–A Guide for Entrepreneurs, Individual Investors, and Venture Capitalists* (Jossey Bass, 2000)

Web Sites

- Financing basics from the SBA: *www.sba.gov/starting_business/financing /basics.html*

- "Startup Journal," the Wall Street Journal Center for Entrepreneurs: *www.startupjournal.com/*

- The Free Management Library, an excellent source for many kinds of business information, including financing, with numerous archived articles and helpful links: *www.managementhelp.org/aboutnml.htm*.

Part One:
Fun &
Fundamentals:
Control What
You Can

Microsoft Small Business Kit

It's the little things that make the big things possible. Only close attention to the fine details of any operation makes the operation first class.

— *J. Willard Marriott, founder, Marriott Hotels (1900–1985)*

Chapter Four
Self-Preservation

The route to start-up includes securing the proper legal licenses, permits, or credentials you might need to operate. You should also review insurance coverage and legal agreements. These guidelines will help safeguard your rights, your opportunities, and your business reputation.

Chapter Four: **Self-Preservation**

Part One:
**Fun &
Fundamentals:
Control What
You Can**

What you'll find:

❑ Investigating licenses and permits

❑ Finding insurance and reassurance

❑ Renting space and signing leases

❑ Tackling contract concerns

❑ Recordkeeping counts

❑ Paying yourself

❑ Creating the right impression

❑ Forming an advisory board

Part One:
Fun &
Fundamentals:
Control What
You Can

Microsoft Small Business Kit

Investigating Licenses and Permits

Before you can legitimately start doing business, you must investigate the government and professional registrations and permits that might regulate your chosen operation. The basics are easy and often flow from applying for an Employer Identification Number (EIN) from the Internal Revenue Service (IRS), as you'll learn in the next section. Plus, most state and local governments require some kind of business license with an annual or a one-time fee or tax that gives you permission to run a business within its geographical limits. Ignoring such regulations can only lead to later confusion or regret or outright trouble. It's worth your time, money, and legal standing to pay attention early.

Federal licensing is required only for businesses that operate across state lines or those involved in specific kinds of nationally regulated transactions—for instance, alcohol, investment services, radio broadcasts, or imports and exports. Other licenses or permits you might need depend on the kind of business you're founding, where you're located, and the individual rules and laws of your state, city, county, or area. State licensing usually covers such services as childcare providers, building and construction contractors, beauty or health services, and more. Local regulations might cover operating commercial machinery, like construction equipment for a landscaping firm or the elevator in the warehouse you've rented to house servers for your Web hosting service. You might also need to take account of environmental protection regulations or worker safety issues regulated by the federal Occupational Safety and Health Administration (OSHA) or some state version of that department.

Some residential neighborhood zoning regulations allow home-based businesses and commercial operations, but others do not. (See the section "Protecting Your Home Business," later in this chapter, for more about home-based businesses.) If you can't turn your basement or a corner of the bedroom into a home office and you must therefore rent commercial space, it will have a dramatic impact on your need for capital. You'll then have to figure out how to negotiate a rental lease, shop for business property insurance, and so on. You see why it's key to know, up front, what you're getting into.

Chapter Four: Self-Preservation

Part One:
Fun &
Fundamentals:
Control What
You Can

You'll further need to check into what's required and what's smart for your particular profession, product, or service. Here are a few guidelines to give you an idea of how you should be thinking:

- Might you need an updated license to practice—for example, as an architect, plumber, bill collector, or psychologist?

- Are you planning to sell products or services that require special licenses or permits, such as lottery tickets, gasoline, and some food-stuffs?

- Will you need a state tax number and advice or information about collecting, reporting, and forwarding tax money to your state government? Usually, state sales tax is levied on retail sales and other services.

- Do you need to ace some test or earn some credential before you can operate—for example, as a real estate broker?

- Does your state grant licenses only for a limited time period? That means you might need to renew your license or update your expertise with some course requirement before being eligible for renewal.

- Does your state use registration and licensing as a way of calculating your business revenue for tax purposes? That means your gross income is tracked and you'll need to map the numbers to your tax payments.

- Do you need local or municipal health code approval to open your business—for example, a coffee bar?

- Although it might not be required, would an industry or professional credential make a difference in attracting customers and establishing your bona fides, such as certification for a financial planner (CFP)?

Federal Licensing Resources

For an overview of federal requirements, visit BusinessLaw, at *www.businesslaw.gov/*.

Check out these federal agencies if your field falls under their regulations:

- Food and Drug Administration (FDA): *www.fda.gov*

- Department of Transportation (DOT), Federal Highway Administration: *www.fhwa.dot.gov*

- Securities and Exchange Commission (SEC): *www.sec.gov*

- Federal Communications Commission (FCC): *www.fcc.gov*

- Bureau of Alcohol, Tobacco, and Firearms (ATF): *www.atf.treas.gov*

- Bureau of Industry and Security: *www.bxa.doc.gov*

Part One:
Fun &
Fundamentals:
Control What
You Can

Microsoft Small Business Kit

State Licensing Resources

For a listing of state government home pages, visit *www.sba.gov/world/states.html*.

For a listing of state licensing Web sites, visit *www.sba.gov/hotlist/license.html*.

If you're just getting up to speed about complying with laws and licensing regulations, it might be worthwhile to tap advice from your local chamber of commerce, your local office of the Small Business Administration (SBA), your state or city commerce department, or any industry or professional organizations you have joined. Most local governments offer free information centers and consulting to help newbie business owners learn about local, state, or federal regulations.

Applying for a Federal Taxpayer ID

Assigned to businesses by the IRS, a federal Employer Identification Number (EIN) or taxpayer ID number lets federal, state, and city governments track your company when you file tax returns, when you withhold taxes from employees (such as income, social security, or Medicare taxes), and when you pay those and other taxes to state and federal authorities. Many states let you use the federal ID number for all filing purposes, but some states require separate, state-issued ID numbers. You'll need to check on that. Federal EINs are also sometimes requested by suppliers or vendors to reassure them that your business is in compliance with tax regulations—although it's not legally necessary for doing business with them.

How to Get an EIN

To apply for an EIN (Form SS-4), call toll free: 1-800-829-3676.If you meet certain conditions, you can also apply online, at *https://sa1.www4.irs.gov/sa_vign/newFormSS4.do*.

Any business structure is eligible to apply for and receive an EIN, whether you're a sole proprietor, a corporation, or a partnership or you operate under a special business name with a Doing Business As (DBA) permit. But an EIN isn't required for all kinds of business. You must have an EIN if you pay any employee salaries, file pension tax or any excise tax (which are taxes based on what you sell, like sales tax or the taxes on automobile gas or liquor), and if your business structure is a C or an S Corporation. Otherwise, you can simply rely on your social security number. Avoiding acquiring an EIN, by the way, is one of the reasons many entrepreneurs prefer to start as a Limited Liability Company (LLC) or as a DBA.

See "Choosing a Business Structure," page 29, to learn more about company formations.

Chapter Four: Self-Preservation

Part One:
Fun &
Fundamentals:
Control What
You Can

Finding Insurance and Reassurance

In recent years, many insurance carriers have pumped up their offerings to attract the growing and lucrative small business market. That's good news for entrepreneurs. It means you can now find better coverage at lower rates than in years past. Despite much more affordable packages, however, insurance is still a pricey proposition for a little start-up. So you might be inclined to skip that expenditure until you're more established or, as you might justify it, until you "really need it." Guess again.

It is simply not worth your while to ignore insurance needs. By avoiding a few hundred dollars of annual expense, you might place your assets, your future, and your enterprise at financial or physical risk. What's more, you could suffer legal consequences. Some states require insurance for certain kinds of operations. Many landlords require property insurance before they will let you lease space. Suppliers might insist on some type of insurance coverage before doing business with you. To find out what kinds of insurance you need, check with your industry association, the state insurance office, or the municipal or county clerk's office.

Beyond the basics of property and general liability insurance, it's up to you to research and determine the risks you and your business are likely to face. In California, you might worry about fire and earthquakes. In the Midwest, there's more chance of floods or tornadoes. And then there are the catastrophes no one can foresee.

Why Insurance Matters

After the terrorist attacks on September 11, 2001, hundreds of downtown Manhattan enterprises were devastated. Many failed utterly, but many more struggled back. Bradley Sacks, a medical malpractice lawyer, rents a second-floor office on Vesey Street, less than a block from the site of the World Trade Center. He was lucky enough to be able to leave his building about 15 minutes after the attacks, walking home over the Brooklyn Bridge. At his Brooklyn home, Sacks found that the office's high-speed lines were still up. He began downloading files until the lines went down late that awful Tuesday afternoon.

The law firm had a habit of backing up its large database every two days. All the client files and calendars were networked to the home office. But Sacks was concerned about irreplaceable paper files—thousands of clients' accident and medical records that served as case evidence.

Part One:
Fun &
Fundamentals:
Control What
You Can

Microsoft Small Business Kit

Late the following week, when occupants of his office building were allowed back in, he got a chance to survey the damage. A hole in one window had acted like a wind tunnel. The 4,600-square-foot office was covered in a foot of ash and soot that could have contained asbestos. A lab test by the insurance carrier determined that it was mostly fine particles of glass silica from pulverized windows and gypsum from wallboards. Copier, scanner, and computers were destroyed. "The place was in bad shape," says Sacks. But the paper records were intact.

"The insurance company stepped up to the plate," says Sacks. He got $15,000 for cleaning and refurbishing, which, he says, was still only a fraction of the costs. He couldn't move back in until December, and claim bills weren't settled until mid-January 2002. He also got about $20,000 in disaster relief grants. He lost business, however. "You can never catch up to where you were," says Sacks. "I'm a sole practitioner working on contingency fees. Everything was pushed forward." A case he was due to argue on September 14, 2001, for example, was postponed until March 2003.

Postdisaster, Sacks has learned a few lessons. "You don't know what will happen tomorrow," he says. He has decided to put all his paper files on disks, although it's an expensive, labor-intensive effort to buy high-speed scanners and hire temporary help to accomplish the job. He installed a back-up phone system. His advice? "Make sure you have personal cash reserves because you could go for several months without income. Don't get lazy. We weren't moving into the digital storage age. We were relying on paper. People have to change." And make sure you have adequate insurance. Sacks has now bumped up his coverage by $50,000.

What Is Business Insurance?

For annual premiums of $500 to $1,000 and up, you can likely find a reasonably good business owner's policy (BOP). This all-purpose package usually bundles major property loss, business interruption, and liability risks in one policy. (Such coverage is also sold as separate policies.) *Property* covers your tangible assets, such as the building, furnishings, and machines and other physical contents. *Business interruption* covers your loss of income in case of a disaster. *Liability* covers your responsibility for injury or harm to people on your property or harm caused by your products and services or something you or your employees do or don't do.

Any BOP insurance package can be customized with add-ons or riders or individual policies to meet your specific needs, covering computer hardware and software as well as electronic data and hard-copy records and files.

Chapter Four: **Self-Preservation**

Part One:
Fun &
Fundamentals:
Control What
You Can

Typically, BOPs might extend to worker compensation insurance, but most do not cover employee benefits insurance, auto insurance, or personal liability coverage.

See Chapter 13, "Providing Benefits You Can Afford," page 370, for more about employee insurance benefits.

Other insurance coverage to consider might include the following:

Professional liability insurance   Sometimes called *Errors and Omissions insurance*, these policies can cover your responsibility for, say, problems caused by software you've designed or lawsuits claiming slander and the like.

Extra expense insurance and/or extra equipment insurance   These options are usually add-ons to property policies that cover revenue lost while your business is down and the damage or loss of key revenue-producing equipment, like servers or printing presses.

Auto insurance   Coverage for any commercial vehicles used in the business. Usually, the insurance protects only the vehicle, not any of the contents.

Umbrella insurance   These policies kick in when any problem goes over the limits of your BOP or other insurance.

Choosing Coverage

When shopping for policies, you're likely to face a maze of insurance options, varieties, and decisions. To explore what you need, try asking your accountant or lawyer for help. Or find an experienced insurance broker who is recommended by trusted friends or advisors. You want the broker to evaluate your needs, run numbers, and make suggestions about carriers and policies, especially for the BOP packages.

To get a handle on the coverage you need, consider these questions:

- What are the sources of your risks? Think about theft, injury claims, employee lawsuits (like wrongful termination or age discrimination), fraud, and the like.

- How much financial risk is posed by each source? Is it frequent and ongoing exposure or one-time risks?

- How best can you lessen or control the risk with insurance and other tactics?

Part One:
Fun &
Fundamentals:
Control What
You Can

Microsoft Small Business Kit

- How often will you reevaluate your business risks? Once a year, as experts recommend? Every six months because you're in fast-growth mode and everything changes quickly? Make a plan.

Ask for bids from three or four carriers before deciding on a policy. Check out the carrier's financial strength, history, and reputation for paying claims and how many claims are filed with the carrier each year. That information is on file with your state's insurance department. If you have any major liabilities or are operating a high-risk business, be prepared for higher rates. For instance, a home renovation business faces the risk of exposure to lead paint in older homes. Also make sure that you don't settle for a BOP that doesn't quite cover your needs. Many carriers will offer policy add-ons to protect a critical asset or machine, such as an earthmover or a database.

Once you've got the basics, ask these questions to make sure you're really covered:

- Does your policy guarantee full replacement costs for your store or factory or office?

- Will the policy insure your equipment or merchandise while it's in transit, say, to a customer or a new location?

- Does your policy protect against water damage, sewer backups, and glass breakage?

- Must you renew your policy every year, which will cause your premiums to spike?

- Will the policy cover your employees' personal property?

- Does the policy cover valuable documents and electronic records?

- Do you have at least $1 million liability coverage? Many experts think any lesser amount is a risk given median jury awards.

Reviewing Life Insurance Needs

You should also consider covering business risks by purchasing life insurance. For business, this is called *key man insurance* because it covers the key person or partners critical to the business' success. (Carriers haven't seemed to notice that these days "key men" are also women business owners.) Such coverage is a guarantee of continuity in case a partner or an owner in a business dies or becomes incapacitated. Banks or other lenders might also require key man insurance as a way of minimizing their risk on capital loans. To figure out how much of a key man policy you might need, think about how much cash it would take to keep your business running without the key player (or yourself). Most major carriers offer such policies, so again, shop around before you choose.

Protecting Your Home Business

Townships, counties, and cities frequently have laws and permits that apply to home-based businesses. To greater or lesser degrees, these distinguish commercial zones from residential zones, dictating where and when you can have an office or a retail shop and more. Likewise, residential developments and subdivisions often have bylaws or covenants that regulate what is and what is not permitted. The more affluent the community, the more likely there are zoning laws or ordinances governing business operations. Generally, if your business won't disturb neighbors or impair or pollute the environment, you're probably OK. But you ought to check. Call your county clerk's office or appropriate state or city office to find out the rules in your area.

When working out of your home, you should also get in touch with your home insurance carrier to discuss your needs and, potentially, to update or adjust your policy. The majority of home-based businesses in the United States could suffer significant financial loss because they do not have appropriate business insurance coverage, according to a recent survey from the Independent Insurance Agents & Brokers of America (IIABA). The survey found that one in every 10 U.S. households operates some kind of full-time or part-time home-based business, yet nearly 60 percent of home businesses lack adequate coverage. When quizzed about insurance, almost four of every 10 home-based business owners (39 percent) said they thought they didn't need insurance or believed they were protected by some other type of coverage.

But don't assume your homeowner's policy automatically extends to business equipment or liabilities. If some electrical spark from your office lighting leads to a fire that burns down your house, you might discover that the insurance company will not cover damages because you didn't tell the carrier you were running a business at home—likewise if the FedEx messenger slips on ice on your front walk. Affordable add-ons or riders to your home policy can take care of such business risks.

Renting Space and Signing Leases

It's a long, tough process to find the right space at a reasonable price and then manage the move. Mistakes can cost time and money. The cost of renting or buying your business property is bound to be among the largest of your ongoing expenses.

You might want to enlist the help of a veteran commercial real estate broker. If so, double-check credentials, get some references, and then choose a broker who is experienced in renting smaller commercial spaces. If you need a 1,000-square-foot office, it will do no good to be working with a broker who usually looks at skyscrapers for big corporations. Remember too that there's no such thing as a "standard" or "regular" lease agreement. Each lease is a legally binding contract, and each lease is customized to the office or space you're renting. That means you must carefully evaluate each lease beforehand. To get through your lease review, consider what's right for your needs and business.

First, be sure that you can handle the cash demands of renting and moving into a commercial space. You must calculate whether your revenue will remain consistently strong enough to cover the fixed costs. Or you must bank on boosting business swiftly enough after the move to meet the monthly rental and other costs of doing business. Don't forget utilities and telecommunications costs. Then there's the drain of one-time expenses for architectural work, furnishings, tech installations and equipment, building fees, insurance, and movers. There's also significant downtime during the move itself and the weeks before and after.

Consider the image and location and what will serve your customers. Let's say you run a professional services company. We all know that prosperous surroundings tend to attract more such business. You must still strike a balance between impressing clients and showing that you know the value of hard work. Consider the customer prospects that will walk through your door, look around, and worry that you'll overcharge them because you squandered money on designer lighting.

Some businesses can leverage being first on the block. A design house, an interactive marketing group, a spa or fitness center, among others, can rent cheaper, bigger space in rundown turnaround districts and use the edgy location as part of their fashion-forward marketing. If your business requires foot traffic, don't jump too fast. Visit the site early and late on weekdays and on weekends. Chat up local retailers and ask about customers—are they your target? Will you want that customer two years from now? Is park-

Chapter Four: Self-Preservation

Part One:
Fun &
Fundamentals:
Control What
You Can

ing difficult? Will talented staff travel to your site? How about security? Call the local police precinct, and ask about crime in the area. Also check into zoning plans and redevelopment projects. A new park or highway could be a boon or the kiss of death, depending on your business.

Before knocking on doors, you should have an idea of where your company is headed for the next 12 months. (It would help to have a plan for the next three to five years as well.) For example, how long do you think you'll stay in this location?

See "Guidelines for Creating Your Plan," page 36, to learn more about business plans.

You might want to get some advice about how to identify the right space. Deconstructing design, staff, storage, IT, and other needs is usually a job for professionals. Until you've investigated what's required to make a space work for your business, do not negotiate the price or other terms of a lease. Otherwise, you might walk away crowing about the $2 a square foot you saved only to find that it will run $10 per foot to wire the office—assuming the building can be upgraded at all. Many old buildings in older parts of town might have a limitation on the number of phone lines that can be installed. Invest in an architect and/or an IT consultant to make recommendations. You can request plans that phase in changes so that you can implement upgrades over time and as cash permits.

Signing a Lease

When you've done your homework and you're ready to commit to a lease, don't accept any first offer. Negotiate. There's always wriggle room, either in price or in free amenities, such as painting, construction, new carpeting, and more. Ask the rental agent or the landlord for a few free months. And try to secure a two-year or five-year option to renew at the same rate and terms, including free months and cost of living increases. That way, you're able to leave, but the landlord can't raise you to market rates if you stay. Be sure to have a real estate lawyer look over the agreement before you sign. You don't want unpleasant surprises after you move in.

Before signing, check answers to these key questions:

■ Is it clear how much square footage you are renting? That number should be listed in the agreement. Usually, when you rent commercial space, you also pay on a portion of the public areas, such as lobbies and hallways. Does your square footage include any other areas? If so, what expenses are you charged to maintain those areas?

Part One:
Fun &
Fundamentals:
Control What
You Can

Microsoft Small Business Kit

- If there's any problem, such as a power failure or fire, and you can't use your office or warehouse space, is the rent waived or can you cancel the lease?

- What kind of improvements or repairs or renovation can you undertake with or without the landlord's approval? How will those improvements influence your rental costs?

- Who are your neighbors, and are they compatible with your business and traffic?

- How are complaints or problems handled? Is there anyone on site to take care of emergencies?

Tackling Contract Concerns

As you move forward in business, you're bound to encounter a number of legal agreements and contracts. Some you will need to draft or customize, and some you'll receive from suppliers, vendors, contractors, or clients. So it's a good idea to develop a relationship with an attorney you can trust, whether a business associate or a friend. You can set up an arrangement to pay a retainer for consultations or agree to an hourly fee to tap his or her advice or expertise for legal agreements you'll need to sign or create.

Many contracts or forms can now be found online as a starting point or a foundation for whatever you require. It's worth searching some of the small business sites (or checking Microsoft's template offerings). You should also always read the fine print, or what's often called *boilerplate text*—that is, the long, small-print paragraphs that usually follow the information that relates to the business at hand. A great deal of what is legally binding can be found in those sections, which many people overlook or ignore.

Some contract forms to consider for your business needs include:

- Contract agreements for sales
- Service contracts
- Distribution agreements—say, between a carrier and shipper
- Agreement to assign rights
- Arbitration or mediation agreements
- Letters of intent
- Promissory notes

Chapter Four: Self-Preservation

Part One:
Fun &
Fundamentals:
Control What
You Can

- Commercial partnership agreements

- Confidentiality agreements

- Confirmation of agreements

- Consignment agreements

- Rental agreements, whether for equipment or other assets

- Letters of credit

- Licensing agreement

- Employee contracts or job offers

Microsoft Office templates

Microsoft offers a full range of business forms and templates that you can quickly download. Visit *office.microsoft.com/templates/default.aspx*.

Recordkeeping Counts

Many entrepreneurs are motivated to start a business because they're tired of the meetings and minutiae that define life at larger corporations. The small biz style, they figure, is more freewheeling and flexible. No question that making your own decisions—and deciding your own fate—is a definite rush, especially if you've labored for years in the vineyards of corporateland. There's obviously a big "but" coming here. You can see it a mile way, right?

But gobs of entrepreneurial gung-ho won't help if you can't keep your paperwork and statements and records in some semblance of recognizable order. You needn't be as buttoned up as all the textbooks insist. But you do need to play for keeps with the basics.

Taxes and all the attendant paperwork, transactions, receipts, and filings are the biggest recordkeeping demand. You need to be fairly meticulous about tax-related records. Keeping records in order will also give you valuable insights into how the business is doing.

See Chapter 5, "Follow the Money," to learn more about finances and records.

See Chapter 6, "Tax Tactics," to learn more about employee, payroll, and tax records.

Part One:
Fun &
Fundamentals:
Control What
You Can

Microsoft Small Business Kit

If maintaining records is your weakness, take a big-deal meeting with your accountant and explain your needs. Delegate. Or hire a bookkeeper to come in one day a week or every two weeks to keep you on the straight and narrow. You'll definitely be glad you did. You're not supposed to be expert at everything, remember?

- The need for specific records varies with each business, especially records for personnel and payroll, but generally this list will get you on the right track: Be sure that your business and personal lives are clearly separate from each other. Don't pay your mortgage out of your business checking account. Likewise, don't pay for business expenses with a personal credit card. Set up separate bank accounts, keep each one rigorously independent from the other, and balance your checkbook every time you get a business account statement. It's a way to make sure you haven't overlooked any expense or transaction.

- Train yourself to be bookkeeper or accountant friendly, which means retaining receipts, filing them in something more helpful than a big paper bag, and being able to document what you spent and why when it comes time to meet with the person who does your books. You can also turn to money management software programs to help track finances, such as Microsoft Money.

- Track your daily income and expenses. Are you up-to-speed on what money is owed to you and how much you must pay out? You won't be able to price your goods and services if you don't have a grasp on the big money picture.

  See "Consider Your Product Price Tag, page 27, for more about setting a product price.

- Are you also up-to-date on invoices and billing? Don't let your statements slide or your invoices pile up.

- Keep clear and organized copies of all your customer transactions and services. That includes sales receipts, invoices, supplies, inventory bills, and so on.

- Can you instantly put your hands on important business documents, such as a lease agreement, insurance policy, city or state permits, tax filings from past years, employee and bank records? You should be able to produce any of these on a moment's notice.

Chapter Four: Self-Preservation

Part One:
Fun &
Fundamentals:
Control What
You Can

Paying Yourself

As the owner of a business, you can pretty much cut your own paycheck, barring some rules that kick in for certain kinds of business structures. Isn't that one of the attractions of being in business for yourself in the first place? How much personal compensation you take out of the business is a subjective choice. There are, however, some considerations to keep in mind, most of them derived from common sense.

See "Choosing a Business Structure," page 29, for more about business structures.

You'll undoubtedly want to balance the needs of the (hopefully) growing business with your own lifestyle and family demands. If your eight-year-old requires orthodontia in the spring, you might want to give yourself a raise. On the other hand, if you're planning to launch an e-commerce channel on the redesigned Web site, you might want to take a pay cut. Straightforward, huh?

There are two driving decisions to make about your pay: First, of course, is the amount and the frequency of payments. Second is the method of payment. Be sure to get the advice of your accountant or your tax preparer before setting up any system for payment.

Records to Track

Keeping up-to-date receipts and statements can help you build the business, secure funding, and avoid trouble with the IRS.

Bank statements and check registers   Keep your business accounts separate from your personal accounts.

Income and sales receipts   Keep at least a monthly account (weekly would be better) of how much money is coming and the sources of revenue.

Expenses and outgoing payments   Likewise, you should have at least a monthly summary of all your outgoing expenses, payments, and transactions.

Big-ticket purchases   Keep receipts for major purchases, such as computers, a car, or one-time payments.

Employee payroll and other records   If you have staff, you'll need to keep tabs on income and social security tax withholding and payment as well as many other employee records.

See Chapter 6, "Tax Tactics," for more about taxes.

Your pay options include the following:

Straightforward salary   Before setting a system for monthly or weekly wages for yourself, consider how you're running the business. If you haven't incorporated and you're using your social security number to report income in the business, you'll be filing a Schedule C, and you can get paid directly. But if you have formed a business structure, how your revenue flows through the company, whether it's taxed, and how much you're allowed to draw will depend on the kind of structure you've chosen.

Part One:
Fun &
Fundamentals:
Control What
You Can

Microsoft Small Business Kit

See Chapter 6, "Tax Tactics," to learn more about filing taxes.

Lump-sum bonus Tax rules are about the same for a bonus as for regular draw or salary arrangements. As an LLC or a sole proprietor, you can add a quarterly or year-end reward for yourself when you've had a good run. Once the business is incorporated, you'll need to check in with your accountant before treating yourself to a big, fat reward. Sometimes, the timing of such bonuses triggers unwanted attention from the IRS.

Dividend distribution As a profitable incorporated business, you might want to pay yourself an annual amount by declaring it a dividend. But if you're a private company—that is, you haven't sold any stock—distributing dividends throws up various challenges, including the fact that you might pay income and employee taxes on the dividends while the company doesn't get to take a tax deduction on the amount. There are exclusions to these rules when you're the sole income provider for the business. Get some advice before setting this up.

Hiring your family If your family members are working for the company just like any other hired staff, you can pay them a salary. If it's your teenager working part-time, you can pay him or her hourly wages or whatever is fair and reasonable market value.

Perks and benefits The IRS permits you to deduct a rash of expenses as the cost of doing business and as the owner of the company. That could include memberships in clubs, company cars, business trips, dining and entertainment for clients, and more. The kicker is that you must show reason why these expenses drive business. You must maintain strict documentation of receipts and records, and you need to be sure that the business expenses aren't muddied with personal ones.

Delayed compensation If you're tightening your belt during the start-up salad days, you might want to delay your compensation for later, when revenue has climbed and the business takes off. In that case, you'll need to document a plan that shows you're forgoing pay early on and intend to reap later benefits. All of this should be recorded in your company accounting books.

Employee benefits Don't forget that putting tax-deductible employee benefits in place can bolster your annual pay. These include health insurance and dental insurance, group life insurance, and more.

Taking a loan This can get tricky because the IRS takes a dim view of owners who use business revenue to fund their personal lives. But when the loan is carefully documented and with a serious repayment schedule and the going rate of interest, you might be able to take a loan from the company.

Chapter Four: Self-Preservation

Part One:
Fun &
Fundamentals:
Control What
You Can

Creating the Right Impression

Presenting an appropriate image and message to the varied groups and audiences a business owner will encounter is a key part of starting your business and assembling the credentials and skills you'll need for operation and growth.

Many entrepreneurs see making presentations, dealing with media representatives, or participating in publicity or marketing efforts as an interruption of their "real work." And if it's not seen as a complete waste of their time, owners still often find the idea of speechmaking scary and nerve-racking. But the truth is, you need top-notch communications skills. Part of the job of any chief executive is to be an effective advocate for the business, especially when it's in start-up mode. If you cannot articulate the mission of your company in a commanding sentence or two, or if you can't deliver energetic speeches or polished presentations, you're short-circuiting your company's future.

The first step is to take the communications process seriously. Donning a power suit instead of jeans won't seal a deal. But graceless moves, inappropriate dress, or being unable to put across your message with confidence can surely lose it. Don't underestimate the power of the impression or image you convey.

So how is a chief executive officer (CEO) supposed to look and talk? Like you, actually, only in a heightened version of how you walk, talk, and communicate.

While your business model might be cutting edge, the business of communicating is far more basic. Over and over, media trainers and coaches advise CEOs to learn how to be themselves while being on public display. It's not easy. "Receiving attention causes enormous tension and paralyzes us," says Laurie Burton, who runs Image Development in Los Angeles and brings 30 years of experience as an actor to communications coaching. "Most people don't think they're interesting enough for an audience. But you need to bring who you are to the speech. You are the experience."

Burton tells of a movie studio sales executive who was referred to her by a career coach. The executive's speaking style was boring, withdrawn, and wooden. "He'd stand in the 'fig-leaf position,' with his hands clasped in front of him, and talk," says Burton. So she asked him what he was passionate about. The answer: his two young daughters. Burton told him to take out a photo of his children, hold the picture in front of him, and talk about his

Part One:
Fun &
Fundamentals:
Control What
You Can

Microsoft Small Business Kit

Brush Up Your Presentation Skills

When you need financial help, you don't think twice about hiring the services of an accountant. Same goes for legal advice. But somehow business owners think it is embarrassing or unnecessary to hire a communications coach or media trainer. If so, three words for you: "Get over it."

■ Before a special appearance or to hone your image, consider hiring a media trainer. You can sign up for an affordable session or two or an entire course. Typically, the trainer videotapes you making a speech and works to improve performance. To find an effective trainer, ask friends for referrals, especially people in media or publicity. Check references, and meet beforehand to make sure you're comfortable.

■ Join a local Toastmasters group. Founded in 1924, Toastmasters is a network of peer-to-peer public speaking workshops. There are now more than 9,300 clubs in some 80 countries and regions. A typical club has 20 to 30 people who meet once a week for about an hour, giving everyone a chance to practice. There's a low fee to join (about $20) and low-cost dues. To find a group in your area, visit *www.toastmasters.org*.

little girls. The sales executive became entirely different. "He grew passionate and animated. And he made the connection. He got it," she says. That energy carried over to his national sales conference speech, and he was a big hit. Says Burton, "You have to trust in your own ability."

Body language and eye contact communicate far more than words—some say 70 percent of all communication is nonverbal. So don't hide behind tables or podiums. Move into the audience and walk around. Ask for a remote control for your screen or Microsoft PowerPoint presentation. Then you can clip on a mike and wander the stage or audience. You'll be a lot more charismatic.

Other expert tips:

Practice, practice, practice, but don't memorize.   Rehearse your remarks before a spouse, partner, or friends or in the shower. Tape or videotape your performance, and then make corrections.

Lower the pitch of your voice.   Often, when people are nervous or tense, their voice tends to go up in pitch, which makes them sound uncertain. Try lowering the pitch of your voice.

Stick to three key messages.   The audience won't really be able to focus on or process more than three significant points. But business owners and chief executives tend to be so knowledgeable about their subject that they include jargon or technical language or drone on and lose the audience's attention.

Develop examples or stories for each point you make.   People remember things much more vividly if there's an anecdote or an emotional context.

Chapter Four: Self-Preservation

Part One:
Fun &
Fundamentals:
Control What
You Can

Create images or pictures, especially for statistics. Don't just say it's big and add a trillion-dollar figure. Pull in a metaphor or a picture that goes with the statistic—say it's the size of the Atlantic Ocean. Similarly, don't clutter slides and presentations with words and numbers—and *never* read from your slides. You might consider simply putting graphics or illustrations on your slides and using those simple slides to support your talk. That way, the focus remains on you and your words, not some numbers on a slide. For instance, show a mountain climber, and then talk about the tough climb ahead you see to build sales.

Smile and be impeccably groomed. People like to identify with leaders and experts. Look like the winner you are.

Prepare takeaway points. Always plan the points or facts you want the audience to walk away thinking about. You might identify these points as the building blocks of your presentation. If someone else prepares your material, discuss the takeaway points first.

A great deal of business is clearly show business. If you don't know how to communicate well, you're limiting your company and your employees.

Forming an Advisory Board

Assembling a network of diverse experts and specialists to offer advice and experience in running your new business can help keep you focused on strategy and the big picture. Such groups differ from a corporate board of directors. Advisory board members do not have voting power. Nevertheless, the seasoned specialists or experts you invite to be informal advisors ought to have significant influence on your actions and thinking. Otherwise, why bother asking them to participate?

Some board advisors are paid for their work with gracious dinners, and some get honorariums, from a few hundred to a few thousand dollars per meeting. Infrequently, advisory board members are compensated with stock or a stake in the company. Most often, advisory boards are a group of active and engaged specialists who want to fulfill the role of mentor. Perhaps later, once the business has developed, you can promise some compensation. The frequency and composition of the meetings is also flexible. You can call on each board member as you need his or her expertise or gather everyone together once a month or once a quarter. Every owner sets his or her own arrangement.

There are many solid reasons to build an informal group to advise you and your top managers. Tapping the objective insights of outsiders can help you

Part One:
Fun &
Fundamentals:
Control What
You Can

Microsoft Small Business Kit

figure out where to hold on and where to let go. A board of advisors can also help you do the following:

- Network
- Boost credibility in your industry or field
- Open doors to strategic partners or customers
- Keep up-to-date on new developments in your field
- Gain access to lenders, angels, and investors

See Chapter 3, "How to Find Backing," for more about financial backing.

To assemble a board, identify four or five experienced professionals who have skills that complement your in-house expertise. Don't choose people just like you. The idea is to broaden your horizon. Look for experience that you or your key partners and employees don't have, from such pros as lawyers, accountants, software consultants, bankers, publicists, chief financial officers (CFOs) of other companies, management consultants, sales trainers, and the like.

Think about getting advice in the five major areas of business strategy and operation:

- Market demand
- Technology needs
- Staffing
- Management depth
- Financing

Be selective about whom you ask. The point is to find people whose advice you respect and heed—in other words, advisers who have both the expertise and good will to help you grow. To find interested gurus, canvas your industry's conferences, association meetings, university or professional school alumni events, and local business or executive clubs. (See the sidebar "Where to Find Advisors," later in this section.) When discussing the possibility of someone becoming an advisor, set up a personal meeting. Be sure that the advisor understands the purpose of the meeting so that he or she won't think you're looking for an investment or an infusion of capital.

Don't forget that you need to gain the advisor's enthusiastic interest. But get clear answers to such queries as:

Chapter Four: Self-Preservation

Part One:
Fun &
Fundamentals:
Control What
You Can

- What kind of experience do you have?

- Have you ever been in business for yourself?

- Do you have experience with a business like mine?

- Can you help with backing or sales or whatever?

- Are you easily accessible?

Once you've assembled a board, don't ignore the board members. Keep them involved and up-to-speed with your business's news and growth.

Where to Find Advisors

You can find a roster of possible advisors at networking groups or executive clubs. Here are two sources:

President's Resource Organization (PRO)
Formed in 1993, *PRO* is a nationwide network that helps executives and owners address challenges in a peer-to-peer forum. PRO helps entrepreneurs form advisory boards. Visit *www.propres.com*.

CEO Club The 25-year-old, nonprofit CEO Club has chapters around the United States. Members must be CEOs of businesses with a minimum of $2 million in annual sales. Visit *www.ceoclubs.org/*.

For More Information

In addition to the resources mentioned in this chapter, you will find links and information on the companion CD. Some books and Web sites particularly useful as you research how to insurance and license your business include:

Books

- Fred S. Steingold and Ilona M. Bray, *Legal Guide for Starting & Running a Small Business,* Seventh Edition (Nolo Press, 2003)

- Gregory C. Damman, *How to Form and Operate a Limited Liability Company: A Do-It-Yourself Guide* (Self-Counsel Press, 2003)

- Judith H. McQuown, Inc. *Yourself: How to Profit by Setting Up Your Own Corporation* (Career Press, 2002)

Web Sites

- Small business insurance tips from the My Own Business Web site, which provides a wealth of other valuable ideas and free online courses as well: *www.myownbusiness.org/s5/*

- Small Business Insurance Primer from American Express, another site with links to many useful resources: *home3.americanexpress.com/ smallbusiness/resources/starting/small_business_insurance/*

- Small business insurance articles from *About.com: sbinformation .about.com/od/insurance/*

Part Two

Profit and Loss: Getting the Facts on Figures

In this part

Chapter Five   **Follow the Money**. 100
Chapter Six   **Tax Tactics** 126
Chapter Seven   **By the Numbers: Analyzing Your
                   Business with Excel**. 144

Thought, not money, is the real business capital.

— *Harvey S. Firestone*

Chapter Five
Follow the Money

As Harvey Firestone tells it, business isn't only about money–there's the creative side of business, the intellectual horsepower it requires, and the relationships you make and build. But you have to follow the money you make and the money you spend if you want to stay in business and keep your business growing.

What you'll find:

❏ Accounting essentials

❏ Preparing financial statements: the balance sheet and the income statement

❏ Using a chart of accounts

❏ Cutting paychecks

❏ Preparing and managing a budget

❏ Managing cash flow

Accounting Software

If you set up a computerized accounting system for your business, you have a number of software programs to choose from, including Microsoft Money, QuickBooks Pro, Quicken, and Peachtree. At the time of writing this book, a free 60-day trial version of Microsoft Money 2004 Deluxe is available for downloading from Microsoft's Web site (*www.microsoft.com/money/deluxe*). Microsoft Money also comes in a small business edition. Some of the features of this version of Microsoft Money include a payroll tax calculator, electronic reminders for tax deadlines, the ability to exchange contact information with Microsoft Outlook, an invoice designer, and all the regular accounting functions you would expect—reports, a chart of accounts, account reconciliation, and the like.

Instead of using an accounting program, you could set up one or more Excel spreadsheets for your accounting needs. Over time, however, you will probably get better results from using a full-blown accounting program. Still another approach, especially if you want to keep all your records in a Microsoft Office application, is to download the Accounts Ledger Database from Microsoft Office Online. (This database is one of the accounting and reporting templates.) To use this database, you need a copy of Microsoft Access, which isn't included in Microsoft Office Small Business Edition 2003. If you have Access, however, or want to purchase the program, this database offers a simple means for entering transactions (deposits and withdrawals) and has some useful built-in reports such as a Transaction Listing report and an Account Summary report.

A lot of small business owners decide early on to turn bookkeeping over to a professional. There are plenty of good reasons for doing this. For one thing, keeping an accurate set of accounts takes time—time you might spend more lucratively marketing your business or selling goods and services to customers. For another, an experienced bookkeeper or accountant is less likely to make a potentially costly mistake, such as forgetting when a tax payment is due, calculating payroll incorrectly, or failing to record a big invoice or payment so that your financial picture is skewed. Finally, when tax time comes around, it's good to know that the information you need to fill out your tax forms is the way it should be.

For tax tips and other tax information for small business owners, see Chapter 6, "Tax Tactics."

On the other hand, few experiences teach you more about the state of your business than working through a stack of monthly bills or preparing invoices to send to your clients and customers. You get a close-up view of where your money's going and where it's coming from. Even if you work with a bookkeeper or an accountant, you're wise to learn about the practices and details that are used to keep track of your business's money.

In this chapter, we'll describe some of the essentials of accounting, including an overview of accounting methods and practices and financial statements. We'll also review some steps you take when creating a budget and how to keep tabs on your cash flow. You won't see examples of any specific accounting software programs in this chapter (although you will learn how to set up a simple budget in Microsoft Excel), but the information presented should prove useful no matter which program you use or even if you choose to keep your financial records by hand.

Accounting Essentials

Balancing your checkbook each month, online or on paper, resembles the work required to keep track of money in a small business, but there's a lot more to it as well. You have different obligations as a business owner. You might need to provide regular financial statements to a bank or to investors or partners, you need a detailed record of income and expenses to accurately prepare your taxes, and you need the same detailed information to make decisions about your business in the future—to prepare next year's sales forecasts and expense budgets, for example—or to perform any meaningful financial analysis.

Accounting systems of one kind or another have been around nearly as long as civilization. It's a discipline with a reputation for having lots of subtle rules and obscure practices. You might keep the books for your business yourself, at least for a while, or you might decide to hire a bookkeeper and an accountant to do the work for you. In either of these situations, however, every business owner should have a handle on the essentials of accounting. With the outline provided in this chapter, you'll be better able to keep up with your accountant when the two of you meet or, if you choose to do the bookkeeping chores on your own, be off to a good start knowing what you need to do.

Chapter 7, "By the Numbers: Analyzing Your Business with Excel," provides examples of how to analyze financial and other business information— how to calculate a breakeven point, for instance, and how to analyze the effect of small changes in prices and costs on your bottom line. Later in this chapter, in the section "Preparing and Managing a Budget," we'll also describe how to set up a simple budget spreadsheet in Excel.

Choosing the Cash Method or the Accrual Method

One of the first decisions you need to consider when setting up an accounting system for your business is whether to use the *cash method* or the *accrual method* of accounting. Your choice of accounting method determines the procedures you'll follow for reporting incomes and expenses.

In cash accounting, you record income and expenses when the cash is actually received or disbursed. Sounds simple enough, but you need to keep a few rules in mind. For tax purposes, for example, there's the idea of *constructive receipt* of money. If you're having a great fourth quarter of the year and receive a big check on December 30, that money must be counted as received in the year that's about to end, even if you wait until the start of January to deposit the check in the bank. Also, you can't necessarily deduct every cash expense immediately. Larger purchases like equipment need to be depreciated over time, with the expense deduction amortized. Rent payments you may have made in advance can't be deducted until the year to which they apply. Also, goods or services provided to you as payment (as trade, instead of cash) must be counted as income at their fair market value. Likewise, if you fulfill one of your own financial obligations by trading goods or services, that transaction counts as a payment.

With the accrual method of accounting, income is counted when a transaction or sale takes place, not necessarily when you get paid. In other words, if you sign a contract for $12,000 that will be paid in installments over the next three months, you record $12,000 of income when the contract is signed, not $4,000 of income when each payment is received, even if one or more of the payments cross over from one tax year to the next. Likewise, you record an expense when you receive the goods or services, even though you will pay for these items at a later date.

For most small businesses, the accrual method of accounting offers a clearer idea of how the business is performing month to month and year to year. Income is accounted for when it is earned (as opposed to only when you receive payment), and expenses are recognized when you become liable for payment.

A small business that has a physical inventory is required to use the accrual method, while service businesses (in general) can use the cash method. A business set up as a C Corporation that has more than $5 million of average annual income must use the accrual method as well, as must any partnership with one or more C Corporations as a partner. Some businesses choose to combine the cash and accrual methods, using the accrual method for sales and purchases of inventory, and the cash method for other accounts. Maintaining your books using a combination of cash and accrual accounting can require more work because you need to keep two different systems in place.

As mentioned, the accrual method is recommended because it provides more accurate information about the state of your business. For one thing, the accrual method is better at matching income to expenses. The accrual method also helps smooth out peaks in income, which might have tax benefits. The cash accounting method, on the other hand, has potential tax benefits because it offers some flexibility to business owners who can juggle certain expenses, prepaying some and deferring others.

Double-Entry Accounting

Anyone who has taken a beginning accounting course somewhere along the line has been introduced to double-entry accounting. At the heart of this system is the rule that for every debit there's a credit. For example, the purchase of new equipment is not only a withdrawal from your bank account (a reduction in cash), it's an expense that increases the amount you've spent on equipment. You need to make two entries in your accounting system to accurately represent a purchase like this. You credit your cash account and debit the account in which you record equipment expense. Making this double entry is what keeps your books in balance.

The main types of accounts you use to track business activities are assets, liabilities, equity, income, and direct and indirect expenses. Asset accounts are debit accounts, which means they are positive numbers. Liability accounts are credit accounts. Liabilities are subtracted from assets to determine a business's value. If you owe $10,000 to the bank, that's −$10,000 to you. In double-entry accounting, you credit a liability account, adding one negative number to another negative number, which increases the amount of the liability.

Most of the time when you're paying bills, the double entries are crediting cash (decreasing the amount of your checking account) and debiting the expense category (increasing the total amount of the expenses—whether that's advertising, rent, office supplies, or payroll). If you charge an item, you would credit your accounts payable (a liability account) and debit the expense account. Again, these entries balance each other.

Accounting Methods and Periods: Help from the IRS

You can learn a lot more about accounting methods and accounting periods in IRS Publication 538, "Accounting Periods and Methods," which is available for download at *www.irs.gov*. For example, when you file your first tax return as a business, you'll indicate whether you're using the cash or the accrual method. After filing this return, switching from one method to another requires the approval of the IRS. Publication 538 gives you the details about why approval is required and what you need to do to get approval. This publication also provides information about accounting periods and tax years. Most small business will use the calendar year (January 1 through December 31) as their tax year. Some businesses will use a fiscal year, which is a period of 12 consecutive months ending on the last day of any month other than December.

Preparing Financial Statements: The Balance Sheet and the Income Statement

A good place to begin learning how to manage the finances for a small business is to create basic financial statements—a *balance sheet* and an *income statement*. The balance sheet shows a business's assets, liabilities, and net worth at a certain point in time. A balance sheet is usually prepared at the end of an accounting period, when you close the books for the preceding month, quarter, or year. A balance sheet is a tool for analyzing trends in your business. For one thing, a balance sheet for one period will show changes in the business's net worth from the previous period, and hopefully this trend is positive. You can also compare cash accounts to the amount you are owed (shown in the accounts receivable line item) and see the amounts of both your short-term and long-term liabilities.

In a balance sheet, assets always equal the sum of liabilities and net worth. Assets include cash and accounts receivable, as well as inventory and equipment of significant value (such as a delivery van or manufacturing machinery). Another type of asset is a prepaid expense such as a security deposit on your rent. Liabilities include items such as accounts payable (the amounts you owe to suppliers, for example), loans you are paying, and tax liabilities. Net worth shows the owner's investment in the business. Net worth is shown with liabilities on a balance sheet because it reflects the amount the business owes to its owners. Owners generally have a long-term expectation of realizing this amount—unlike suppliers, who expect to be paid on regular terms. In the next section, we'll take a look in more detail at some of the accounts that appear on a company's balance sheet.

The other standard financial statement is the income statement (which is also known as a *profit-and-loss statement*). While a balance sheet shows the cumulative assets and obligations of a business at a certain point in time, an income statement shows how profitable a business has been over a period of time by reflecting all the income and expense transactions that occurred during that time period.

Most accounting programs can produce a balance sheet and an income statement as two of the reports they generate. When you set up your accounting program, you will designate an account as an asset account (inventory, for example) or a liability account (taxes payable). Transactions that affect these accounts will be summarized when you produce a balance sheet. Likewise, income and expense accounts, after a month's or quarter's worth of data is entered, will be summarized in the income report.

At the start of your business, you might want to prepare a balance sheet that shows the state of your business's finances as you get ready to open the doors. One of the financial and accounting templates available from Microsoft Office Online is the Opening Day Balance Sheet, an Excel spreadsheet (with instructions) provided by the Service Corps of Retired Executives (SCORE). Figure 5-1 shows part of the balance sheet open in Excel.

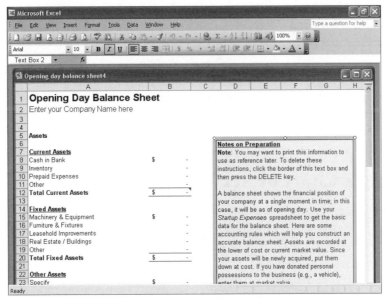

Figure 5-1   The Opening Day Balance Sheet template is a tool you can use to examine the financial state of your company as you open for business.

SCORE

The Service Corps of Retired Executives (SCORE) is a nonprofit group that provides information and business counseling to entrepreneurs. (The organization's Web site is *www.score.org*). SCORE's Web site also has a template gallery, as well as online workshops and other resources.

The Opening Day Balance Sheet template refers to another Office Online financial template, the Start-Up Expenses worksheet. You use this worksheet to gather the basic financial information you use to build your initial balance sheet. Among the start-up expenses you list are your sources of capital, the cost of equipment and improvements to the space you've rented, and administrative expenses. The Start-Up Expenses worksheet also includes instructions prepared by SCORE.

The instructions that accompany the Opening Day Balance Sheet template provide definitions of the various financial categories. The worksheet is also set up with formulas that calculate subtotals and totals for each main category as well as *owner's equity* (another term for net worth). If you are working with an accountant or a financial planner in setting up your business, you might consider working through this template before your initial meeting.

Financial statement templates

The Office Online templates for financial statements also include an Excel worksheet you can use to prepare a sales forecast, an income statement, and cash flow projections. We'll look in more detail at one of the templates for cash flow projections in the section "Managing Cash Flow," later in this chapter.

Using a Chart of Accounts

Accurate accounting requires attention to lots of details. The framework that supports detailed recordkeeping about each of your business's transactions, whether income or expense, asset or liability, is a chart of accounts that reflects your business's operations. Building a chart of accounts is one of the first tasks you'll perform when you set up an accounting program. In Microsoft Money, for example, creating your accounts is one of the steps you follow when you use Money's Setup Assistant. (You can, of course, skip the Setup Assistant and start building your list of accounts by using Money's standard menus and commands.) Many accounting programs have charts of accounts already defined for different types of businesses.

In a chart of accounts, each account is numbered. The first number in the sequence identifies the type of account (an asset account, a liability account, and so on), and the numbers that follow are used to list the accounts in the order you want. Here's an example of a numbering system that's often used for a chart of accounts:

- Asset accounts are numbered 1000 through 1999. These accounts include your bank accounts, inventory, accounts receivable, and others. Asset accounts are listed at the top of your balance sheet.

- Liability accounts are numbered 2000 through 2999. Liability accounts are listed after asset accounts on the balance sheet. They include accounts payable, loans, tax liability, and so on.

- Income accounts, from sales, for example, are numbered in the 3000s.

- Direct expense accounts use the range 4000 to 4999.

- Indirect expense accounts are numbered starting with 5000.

- Nonoperating accounts such as earned interest and the like are numbered 7000 through 8000.

Strive for details

Although miscellaneous expenses are a valid category, it's best to set up an account for each type of expense you have and resist the temptation to lump too many expenses together in a category with a name such as Other Expenses.

Direct and indirect costs

Many businesses have direct costs such as labor, materials, and shipping. These expenses fluctuate depending on the volume of business activity. Businesses also have expenses such as rent and standard utilities that are not tied directly to the volume of products or services they sell. These costs remain fairly static. One reason to separate direct expenses and indirect expenses is to calculate your overhead (your indirect expenses), which can be a factor in how you determine the price at which you sell products and services. When setting up a chart of accounts, any cost that's related to manufacturing a product or to the actual service you provide should be considered a direct expense.

In the following sections, we'll take a look at some specific accounts in more detail.

Accounts Receivable

Accounts receivable is an asset account (along with cash, inventory, and others). For any business owner, reviewing the amount that customers owe you always sheds light on the state of your business, even if what you see can sometimes appear challenging. You create a receivable by selling a good or service to a customer on terms. The customer is then obligated to pay you 30 days from the date of the sale, for example. The aim is to turn each receivable into cash. If you notice a sizable change in the amount of receivables from one accounting period to the next, consider that an invitation to dig deeper to see which customers are paying on time and which are not. A steady increase in receivables could mean your business is growing, but it might also mean that too many customers (or a few of your larger ones) are falling behind in their payments. In a situation such as this, you could run short of cash. Don't look at your accounts receivable in isolation—examine them alongside your cash accounts.

You'll also want to maintain an accounts receivable *aging report*. In an aging report, you keep track of how much your customers owe you, when they paid you last, and the amount (if any) that's past due. Figure 5-2 shows another of the accounting templates from Office Online, the Accounts Receivable Aging Workbook, an Excel worksheet you can use to track the aging of your accounts receivable. (The template is provided by Template-Zone by KMT Software.) This spreadsheet uses a single formula in the column labeled Total Due to calculate the total of the amounts you enter in the Current and Past Due columns. As you can see, you can also record the amount and date of a customer's last payment. This relatively simple, easy-to-use worksheet captures information vital to your business's financial health.

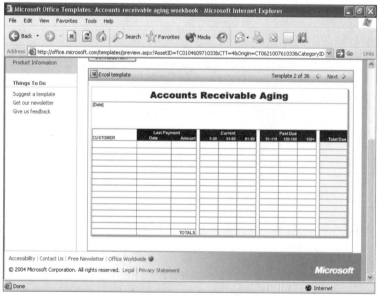

Figure 5-2   You can use this Excel template to track accounts receivable that are current and past due.

Inventory

Inventory is the physical stock a business purchases and resells, in some form, to its customers. Your inventory might consist of raw materials that you convert or manufacture into saleable products, or it might be already-finished goods that you purchase at a quantity discount and then mark up and sell for profit. When you sell some of your inventory, you don't necessarily put money in the bank right away. If you're selling the inventory on terms, you create a receivable.

Evaluating your inventory and managing how much inventory you purchase and hold are important business activities. You don't want to hold an excessive amount of inventory because that could deplete your cash and reduce your profits. However, you need enough inventory to fulfill orders and purchases, attract customers, and generate cash sales and receivables that you can collect. In the double-entry accounting system, when you purchase inventory, you likely spend cash, so one entry is to credit cash and the other is to increase inventory (by debiting) the inventory account.

Fixed Assets

Cash, receivables, and inventory are a category of assets known as *current assets*. A business is expected to realize the cash value of current assets within a year. *Fixed assets*, on the other hand, are physical assets such as land, real estate, machinery, equipment, furniture, and fixtures that need to be accounted for on a balance sheet when you're computing the net worth of your company. Fixed assets have a life greater than one year. Also, for accounting purposes, the cost of fixed assets is expensed over time through depreciation.

If your business includes a lot of equipment and machinery (including items such as delivery vans or other vehicles), you should learn a little bit about depreciation—and then talk to an accounting expert. Depreciation not only refers to how the cost of a fixed asset is allocated over time, it also marks the decrease in the value of the asset because of wear and tear, age, and even market conditions. Depreciation affects your business's bottom line because you will eventually have to replace items that do wear out. When you or your accountant record depreciation, the double entry made is to debit depreciation expense (although no cash is actually spent) and to credit accumulated depreciation. The total accumulated depreciation should give you an idea of the amount you'll need to spend to replace these fixed assets someday.

If you browse through the financial templates on Office Online, you'll see several Excel templates designed to record information about fixed assets. The names of the templates reveal a little about the rules of accounting for depreciation:

- Fixed Asset Record With Straight-Line Depreciation
- Fixed Asset Record With Double-Declining Depreciation
- Fixed Asset Record With Fixed-Declining Depreciation

With *straight-line depreciation*, an asset's value is reduced by the same percentage each year. To calculate the amount of depreciation for a single year, you estimate the value of the asset at the end of its useful life (called the *salvage value*), subtract this amount from the purchase price, and then divide the remainder by the number of years you expect the asset will be used. *Double-declining depreciation* means that twice the amount calculated through straight-line depreciation is taken in the first year. In the following years, that same percentage is applied to the remaining value of the asset. *Fixed-declining depreciation* uses a fixed rate to compute depreciation of an asset.

The intangibles

A nice name for a rock group, but intangibles are also another category of assets that pertain to some small businesses. An example of an intangible asset is a patent. The value of an intangible is difficult to measure, so they are often not counted as part of a business's net worth. If your business relies on a patent or you conduct regular research and development, you should consult with an accounting professional to learn more about how to assign a value to and keep track of intangible assets.

Liabilities

Liability accounts record the amounts a business is obligated to pay—everything from the $23.57 charge for photocopies you made last month at the downtown copy center, to next week's payroll, to payments to people or financial institutions that have loaned money to the business over a short or a longer period of time.

Current liabilities are those amounts owed to suppliers, employees, financial institutions, and government tax authorities. These amounts are usually due within a 12-month period. One measure of a business's health, of course, is how well it keeps up with its current liabilities. Think of a supplier that provides your business with goods or services as an investor—an investor who expects a return over a short term and who will continue to invest as long as the return (your payments) keeps coming.

Long-term liabilities (or *noncurrent liabilities*) are financial obligations that are not due and payable in the next 12 months. These likely would be a loan on which you pay interest periodically but aren't obligated to repay the entire principal amount until some point in the future.

Accounts Payable and Accrued Expenses

The supplies and services you purchase and use each month and pay for on terms should be recorded as accounts payable. While doing your bookkeeping, enter each invoice you get, making a debit entry in the appropriate expense account and crediting the accounts payable account. When you sit down to write checks and pay these bills, the accounting entries you make are to debit accounts payable, decreasing the amount of that account, and credit cash, which decreases the amount of cash you have as well. After you finish paying the bills, the amount of accounts payable should be zero (or the amount of the bills you didn't pay that month).

In addition to accounts payable, current liabilities include expenses that you accrue—payroll and related expenses, for example. For every hour an employee works, a business accrues the cost of that labor—the salary or wages, payroll and other taxes, and even contributions to pension funds and payment of employee benefits. The interest due on a loan is also an accrued expense.

Pay early and often

If the terms offered by some of your suppliers allow you to deduct a small percentage from an invoice by paying the invoice early, try to do so. A savings of a few percent, for example, might not sound like much, but as you record the savings that early payments bring, you'll begin to see a difference. In your chart of accounts, set up a cash discount account. When you're recording an invoice you've paid early, debit the entire amount of the invoice to the expense account—not the discounted amount you actually paid. The amount you actually paid is credited to your cash account, which leaves the amount of the discount. Credit this amount to the cash discount account. Over time, as the amount of the cash discount account increases, you'll see the positive effects of paying bills early.

Notes Payable

If you have a short-term loan (a loan payable on demand or within a term of between 30 days and 3 years), the principal amount of the note is considered a current liability. The interest you pay on the note is counted as an accrued expense. In general, you should use money that you borrow over a short term to buy current assets such as inventory. Because you're borrowing the money over a short term, you want to use that money to secure an asset that you expect to turn into cash over a comparable period of time. You might use short-term loans to purchase more inventory during a hot selling season or to take advantage of a discount offered for early payment of an item among your accounts payable.

Long-Term Liabilities

Liabilities that aren't due over the next year include such items as the principal amount of a long-term loan that isn't currently due or a loan made by an owner or a shareholder. A small business might use the amount of money it borrows through a long-term loan as working capital or to purchase an asset such as real estate or expensive machinery. When an owner makes a loan to his or her business to increase the owner's stake (instead of by purchasing more shares, for example), a portion of the loan payments—when the business can afford to pay them—is deductible as an interest expense.

Contingent liabilities

Contingent liabilities include amounts that might be due as the result of lawsuits or warranties a business makes. Because the amounts of contingent liabilities might never have to be paid, contingent liabilities are usually added to a balance sheet in the form of footnotes rather than as a main entry.

Net Worth

Net worth (or equity)—the owner's share in a business—is calculated by subtracting the amount of your liabilities from the amount of your assets. (Remember that the rule of a balance sheet is assets equal liabilities plus net worth.) The particular items that make up owner's equity—items like retained earnings and investment capital—are different for different kinds of businesses. Calculating the components of owner's equity is one topic about which you should consult with an experienced accountant.

Cutting Paychecks

Recording the amounts you pay in wages and salaries, especially because of payroll taxes and other related taxes involved, requires entries in several different accounts. Wages should be debited to a wages expense account. Federal withholding taxes and an employee's share of FICA taxes are taken out of the employee's paycheck. (FICA, which stands for Federal Insurance Contributions Act, represents taxes that fund the U.S. Social Security program.) Employer's must pay their share of FICA taxes as well, along with applicable state and federal unemployment taxes. For accounting purposes, taxes that an employer pays should be debited to a payroll tax expense account and also credited to a corresponding liability account—something like FICA Payable, FUTA (Federal Unemployment Tax Act) Payable, and so on. These liability accounts are among the accrued expenses that show up on a balance sheet.

Payroll taxes are calculated as a percentage of the amount of an employee's gross wage. As of 2004, FICA and the Medicare tax is 7.65 percent of gross wages. The U.S. government provides a chart that you can use to calculate the amount of income tax withholdings. (For states with a tax on income, you can likely obtain a chart for state withholding as well.) Unemployment and worker compensation taxes are based on indexes that take into account the state in which your business operates and historical data about your business's unemployment record. (For a new business, of course, no history will be established.)

When you're looking at the cost of hiring someone, don't look only at the hourly wage and the number of hours you expect the employee to work. You need to include in your calculations the taxes that an employer is obligated to pay as well as the cost of any employee benefits you plan to offer. Taxes and benefit costs add up quickly, of course, and can make a significant difference to the total cost of employing someone.

Closing Your Books

At the end of accounting periods—the end of a month, the end of a quarter, and especially the end of the year—you need to go through your accounts to check whether everything is in balance. In part, this task is a matter of instinct. Over a period of a month, for a new business owner at least, you should probably have a sense of how things went—what your major expenses were and how much you took in. You can probably recognize whether the amount of a particular account looks odd by reviewing your monthly financial statements and other reports. You will probably want to review critical accounts—sales, inventory, and the like—in detail. Using your balance sheet from last month, compare how accounts have changed. Does the ending balance for this month equal the beginning balance plus current activity? Also, if your business holds inventory, you'll need to take stock of all you have at the end of the year (and possibly other times during the year as well) and assign a value to the inventory you have.

Most accounting programs let you run what's known as a *trial balance*. A trial balance essentially points out where debit and credit entries aren't in balance. You can then go back and find those entries that are missing their double. An accounting program should also produce for you an item-by-item transaction report that lets you see all the account activity for the month or the year, including account balances. An item-by-item report might help you see an expense that was recorded in an incorrect account or a transaction you missed classifying altogether.

Preparing and Managing a Budget

Budgets help a business set the stage for its financial future and track its performance to date. Establishing a budget helps you define financial priorities and set goals for how much you can spend and how much you need to make. Budgets also help you allocate money when you don't have much to spare. If you're in business with partners, budgets can also represent the outcome of negotiations—a plan of action the partners agree to—for times when the partners don't see precisely eye to eye.

But remember that budgets are plans; they aren't set in stone. Like many other plans you make, budgets can be changed. If you've budgeted a certain amount for advertising but come upon a great marketing opportunity that will cost a little more, you'd probably be unwise to say "But we've budgeted only X amount" when the extra marketing might earn you 10 times the additional amount you decided to spend.

You should follow a couple of principles when beginning a budgeting exercise. First set some specific goals. How much income do you need, for example? Is your goal to increase sales by 10 percent over last year while reducing costs by the same amount? If you need to upgrade your physical plant, what are the priorities and how much can you allocate to the improvements you need? Use as much actual data as you can to formulate a budget. Although you might need to make an educated guess for some categories, legwork and planning make the information you include in a budget more accurate. Go over statements and invoices, for example, and use those as the basis for the next round of estimates.

When considering the expense side of a budget, be sure you recognize whether each expense category is a fixed expense, a variable expense, or a periodic expense. Fixed expenses, of course, are those that occur regularly (every month, for example) and possibly on a set date and for the same amount (an expense like your rent). Variable expenses (a category like advertising, for example) can be controlled more easily by reducing or increasing the amount you spend. Periodic expenses might be a fixed expense or a variable expense, but because they don't occur regularly, it's easy to overlook them. You need to be sure you have enough money set aside to cover a periodic expense when it falls due.

Once you've set up a budget, you should return to it (perhaps every month or every quarter) to check your actual expenses against the financial plan you developed. Has anything changed in your business in the past few months that should lead you to revise the budget? If you're under budget in one category, do you want to allocate that amount to another line item? If you're over budget in another category, what's the reason? Is the difference a one-time expense you didn't expect, or did you underestimate that prices for this good or service went up across the board?

You also need a budgeting tool—whether that's a component of your accounting software program, a ledger you keep by hand, or a spreadsheet you develop. Microsoft Office Online includes an expense budget in which you can track budgeted amounts, actual amounts, and differences between them (both the amount of the difference and the percentage difference). The Office Online expense budget is best suited for a budget that covers a single accounting period—one month, for example. You might also want to compare budgets for several months side by side on a single spreadsheet. You can set up a budget in Excel that offers this view of your business with a few formulas and the help of Excel's ability to rapidly fill in data in a well-known series—like the names of the 12 months. The formulas make the budget easy to maintain, providing you with some good historical data as your business grows and changes year to year.

If you want to create your own budget worksheet in Excel, here are the steps. Remember that the accounts created for this sample budget are provided as an example. If you use this example in your own business, you'll probably need to change the set of accounts—adding or deleting some—and modify some of the instructions accordingly.

Create a simple budget in Excel

1. From the Windows Start menu, open Excel. You'll see a blank worksheet window and the Getting Started task pane. You can close the task pane if you want to.

2. In cell A1 of the worksheet, enter your business's name and the label **Budget**. In cell A2, enter the date. Each time you update the budget, edit this cell so that it shows the last date the budget was changed.

3. In cell B3, enter **January** (or whichever month marks the beginning of the period you're creating the budget for). The spreadsheet should now look something like this:

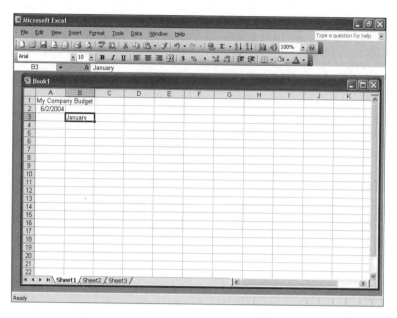

4. Select cell B3 (the cell containing *January*) and cell C3. On the Format menu, click Cells. In the Format Cells dialog box, click the Alignment tab, and then select Merge Cells in the Text Control area. From the Horizontal list under Text Alignment, select Center Across Selection. The dialog box will look like the following:

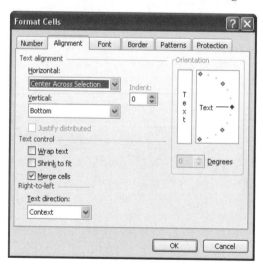

5. Click OK in the Format Cells dialog box, and then select the merged cells (cells B3 and C3). Position the mouse pointer on the fill handle (the black square at the bottom right corner of the selected cell; the

pointer will appear as a plus sign), and then drag the fill handle to the right to fill in the rest of the months. If you start with January in columns B and C, December will end up spanning columns X and Y.

6. In cell B4, enter the label **Budget**. In cell C4, enter **Actual**. Select these cells, and then use the fill handle again (as in step 5) to copy these labels to the cells beneath the other months you entered. The first portion of the worksheet should now look like this:

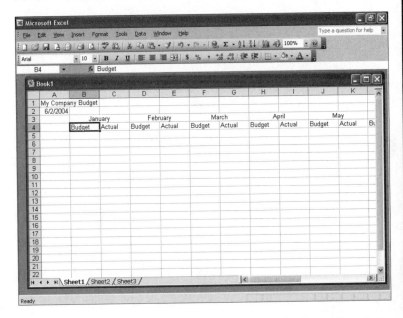

7. Use the rows in column A to list the accounts the budget will track. In cell A5, enter **Sales**. (You might have only one income entry, as here, or several if you budget income from more than one source—several different products, for example.)

8. In rows A7 through A18, enter the following expense categories. Again, these are only examples. You should enter your own accounts in this step if you want to.

- Advertising

- Dues and Subscriptions

- Insurance

- Legal and Professional Fees

- Licenses and Fees

- Office Expense and Supplies

- Payroll Taxes

- Postage

- Rent

- Repairs and Maintenance

- Telephone and Utilities

- Wages

Select column A, and then click Format, Column, AutoFit Selection. This command will widen the column so that it shows the longest string of text you entered in the column.

9. In cell A20, enter the label **Total Expenses**. Then, in cell B20, enter the formula **=Sum(B7:B18)**. This formula will add up any numbers you enter in the expense rows in column B. Select cell B20, and then use the fill handle again to copy this formula to the other Budget and Actual cells to the right. At this point, you've created a worksheet in which you can enter month-by-month budgets and track actual amounts spent as each month's activity is recorded. The worksheet should now appear as follows:

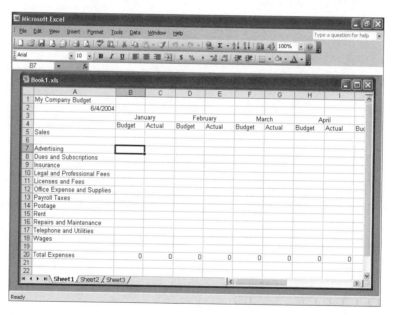

You could modify this worksheet in a couple of ways. If you have more than one income category, you could use a row to show the total of those categories.

Use Excel's SUM function again (as in step 9) to make this calculation. You could also insert a couple of columns for each month—one that would calculate the difference between the budgeted and actual amounts and one that would calculate the percentage difference. The formula to calculate the difference would be something like =B7−C7. The formula to calculate the percentage difference would be C7/B7*100. (The slash is the character Excel uses to divide two values, and the asterisk is the multiplication operator.)

Managing Cash Flow

Money in, money out. That's the nature of cash flow. The pattern of money coming into and going out of your business will influence (if not determine) whether you stay in business. Regularly reviewing when you expect to receive money and when you expect to have to pay it out—you might perform this exercise every month or at least a couple of times each year—will help you determine how to sufficiently balance and manage your cash flow.

Some of the key accounts to study when you're looking at cash flow are accounts receivable, accounts payable, and inventory. You also need to examine the credit terms under which you sell goods and services to customers and the terms under which you purchase materials from your suppliers. An understanding of how these accounts relate to one another will help identify potential problems and keep cash flowing more smoothly.

The most basic analysis you should do is to compare accounts payable and accounts receivable at the end of each month. Obviously, if the amount of your accounts payable exceeds the amount of income you're scheduled to receive, you'll have to dip into cash reserves to make up the difference.

Because you can be sure that you'll always have cash flowing out—rent, inventory purchases, fees, and the like—you need to be active in setting up processes that will help assure that cash keeps flowing in as well. For example, don't wait until the end of the month to send out all your invoices. If you make a sale on June 3 that is payable 30 days from the date of the invoice and then wait until June 30 to send the invoice, you've added nearly a month to the time frame for being paid. Also be sure that you keep a close eye on how customers are doing with respect to payment. If a customer is already behind in paying you, make sure you get some of the amount the customer owes you, and preferably all, before you ship the next order. You can also offer a discount of a few percentage points as an incentive to customers to pay invoices early—say 10 to 14 days after the sale rather than 30 days. Ask for payment of a portion of work you plan to do or the goods you'll deliver as part of the initial order. You can put that money to use while you complete the rest of the job. And finally, act quickly in collecting amounts that are past due. Document your request for payment with letters or faxes, and specify the steps you'll take if payment isn't received, including turning the account over to a collection agency.

Microsoft Office Online's financial statement templates include a couple of Excel worksheets designed for tracking cash flow—the 12 Month Cash Flow Statement (one of the templates provided by SCORE) and the Small Business Cash Flow Projection. Both of the worksheets are set up to calculate the amount of cash you'll have on hand based on when you estimate you'll receive income and when you'll incur related costs. Figure 5-3 shows a portion of the Small Business Cash Flow Projection template for small businesses.

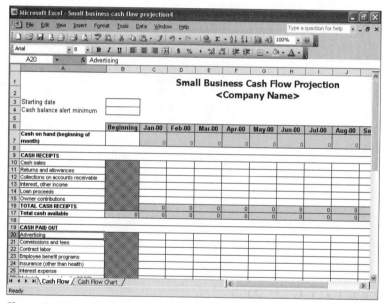

Figure 5-3 Analyzing cash flow regularly will help you estimate the peaks and valleys for the amount of cash you'll have on hand.

The shaded cells in rows such as those labeled Total Cash Receipts and Total Cash Available contain formulas that add up the amounts you enter in the accounts and categories listed in the rows under Cash Receipts and Cash Paid Out. This worksheet also uses *conditional formatting*, a feature in Excel that you can use to apply special formatting to information that meets conditions you specify. In this worksheet, for example, any time cash balances are less than a certain amount, the cash balances are displayed in red so that you'll be sure to notice them. In cell B4, labeled Cash Balance Alert

Minimum, near the top left corner of the worksheet, you can enter the amount you want to use as the basis of the condition. To apply conditional formatting to the information in a worksheet, click Conditional Formatting on the Format menu. You then specify the conditions under which special formatting will be applied and the formatting properties themselves—a font size and color, for example, or a background pattern in the cell.

You can modify the account and category names listed in column A, and you can also insert (or delete) additional rows. If you insert an expense account between rows 20 and 44 (by using the Insert, Row command), the formula that calculates the subtotal is updated by Excel so that all rows in the new range are included.

Remember that some people love to manage money. They do it professionally. You need to consider whether your time as a small business owner is well spent keeping your own books or whether that's a job you can and want to entrust to someone else. You might not be able to afford a bookkeeper or an accountant from the very start, and that's where the use of an accounting program, as well as one or more of the financial and accounting templates on Office Online, can help. The basic task is to keep on top of your financial records—whoever does the work—so that you have a realistic understanding of how well your business is doing.

List of Resources

Here's a list of the Web sites mentioned in this chapter, where you can find information and job aids that will help you manage your business's finances:

- You can find a number of financial and accounting templates at *www.office.microsoft.com.*

- You can download a 60-day trial version of Microsoft Money, a computer accounting program, at *www.microsoft.com/money/deluxe.*

- For information about accounting methods and other information about accounting requirements for small businesses, visit *www.irs.gov.* IRS Publication 538, "Accounting Periods and Methods," is particularly helpful.

- At *www.score.org*, you can find financial statement templates and lots of other relevant information provided by the Service Corps of Retired Executives (SCORE).

For More Information

In addition to the resources mentioned in this chapter, you will find links and information on the companion CD. Some books and Web sites particularly useful as you learn about accounting principles and practices for your business include:

Books

- Angie Mohr, *Bookkeepers' Boot Camp: Get a Grip on Accounting Basics* (Self-Counsel Press, 2003)

- Linda Pinson, *Keeping the Books: Basic Record Keeping and Accounting for the Successful Small Business* (Dearborn Trade, 2004)

- Suzanne Caplan, *Streetwise Finance and Accounting: How to Keep Your Books and Manage Your Finances Without an MBA, a CPA, or a Ph.D.* (Adams Media, 2000)

Web Sites

- The Small Business site within the Nolo Legal Encyclopedia is a great starting spot for many topics, including bookkeeping and accounting: *www.nolo.com/lawcenter/*

- The bookkeeping and accounting guide at the Online Women's Business Center of the SBA: *www.onlinewbc.gov/docs/finance/bkpg_acct.html*

- The Microsoft Office Templates home page: office.microsoft.com/templates/default.aspx

The hardest thing in the world to understand is the income tax.

— Albert Einstein

Chapter Six

Tax Tactics

As the old saying has it, the only things certain are death and taxes. Although you can't avoid paying taxes, questions about taxes abound: when do you need to pay them as a business, what can you deduct, when do you need an expert? Getting advice from a tax professional is often the best course to take. When you have a question about taxes, you don't want to guess at the answer.

What you'll find:

- ❏ Tax strategies for major business expenses
- ❏ How to interview a tax pro
- ❏ When to manage taxes on your own
- ❏ Secrets tax pros never share
- ❏ Frequent tax and bookkeeping mistakes
- ❏ Travel expense deduction strategies
- ❏ When a PC at home isn't a home PC

Taxes, of course, are an enormous topic, from business income tax to state unemployment tax, and nearly every business will have its own tax situation and its own set of questions. In starting and running a business, you venture into a far different tax world than the one inhabited by individual taxpayers—rules about deducting business expenses, rules for the use of your car for business purposes, rules about what records you need to keep when you travel and entertain for business. Taxes are one area for which many small business owners will seek professional advice.

This chapter presents a collection of articles about small business tax issues published on *www.microsoft.com/smallbusiness*. You'll find tips for how to select a tax professional, tax and bookkeeping mistakes to look out for, guidelines for travel deductions, and lots of other useful advice. Check the Microsoft small business Web site and the other resources mentioned in this chapter for more information.

Tax Strategies for Major Business Expenses

In a simpler tax world that we can only imagine, the way small businesses write off major expenses would be, well, a lot simpler. You'd deduct the costs of all your major purchases in the same year you made them. The tax laws passed by the U.S. Congress in 2003 go a long way toward creating that world for most small businesses.

Here are four points to remember when trying to figure out how major purchases will affect your business's tax bottom line:

Up to $100,000 is allowed in personal property write-offs. As a small business, you can expense, or write off, up to $100,000 of business personal property in 2004 and 2005. Business personal property is stuff like furniture, office equipment, and computers. Writing off the full cost in one year is called a *Section 179 election*, and the election has to be made in the year of purchase. That means you cannot buy a computer this year and then try to expense it next year, or take the personal computer you bought for your home in 2003 and try to write off the full cost when using it in your business in 2004 or 2005.

You have to use the property more than half the time for business for it to qualify for Section 179 treatment, and the deduction is proportionately reduced for anything not used solely for business. That means that if you buy a $2,000 computer and use it 75 percent for business, the maximum amount you can write off is $1,500.

If you want to see how much small businesses love the Section 179 deduction, take a little time between Christmas and New Year's Day to peek inside any store that sells office furniture or equipment. Chances are you'll see lots of buyers racking up some year-end deductions.

Exceptions to the rules

The $100,000 maximum is reduced for businesses that buy more than $400,000 worth of personal property in a year. The reduction is dollar-for-dollar for amounts over $400,000. So, for example, if your business spends $410,000 on equipment, the maximum Section 179 write-off is $90,000.

An office building is not personal property. You'll notice that this $100,000 deduction opportunity refers to *personal property*. This is important to note: real estate is not personal property. (Apologies to anyone who thinks that statement is obvious, but people have bought office condos thinking they could write off a big chunk of the cost in the first year.)

Nonresidential real estate, such as office or industrial properties, has to be depreciated over 39 years. And only the building qualifies for depreciation (that is, you cannot depreciate unimproved land). Add it all up, and it means that your first-year depreciation write-off on a business building is probably going to be less than 2 percent of the purchase price.

Cars aren't personal property, either. The rule on deducting the cost of a business vehicle you own used to be simple—and onerous: the deduction in the year of purchase was limited to $3,060, plus business-related operating expenses.

Now the rule is more liberal, but also more complicated. Automobiles purchased in 2003 or 2004 qualify for a special *bonus depreciation* of $7,650, on top of the $3,060 limit, for a total first-year depreciation deduction of up to $10,710.

However, there are some exceptions to this rule for vehicles that are not considered ordinary passenger cars. Most significantly, you could apply the full Section 179 expense deduction (assuming you had no other business equipment purchases) against the purchase of a vehicle that qualifies as a truck. You could even deduct the entire purchase price of the vehicle in the year that you buy it.

Spent more than $100,000? You could still get a larger deduction. You could wind up with more than $100,000 in equipment deductions for 2004, even with the Section 179 limit in place. Here's how. (It's also complicated.) Let's say you're a physician, video producer, or other professional who might have to spend $150,000 in a year on business equipment that qualifies for the Section 179 deduction. You could get a write-off of $100,000 in equipment under Section 179. You also could get a special bonus depreciation of 50 percent on the remaining balance, for a write-off of an additional $25,000.

And then you'd still get your regular depreciation on the remaining $25,000 worth of equipment. The overall result is that even if you spent as much as $150,000 on qualifying business equipment in one year, you could still take a first-year write-off of more than 85 percent of those costs.

Confused? See a Tax Pro

There are other rules and restrictions on writing off major business purchases. For example, farmers can get special treatment for certain single-purpose agricultural buildings such as greenhouses. Your Section 179 deductions can be limited by your overall taxable income from a trade or business; limitations also apply if you're reporting Section 179 expenses from multiple businesses. And these liberal deduction rules are expected to be tightened again after 2005.

Already, several states have acted to restrict the up-front deduction on 6,000-pound SUVs, which means that you could wind up having to keep track of different depreciation schedules and deductions for your state and federal income taxes.

This stuff isn't simple. Talk with a tax pro before year-end if you need more help with your major purchases.

How to Interview a Tax Pro

Be sure to interview a tax pro before you hire him or her—just as you'd interview a lawyer, an architect, a doctor, or any other professional. Sure, you're not an expert in the field, but you can still learn a lot and at least screen out some candidates with an initial meeting.

Your interview goals? You want to determine not only how the tax pro's business meshes with your needs, but also whether you'll have a good emotional "fit" or comfort level.

Here are seven questions you should ask a tax pro before hiring him or her:

What kind of credentials do you have? Tax pros usually are certified public accountants (CPAs), enrolled agents (EAs), or unenrolled preparers. CPAs by definition are public accountants; many focus on tax issues, but some specialize in other areas. Most CPAs are state-licensed by the states and have broader powers with regard to IRS audits than unlicensed CPAs (public accountants who have passed the Uniform CPA exam but who have yet to receive a state license). EAs are licensed by the federal government, and so by definition specialize in tax issues. Unenrolled preparers are, basically, everyone else. They might or might not have had any formal training.

Do you have an area or type of client in which you specialize? You're looking not just for a tax pro, but also for someone who is very familiar with and hopefully an expert in the issues affecting you. An EA who spends most of his time handling audits might not be right for you if your main reason for hiring a professional is that you have several real estate investments. A CPA who handles returns for trusts or large businesses isn't likely to be the best fit if you have a small business with a handful of employees. Both tax pros could be qualified to handle those returns, but you'll probably be happier with someone whose client base is similar to your own profile.

How much professional education do you get annually? Just passing the test to become a CPA or an EA isn't enough. With the tax code and interpretations of the code changing every year, continuing education is really essential. EAs are required to complete 72 hours of continuing education in a three-year period. Each state sets its own requirements for CPAs. In Oregon, for example, CPAs must take 80 hours of continuing education within a two-year period.

Many tax professionals take more than the minimum requirement for continuing education. Although more training doesn't necessarily mean the tax pro will be superior, it's certainly not a bad sign.

Who will I be interacting with?   Many tax firms assign more than one person to a client's return. You probably don't need to know how the "back room" operates, but you do want to know whether the person you're interviewing is the one who will be able to answer your questions about your return.

What's your policy on returning phone calls?   One of the complaints heard most often from consumers about their tax pros: "She doesn't return my calls." What can we say? Tax pros aren't famous for their communications skills. It's not unreasonable to ask how long you should expect to wait to have a call returned. Asking also lets the tax pro know that you do want your calls returned.

Are you available outside of the tax season?   Some tax preparers are seasonal: they are available only the first four months of the year, or their offices are closed for a few months each year. If you expect year-round access, you need to make sure the tax pro will be available.

How much are you going to charge me?   Don't be afraid to discuss fees. After all, it's your money. Tax pros might bill by the hour, the form, the overall return, or some combination. After reviewing your previous returns and interviewing you, a tax pro should be able to give you a good-faith estimate of costs.

When to Manage Taxes on Your Own

In the previous section, we listed seven questions you should ask a tax professional before hiring him or her. Many of you might be wondering, "Do I really need to hire a tax pro?" It's a good question, but know this up front: We're a little biased in favor of using a tax pro. We've seen some of the problems taxpayers can wind up with when they do their own returns and don't understand some of the gray areas of the tax rules.

That said, millions of people do their own tax returns, and most of them get no negative feedback from the IRS or state taxing agencies. Here are six signs that you can survive without a tax pro:

You're not afraid of numbers.   Obvious, but important. We're not just thinking about adding and multiplying here. We're also thinking about the basic issue of entering or writing down the numbers properly. An innocent mistake such as transposing two digits from a wage statement can result in more hassles than you would think possible.

You've got a simple return.   A "simple" return doesn't mean it has to be a Form 1040-EZ. Most people who have little more going on in their financial tax lives than having a full-time job, owning a home with a mortgage, contributing to a fully deductible retirement account, and making contributions to charities can do their own returns. "If you're good at simple math, and the most complicated calculation you'll have to do is figure out the taxable portion of your Social Security, you may be a good candidate for doing your own returns," says Gretchen Beck, an EA in San Francisco.

You understand your own returns.   You can use a computer program, so you say it doesn't matter whether you understand your returns. Maybe. You can certainly produce a very good return using a computer program, but it's still GIGO (garbage in, garbage out). If you enter something incorrectly or don't understand the question being asked, you're not going to have as accurate a return as you could. That leads to the next point.

You're good at double-checking.   The more information you have to enter on your return, the more possibilities for forgetting something or entering it in the wrong place or entering the wrong numbers. So having the patience to double-check your own work does matter. Leon Taylor, a CPA in Portland, Oregon, recalls having to amend several years' worth of returns for an intelligent high-tech employee. "This was a smart person with nothing more on the returns than wages, interest, dividend, mortgage interest, taxes, and contributions—and there were significant errors on every year," Taylor says. "If someone is detail-oriented and good at following directions, they could probably handle a basic return. Otherwise, they should hire a pro."

Your life hasn't changed from the previous year.   Many people first go to a tax pro when their lives change. They might be getting married, getting divorced, buying investment property, selling a house that had a home office, starting a business, or pulling money out of retirement plans— the key is that something new and different is happening in their lives and it affects their tax returns. You're a better do-it-yourself candidate if there was nothing new in your life last year and your return is likely to look pretty similar to what you filed in previous years.

Money is more important to you than time.   Ultimately, the issue for some people becomes simply one of time. They are capable of doing their own returns, but they would rather pay a tax pro and have those several hours or days they might spend on their returns available for other things.

That sentiment is reasonable. You also might know how to do a lot of repairs around the house or how to work on your own computer, but you'll often spend money on a professional repairperson or tech expert instead. A pro who does something all the time is likely to know some things you don't and will do the work faster and better than you can. The money you spend is more than made up for by the time that gets freed up for other things—like running your business.

Secrets Tax Pros Never Share

According to statistics from the IRS, more than half of you will pay someone to prepare your tax returns this year. Tax professionals from around the country talk to each other, and because they do what they do, they talk shop and share insights. They tell each other things they won't tell you, including stuff that could help you deal with your own tax pro and maybe even save you money, if only you knew.

Here are some things you've probably never been told by a tax pro:

That first meeting? You'll probably get charged less if you've got your stuff together. Most tax pros charge based on some combination of hourly rates, complexity of the tax return, and the so-called hassle factor.

Having information dribble in—one form this week, a couple of necessary numbers next week—increases the hassle factor, and the amount the tax pro is going to want to charge. As one tax pro said, "I wish there was a nice way I could tell clients to wait until they think they've got all their information and not bother sending me part of it now and part later. I cannot complete the puzzle until they give me all the pieces."

Another tax pro was more direct. "Every time I open up a client's file to add another form or another piece of information, the cost of preparing the return goes up. I charge for my time. How else can it be?"

The early bird gets more attention. It's human nature. Early in the tax season, tax pros feel like they have more time. This doesn't necessarily mean you're going to get a "better" return—a good tax pro should go through the same questions and processes regardless of when the return is done. But you have to figure that if your return is being worked on early in the tax season, a little more time (including time talking with you) is going to go into it than would otherwise be the case. If you're going to use a tax pro, see him or her in mid-February.

Each tax office has its own "crunch" period, but for most, the worst weeks fall somewhere between March 15 and April 15. Interestingly, Tax Day itself, April 15, often is not that bad a day. Many tax professionals leave that day open for any last-second calls and clients picking up their returns. All the returns that are going out will have been finished by the 13th or 14th of the month.

Avoid last-second rush jobs.   Tax pros want to do a good job for all of their clients. If you call a tax pro you've never talked to before on April 12, saying you need to file by April 15, the tax pro is probably going to refer you to someone else. The tax pro won't want to take on a new client that close to the deadline and potentially take time from existing clients.

Extensions are fine.   Many taxpayers worry that they're going to have trouble with the IRS if they file an extension. There's little evidence of that. In fact, extensions are the perfect solution for the taxpayer who would otherwise be a "rush job." It's much better to file an extension and send in an accurate return later than it is to rush to meet the April 15 deadline and later discover things you missed that require you to amend the return.

With the extra time afforded by an extension, a tax pro can go over a client's tax situation after April 15 and make sure all the documentation has been collected and all the questions asked that could help trim the client's tax bill. Individuals can get an extra four months to send in their return by filing Form 4868 by April 15.

Don't ask a tax pro to help you cheat.   They don't want to do it. They can't do it. And in a legal proceeding, a tax pro might even have to testify that you wanted him or her to help you evade the law. (Tax professionals maintain the confidentiality of their client's information, but they generally do not have the same kind of attorney-client privilege that lawyers enjoy.)

"One client wrote me a letter telling me he was going to have some income that he would not be declaring," remembers one tax pro. Yikes.

There's a lot a good tax pro can do to help you pay no more in taxes than you are legally required to pay. There's nothing a good tax pro can do to help you cheat. If that's the kind of "help" you want, you should just do your own returns.

The person preparing your taxes might make less than a fast-food worker.
Some tax preparers work only during the tax season for one of the big tax
return chains. For this part-time, seasonal work, the tax preparer
might make about $9 an hour—pretty low for someone doing work so
closely related to your financial life. In some cases, the tax preparer
won't be a CPA or an EA—professionals recognized as specialists. The
preparer might not have any formal training beyond the coursework
offered by the company that hired him or her.

Firms might have more highly trained or experienced people reviewing
the work of low-paid assistants. If you want to know, you'll have to ask.

Frequent Tax and Bookkeeping Mistakes

The U.S. tax code is so complicated that it's no surprise many small businesses and individuals make mistakes in their bookkeeping and filing. But
don't count on any mercy from the IRS. Here are several of the more common mistakes, and what you need to do to avoid them:

Not saving receipts of less than $75   People sometimes get excited when
they hear that the IRS doesn't require receipts for meal and entertainment expenses of less than $75. Don't fall into this trap. You might
not need the receipt, but you still need to have some sort of record
documenting where you went, when you went there, who you were
with, the business purpose of the meal or entertainment, and the
business relationship between you and the people you were with.

When you look at the list of requirements, what could be better for
documentation than a credit-card charge receipt? In most cases, the
charge slip will already have printed on it the name and address of the
restaurant and the date and time you were there. All you have to do is
write on the slip who you were with and what the business relationship and purpose was of the event. While a receipt might not be
required, for many people, hanging on to the receipt is going to be easier than keeping an entirely separate log of the expense information.

Lumping equipment with supplies   Equipment is a capital expenditure,
and capital expenditures have to be depreciated. Special rules do
allow most small businesses to write off up to $24,000 in capital
expenditures for tangible personal property (such as computers and
office furnishings) in the year the property is purchased. However,
you still have to report these purchases as capital expenditures and
elect to use this special method of expensing the costs.

What if you don't report the purchases properly and instead just deduct your computers and other capital items as supplies? The IRS could rule that you improperly characterized the expense and are not entitled to the deduction you claimed.

Not only that, but since you failed to properly categorize the property or make an election, you could also find that you're required to add the cost of the property to your overall investment in your business. Result: no current deduction at all.

Forgetting to track reimbursable expenses   Many small business owners pay for some business expenses with cash out of their own pocket or through a personal credit card. That's fine. The mistake is if you don't track those costs and submit the expenses to your company for reimbursement. Also, the company must have an established plan that does deduct the expenses and enables reimbursements to be nontaxable to employees.

But if you don't keep track of and substantiate the expenses, you will at best have a nonreimbursed business expense. These can be deducted on your personal tax return only to the extent that all of your miscellaneous Schedule A expenses exceed 2 percent of your adjusted gross income.

Miscalculating automobile deductions   Part of the problem here is that there are many ways to calculate deductions for business use of a car. Here are some brief guidelines that can help you:

■   You can take a standard mileage deduction per business mile, or you can take a deduction for actual expenses, including depreciation of the car. But you cannot claim the standard mileage deduction and the depreciation for actual expenses.

■   You can switch between the two methods. However, if you go from standard mileage to actual expenses, you cannot take depreciation using the modified accelerated cost recovery system (MACRS) depreciation system. You have to take a straight-line depreciation, which typically yields a smaller initial deduction.

■   If the car is owned by the corporation, 100 percent of the costs can be deducted. However, any personal use by an employee has to be included as taxable income to the employee. Your tax pro or IRS Publication 917, "Business Use of a Car," can help you figure out how to determine the value of personal use.

Small Business Tax Resources at *www.irs.gov*

The IRS's Web site has a number of small business tax tools as well as a wide array of information and other resources. The site includes links to online tax workshops that cover topics such as employment taxes, business use of your home, and tax incentives for employers. You can watch these workshops over the Internet (the IRS site recommends that you have a high-speed connection) or order a CD that contains the workshops. The site also contains links to small business tax forms and publications, a small business resource guide, a tax calendar for small businesses, and a list of changes for businesses in the current tax year.

Giving more than you can receive, tax-wise Every year you can hear tax pros talk about having at least one small business client that says it had a couple thousand dollars in deductible business gifts in the previous year. There's no problem with offering gifts to clients and business associates. But a four-figure deduction for gifts gets people's attention because the IRS allows deductions only up to $25 worth of gifts to any individual per year. So $2,000 in deductions would mean that gifts were given to at least 80 different people. That's a lot of gifts.

Usually it turns out that while the money was indeed spent, it was divided into several gifts that were more than $25 apiece. There's nothing wrong with being generous. But only that first $25 per recipient is a deductible business expense. The rest is a nondeductible expense. (Sometimes it does seem as if no good deed goes unpunished.)

Travel Expense Deduction Strategies

When you hit the road for business trips, you have to know the rules for deducting your hotel and meal expenses. While the rules haven't changed much lately (proposals to increase the percentage of a meal that can be deducted haven't gone anywhere), they're still a little tricky.

There are several different ways to deduct meal and lodging expenses when you or your employees are on the road. The method you use could make a difference in terms of how much money—and time—you save.

Here's a breakdown:

The basic method: tallying actual costs. Keeping careful track of actual food and lodging costs is the method with which most small businesses are familiar. Save your receipts, document your costs and the business purposes of your activities, and take your deductions.

Alternative No. 1: per diem for businesses (the high-low method).   You, as the employer, can give your employees a per diem allowance. The simplest way of doing this, known as the *high-low method*, lets you choose from only two different rates for meals, hotels, and incidental expenses for business trips within the continental United States.

Per diem allowances within the United States under this method are $207 per day in so-called high-cost areas, which include major cities such as New York, Chicago, San Francisco, and Washington, D.C. Most of the country, however, falls under a per diem rate of $126 per day. For more details on per diem rates, go to the IRS Web site (*www.irs.gov*) and search for *per diem rates.*

One advantage of the per diem route is that you don't have to keep track of the actual receipts for meals and hotel costs. However, the paperwork burden is not entirely eliminated. You and your employees still have to keep track of the time, place, and purpose of each business expense.

If you decide to use the high-low method, you have to use it for all travel for the entire year.

Alternative No. 2: per diem for businesses (the federal meals-and-lodging travel rate method).   Instead of the high-low method, you can choose to take per diem deductions, or reimburse your employees, based on the federal per diem rates, which vary depending on the location. These per diem rates actually can be more favorable than those under the high-low rate, but you'll want to take a look at the rates in the cities you are traveling to and do a comparison before deciding which works to your advantage.

Per diem for sole proprietors.   If you're an unincorporated sole proprietor, you also are entitled to take per diem deductions for meals, but not per diems for hotels.

This fact might tick off more than one sole proprietor, but these are the rules: You can use the government's meal per diem rates (which, until September 30, 2004, are $31, $35, $39, $43, $47, and $51 per day, depending on the city), but you cannot use the federal travel rate method or the high-low method for taking lodging deductions. You'll have to keep track of those actual hotel expenses regardless of whether you use the per diem rates or deduct actual meal expenses.

On the other hand, as a sole proprietor, you're not locked into taking either the per diem deduction or actual meal expenses for all your trips for the whole year. You can decide with each trip which method to use for that trip. You do, however, have to be consistent in using the same method for the entire trip.

Foreign travel per diems.   Foreign trips are subject to different rules and per diem rates and requirements. If you happen to have a qualifying business trip overseas—and the rules for deducting overseas travel differ significantly from those governing domestic business travel—you can check out the foreign per diem possibilities at the Web site for the U.S. Department of State (*www.state.gov/m/a/als/prdm/*).

Don't Forget the Basics

Regardless of the method you use, meals have to be considered ordinary and necessary expenses for your business. You don't have to actually conduct paying business during the meal, but you do have to have either a more-than-general expectation of getting some sort of business benefit in the future, or a substantial business discussion either immediately before or after the meal.

A couple of other things: You generally cannot deduct meals with your business partners or coworkers unless you establish a clear business purpose for the meal. You cannot deduct anything that would be considered lavish or extravagant under the circumstances. And you also are restricted, regardless of the meal or deduction method, to getting a tax break for only 50 percent of the deduction.

When a PC at Home Isn't a Home PC

The IRS regulations about deducting computers used in your business can take on an almost Alice-in-Wonderland quality. But if you hope to write off the purchase of PCs for your small or home-based business, you need to know something about these rules. Here are some of the high points.

The World of Listed Property

Computers, along with passenger autos, cell phones, cameras, and some other types of equipment, are generally subject to more recordkeeping and substantiation for tax deductions. These types of items are known as *listed property*. In fact, there's a special section for them on the tax return: Part V of Form 4562, "Depreciation and Amortization."

It makes sense for the IRS to want more recordkeeping than usual for these types of business purchases. Cameras, video equipment, and other high-tech toys are widely used for personal purposes and entertainment. The IRS is well aware of this, so it wants to make sure that you'll include as a business expense only 90 percent of the cost of your hand-held camcorder if you're using it 10 percent of the time for vacations and parties.

Typically, you're supposed to keep track of the business use of each of these types of property. The most common way of doing this is by keeping a usage log. For your computer, the most complete method of recordkeeping would involve noting on a daily basis how much time you've spent using the computer and how much of that time was business usage.

An Exception to the Rule

However, there is an exception to these requirements for some computers. (You must know that a tax professional's list of five favorite phrases always includes, "But there is an exception to that rule.")

If you use your computer exclusively at your business location, the computer does not have to be considered listed property. Therefore, you would not include it with cell phones, automobiles, and other listed property on your tax return.

This doesn't mean that you won't include the computer expenses on Form 4652 of your tax return. But if you're depreciating a new computer, the equipment will be included with expenses in Part II of the form, instead of Part V.

So far, so good. You have your computer in your home office, you don't take your computer out of your home office, and you get out of some of the more onerous recordkeeping requirements attached to deducting a business computer.

When Home PCs Aren't Home PCs

Here's where things get a little weird. Let's say that you're one of the many small business owners or small proprietors with a home office. You have a computer in your home office, and you use the computer exclusively for your business.

You think of this equipment as your *home computer*. The folks who sold it to you probably referred to it as a home computer. But in the lingo of the tax world, it is not a home computer. It is a computer being used in a regular business location, and thus it is not subject to the difficult recordkeeping requirements of home computers.

Now, let's consider that six-pound, two-inch-thick high-tech machine that you lug with you when you go to see clients or have other business meetings. You probably think of that as your laptop PC. You paid a lot for it—probably more than you would pay for a desktop PC—precisely because it is lightweight and portable and allows you to work from just about anywhere, instead of being tethered to your office desk.

You probably wouldn't have even bought this laptop if you didn't have a business. So you surely think of it as a fully deductible piece of business equipment. But when it comes to tax returns, that laptop is subject to the rules in place for home computers. That's right—it is listed property, which means that you're supposed to keep track of and report the business use of the computer on your tax return.

Employees Get Different Treatment

Don't use this story as a guide to deductions if you are an employee trying to write off a personal computer that you use to do work at home for your boss. The rules about deducting those kinds of purchases when you are an employee are much stricter—most employees don't get to deduct anything for home computer purchases.

Finally, a warning: While computers used solely in a home office or other business setting are not considered listed property, there has been at least one tax court case in which a taxpayer's deduction for computer equipment used in a home-based business was denied, at least in part because there was no evidence offered about the business use of the computer.

So despite the way the tax laws read, if you want belt-and-suspenders security, keep some type of a log. You also should be careful to note in your records the dedicated home-office space and the computer's placement within that space.

Taxes are something you need to get right. Doing some tax planning with a tax pro or on your own is one of the tasks you should make a priority when you own a small business. There's nothing to be gained by paying more taxes than you owe—you can work to make your taxes as low as possible as long as you pay your taxes in the amount the tax rules demand. Working with a tax professional—one who understands something about the business you're in—is often the way to go.

For More Information

In addition to the resources mentioned in this chapter, you will find links and information on the companion CD. Some books and Web sites particularly useful as you tackle the thorny issue of taxation include:

Books

- Frederick W. Daily, *Tax Savvy for Small Business: Year-Round Tax Strategies to Save You Money* (Nolo Press, 2003)

- Michael Savage, *Don't Let the IRS Destroy Your Small Business: Seventy-Six Mistakes to Avoid* (Perseus Books, 1998)

- Stephen Fishman, *Working for Yourself: Law and Taxes for Independent Contractors, Freelancers and Consultants* (Nolo Press, 2002)

Web Sites

- The IRS's small business portal site: *www.irs.gov/businesses/small/*

- *Business Week* magazine's Small Business Center has useful advice on taxes, as well as a range of other resources and articles: *www.businessweek.com/smallbiz/index.html*

- The CCH Business Owner's Toolkit includes extensive information on taxes: *www.toolkit.cch.com/*

Drive your business or it will drive you.

— *Benjamin Franklin*

Chapter Seven

By the Numbers: Analyzing Your Business with Excel

Keeping track of the money that flows into and out of your business is important work. But those aren't the only numbers you need to pay attention to. You need to analyze numbers to set sales goals and to determine how much you need to charge. You need to examine trends in your business so that you can plan ahead and take advantage of the opportunities to come.

What you'll find:

❏ Excel training and assistance

❏ What data should I collect?

❏ "What if...?": tools for analyzing common business questions

❏ Spotting trends: sorting, filtering, and charting information

❏ Slicing and dicing your business data: why should you use a PivotTable?

❏ Two important Excel functions

How many units of your product do you need to sell each month for the next six months to stay current on your rent, pay the two employees you hope to hire, and have something left over for yourself? How would a 5-percent increase in the price you charge affect your overall financial picture? How much do you need to charge per hour—and how many hours do you need to bill each month—to meet your annual revenue goal?

Many questions like these can be answered using Microsoft Excel. When you're starting a business or taking stock of what's gone on in your business for the first year or two, you'll want to do some data analysis. Basic data analysis will help you clarify the goals in front of you and also help you see important trends once you've been in business for a while. Knowing how to make sense of the business and financial information you collect leads to better decisions.

You can use Excel for many business tasks—everything from maintaining a list of customers, to tracking the sums of money you spend each month, to preparing sales forecasts and budgets. Excel also has a number of features designed for analyzing business information. You can easily run what-if scenarios, for example, or set up tables that let you test how small changes in cost or price affect the margin between your income and expense. In addition, you can see what's required to meet certain financial or other business goals. We'll take a look at these and other features of Excel in the sections ahead.

Excel Training and Assistance

To make the most of the data analysis tools in Excel, you should know the basics of how to enter data in an Excel worksheet and use simple formulas. You should also know how to refer to cells and cell ranges in formulas, edit data in worksheets, move and copy data, and format data so that you can emphasize and present the information that's most important.

You can use the online training and assistance available through Microsoft Office Online (*www.office.microsoft.com*) to learn about the basic features of Excel or to sharpen the skills you already have. If you're a beginner, click Microsoft Office Online on the Help menu in Excel, and then click the link for Assistance near the top left corner of the Microsoft Office Online home page. In the Browse Assistance area, click on Excel 2003, and take a look at the topics listed under the sections "Workbooks and Worksheets" and "Working with Data." You can also consult numerous books about Excel, including these two books from Microsoft Press:

- *Microsoft Office Excel 2003 Step by Step* (2003), by Curtis Frye. This book is a self-paced guide that covers all the basic features in Excel.

- *Microsoft Office Excel 2003 Inside Out* (2003), by Mark Dodge and Craig Stinson. Choose this book if you want a comprehensive reference that describes basic features as well as the tools you use in Excel to perform complex analyses.

If you already have a good grasp of how to work with Excel, Microsoft Office Online also provides training and assistance that relates to Excel's data analysis features. Here are a few of the training modules you can work with online:

- Excel Statistical Functions

- PivotTable I: What's So Great About PivotTable Reports?

- PivotTable II: Swing into Action with PivotTable Reports

- Charts I: How to Create a Chart

- Charts II: Choose the Right Chart Type

Two additional books from Microsoft Press provide in-depth coverage of the data analysis techniques available in Excel:

- *Accessing and Analyzing Data with Microsoft Excel* (2003), by Paul Cornell. If you know the basics of Excel, this book will teach you more about working with features such as PivotTables, sorting, and filtering.

- *Microsoft Excel Data Analysis and Business Modeling* (2004), by Wayne Winston. This book provides numerous examples of how to set up spreadsheets for business forecasting as well as for complex statistical analysis.

What Data Should I Collect?

The kind of data you choose to collect depends a great deal on the kind of business you're in. A retail store doesn't have the same requirements as a small manufacturer or a self-employed professional. A retail store might be interested to know how many customers enter the store and the percentage of customers who then make a purchase. A manufacturer would want to collect data about the rates at which they use their inventory of parts and raw materials. Most all types of businesses benefit from collecting information about their customers, but you need to be considerate and careful when you collect personal information about your customers—even their names and addresses.

At the start, you won't have historical sales and expense data to analyze, but you'll still want to test financial models that compare what you've budgeted with what you think you can earn. You need to determine sales goals so that you can understand whether your business is on track. And over time, you'll want to collect information that can lead you to know more about who your customers are, what they buy from you, and what services they want. Do customers purchase some products or services more often than others? Are sales peaks tied to different times of the year? Are discounts of any value to your business, and at what quantities do discounts pay off?

Collecting and analyzing information such as this eventually leads to decisions about which products and services you should keep offering and which you should discontinue, when to buy extra inventory and when to hold a clearance sale. Do you have all the employees you need? Do you need to find another supplier because the one you've been working with can't keep up with demand? Pricing, sales forecasting, and managing expenses—these and other areas of your operation will benefit from analysis up front as well as periodically as you measure your success.

For examples of using Excel worksheets to create and manage budgets and analyze cash flow, see Chapter 5, "Follow the Money."

"What If I...?": Tools for Analyzing Common Business Questions

Sometimes, very little seems certain when it comes to running a business. Questions like "What if I raise my prices?" "What if I borrow $10,000 more?" or "What if I add a new employee's salary to overhead?" need careful consideration. Excel includes various tools that you can use to perform what-if analysis. In general, to do what-if analysis, you set up a spreadsheet with the information you want to study and then change some of that information to see what effect the changes have. Three of the tools you can use to answer "what-if" questions in Excel are the Goal Seek command, data tables, and Scenario Manager. We'll describe how to use these tools in the following sections.

Knowing What You Need to Meet Your Goals: Using the Goal Seek Command

When you're striking out on your own to start or expand a business, you need to know what volume of sales will cover your costs—in other words, how many units need to go out the door, or how many hours do you need to bill? You need to know how much to charge for your time and the prices to charge for the products or services you sell. If you're taking out a loan for your business and your goal is to pay no more than $1,000 each month in principal and interest, you need to figure out how much you can borrow.

Questions such as these can be analyzed and the answers refined by using the Goal Seek command, which you'll find on the Tools menu in Excel. The Goal Seek command lets you calculate the value that makes the result of a formula you've written equal to a goal you've set. For example, how many units do you need to sell if your goal is $100,000 of income? When you use the Goal Seek command, you enter information in the dialog box shown in Figure 7-1.

Figure 7-1   The Goal Seek command in Excel is designed to calculate answers to questions such as "What is my breakeven point?"

Here's a description of the information you need to provide:

Set Cell   In the Set Cell text box, enter a reference to the cell that contains the formula that computes the information you're seeking. If you're calculating your profit (or your breakeven point), for example, you would enter a reference to the cell in which you've entered the formula that calculates profit. (The formula would be something like *Revenue – Variable Costs – Fixed Costs*.)

To Value   In the To Value text box, enter the value for the goal you're seeking. For a breakeven analysis—where you want to know how much you need to earn to cover all your costs—you would enter 0. If you want to cover your costs and take home $20,000, enter 20000 in the To Value text box.

By Changing Cell   In the By Changing Cell text box, enter a reference to the cell whose value will change so that the goal you've defined (the number entered in the To Value text box) is met. In a breakeven or profit analysis, you might enter a reference to the cell in which you've recorded the hourly rate you charge, the number of hours you need to bill at a certain rate, the price for a certain product, or the number of units you need to sell at a particular price.

Here are two brief examples of using the Goal Seek command. The first is a breakeven analysis, and the second shows how to determine how much money you can afford to borrow.

Analyzing Your Breakeven Point with Goal Seek

Take a look at the expense and income information shown in Figure 7-2. This information is fictional, of course, but at the current level of expense and income, this business will fall behind pretty quickly, as you can see by the fact that the profit shown in cell B17 is a negative number. How many more hours does the business need to bill (or how much more does it need to charge per hour) to at least cover its costs?

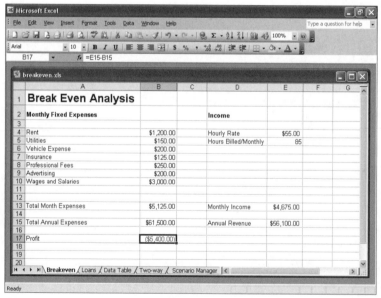

Figure 7-2   You can use Goal Seek to calculate how many more hours this business needs to bill each month to break even.

To make this calculation using the Goal Seek command, follow these steps:

1. On the Tools menu in Excel, click Goal Seek.

2. In the Set Cell text box, enter the cell reference **E13** .

3. In the To Value text box, enter **5125**, and in the By Changing Cell text box, enter the cell reference **E5**.

    We want to set cell E13, which calculates monthly income using the formula E4*E5 (the hourly rate multiplied by the number of hours billed) equal to the amount of monthly expenses ($5,125) by changing the number of hours billed, recorded in cell E5. Here's how the Goal Seek dialog box looks when it's set up to solve this problem:

    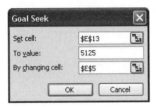

    Cell references

    The dollar signs included with the cell references in the Goal Seek dialog box (E13, for example) are added by Excel. They are used in formulas to create an *absolute cell reference*—a reference to a cell in a specific location. If the cell that contains the formula is moved, the cell reference remains the same. Excel also uses *relative references* and *mixed references*. A relative reference takes the form A1, for example. If you move a cell containing a formula that includes a relative reference, the cell referred to in a formula changes relative to the position of the cell with the formula. Relative references let you easily copy related formulas across rows and columns of numbers. Mixed references let you control the reference to either a column ($A1) or a row (A$1).

    ---

4. Click OK in the Goal Seek dialog box. Excel calculates the number of hours the business needs to bill to break even, which turns out to be a fraction above 93 hours, as you can see in the figure that follows.

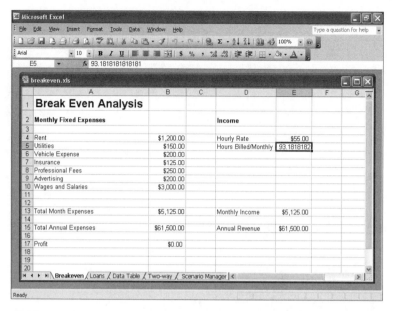

You would use a similar setup when the goal you're trying to meet involves the price you charge or the expected demand of a product you sell. For example, you could change the value in the cell where you've listed the price to see how much you have to charge to achieve the level of profitability you want. You could also calculate a target for the cost of manufacturing or purchasing a product you sell by referring to the cell that contains that information in the By Changing Cell box.

The smaller, the better

If you are using Goal Seek for precise analyses, you need to set an option before performing the calculations. Choose Tools, Options in Excel, and then click the Calculation tab. In the Maximum Change text box, enter a number something like .000001. Entering a value smaller than the default value (which is .001) means that the Goal Seek command will use values within that range of the goal.

Using Goal Seek for Loan Calculations

Another business calculation for which Goal Seek comes in handy is determining the amount of money you can borrow given a set monthly payment of principal and interest. In an Excel spreadsheet, list the term of the loan (how many monthly payments you'll make to pay back the loan), the interest rate you expect to pay, the loan amount (you'll use a dummy value to start), and the amount of the monthly payment you want to make. An example is shown in Figure 7-3. With this information, Goal Seek can tell you how much you can borrow given the amount you want to spend each month.

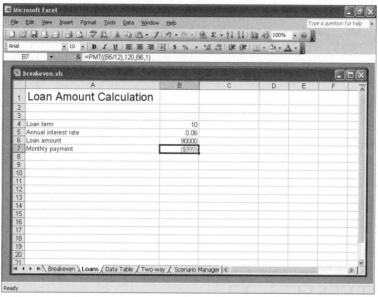

Figure 7-3 Goal Seek can take the information shown in this spreadsheet and calculate the amount of money you can borrow given a monthly payment you want to match.

The monthly payment is calculated with a formula that uses the PMT function in Excel. The basic formula is =PMT(*annual interest rate, number of payments, loan amount*). Before you use Goal Seek, enter any number for the amount of the loan. Excel will use this amount as a starting point in its calculations.

Using the information in the spreadsheet shown in Figure 7-3, here are the steps you would take:

1. In the Set Cell text box, enter **B7**. This is the cell that contains the formula that calculates the monthly payment.

2. In the To Value text box, enter the amount you want to spend on the loan each month. In this example, we entered **-1200**, as you can see below. The value is a negative number because this is money you spend.

3. In the By Changing Cell text box, enter **B6**, the cell that contains the loan amount. The Goal Seek dialog box should look like this:

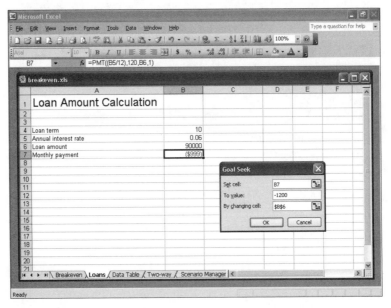

4. Click OK in the Goal Seek dialog box. Excel calculates the amount you can borrow given the monthly payment and interest rate you specify. With a payment of $1,200 per month, you can borrow about $108,000 on a 10-year loan at 6 percent annual interest rate.

A Little Change Can Make a Difference: Sensitivity Analysis with Data Tables

Keeping a business profitable isn't easy. In many businesses, the margin between what it costs to stay in business (everything from rent to the cost of raw materials) and revenue (all the money you take in) is pretty thin. Even small changes in the number of units you sell, the prices you charge, or the number of hours you bill can have a significant effect on the bottom line. But determining how sensitive your business is to small changes in price and costs, to the amount you spend to increase your inventory, or to the number of units you need to sell to remain profitable isn't always easy. And when you're starting a business, being able to look ahead and see that incremental changes in costs, demand, and price can matter greatly is important. For example, knowing that if you sell 4000 units you'll lose money, but if you sell an additional 500 units you'll be in the black, is vital.

To do a thorough job of analyzing the financial picture of your business, you want to test a range of assumptions about the effects of price and productivity. Setting up what's known as a *data table* in Excel makes this work easier and can provide useful number crunching as you seek to understand your business.

For example, imagine that you want to study how fluctuations in demand for a product affects your business's profitability. You might have information similar to that shown in Figure 7-4, which lists monthly expenses as well as price, the demand you've assumed for the product, the cost of purchasing or producing one unit of the product, variable costs (demand multiplied by the single-unit cost), revenue, and profit. As you can see, if demand is 4500 units, the business is falling behind.

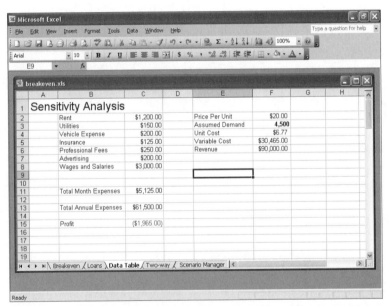

Figure 7-4   To work with a data table, first enter information you want to analyze.

Suppose that your research shows that you'll sell between 3500 and 6000 units each year. We want to see, in one easy view, the effect that varied demands have on the bottom line. Here are the steps you follow to set up a data table that lets you analyze how different levels of demand affect your business, assuming that you're working with a spreadsheet that contains information like that shown in Figure 7-4.

1. Enter the values you want to test (demand is between 3500 and 6000 units in this example) in a column in a blank area of your worksheet. This range of values defines the rows for the data table. As shown here, the range of possible demand is entered in cells E12 through E22.

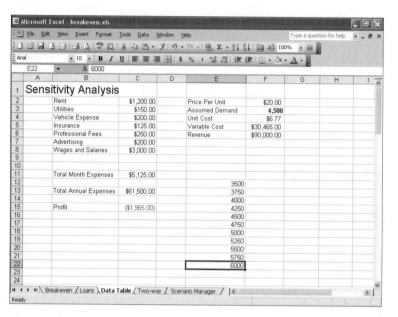

2. The next step is to set up the columns for the data table. The columns correspond to the values that change depending on the level of demand. In this example, that's variable costs, revenue, and profit. Since these three values are calculated by formulas in other cells in the spreadsheet, you can use references to those cells in defining the data table's columns. Enter the references for the column headings in the row above the first value you're testing. In this example, you would enter **F5** for variable costs, **F6** for revenue, and **C15** for profit. The results are shown here:

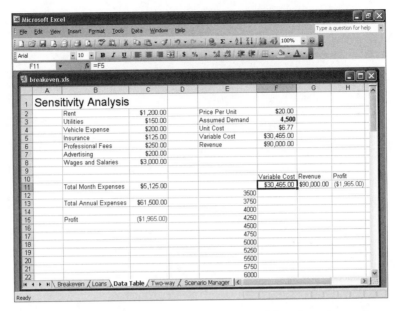

With the rows and columns of the data table defined, you're ready to have Excel fill in the values for each cell in the body of the data table.

3. Select the range of cells that make up the data table. Start in the cell above the first row in the table, and then drag to select the cells, ending with the cell at the intersection of the last row and column, as shown here:

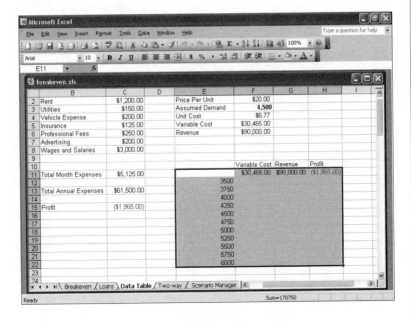

4. From the Data menu, choose Table. You'll see the Table dialog box, shown here:

Because the values we're examining are listed in a column, we need to enter a column input cell in the Table dialog box. The input cell corresponds to the value we're testing, which in this case is demand. The value for assumed demand is in cell F3.

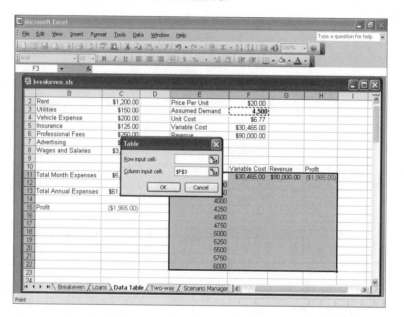

5. After entering the column input cell, click OK in the Table dialog box, and Excel fills in the data table as shown here. The table now lists the values for variable costs, revenue, and profit for the different levels of demand. Notice that the business becomes profitable once demand reaches approximately 4750 units.

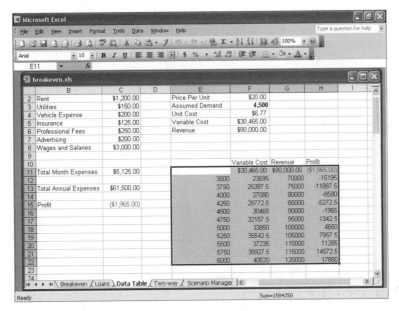

Now that the data table is complete, you can make other adjustments to the information in the spreadsheet and see how those changes affect your bottom line. For example, you could enter a new value for the unit cost and see the effects on profitability at different levels of demand. You could enter a different price or make changes to fixed costs as well.

The data table we've been looking at is an example of a *one-variable data table*. The amounts in the data table are calculated using a single range of values (the different levels of demand), and the table shows changes to revenue, variable costs, and profitability. A *two-variable data table* shows the effect that two different items (price and demand, for example) have, but you can see the changes for only one amount. Profitability would be used in many cases.

If you want to see how combinations of price and demand affect profitability, you could set up a data table such as the one shown in Figure 7-5. As before, the range of possible demand is listed in column E, and to this a range of prices (from $17.50 to $22.00) is added in a row at the top of the table.

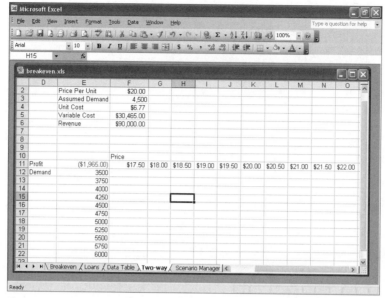

Figure 7-5   A two-variable data table lets you analyze the effect of both price and demand on your bottom line.

To fill in the data table, follow these steps:

1. Enter the formula you want to calculate (or a reference to the cell that contains the formula) in the cell at the top left corner of the table. Profit is used in this example.

2. Starting with the cell in which you entered the formula in step 1, select the cells in the table, ending the selection at the cell where the last row and column intersect.

3. On the Data menu, click Table. In the Table dialog box, enter both the column and the row input cells. Here, the column input cell is again F3 (assumed demand), and the row input cell is price (cell F2).

4. Click OK in the dialog box, and Excel fills in the data table with the array of values that would occur if you sold a particular number of units at a particular price, as shown here:

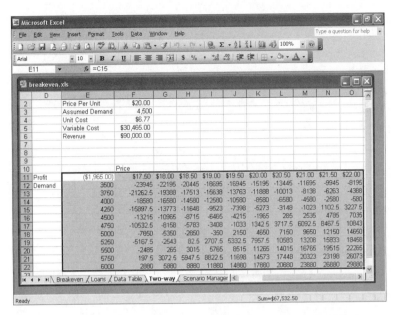

Once the data table is filled in, you can make changes to other cells that affect the values in the table (unit cost would be one in this example) and see how the changes trickle through.

Using data tables to calculate loan amounts

You can also use data tables to examine the ramifications of securing a business loan. You could test a range of different loan amounts or interest rates, for example, in a one-variable data table. A two-variable data table could be set up to show the effect of interest rates as well as the term of a loan. The Excel online help provides brief examples of how to set up a data table to make calculations of this sort. Look for the help topic titled "About Data Tables."

Managing Business Scenarios

Data tables and the Goal Seek command are useful when you want to see the effect that changes to one or two variables have on your business. Excel has another tool, Scenario Manager, that lets you perform sensitivity analysis using additional variables—as many as 32. You can save scenarios produced by Scenario Manager so that you can alter and adjust the values you used in the original models. A worksheet can contain more than one scenario as well, which means that you can switch between scenarios you define to see how the scenarios compare.

Let's suppose that you want to use Scenario Manager to take account of how different assumptions about demand, sales growth, and product price affect the first three years of your business's operation. You'd need information similar to what's shown in Figure 7-6.

	A	B	C	D	E	F	G	H	I
1	**Sensitivity Analysis**								
2		Rent	$1,200.00		Price per unit	$21.00			
3		Utilities	$150.00		Demand, year 1	5,250			
4		Vehicle Expense	$200.00		Sales growth	0.07			
5		Insurance	$125.00		Unit cost	$6.77			
6		Professional Fees	$250.00		Variable cost	$35,542.50			
7		Advertising	$200.00		Revenue	$110,250.00			
8		Wages and salaries	$3,000.00		Price increase	0.02			
9					Cost increase	0.04			
10									
11		Total Month Expenses	$5,125.00						
12									
13		Total Annual Expenses	$61,500.00						
14									
15		Profit	$13,207.50						
16									
17			Year 1	Year 2	Year 3				
18		Demand, year 1	5,250	5,618	6,011				
19		Price per unit	$21.00	$21.42	$21.85				
20		Unit cost	$6.77	$7.04	$7.32				
21		Variable cost	$35,542.50	$39,551.69	$44,013.13				
22		Revenue	$110,250.00	$120,326.85	$131,324.72				
23		Profit	$13,207.50	$19,275.16	$25,811.60				
24									

Figure 7-6   With information such as this in a spreadsheet, you can use Scenario Manager to test assumptions about key business metrics like demand, sales growth, and price.

This spreadsheet lists the details of monthly expenses in column C, as well as the totals for monthly and annual expenses and profit. The amounts in column F show the per-unit price, initial demand, unit cost, variable cost, revenue, and assumptions about expected sales growth and price and cost increases. Formulas calculate the values for variable costs (*Unit Cost * Demand*), revenue (*Demand * Price Per Unit*), and profit (*Revenue − Variable Costs − Annual Expenses*).

The assumptions entered in the spreadsheet indicate that sales are expected to grow at 7 percent each year (cell F4) for years 2 and 3 from an initial demand of 5250 units (entered in cell F3). The price for this product is expected to increase 2 percent each year, and the cost of producing or purchasing the product is expected to increase at 4 percent. You can see these amounts entered in cells F8 and F9.

The results of this first scenario (sales will increase by 7 percent, price by 2 percent, and costs by 4 percent) are shown in rows 18 through 23 for the first three years in business. With these assumptions, profit (shown in row 23) increases from about $13,000 in the first year to nearly $26,000 in year 3.

Now let's say that we also want to test a few other sets of assumptions. For example, what happens if our sales stay nearly flat over the next two years (say, only a 1 percent increase in demand rather than 7 percent), we keep the price we charge the same because demand is sluggish and the economy is tight, but the cost of producing the product increases more rapidly (6 percent rather than 4 percent) because a key component is now more scarce? That scenario is somewhat pessimistic, but a good one to test. We want to imagine a rosier view as well. Our product is popular and sales take off, increasing by 10 percent for each of the next two years. Because demand is growing, we can charge a bit more, so we plan to increase the price by 5 percent. And because we're buying more from our suppliers, they're giving us a better price. The cost of producing the product goes up, but only by 2 percent instead of 4.

After these scenarios are defined in Scenario Manager, Excel will calculate the associated values for expense, revenue, and profit and produce a well-formatted report that shows how each scenario affects the bottom line. To fill in the information Excel needs to make these calculations, follow these steps:

1. In Excel, choose Scenarios from the Tools menu. The Scenario Manager dialog box is shown here:

2. Click Add to enter the information for the first scenario. In the Add Scenario dialog box, shown here, enter a name for the scenario, and then identify the changing cells—in this example, cells F4 (sales growth), F8 (the percentage increase in price), and F9 (the percentage increase in cost). To enter noncontiguous cells such as these, separate each cell reference with a comma (F4, F8, F9).

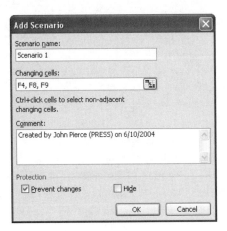

3. Click OK in the Add Scenario dialog box. You'll see the Scenario Values dialog box, shown here. For Scenario 1, we don't need to make any changes to the values for the changing cells because those assumptions are already entered in the spreadsheet.

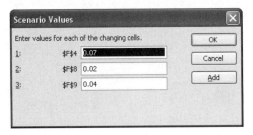

4. To enter the next scenario, click Add in the Scenario Values dialog box, and then enter a name for the second scenario in the Add Scenario dialog box. The changing cells stay the same.

5. Click OK in the Add Scenario dialog box, which takes you to the Scenario Values dialog box again. This time, enter the assumptions for the second scenario—1 percent growth in sales, no change in price, and a 6 percent increase in costs—and then click Add again.

6. Enter the information for the third scenario. After entering the assumptions in the Scenario Values dialog box, click OK.

7. Back in the Scenario Manager dialog box, select the scenario you want to view, and then click Show. The calculations in the worksheet are updated to reflect the scenario's assumptions. Scenario 3 (the rosy view) increases profit in year 3 from roughly $26,000 to more than $40,000. The pessimistic scenario reduces profit by just over 60 percent. You need information like this when you're setting goals or forecasting what might happen in the years to come.

To see a summary report of the scenarios, showing the values and the results, click Summary in the Scenario Manager dialog box. Excel creates a report similar to the one shown in Figure 7-7. The report is formatted well enough to share with prospective business partners, insert into a presentation, or just save for your own reference when you want to update the scenarios.

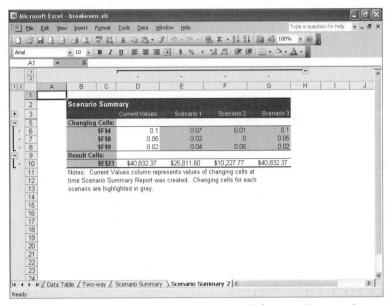

Figure 7-7 Scenario Manager can create a well-formatted report that summarizes the results of the scenarios you define.

Spotting Trends: Sorting, Filtering, and Charting Information

After your business is up and running for a period of time, you'll want to identify and understand trends. Why are sales up or down? Who are your best customers? Which of the products you sell do best in the spring, and which in the holiday season? What percentage of the orders you received are more than $500?

You can start examining these and many similar questions simply by sorting the information in a spreadsheet. You can capture a close-up view by applying a filter to a spreadsheet because a filter lets you select just the information you want to see. And if you're someone whose understanding of numbers is enhanced when they're compiled in a chart instead of listed in rows and columns, you can also use a number of different charts in Excel to see how your business is doing.

Sorting to See Groups and Patterns

When you sort information in a spreadsheet, the information is presented in an order that lends itself to more meaningful analysis than you can easily perform by combing through an unsorted spreadsheet. Let's say you have a list of customers in a spreadsheet and want to see how the customers are distributed geographically. If they come from around the country, you could sort by city or state. If your customer base is more local, you could sort by ZIP Code to group customers from a certain neighborhood in consecutive rows. You can sort a list of orders by product to see which customers bought a particular item. You can sort the same list by customer to see each product a particular customer buys, and sort again by the order date to see trends in customer orders week by week or month by month.

The Sort dialog box, shown in Figure 7-8, is displayed by clicking Sort on the Data menu. Notice that the dialog box lets you sort by as many as three columns, each in either ascending or descending order. If the spreadsheet you're sorting has column labels, be sure to select Header Row at the bottom of the dialog box. Otherwise, the column labels can be included in the sorted list.

Figure 7-8   Use the Sort command on the Data menu to arrange the information in a spreadsheet in the order you want.

Sorting options

Sorting options include list orders such as January, February, March for a column of dates. Without this option, the names of the months would appear alphabetically rather than chronologically.

Filtering Information to View Selected Records

If you want to look at only some of the rows of data in an Excel spreadsheet (at a single customer's orders, for example), you can apply a filter. Depending on the information you want to see, you can use a couple of different methods for applying a filter.

Excel's AutoFilter

The Filter command on the Data menu has three subcommands—AutoFilter, Show All, and Advanced Filter. An AutoFilter adds an easy-to-use drop-down list to the top row of a spreadsheet where the column headings appear. Click the arrow to open the list and select the value that you want to use as a filter. For example, if you want to see the orders for a certain date, select that date from the drop-down list, as shown in Figure 7-9.

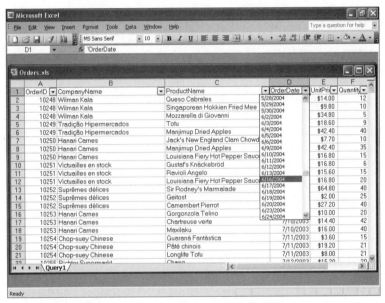

Figure 7-9 By applying an AutoFilter to a list of data, you can view the data for a particular date, customer, or product.

The drop-down list also includes entries named All, Top 10, and Custom. Choosing All removes any filter you've applied to a column so that each value in the column is visible again. In columns that contain numerical data, the Top 10 item does just what its name implies—it leads you to the top 10 values in that column and provides an easy way to see a list of best-selling items, the 10 customers who purchase the most, the 10 months in which your expenses were greatest, and so on. Choosing Top 10 can also lead you to the bottom of things. When you pick Top 10 from the list, Excel displays a dialog box in which you can choose Bottom 10, adjust the number of items you want to see, or choose to base the list on the number of items or on a percentage.

The Custom item in the AutoFilter list lets you refine a filter. You can indicate a particular item to filter for—for example, you can find dates that are later than or earlier than another date, dollar values greater than or less than an amount you enter, or all the products you have that begin with the letter C. Figure 7-10 shows how you could set up the Custom AutoFilter dialog box to see the orders for the third calendar quarter:

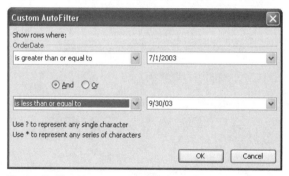

Figure 7-10   You can use criteria such as a date range when creating a custom AutoFilter.

When you want to remove the drop-down lists that the AutoFilter command created, click Filter on the Data menu, and then click AutoFilter again. (The check mark beside the command's name is now cleared.)

Advanced Filters

The AutoFilter command sets up an easy mechanism for filtering columns of data in place. Using an advanced filter (click Filter on the Data menu, and then click Advanced Filter), you can filter the list in place or copy the filtered values to a different worksheet or to a different location on the worksheet you're viewing. You also specify the values in a range of cells as criteria for a filter. The values in a criteria range let you use a specific list of items as a filter (say, four products you think you might discontinue) or use a combination of items (a product name and an order date). Figure 7-11 shows what the Advanced Filter dialog box looks like.

Figure 7-11 Use an advanced filter to copy the records the filter selects to a different location and to specify a range of filter criteria.

To work with a criteria range you want to use as an advanced filter, follow these steps:

1. Enter the values you want to use in a blank column in the spreadsheet (column H in this example), as you see here:

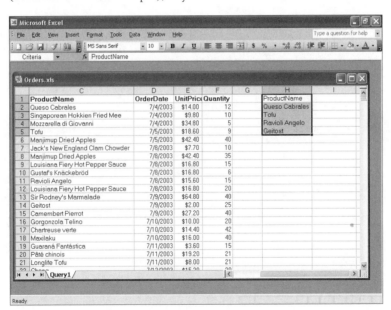

Notice that the criteria range is identified by ProductName, the same label used in the list of items to filter (the list of products in column C). Because each product name appears in the same column, the filter is set up as *ProductName equals Queso Cabrales* or *Tofu* or *Ravioli Angelo* or *Geitost*. That way, the filter selects information about all four products.

2. If you want to join values in a filter with *and* rather than *or*, place the values in separate columns in the same row, as you see here:

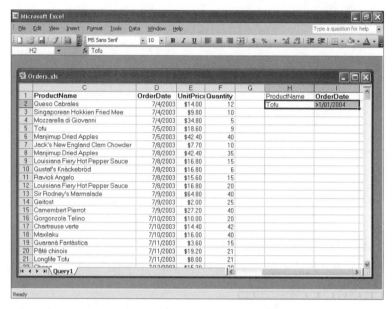

With this filter, Excel will show you the records in which the product name equals tofu *and* the order date is later than January 1, 2004. Here are the results of applying the filter:

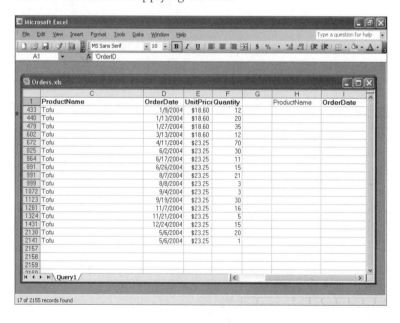

Be sure to include column headings

When you enter the cell references for the criteria range in the Advanced Filter dialog box, be sure you include the cells that contain the column headings for the range. Otherwise, Excel won't find the records that you're looking for.

3. To set up a filter that uses *or* as well as *and* in its criteria, enter the column headings (ProductName, OrderDate, and Quantity, for example) in the first row of the criteria range. You can then enter two or more product names, a date range you want to use, and the quantities you want to filter for in the rows that follow. Criteria ranges in advanced filters are an excellent means for selecting a detailed set of records you need to study.

Charting Data

Another way to identify and examine trends in your business is to plot your business information on a chart. You can use a bar chart to see a comparison of sales and expenses over a six-month period. With a pie chart, you can see the relative proportion of each category of expenses as a part of the whole, and a line chart is well suited for plotting sales over time.

Creating a chart in Excel is straightforward thanks to the Chart Wizard, shown in Figure 7-12. To display the Chart Wizard, click Chart on the Insert menu or click the Chart Wizard button on Excel's Standard toolbar. As you can see, the Chart Wizard offers a variety of chart types and sub-types. The name and use of each sub-type is briefly described at the bottom of the wizard when you select the sub-type in the Chart Sub-Type list.

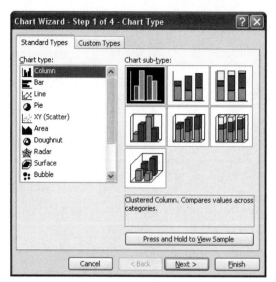

Figure 7-12   The Chart Wizard leads you through the steps required to create a chart.

Building effective charts requires some preliminary work organizing the data. In general, enter the data in a single area of the spreadsheet rather than spreading out the data in different columns and rows. Many chart types don't easily present a large amount of detailed data. Charting a whole year's worth of expenses in 12 different categories will create a chart that is more busy than helpful. Figure 7-13 shows an example of a pie chart that captures the relative proportion of different expense types for the month of January 2003. (Notice the descriptive ScreenTip that's displayed when the mouse pointer is placed over a segment of the chart.)

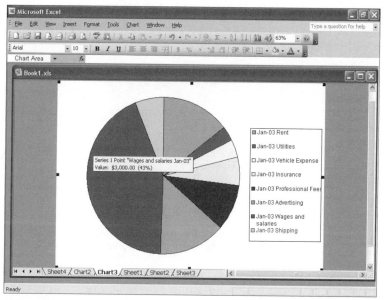

Figure 7-13 Here's one example of the types of charts you can create in Excel.

Slicing and Dicing Your Business Data: Why You Should Use a PivotTable

A PivotTable is one of the ultimate tools for data analysis in Excel. PivotTables are especially helpful when you need to make sense of a mountain of detailed data—a spreadsheet in which you've recorded three years' worth of sales or expenses, for example, or have listed the homes for sale in your region together with their sales price, square footage, and other details. PivotTables (and PivotCharts) are designed to let you see information from different views (in detail or as a summary, for example) without you having to set up multiple spreadsheets. You can also rearrange ("pivot") the layout of a PivotTable to gain different perspectives on the data it presents. For example, you might set up a PivotTable initially to see expense information by category. In the same PivotTable, you can then adjust the layout to see expenses by month or filter the information to see the expenses for a single year.

The steps to create a PivotTable are made easier by using the PivotTable And PivotChart Wizard, shown in Figure 7-14, which you run by clicking Pivot-Table And PivotChart Report on the Data menu. In this three-step wizard, you indicate the type of data you want to present in the PivotTable, whether you want to create a PivotTable or a PivotChart, the cell range in which the data you want to analyze appears in the spreadsheet (something like A2:H101), and the location where you want the PivotTable to appear (in a new worksheet or the worksheet in which you're working).

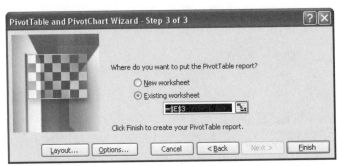

Figure 7-14 The third step in the PivotTable And PivotChart Wizard. A PivotTable lets you analyze large amounts of detailed data from multiple perspectives in a single spreadsheet.

Here are the steps you follow to build and work with a PivotTable once you've stepped through the wizard:

1. After you click Finish in the PivotTable Wizard, you're provided with a blank PivotTable similar to the one shown here:

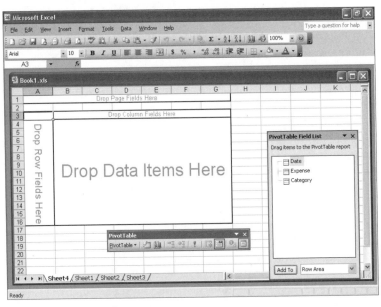

2. To lay out the PivotTable, drag fields from the PivotTable field list to the drop zones in the table itself. In this example, you could set up the PivotTable by dragging Category to the Drop Row Fields Here area,

Date to the Drop Column Fields Here area, and Expense to the Drop Data Items Here area. The PivotTable would appear something like the following. Notice that the PivotTable provides a grand total for each month of expenses.

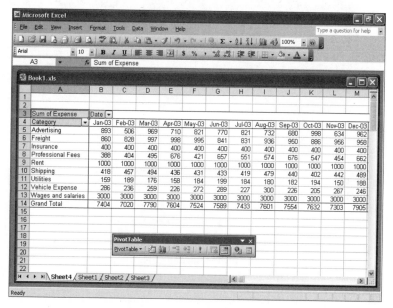

3. To get a different view of the data, you could rearrange the data in the PivotTable and use expense categories as the columns and the dates as the rows. To do this, drag the fields off the PivotTable and start again by using the field list, or you can click the field label in the PivotTable itself and drag it to the area where you want to see the data. The following figure shows how the revised PivotTable would appear.

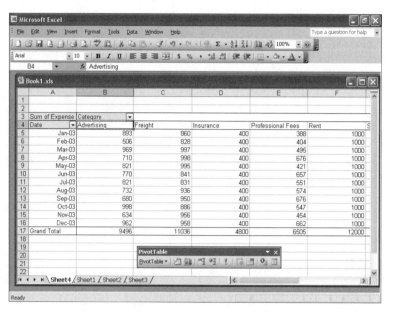

4. Using the arrows beside the Category and Date fields, you can filter the data in the PivotTable. Clicking the arrow displays a list that lets you select a single value or a combination of values (as well as all values), as you see here:

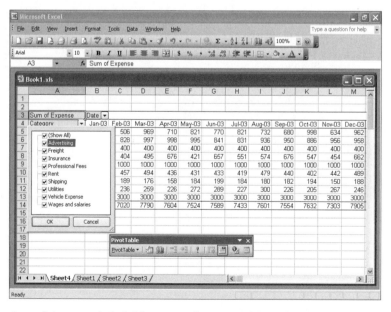

One of the most helpful features of a PivotTable is the group of options you can set in the PivotTable Field dialog box. These options let you see values as a percentage of the row or column, as a running total, as a percentage of the total, and so on. In this example, rather than see the total expense for each category in each month, you can view each category as a percentage of the total expenses for a month or as a percentage of the total expenses for a year.

5. To set these options, click Field Settings on the PivotTable menu (which you open by clicking the PivotTable button at the left end of the PivotTable toolbar).

6. In the PivotTable Field dialog box, click the Options button.

7. Open the Show Data As list to see the variety of ways in which you can present the data, as shown here:

8. To see the category amounts as a percentage of monthly expenses, choose % Of Column, and then click OK. The figure that follows shows the new view of the data you'd see.

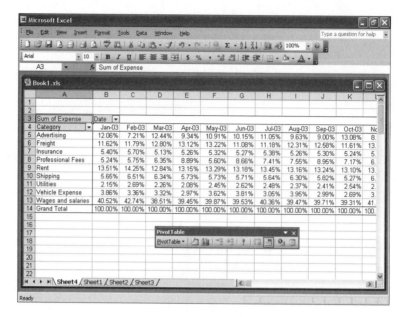

Two Important Excel Functions

If you've worked with Excel much at all, you've likely used at least a few of its standard functions, such as SUM, to add up a column of numbers, or AVERAGE. Earlier in this chapter, we mentioned the PMT function, which is used to determine loan payments.

Two other functions you might find useful from time to time are the PV function and the FV function. The PV function calculates the present value of an investment. You could use the PV function to help decide whether to pay cash for a piece of equipment today or pay for the equipment over time. To use the PV function, you need the following information:

- The interest rate that applies on each periodic payment (an annual interest rate of 8 percent would be 8 divided by 12 (or .67 percent) per month.

- The number of payments you'll make. On a five-year loan with monthly payments, the number of payments would be 60, for example.

- The amount of each payment (principal and interest combined).

- Any cash balance you want at the end of the period. If you're planning to pay off the loan, this amount is 0.

- Whether you make the payment at the start of each period or at the end of each period.

When you use the PV function in Excel, you would enter information similar to that shown in Figure 7-15.

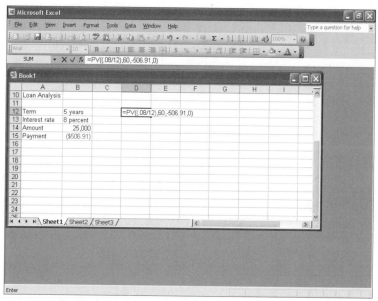

Figure 7-15 The PV function in Excel helps you determine whether to pay cash for a piece of equipment today or pay for the equipment over time.

By making this calculation, you can see how much you'll end up paying with interest over the life of the loan. You can then determine whether paying cash today is more economical.

The FV function, on the other hand, calculates the future value of an investment. You can use the FV function to determine how much an investment will earn through the years as you contribute to it. To use the FV function, you need to know the following:

- The rate of return on the investment.

- The term of the investment (the number of periodic contributions you will make to the investment).

- The amount you pay in each period—for example, adding $750 each month to a savings account.

- Whether the investment is made at the beginning or the end of each period.

A formula using the FV function would look something like =FV((.05/12), 120,750,0). In this formula, we're calculating how much we'll have saved in

10 years (120 periods) if we contribute $750 to an investment at the end of each month, earning 5 percent annually.

With some basic data analysis like the examples we've described in this chapter, you're better able to see sales patterns, differentiate strong products from weaker ones, understand the effect of pricing and demand on your bottom line, and see how you spend the money you take in. Once you understand the fundamentals of Excel, using one or more of the data analysis tools is an important step toward clarifying the financial goals and trends of your business.

For More Information

In addition to the resources mentioned in this chapter, you will find links and information on the companion CD. Some books and Web sites particularly useful as you learn to use Excel to help you manage your business include:

Books

- Curtis Frye, *Microsoft Office Excel 2003 Step by Step* (Microsoft Press, 2003)

- Curtis Frye et al., *Microsoft Excel 2003 Programming Inside Out* (Microsoft Press, 2003)

- Joseph Rubin and Bill Jelen, *Mr. Excel on Excel* (Holy Macro! Press, 2003)

Web Sites

- Ozgrid—Microsoft Excel Training & Tutoring, Add-ins, Templates & Software: *www.ozgrid.com/*

- Excel Business Tools: *www.excelbusinesstools.com/*

- Template Zone.com: *www.templatezone.com/*

Part Three

Makes and Models: How to Stand Out from the Crowd

In this part

Chapter Eight   **Branding Basics** 182

Chapter Nine   **Crafting Your Message** 208

Chapter Ten   **Go to Market with Publisher, Make a Pitch with PowerPoint** 244

Part Three:
Makes &
Models: How to
Stand Out from
the Crowd

Microsoft Small Business Kit

A branding program should be designed to differentiate your cow from all the other cattle on the range. Even if all the cattle on the range look pretty much alike.

— The 22 Immutable Laws of Branding, *Al Ries and Laura Ries (HarperCollins, 1998)*

Chapter Eight

Branding Basics

Creating a powerful brand spreads the word about your business, building recognition, credibility, and the trust of customers. Here are the steps you can take to develop your company identity.

Chapter Eight: **Branding Basics**

Part Three:
**Makes &
Models: How to
Stand Out from
the Crowd**

What you'll find:

- ❏ Developing brand personality
- ❏ What is the mission of your business?
- ❏ Focusing on your point of difference (POD)
- ❏ Finding the right image: logos and icons
- ❏ Mastering your domains: two steps for building a presence on the Web
- ❏ Building credibility
- ❏ Protecting your intellectual property: trademarks, copyrights, and patents

Part Three:
Makes &
Models: How to
Stand Out from
the Crowd

Microsoft Small Business Kit

Developing Brand Personality

Imagine you belong to a monthly networking group and there's one business owner who shows up looking utterly different every time you get together. One month she arrives with wind-tossed blond hair, a flamboyant red dress, and stiletto-heeled shoes. A month later, she's back in a conservative navy pantsuit and low-heeled oxfords and has sleek brown hair. Then there's the jeans and sweater ensemble, complete with girl-next-door ponytail. And so it goes.

At each meeting, you and the other business owners keep mistaking this chameleon for someone else. You can't get a fix on who she is, what she represents, or whether an association with her might yield benefits. In fact, if you checked into her background, you'd learn she's a crackerjack realtor and exactly the professional you need to find the office space you've been seeking. But even though you've heard some rumors about her abilities, you give her a wide berth. Why?

She has no recognizable profile. She's hard to define. She's way too changeable and demands too much investment in time and talk and energy to understand. Added together, she appears untrustworthy and unreliable, whether it's deserved or not. No one likes the idea of doing business with a new face at every transactional encounter—that is, at what marketers like to call the *customer touch points*. Ms. Chameleon provides no consistent identity, and it's costing her business.

Customers evaluate your business in similar ways. How you "dress" your firm expresses the core of the company. It's the brand's message. If your message is clothed in dramatic red one day and conventional blue the next, your brand is altogether confusing.

Image Counts

Consider the business implications of such instant judgments as the real estate broker provoked:

- Clients and customers will make critical financial judgments based on your packaging, looks, and image—no matter what kind of skills or expertise you might have.

- Public perception has an enormous influence on the course of business success.

- An inconsistent identity can quickly kill your relationship with customers.

Chapter Eight: **Branding Basics**

Part Three:
Makes &
Models: How to
Stand Out from
the Crowd

Let's Get Down to Business

The look-at-me red dress is not the issue. Such style might be perfectly acceptable for an outgoing salesperson. Your business image needn't be drab or low-key to be taken seriously. Just think of Sir Richard Branson and the global empire he's built. Not only has the unconventional Virgin brand expanded to include Virgin Airlines, Virgin Records, Virgin Megastores, and Virgin Mobile, but Sir Richard, in his mid-fifties, is also not above dressing up as Eminem to emphasize his company's rebel-with-a-cause character. Such stunts also generate publicity for the Virgin brand, which lacks the reach and resources of its giant competitors and must find creative ways to attract notice.

Depending on what you're selling, of course, an image of fireworks and fun can be just as effective as pinstripes and solemn assurances. It's constant change that works against trust, not necessarily a light-hearted or humorous approach.

Don't make the mistake of assuming that this is all about some external display or superficial image or colors. Just as the clothes and style of communication you choose make up your "personal brand"—who you are, your inner values and sensibilities—so it is with the business brand. The external image or marketing message must telegraph the values of the company.

Consumers today are skeptical and knowledgeable. They're not likely to trust products or services that shape-shift, if, in fact, they even remember you. Your message must have staying power. And that comes from having a brand strategy. Here's how to carve out your company's brand personality and then put that to use in standing out among your competitors.

A lot of hard-charging, impatient business owners pooh-pooh branding because they're too busy chasing sales, impressing investors, or recruiting talent. Who has time for such stuff, they say. But business gets a whole lot easier when you have a recognizable brand.

Think about BMW or Burger King, for example. All you need do is mention those globally recognized names and people have immediate perceptions and expectations. There's an emotional connection that rises to the surface, fostered by the brand personality, and, of course, supported by marketing and advertising.

See Chapter 9, "Craft Your Message," to learn more about marketing messages.

Part Three:
Makes &
Models: How to
Stand Out from
the Crowd

Microsoft Small Business Kit

With a strong brand, you don't have to sell nearly as long or as hard. Customers know what you stand for before you even begin your pitch or proposal. If you take the time to brand—that is, define who you are, what you sell, and which customers to target—all efforts become more focused and more efficient.

What Is the Mission of Your Business?

In the course of investigating what it takes to run a business, you've probably already heard something about needing a *company mission statement*. A mission statement is a useful tool to have. Figuring out what your company does at its core—in other words, the "mission" thing—fuels your branding process (and helps focus your staff as well). Let's put aside the jargon for a moment, however.

Of course, you're in business to make money. But turning a profit comes as a result of your mission. It is not the mission itself. Concentrate specifically on what it is your company stands for. What do you want to be known for? What are you truly in business to accomplish? Another way to view a company's mission is that it's likely the main reason you got into business in the first place. Think through exactly what it is you're producing and why customers will want to choose your product. What's the heart and soul of what you sell? It could actually be a feeling, even when your company markets tangible products.

For instance, you might manufacture vacuum cleaners, but what you're really selling is a better, faster, and easier way to clean house. You might produce fancy colored balloons, but what you're really selling is the joy of celebration. That means your tag line or marketing message shifts from "Get a lot of contained hot air, cheap!" to "It's time to party!" You must also define what makes your product more desirable than that of your competition (which is discussed in the section below, "Focusing on Your Point of Difference (POD)").

A frequent misconception is that "personal values" have little place in business. But that makes no sense. Obviously, your company is defined by the way you do business. How you run it—what stamp you put on it—counts enormously and is certainly part of your mission statement, not to mention an important factor in attracting top talent and loyal customers. The past few years of corporate upheavals and scandals has emphasized how aligning profits with good corporate citizenship goes a long way to standing out in the marketplace.

Stripped to basics, your *brand* is the promise you make to customers combined with the judgment customers make about how well you deliver on that promise, sometimes called *customer perception*. Think of branding as the personality and values you communicate to customers, vendors, investors, and the outside world. But mission gets you to the brand. It's the process of delivering on those values and promise—the definition of the way the company operates. Start-up business owners like to jump to the cool parts of branding, creating the cute characters and fancy logos. But none of that will matter a whit if you can't develop a mission for your company that supports the promise that attracts customers.

Invest some time in figuring out your mission. Don't get off track or bogged down by formulating a list of goals or marketing strategies—that's for another time. And don't be concerned with turning it into formal bizspeak. Your mission should be clear, concise, and perfectly to the point. It should sum up the company's defining characteristics quickly, succinctly, and memorably.

Consider these questions when crafting your company mission, whether you end up writing a formal "statement" or jotting notes on an index card:

- What need does your business satisfy?
- Why are you launching the company?
- What is the rationale for your business?
- What are the principles and values that support the business?

Home Depot's company mission, for example, reads like this:

Our mission is to form mutually beneficial partnerships with diverse businesses that allow us to deliver superior products and services and superb customer service, which ultimately increases shareholder value.

A data recovery company has adopted a mission statement that says:

Using our innovative tools, quality facilities, and expert engineers, we strive to provide our clients with the fast, secure, and affordable data recovery services they need in order to maintain business continuity.

And the Tribune Company, a media company that publishes, among other things, the *Chicago Tribune* and the *Los Angeles Times*, has this mission:

Build businesses that inform and entertain our customers in the ways, places, and at the times they want.

Part Three:
Makes &
Models: How to
Stand Out from
the Crowd

Microsoft Small Business Kit

Try writing your company's mission now in 30 words or less.

If you can define the mission, the brand and all the "dressing"—such as the logo or icon, the company colors, tag lines, promotions, and marketing messages—will follow. The mission leads you to a meaningful and commercial brand. When successful, the brand becomes the emotional embodiment of the company mission, creating bonds with customers that will make them loyal to you.

Important Why should customers seek out your brand and pay you for the service or product you provide? That's the key question to ask and answer in developing your company mission.

Translating Mission into Brand

When you've decided what the company stands for, from the inside out, the effort to create marketing tag lines and messages to customers gains clarity. Some examples of company tag lines that communicate the company mission and also identify the brand include FedEx's "Relax, it's FedEx," or General Electric's "imagination at work."

Too often, companies equate the name or tag line with the brand identity. But "Just Do It!" and "All the news that's fit to print" resonate with consumers not because they're hip or authoritative. Nike and the *New York Times* must deliver products and services that make those catchphrases ring true. When consumers can depend on the experience you promise—consistently—the tag lines evoke emotional buy-in. You can't simply make up a mission and assume customers will come running. It takes time to build a brand. It takes forging an emotional connection, often referred to as the *customer relationship*.

Focusing on Your Point of Difference (POD)

The next step is to determine what's distinctive about your offerings. What makes your business special and different from any other company? Why should anyone care about your product or service? Do you emphasize customer service? Do you offer the best value in your category, or in your town, or on the Web? Not the lowest price, mind you, but the best value. Is it the considerable luxury of soup-to-nuts convenience, for which you can charge a premium price? Have you chosen to fill an underserved niche—say, a

Chapter Eight: **Branding Basics**

Part Three:
Makes &
Models: How to
Stand Out from
the Crowd

middleware software application that seamlessly connects popular applications, or a business newsletter that keeps professionals in the Hispanic entertainment industry informed?

This is where you elaborate on the marketing overview and big-picture strategies that you set out in your business plan. When you're ready to formulate the positioning for your marketing and to develop a working strategy for standing out in the marketplace, you might want to get some advice from one of the many nonprofit small business advisory groups, such as SCORE, the Service Corps of Retired Executives, at *www.score.org/*. This nonprofit association offers free and confidential counseling, both face-to-face and via e-mail. SCORE currently has nearly 400 chapters around the country.

See "Ready, Set, Go," page 18, for some other small business advisory resources and Chapter 2, "Developing a Business Plan," to learn more about thinking through your plan.

Another rich resource is your local U.S. Small Business Development Center (SBDC, at *www.sba.gov/sbdc/*), often located on college campuses. These programs, which provide small businesses with free management and technical assistance, are supported by the combined efforts of private corporations, educational facilities, and governments. There are currently about 65 SBDCs, with one in every state and a network of more than 1,100 service locations at universities and community colleges as well as vocational schools and chambers of commerce.

In formulating your marketing POD, also called the company's *unique selling proposition* (USP), it often helps to brainstorm with friends, associates, or employees. Don't forget to survey customers, too. You want to leverage the way they see you. You can invite everyone to a brown-bag lunch or a virtual get-together online and let all the ideas ripple out. Try not to judge or censor until afterward.

Whether you're working on your own or in a group, keep written notes of all the points or benefits discussed. Later that written list will make your branding and tag-line choices easier and more organic. In general, to work out your POD, develop well-thought-out responses to these marketing issues:

- ■ **Identify your customers.** Describe your ideal or target customer, including his or her age, income level, geographic region, education level, and other defining demographics. You ought to address specific ways you can outshine the competition, including what will make your product or services more attractive to customers. Put yourself in

Part Three:
Makes &
Models: How to
Stand Out from
the Crowd

Microsoft Small Business Kit

your customer's shoes and get inside his or her mind. What consumer need will you satisfy?

- **Research customer preferences.** Discover what makes your target customer or target groups tick. That means how targets think, what they need, why your product works for them, when they use it, how they prefer hearing from you, which messages press their buttons—the works.

- **Define your competitive advantages.** Explain in a few sentences what it is your company is good at doing. You might also want to include what it is you like to do—which will help you stay focused. How can you sell your strengths in a competitive environment? What are the product's weaknesses, and does that influence the branding?

- **Relate to emotional buy-ins.** Now try and turn all these characteristics into emotional buy-ins. What words, feelings, and emotional reasons will make your product appeal to your target audience?

Make sure you spend some time checking out the competition. Analyze each competitor's mission and brand promise to see how successful that company is at reaching its customer. What can you do better? What's the difference between what your competitors promise and what you want to do?

When your POD list is honed, it's at last time to move on to the tangible look and feel of your brand. To do this, you'll need to figure out:

- Who your customers are
- What your customers are searching for
- How you can provide what they want better than the competition

Finding the Right Image: Logos and Icons

Your corporate identity is communicated and represented by individual graphical designs and words: logos, tag lines, letterheads, brochures, business cards, Web sites, posters, direct-mail fliers and postcards, press releases, word of mouth, TV and radio ads, CD promotions, highway billboards—in short, the works. The overarching goal in creating this brand image and its graphic representations is clarity. Resist the impulse to get fussy or complicated. You want to communicate an emotion and your company name or product in less time than it takes to sneeze.

Chapter Eight: **Branding Basics**

Part Three:
Makes &
Models: How to
Stand Out from
the Crowd

Also be careful to match the image to your mission. A family medical practice, for instance, wouldn't get far by selecting a motorcycle as its icon. That's an outlandish logo for doctors. But how many companies have you come across with names or logos totally at odds with their selling propositions?

Getting too cute might make customers nervous, depending on your wares. Likewise, the reverse. An up-market image won't work when your unique selling proposition is the cheapest price on the market. Gray and blue corporate colors wouldn't do for a kicky fashion boutique. But they'd be great for a financial services company, which should project stability and responsibility.

Another brainstorming session with family advisors and the staff might be warranted to kick around logos and tag lines. Certainly, don't rush into a decision without trolling the Web to check out the palette, words, pictures, and feel of companies that are similar to yours. You might even mount a low-budget contest that asks customers (or suppliers, if you haven't yet launched) to send in their best ideas for a tag line. Winner gets a free dinner or a free sample or a discount. See—you're marketing already.

Using Branding Tools

When you're ready, desktop publishing programs like Microsoft Publisher can help to conveniently create the visual look of your brand personality. Typically, desktop publishing software offers selected sets of design ideas, like colors, styles, and fonts that complement each other. You can choose among the offerings or customize your own ideas. Then simply save the templates and use them whenever you create forms or marketing material, from newsletters and catalogs to postcards and Web sites. You can also use the desktop publishing program to create prototypes that you take to a printer for professional reproduction. The colors, images, templates, and designs you choose in the software program, which can be accessed by everyone on staff, become the custodian of the brand by assembling all your brand elements into a convenient and cost-effective toolkit.

To create a logo in Publisher, use one of the 45 professionally designed Master Sets designs (found under Design Sets) to identify and integrate all your chosen brand elements, including key marketing messages and tag lines, product logos, fonts, product trademarks or names, and more. The Master Sets design you choose can carry that consistent look across various media. To make it easy, each Master Sets design in Publisher includes coordinated colors, fonts, and layouts for commonly used business

Part Three:
Makes &
Models: How to
Stand Out from
the Crowd

Microsoft Small Business Kit

publications—from newsletters and brochures; to flyers, postcards, and business cards; to e-mail and Web sites. These designs can also be quickly and easily imported into other Microsoft Office applications, such as Word and PowerPoint.

Microsoft Publisher also has third-party vendors, many available via the Office Marketplace (*directory.partners.extranet.microsoft.com/*), to create Master Sets designs, if that's what you prefer.

In Chapter 10, "Go to Market with Publisher and PowerPoint," you'll see examples of some of the work you can do with Microsoft Publisher, including how to build a simple Web site and marketing materials to print.

Appointing a Brand Cop

Educate everyone on staff, from assistants to the chief financial officer, to understand the brand and its tools as well as you do. Otherwise, each employee, including the all-important sales team, could create his or her own version and confuse your customers. Once you assemble the brand toolkit, every employee can then access it and draw upon whatever he or she needs.

Even so, over time, logos tend to shift color or size. Someone adds a bit of blue sky around the gray goose logo of your down jacket business. Someone else feels creative and redraws the goose so that its wings are stretched out in flight. Pretty soon, your little gray goose is lost in the wilderness. Make sure you keep policing your brand image. Put a designer or staffer in charge. Especially if you work with outside vendors, write down guidelines about what can be adjusted and what's not allowed. Specify the colors you've selected, the font, the size of any images or character, and every other detail. Consider your branding toolkit as part of the intellectual capital of your burgeoning business. (See the section below, "Protecting Your Intellectual Property," to learn more.)

Mastering Your Domains: Two Steps for Building a Presence on the Web

In this day and age, whether you use a Web site to collect and process orders or simply as a yellow pages ad that lists your business's name, address, and phone number, establishing a presence on the Internet is an important part of building and managing a business brand. The Internet

Chapter Eight: Branding Basics

Part Three:
Makes &
Models: How to
Stand Out from
the Crowd

has the potential to increase by many times the reach of your business's identity.

Part of using the Internet to help develop and build a business is knowing what you want to accomplish with a Web site—in effect, writing a mission statement for your site. Do you plan to use the site mostly as an advertisement—either a simple online business card or a place where customers can find out about your goods and services? Do you want to provide a list of frequently asked questions (a product FAQ) on your site or describe how your products or services are supported? Is your business well suited to online transactions? Will you conduct your business exclusively online or is your site an extension of your physical location? How you plan to use a Web site affects how much effort you need to apply to developing your brand online.

For more information about how to build a Web site, you can find references on the companion CD.

The way your business will be identified on the Web is wrapped up in the Internet domain name you use—for example, a name such as Amazon.com, MSN.com, or NPR.org. In the following sections, we'll describe two steps you need to take to start making a name for yourself on the Internet: registering a domain name and determining where you'll host your Web site.

Registering a Domain Name

A domain name (such as MSN.com) is associated with a computer that's connected to the Internet. However, computers connected to the Internet actually find each other by using an address such as 123.444.55.66. It's pretty clear that your business will benefit more by asking customers to visit *www.*[mycompany].*com* (where "mycompany" is the name of your business) than by asking them to remember a series of numbers.

When you register a domain name, you specify the computer your domain name will correspond to. That's the computer on which your Web site is hosted. A domain name also provides the means for receiving e-mail messages at an address that identifies you and your business (*theboss@cohowinery.com* or *orders@cohowinery.com*).

Domain names can be registered either by individuals or by a company. You register a domain name through one of the registrars that are accredited by the Internet Corporation for Assigned Names and Numbers (ICANN), which is one of the agencies that govern the Internet. In addition to the domain name you want to use, you provide the registrar with contact and

Part Three:
Makes &
Models: How to
Stand Out from
the Crowd

Microsoft Small Business Kit

technical information, and then the registrar submits the name for registration. You also need to sign a registration contract with the registrar, which spells out the terms and conditions of registering a domain name. You can review the terms and conditions online. The agreement usually specifies the costs of registration, the procedures for resolving disputes over a domain name, and how the registrar will use the contact information you provide. After your domain name is included in the registry, computer users can access a Web site using that name.

You're probably familiar with several of the abbreviations that are known as *top-level domains*—.com, .net, .org, and others. Most small businesses choose .com as the top-level domain because this domain refers to a commercial enterprise (as opposed to .org, for example, which is usually associated with not-for-profit organizations). However, new top-level domains have recently been approved. For example, you can now register a domain name that uses .biz, which is restricted to businesses, or .name, which is reserved for individuals. If your business is deeply identified with your personal name, you might consider registering your domain name with .com (or .biz) and .name. You might also want to register a domain name using .com and another using .biz for your business to help preserve the online identity of your company.

Domain name registration scams

The ICANN has recently made new top-level domains available, including .aero, .biz, .coop, .info, .museum, .name, and .pro. The U.S. Federal Trade Commission (FTC) has warned of a scam that offers owners of domain names, via fax or e-mail, a chance to preregister their name with a new top-level domain, for a fee, of course. Be leery of a service that promises to preregister new names, especially if the offer is unsolicited. You can stay up to date about the use of top-level domain names at the ICANN Web site, *www.icann.org*.

Domain name registrars work competitively, so you can choose which registrar you want to use, and you can probably find offers that keep down the cost of registering your domain name. You can find a list of accredited domain name registrars at *www.internic.net*. This Web site, which is operated by ICANN, provides a search tool that you can use to check whether the domain name you want to use is already registered. (The InterNIC site also provides the means to lodge a complaint about a domain name registrar, but hopefully you'll never need to do that.) You'll find similar search tools on the Web sites of many domain name registrars, and some require

Chapter Eight: Branding Basics

Part Three:
Makes &
Models: How to
Stand Out from
the Crowd

you to conduct a search for the domain name you're considering as the first step in registering.

Many registrars charge about $30 per year, an amount that can be made up quickly if your presence on the Web brings in a little new business. The price of registration might also include services such as a free "under construction" Web page that's displayed while you put a site together. Domain name registrations can be obtained in one-year increments, but 10 years is the maximum length for any unexpired term.

The list of registrars available at *www.internic.com* provides links to the various registrars' Web sites. Using those links, you can look over and compare the offers from various registrars. After you choose a registrar, follow the online registration processes (or print out the forms you need and submit them).

Choosing How and Where to Host a Web Site

Registering your domain name is the first step in building an identity on the Internet. You also need a place to host your site—a computer where you store the images, text, and other content that make up your Web site.

You can host your own site if you want to purchase the computer hardware and software that's required and if you have the technical know-how to support a Web site. You also need a high-speed connection to the Internet, such as a T1 line, that provides more speed than a Digital Subscriber Line (DSL) or cable connection. Hosting your own Web site might make sense if you plan to conduct all or most of your business transactions through a Web site and you anticipate a high volume of visitors (hundreds of thousands) each month.

The approach many small businesses use is to purchase a Web site hosting package from an Internet service provider (ISP). ISPs such as EarthLink or AOL provide hosting services. You can find details about the hosting packages provided by Microsoft at the Microsoft Small Business Center (*www.microsoft.com/smallbusiness*). Many smaller companies provide hosting packages as well.

The costs of a hosting package vary. A basic package, which typically includes a setup fee, a limited amount of storage space, and a small number of e-mail mailboxes, might be as little as $25 per month. A more comprehensive package—one with more mailboxes, for example, more storage space, and some e-commerce features such as an online catalog—will cost in the range of $100 or more per month. Through some ISPs, you can register a

Part Three:
Makes &
Models: How to
Stand Out from
the Crowd

Microsoft Small Business Kit

domain name as part of a hosting package. Some packages might also include reports of traffic on your Web site that you can use to analyze trends in your business.

Free Web site hosting

On a limited basis, an ISP might provide a "free" (except for the cost of Internet access) Web site, although these offers restrict the amount of space your Web site can occupy, so you won't be able to do much more than host a few pages. You could not expect to provide a feature such as online sales on a free site.

There are also a variety of places on the Internet that offer hosting at no charge, but before you host your Web site with one of these services, be sure you understand the details of the hosting agreement. You might be required to place a banner advertisement for the hosting service on either the top or bottom of each page of your Web site. Also, the free hosting package might require that the activities of people who visit your Web site be tracked online and the data collected sold to marketing services. If you're concerned about the privacy of customer data, you won't want to use a service such as this.

A great advantage of using a hosting package offered by an ISP or by the Microsoft Small Business Center is that you don't need to deal directly with as many technical issues and you don't need to purchase the computer and software necessary to host a Web site. Instead, with the hosting company managing the technical chores, you can apply your efforts to developing the content for your site and refining how the site presents and advances your business.

Web site forwarding

Another feature you might want to look for in a hosting package is *Web site forwarding*. Let's say you host your Web site on the members page of your ISP, so the address is something like *www.contoso.com/members /cohowinery*. That's not a very memorable name. You'd rather your customers and clients simply use *www.cohowinery.com*. When someone looking for your site types **www.cohowinery.com** in their Web browser, Web site forwarding sends them to your complete address.

Chapter Eight: **Branding Basics**

Part Three:
**Makes &
Models: How to
Stand Out from
the Crowd**

When you research Web hosting packages, be sure you consider the following:

- What sort of security features does a host provide? Has the host implemented a firewall? How often do they back up data? Are the Web servers themselves physically secure? Are antispam and antivirus features provided for e-mail?

- 100 Web pages equals approximately 10 megabytes (MB) of disk space, although the amount of space varies depending on the composition of a page—the number of images, graphics, and sound files, for example. You can use this rough ratio to calculate how much disk space you need.

- Most packages place a limit on how much data can be transferred each month. Each visit to your site will affect this limit, and you could be charged more if you exceed the amount provided by your hosting plan.

- Check out the reliability of a host's Internet connection. Make sure the host has multiple connections so that in the event one line goes down, customers don't lose access to your site. A host should offer a guarantee of service, meaning the host pledges that your site will always be available (more or less)—a guarantee of 99.9 percent service is preferable.

- If you're not an expert on creating Web pages, Web site hosting packages often provide software tools that make designing and implementing a Web site quite easy. See whether you can find a demonstration of the tools.

- E-commerce features such as a built-in shopping cart and credit card authorization are often available. Determine how much extra these features cost if you plan to make use of them on your Web site.

- What level of technical support is provided? You should seek a host that provides support 24 hours a day every day and that responds to emergencies promptly.

You can find lists of Web hosting companies (if you don't already have an ISP you want to work with) at several sites on the Internet. A good list is available through *www.webservices.cnet.com*.

Part Three:
Makes &
Models: How to
Stand Out from
the Crowd

Microsoft Small Business Kit

Building Credibility

The next challenge is to reinforce brand recognition so that you build business at every moment and in every channel of customer contact. Each customer must receive a consistent message that represents your brand—that is, your promise to the customer. You want the company personality to be easily identifiable at every customer touch point, from word of mouth to final sale. Every bit and byte of packaging, presentations, communications, and marketing should speak with a brand-consistent look and voice.

The same branding should appear on your entire range of advertising and promotional options, not just stationery or sales material. That includes press releases, e-mail signatures, trade show displays and booths, shop or office signage, banners and posters, print ads, and marketing for sponsored or charity events—in other words, everything.

Still, brand credibility obviously takes a lot more than having the right color code. You must honor what your brand symbolizes. The greatest tag line in the world won't get customers to come back if you don't fulfill your marketing promises. None of this, by the by, requires gobs of money. It's the discipline of staying on-message and building your identity that's key—not a big budget.

Brand Your World

Don't miss an opportunity to brand your company communications. Use the logo on:

- Stationery, labels, and envelopes
- Invoices, receipts, and bills
- Fax cover sheets
- Web site channels
- E-mail signatures
- Shopping bags
- Office or store signage
- Conference, trade show, and seminar signage
- Highway billboards
- Brochures, advertising, and flyers
- Clothing and specialty products (like pens or calculators)

Chapter Eight: Branding Basics

Part Three:
Makes &
Models: How to
Stand Out from
the Crowd

Protecting Your Intellectual Property: Trademarks, Copyrights, and Patents

After you've defined and designed your print and digital branding elements, you might want to consider protecting the graphics, words, or names that now represent your company's identity. Such protections can be smart not only for your overall company icon, logo, or tag lines, but also to safeguard special product names—say, GripnGlug plumbing chemicals—or unique branding you've developed to market services—say, 4EverYoung spa treatments.

The wonder of digital technology, of course, is always double-edged. On the one hand, easy-to-use technologies give small businesses unprecedented power and worldwide reach for mere pennies a day. On the other hand, it has spawned a marketplace rife with cut-and-paste imitators and burn-a-disk copycats. It's increasingly easy to adopt or appropriate another company's branding and marketing personality to make customers think an imitation is the real thing. Think, for instance, of the huge market in fake designer handbags.

As a result, business owners are increasingly looking for ways to protect their intellectual property. They do this for the same reason you lock up the office when you're not around. It might not totally prevent theft, but it certainly helps to discourage thieves.

What Is Intellectual Property (IP)?

Roughly defined, *IP* refers to intangible assets that are the result of human brain power and knowledge. But IP doesn't include every stray thought or concept. Typically, intellectual assets aren't considered IP unless they have clear market or commercial value. IP can include:

- An idea
- An invention
- A singular expression
- An industrial process or business method
- A creation, whether literary or conceptual
- A unique name

Part Three:
Makes &
Models: How to
Stand Out from
the Crowd

Microsoft Small Business Kit

- A mathematical or chemical formula
- A computing process or program
- A unique presentation or display

Choosing Legal Protections

There are three main ways to legally register your company's IP: trademarks, copyright, and patents, which are outlined in the following sections. In each case, application fees will run a few hundred dollars, depending on the kind of registration protection you want and the documents you request. Remember that IP protections, especially in the digital age, are fluid and open to judicial interpretations. If you're serious about applying for such registrations, you ought to consult an IP attorney or expert. Don't hire anyone without first asking about fees and checking references. Attorney fees vary as well.

To find an IP attorney:

- Ask your local chapter of the American Bar Association (ABA), found in local phone directories.
- Use the ABA's online lawyer locator: *www.abanet.org*.
- Ask for referrals from your business associates, accountant, or professional association.

Trademark, copyright, and patent application and other fee schedules change regularly. Check the U.S. Patent & Trademark Office (USPTO) and U.S. Copyright Office Web sites to find current fees:

- *www.uspto.gov/main/trademarks.htm*
- *www.copyright.gov/*

Registering Trademarks and Service Marks

Generally, a *trademark* is used to protect distinctive or unique words, names, symbols, or designs. You can also trademark distinguishing sounds or colors that set your goods and services apart from those of other makers and marketers. Trademarks can be renewed in perpetuity as long as you keep using them for commercial purposes. When you're selling a service rather than a product, you'll need a *service mark* instead of a trademark. The terms *trademark* and *mark* are often used interchangeably to refer to either trademarks or service marks.

Chapter Eight: Branding Basics

Part Three:
Makes &
Models: How to
Stand Out from
the Crowd

There are three types of trademark symbols:

- ™ Trademark
- **SM** Service mark
- ® Federal registration symbol

You don't have to register a trademark or mark with the USPTO to establish your legal rights to the mark. You establish that right simply by doing day-to-day business with your unique products, symbols, services, or whatever. "Any time you claim rights to a mark, you may use the 'TM' (trademark) or 'SM' (service mark) designation to alert the public to your claim, regardless of whether you have filed an application with the USPTO," explains Ruth Nybold at the Patent & Trademark Office.

Search and protect

Trademark search and application processes are complicated. Hiring an attorney who specializes in trademarks will save you time and potential trouble later on. You can, however, get an idea of marks that are currently registered by searching the USPTO's free database, which includes both registered marks and marks with pending applications: *www.uspto.gov/main/trademarks.htm.*

Why Bother to Register: Trademarks

Formally applying to and registering with the USPTO offers some additional benefits. The advantages of formal federal trademark registration are as follows:

- Your registration is put in a database, letting other potential users know that the mark is yours and not to be used even if they have never seen your trademark.

- Registration provides documented evidence that you're actually using the mark in the course of business and that you're the owner.

- Registration gives you the ability to bring legal action concerning the mark in federal court against anyone who uses it.

- You can file a registration with U.S. Customs Service that prevents an importer from bringing in products or services made abroad that infringe on your mark.

- Although the registration only covers use of the mark in the U.S. and its territories, registration here serves as the basis to register your mark in other countries.

To register your trademark, you must first search all existing federally registered marks. You need to make sure no other mark is like yours and there's no possibility of conflict or what the USPTO calls "likelihood of confusion." If conflicting marks are not found, you submit an application to have your mark registered with the USPTO.

Once registration is granted—which you then signify by using the ® mark—you must renew it every 10 years. Every 5 years, however, you must present an affidavit to show that you're still using the mark.

Part Three:
Makes &
Models: How to
Stand Out from
the Crowd

Microsoft Small Business Kit

For more information, check the USPTO Web site (www.uspto.gov/main/trademarks.htm) and the International Trademark Association Web site (www.inta.org/).

Registering Copyrights

In contrast to a trademark (which protects symbols, words, or designs that identify the company that produces goods or services), *copyrights* protect original works of authorship of published and unpublished works, whether digital or print. That protection permits the "author" to have exclusive right to reproduce the work, produce any derivative form of the original, and publicly perform or display the work.

Copyright protection covers:

- Literary works, published and unpublished.

- Dramatic works, including any accompanying music or vice versa—musical works that include accompanying words.

- Pantomimes and choreographic works.

- Sound recordings.

- Motion pictures, both the script and the film itself.

- Architectural works, including the design and the plans.

- Pictorial, graphical, or sculptural works.

- Recipes. Merely listing ingredients in recipes, formulas, compounds, or prescriptions is *not* protected by a copyright. But when the ingredients are combined and used together—say, to form a cookbook, a set of directions, or a set of explanations—copyright protection kicks in.

- Computer software. The U.S. Copyright Office defines *computer software programs* as "a set of statements or instructions to be used directly or indirectly in a computer in order to bring about a certain result." So copyright protection extends to all of the expressions in the program. There are special limitations on computer program copyrights. Check with the U.S. Copyright Office (*www.copyright.gov/title17/92chap1.html#117*).

- Web pages. Protection extends to works transmitted online, including text, artwork, music, audiovisual material, sounds and sound recordings, and more.

Chapter Eight: **Branding Basics**

Part Three:
Makes &
Models: How to
Stand Out from
the Crowd

Like trademarks, you needn't notify the U.S. Copyright Office to secure a copyright. Copyright is automatically extended as soon as the work is in some kind of fixed form, such as a printed manuscript, sheet music, CD, DVD, or Web site. For example, if you compose a song, it's not considered a "work," and it will not be protected by copyright until and unless you record it on a tape or a disk or write its notation on a sheet music form. Typically, only the author of a copyrighted work can claim ownership. The exception is when a work is commissioned as a *work for hire*, which is established at the outset, usually with a contract. In that case, the commissioning employer is the copyright owner, not the author himself or herself. Work-for-hire commissions and contracts can get tricky. It's worth consulting an attorney before signing one or assuming it affords you protection.

Once you've put the work into a fixed form, you might place a notice where it can be easily seen and understood to signify that you have copyright ownership. Copyright notice consists of the symbol © or the text *copyright* or *copr.*, the year of first publication, and the name of the copyright's owner, as in this example:

© *2004 Eva T. Kuhn*

The same format should be used for phonorecord, audio, or sound formats. In that case, you use the symbol of *P* with a circle around it, the year of the publication of the sound recording, and the copyright owner, as in this example:

(P) 2004 Eva T. Kuhn

Authors or copyright owners can place a copyright notice on any unpublished copy or phonorecord of their work that leaves their control, as in this example:

Unpublished work © 2004 Eva T. Kuhn

Copyright doesn't extend to facts, ideas, or the way something is produced, such as a method or process of operation, but it can be harnessed to protect the way such things are expressed—for instance, in a manual or a handbook.

Part Three:
Makes &
Models: How to
Stand Out from
the Crowd

Microsoft Small Business Kit

Why Bother to Register: Copyright

There is a difference between simply putting a notice on your work and actually registering a copyright. The advantages of formal federal copyright registration are as follows:

- Registration creates a public record of your claim of copyright ownership.

- Registration gives the owner power to file an infringement suit and defend the ownership in federal court.

- Registration establishes evidence of the facts stated in a copyright certificate—if registration is made within five years of publication. *Publication* is defined as the date of the first distribution of the copied work to the public. Simply showing or performing the work publicly is not considered publication.

- Registration protects the owner against the importation of infringing copies from other countries by allowing registration with the U.S. Customs Service.

- A copyright owner can transfer copyright to someone else. The transfer must be in writing and signed by the owner and then recorded in the Copyright Office.

- A copyright owner can bequeath ownership or transfer it as personal property—subject to state laws regarding estate succession.

For works published and registered on or after January 1, 1978, copyright protection is in force for the life of the author, plus an additional 70 years. For a work for hire, copyright extends 95 years from the date of publication or 120 years from the date of creation, whichever is shorter. For works published and registered before January 1, 1978, copyright was good for 28 years, with the option of a renewal term with the Copyright Office for up to 95 years.

For more information, check the U.S. Copyright Office Web site: www.copyright.gov/.

The limits of protection

Keep in mind that if you write a book or manual about how to build a car, the manual can be copyrighted. But that will only prevent others from copying your particular book. It will not prevent anyone from writing his or her own book on that very topic or even building a car based on your book's instructions. You can copyright the manual, but if you want the machine to be protected, you need a patent. (See the section below, "Registering Patents," to learn more.)

Registering Patents

A *patent* is a property right granted by the USPTO to an inventor for a period of 14 or 20 years (depending on the type of patent), giving the holder the exclusive right to exclude others from manufacture, use, or sale of the invention. After the 20-year period, the invention is available to the public, and the inventor loses his or her exclusive right to profit from the invention.

There are three kinds of patents:

- **Utility patents**   Covers discoveries of new and useful processes, whether industrial, mechanical, or technical, including improvements

- **Design patents**   Covers original and ornamental design for manufactured items

- **Plant patents**   Covers inventions or discoveries of distinct and new varieties of plants

Chapter Eight: Branding Basics

Part Three:
Makes &
Models: How to
Stand Out from
the Crowd

The length of patent protection varies. Utility and plant patents last for 20 years from the date the application was filed. A design patent runs 14 years from the date the patent is granted.

You cannot patent any inventions that are not considered useful, like a special container for liquid that has a hole in the bottom. You further cannot patent laws of nature or physical phenomena, although patents can apply to new methods or devices that harness natural laws. There are other minor exclusions as well.

The USPTO encourages inventors to conduct initial searches of their discoveries before applying in order to make sure their invention is actually new and no others are like it in scope or design. To run an initial search, check with one of the many patent and research libraries found across the country or on the USPTO's online database. If what you find or don't find seems encouraging, you should probably rely on an experienced patent attorney to investigate further. An attorney can quickly help you decide whether a patent is worth pursuing, saving you time, money, and research effort.

After the patent application is submitted, a patent examiner starts the legal process of determining whether eligibility requirements are met and whether the invention is indeed new and original. While the application is being considered, an inventor may use *Patent pending* or *Patent applied for* on products or marketing material.

What happens when the application is approved? A patent number is granted, and the inventor is required to put the word *Patented* and the patent number on the product. Failure to do so can incur a penalty.

Patents can also be revoked if you don't pay required maintenance fees. For utility and plant patents, maintenance fees are due at 3.5 years, 7.5 years, and 11.5 years. The USPTO does not send out notices about these fees, which means you're on your own to remember them. But if you do miss a payment, there's a six-month grace period in which to pay, with a surcharge, of course. If a maintenance fee is not paid, the patent expires. Maintenance fees are not required for design patents.

Hire an experienced pro

IP lawyers can help with trademark, copyright, and patent preparation; searches and applications; trade secret enforcement and defense litigation; new media and cyberlaw; and any legal claims that may arise.

Part Three:
Makes &
Models: How to
Stand Out from
the Crowd

Microsoft Small Business Kit

Why Bother to Register: Patents

Aside from the obvious protection of avoiding theft or imitators, registering a patent gives you the right to transfer your exclusivity. Patents are considered personal property, like copyrights. A patent right can be sold to others, mortgaged, or bequeathed by a will. You can pass the patent to your heirs. This is accomplished by a written assignment that transfers the patent to someone else.

For more information, check the USPTO Web site: www.uspto.gov/.

List of Resources

- **E-commerce primer** The U.S. government's Small Business Administration (SBA) Web site (*www.sba.gov*) includes links to online presentations that introduce you to Internet technologies and provide tips for setting up and managing your business on the Internet. On the home page of the SBA Web site, click Starting Your Business or Managing Your Business to locate the links to this material.

- **List of domain name registrars** A list of accredited domain name registrars is available at *www.internic.org.*

- **Lists of ISPs** You can find lists of ISPs with Web hosting packages at *webservices.cnet.com.* You can find descriptions of the hosting packages available through the Microsoft Small Business Center, at *www.microsoft.com/smallbusiness.*

- **Reference for how to build a Web site** *Faster Smarter Web Page Creation* (Microsoft Press, 2002)

For More Information

In addition to the resources mentioned in this chapter, you will find links and information on the companion CD. Some books and Web sites particularly useful as you consider how to position and identify your business include:

Books

- Al Ries and Jack Trout: *Positioning: The Battle for Your Mind* (McGraw-Hill, 2000)

- Cheryl Cullen and Amy Schell, *Identity Solutions: How to Create Effective Brands With Letterheads, Logos and Business Cards* (How Design Books, 2003)

- Marty Neumeier, *The Brand Gap: How to Bridge the Distance Between Business Strategy and Design* (New Riders, 2003)

Chapter Eight: **Branding Basics**

Part Three:
Makes &
Models: How to
Stand Out from
the Crowd

Web Sites

- Useful articles and information from AllAboutBranding.com: *http://www.allaboutbranding.com/*

- An interactive online quiz to check your branding knowledge: *http://chadwickcomm.com/brandiq/*

- "All About Trademarks" from an IP lawyer, with many useful articles and links: *http://www.ggmark.com/*

Part Three:
Makes and
Models: How to
Stand Out from
the Crowd

Microsoft Small Business Kit

It's not just what you say that stirs people. It's the way that you say it.

— Bill Bernbach Said, *Bill Bernbach (DDB Needham Worldwide, 1989)*

Chapter Nine
Crafting Your Message

Make sure your customer knows who you are and what you offer at every point of every interaction. More often than not, sales grow from building the relationship, rather than trying to close the deal.

What you'll find:

❑ Disciplined messaging and the seamless sell

❑ Developing a marketing strategy

❑ Selling benefits, not features

❑ Making messages work across channels

❑ Marketing Return on Investment (ROI)

❑ Low-cost, high-impact marketing ideas

❑ Generating sales leads

Part Three:
Makes and
Models: How to
Stand Out from
the Crowd

Microsoft Small Business Kit

Disciplined Messaging and the Seamless Sell

On the silver screen, the Hollywood version of a business success story typically opens with a forceful entrepreneur tinkering in his garage with, say, a sputtering combustion engine. In the hip remake, the engine morphs into a circuit board. Either way, the story runs through roadblocks and jumps the potholes until, inevitably, we freeze-frame on our young hero beating out Mr. U. R. Smug for fame, fortune, and lucrative patent rights into the next millennium.

In this fabled version—a story line most of us grew up with—the budding CEO manages to win the day, not to mention riches and glory, by utterly believing in his innovative product. Passion—the resource entrepreneurs never run out of—sees him through. So what's wrong with this picture?

No one ever mentions marketing.

If the concept surfaces at all, some snappy Joan Friday character comes up with an even snappier tag line over repartee at lunch. In short order, the line is fed to the wide-eyed media, and boom! Sales skyrocket and the company is off and running.

Back here on earth, off-screen, it doesn't quite work that way. Marketing is a slow process of building recognition and forging customer relationships. Like Hollywood, the fairy tale of overnight success is exactly that—a myth. Marketing a small business does not translate into cinematic one-liners or, at the other extreme, blockbuster TV campaigns. Too often, business owners blur the lines between advertising and marketing, between public relations and marketing, and between promotion and marketing, and not just the owners of small businesses, either. That's because advertising is so ubiquitous. It's typically mass media and the most visible form of marketing so it is the most familiar to everyone.

But marketing messages can be delivered in many ways via dozens of channels, from direct mail to free publicity in professional or business journals, newsletters and magazines, from paid search engine listings to, for that matter, skywriting by an airplane. Whatever the channel, if your message does not have a clear target and does not clearly distinguish your company's products and services from everyone else's, however memorable and expensive the channel might be, you're simply throwing away money and opportunity. That goes for a $100 postcard mailing or a multimillion-dollar multimedia advertising campaign.

Chapter Nine: **Crafting Your Message**

Part Three:
**Makes and
Models: How to
Stand Out from
the Crowd**

Consider, for example, the rise and fall of the lonely Sock Puppet. This was—what shall we call it?—the spokesdummy for San Francisco online retailer Pets.com. During the heyday of the Internet bubble, back in 1999 and 2000, the feisty little tube sock made a splash in Super Bowl ads, got interviewed by ABC-TV's Diane Sawyer, and even wrote his autobiography, *Me by Me: The Pets.com Sock Puppet Book* (I Books, 2000). You couldn't ask for more amazing exposure and recognition for a small, unknown retailer.

Yet the upshot, in case you were out of the country, was that while the Sock Puppet fan club kept growing, Pets.com went spectacularly bust.

The lesson: The Sock Puppet fueled buzz and inspired cute ads, but it definitely wasn't marketing.

Marketing mandate

The goal of marketing is to grow the business by boosting sales or building credibility for your brand and wares. Keep your eye on the prize.

What's the Right Message?

The goal of marketing is to open minds and markets over the long term. The best way to accomplish that requires careful and upfront analysis. Marketing paves the way for the sales that follow. Marketing asks the customer to take some kind of action—say, select a product or try a service or make a telephone call, or in the case of corporate or image marketing, buy into a company's integrity and good will.

You can't make a sale without first getting out an appropriate message. The message should be consistent and clear in every marketing channel you choose. If you've gone through the branding process, your next challenge is spreading the word and deciding who is best suited to respond to your message.

See "Developing Brand Personality," page 184, to learn more.

As a small business, you can't afford to be all things to all people. It's way too expensive and demands resources you do not have. Early on, decide which customers you intend to serve and realize you can't please everyone. Pick your targets. Don't confuse true marketing with the tag line, message, or logo you've created. That's just a platform to build on. The smart route is a strategic one.

Part Three:
Makes and
Models: How to
Stand Out from
the Crowd

Microsoft Small Business Kit

Developing a Marketing Strategy

To begin developing your marketing strategy, try answering these questions:

- What are we really good at?
- How do we discover our core strengths?
- What do we like to do?
- What do customers want from us?
- How can we sell our strengths in a tough environment?
- What do we stand for?

Effective marketing requires you to develop a strategy for each of the areas that define marketing: product, price, promotion, and place. In addition, if you have more than one target market, you'll need to adjust your strategy for each of those targets. For instance, if you sell clip-on reading lights for books, one target market might be corporate road warriors who would use your product in airports, hotels, and so on. Another target might be backpackers and campers who use your product when sleeping under the stars. Those are two distinct customer groups. They don't think, walk, or talk alike, yet each group is an equally viable target for your product. You need a thought-out strategy and a message that effectively reaches both.

Marketing Defined

Classroom definitions of marketing, say the professors, boil down to the 4 Ps:

- **Product** Providing the right product or service for your market
- **Price** Selling for an amount deemed worth it by your target customer
- **Promotion** Creating or communicating an appropriate user perception
- **Place** Distributing or moving your product or service to locations where users can readily find it

In other words: Get the right product or service at the right price in front of the right customer, and you'll be cooking. After that, you might decide to rely on public relations work (getting free messages into media over which you have no control), or advertising (paid messages for space you do control), or other methods, such as direct mailers or sponsored events.

Make sure everyone in your organization, from the IT manager to the customer service rep, clearly understands the marketing strategy you develop and, just as importantly, also buys into it. If your receptionist doesn't understand how to satisfy customers and that he or she, along with every other staff member,

Chapter Nine: Crafting Your Message

Part Three:
Makes and
Models: How to
Stand Out from
the Crowd

is a company marketer, you, not the receptionist, had better be there to greet Ms. Strategic Alliance when she walks through the door.

Once you've put a smart strategy in place, you can afford to be flexible about tactics. The best marketing is a work in process: a throttle that you regulate as the economy and your industry shift speed. When something isn't working, don't immediately assume you need a major strategic overhaul, either. Sometimes, small changes or refinements can quickly correct course.

For example, Lisa Kimball is the founder of Group Jazz. Based in Washington, D.C., her consulting firm develops online communities and projects. About a year after launch, Kimball found that marketing the company's services at trade shows and conferences was draining significant dollars. "It never paid off," she says. "By the time we added up the couple thousand in registration fees and the costs of airfare, hotels, food, and materials to have people there to staff the booths, it wasn't worth it." It was clear, however, that her target customers attended the shows. She could definitely raise the profile of her business and reel in interested clients at such venues, but not at a rate that was cost-effective.

So Kimball switched gears. She and senior staffers developed industry-smart presentations and began volunteering to be speakers and panelists. That, says Kimball, not only cut conference costs but also proved more effective in luring business. "There's no point in us setting up a booth—we look too small against the global consulting companies. Now if we're not invited to speak," she continues, "we send someone just to ask smart questions at the sessions and to network. It works."

Classic Marketing Strategies

Big or small, shoestring or lavish, all marketing should have similar goals. Whether you are ramping up a major campaign, creating a one-time postcard mailer, or developing a company logo, keep in mind that you want to

- Get attention.
- Generate interest.
- Call for specific action.

Selling Benefits, Not Features

In the big picture, of course, textbook definitions leave out the spirit or emotional component of marketing. Modern marketing and its latest buzzword, *integrated marketing* (a full-service, comprehensive marketing plan), mean that you attract new customers by promising absolutely terrific value and that you keep all efforts consistent. Then you retain those customers by fully delivering on your promise in every customer exchange or transaction

Part Three:
Makes and
Models: How to
Stand Out from
the Crowd

Microsoft Small Business Kit

in every hour of every day you do business. The name of the marketing game today is customer satisfaction—that is, how well your product or service's performance meets your customer's expectations.

The way to motivate customers is to identify the advantages they gain from buying your products or services. You've got to sell benefits, not features. So the first lesson is to avoid shaping messages that merely echo headlines or fast-fading fashions. Even when you market products that piggyback on a fad—for instance, the must-have toy for a holiday season—you still need a reliable message year-round that will attract customers to you and not to your competitors. Instead, stay a steady course and own the space you've chosen. Most businesses these days—large or small—do not have the resources to fund marketing that only builds awareness—or, as pundits put it, campaigns where you "spray and pray."

Let's imagine that you've come up with an absolutely revolutionary widget. Should your marketing message announce that fact? It's the better mousetrap syndrome, isn't it? You can sit back and wait for customers to start pouring in. Yeah, right.

Truth is, people don't much care whether you build your business—be it a breakthrough widget factory or a crackerjack service firm. It's up to you to provide reasons for customers to find you. Features are the mere facts of what you sell, such as size, price, color, name, or category of your offerings. Features are "navy or black," "antilock brakes," or "T1 line." They're an announcement that says, "Build it, and they will come." Benefits are what customers derive from a purchase, like saving time or money or both. When you market benefits, the emotional transaction counts as much as the financial one. To give potential customers reason to choose your products, you must develop marketing materials that play up what customers will get out of your offerings—whether that's a practical benefit, the status of being an early adopter, or because the product makes the customer feel special. No one needs or wants a color or a size. But everyone craves a great experience or a money-saver. Emphasize the emotion of what you sell so that customers feel good after buying your wares.

For instance, a home appliance store might want to promote a sale on refrigerators. The store's owner can easily get out the word by designing distinctive and very affordable postcards that can be printed on a color desktop printer and mailed to customers. What's the right message for the card?

Chapter Nine: **Crafting Your Message**

Part Three:
**Makes and
Models: How to
Stand Out from
the Crowd**

- **The features sell:** "This week only! Brand-name refrigerators now 35 percent off! Your choice of avocado green, white, and beige—includes energy-efficient freezers."

- **The benefits sell:** "Save on top-of-the-line refrigerators. Convenient upper-level freezers eliminate bending. Energy-efficient cooling systems cut utility bills by 10 percent. Adjustable shelves make storage easy. We deliver free and cart away your old model. Sale ends Saturday!"

Which store would you buy from?

All marketing material, whether brochures, direct-mail postcards, flyers, print or online ads, billboards, media kits, and the rest, should be viewed through the minds, hearts, and shoes of the customer. Understandably, business owners must put intense focus on developing and honing company products or services. Smart, convenient, and innovative *features* are what drive successful products. But selling customers on the *benefits* of those features is what drives sales.

When crafting your marketing messages, be sure to emphasize feel-smart and feel-good emotional reasons for customers to reach for their wallets. While you're at it, keep in mind these three marketing myths and the corresponding reality checks. The thinking behind the myths tends to produce marketing that relies on features. The reality checks will push you into identifying the benefits customers get from buying your product.

- **Myth:** Always offer several options so that you appeal to a broad range of customers.

- **Reality:** Customers want one, convenient solution that works for them.

When creating marketing materials, such as a brochure or a Web site, it's easy to fall into the trap of including everything you can possibly do in order to account for every customer need and desire. A financial services firm, for instance, might produce a bulleted list of offerings, such as "investing, tax-preparation, estate planning, financial planning, saving for college, retirement planning," and so on. But such lists tend to overwhelm people, who might not want all the services. What's the real benefit here? "Comprehensive planning for financial security."

A menu of services or product options usually causes confusion. Instead, make sure your material promises one-stop-shopping solutions.

Part Three:
Makes and
Models: How to
Stand Out from
the Crowd

Microsoft Small Business Kit

- **Myth:** Products sell best at the lowest possible price.
- **Reality:** Customers want value, not bargains.

Typically, people buy on emotion and then look to justify those feelings with some intellectual rationale. Price alone won't do the trick. Look at Wal-Mart. Even with very low prices, the discount chain emphasizes friendly, personalized customer service.

But you don't have to be a nationwide chain to emphasize service at a good price. Service and savings will motivate customers, not merely cut-rate prices.

- **Myth:** Completely unique products are the easiest to market.
- **Reality:** The majority of customers don't want to be first on the block to try something.

Entrepreneurs who start up businesses sometimes forget that everyone else is not as innovative as they themselves are. The result is that they market the launch of their product, the "grand opening" (think *feature*) rather than how the product can help customers. Most people want tried-and-true products. No one wants to experiment with hard-earned dollars (unless, of course, you're appealing to niche markets, like the status-conscious or the early adopters). Use marketing to educate your customer before the pitch.

Making Messages Work Across Channels

Customers now expect companies and services to be transparent and fully informed across all channels. You cannot divide your business—or your marketing messages—into online and offline, or into phone vs. in-store vs. catalog. If you call your bank, for example, to complain about a problem that occurred in an online transfer, you expect the customer service rep on the phone to be fully up-to-speed about online transactions. Your customers have the same expectations.

This does not mean you don't segment and target different customers— remember the backpacker and the road warriors that each might want that reading light. It does mean that when you market to each segment, the targeted message is consistently recognizable in every channel, from radio to direct mail to trade show signage or shopping bags.

See "Focusing on Your Point of Difference,"" page 188, and "Identifying Your Best Customers: the 80/20 Rule," page 288, to learn more about customer segmentation.

Chapter Nine: Crafting Your Message

Part Three:
Makes and
Models: How to
Stand Out from
the Crowd

Here are some ways you can quickly and efficiently cross-market.

- **Market your theme with variations.** One Web-based service that sells real-time Internet monitoring capabilities faced the dilemma of marketing their services to several very different markets, including families, corporations, government agencies, and nonprofits. Rather than create a dozen different marketing kits, the company produced a single general product brochure. They then bolstered that overview with stand-alone inserts—slickly designed one-pagers about the advantages of their service for each of their specific market segments. The inserts slipped into a holder in the marketing kit. The company can now quickly customize packages for any client, but the overall message remains consistent.

- **Take advantage of every opportunity to cross-market.** Small businesses should be trying to harness every bit of customer attention. When you've created the tag line you like, make sure it's on every e-mail message, brochure, business card, letterhead, voice-mail message, Web banner, newsletter, and everything else that goes out the door.

- **Bridge the communication gaps.** Keep in mind that creating channels or messages does not add up to marketing unless it actually reaches customers and hits nerves. What you need is seamless messaging available throughout the company. That means you must coordinate and fully brief your entire team—both staff and outside contractors.

Marketing Return on Investment (ROI)

Increasingly, companies big and small are harnessing marketing to drive sales rather than to simply differentiate their brand identity. Sales leads are the most frequent goal of such *target marketing.*

Whatever the goal, you don't want to squander limited money and effort on marketing campaigns that are hit or miss. Instead, you need to learn what works and then jettison what doesn't. That way, you concentrate your efforts

Focus Your Marketing on Targets

Target marketing has quantifiable goals rather than simply trying to heighten brand awareness. That strategy can translate into:

- Increasing sales
- Deepening customer satisfaction
- Attracting investor interest
- Garnering publicity
- Extending a product line

Part Three:
Makes and
Models: How to
Stand Out from
the Crowd

Microsoft Small Business Kit

on tactics that move the needle. You should be getting clear ROI on all your marketing.

In the start-up phase, marketing is always about acquiring new customers (while making sure that the ones you have remain happy, of course). When marketing to find new customers, one way to control costs and make them pay off is by running net present value (NPV) analyses of your customer's worth. Basically, NPV lets you calculate the value of money over time—that is, how much a project costs in today's dollars vs. how much it will net you in the future.

Calculate the NPV of your marketing

For instance, if each new customer costs you $1,000 to acquire, 15 customers will cost $15,000. And if attending a trade show adds up to $15,000 in expenses, you ought to be very sure that attending that show gains you at least 15 new, paying customers. Otherwise, don't attend that show, and find a more cost-effective way of marketing.

Here are five steps to getting the maximum return on your marketing dollars:

1. **Identify targets.** First, evaluate your market to define the target customers you will benefit from reaching. Remember that target markets are not your core market. Targets shift depending on strategy and goals while the core customer typically remains stable. For example, let's say you sell kerosene camping stoves. Your core market is people who like to go camping. But your target might be Girl Scout troop leaders in the Northwest.

   Further, instead of one-size-fits-all marketing to every user of your product, consider targeting heavy, light, and occasional users. That way, you can customize messages more likely to hit nerves and drive response.

2. **Research customers.** There's little mileage in launching marketing efforts until you know the characteristics of your target customers. Presumably, you gained significant customer intelligence when you researched the marketing section of your business plan. Perhaps that was detailed enough and still current enough to support your campaign now.

   See "Planning Affordable Market Research," page 24, to learn more about assessing your market.

Chapter Nine: Crafting Your Message

Part Three:
Makes and
Models: How to
Stand Out from
the Crowd

But if you think the climate might have shifted since you found funding and launched, or if your plan sketched an overview and you now need more focus, it's worth your effort to investigate. Find out what your target customers think about your product, why they buy it, plus how and when they use it. You especially want to know how customers want to hear from you–direct mail, e-mail, phone, or online–as well as how often. Don't overlook research into what more you can potentially supply that they might need.

You can gain such insights in several ways. When talking to customers, ask them questions. You can also create simple surveys, questionnaires, and customer satisfaction queries with return mail postcards or online forms. Offer a gift or benefit for customer participation, like a coupon for discounted services or a gift that participants can claim. You can also do phone research. You might be surprised by the results.

3. **Quantify success.** Make sure you define the results you want and set expectations that are appropriate for the marketing you choose. To help set goals, you can get advice from industry groups, small business divisions at local colleges, or fee-based marketing agencies.

    You might set the mark at a certain sales revenue or a specified number of generated leads per month. Your goal could be a total number of acquired customers within a year or one new investor by the end of your fiscal year. Success could mean a shift in consumer perceptions or deeper customer satisfaction. Whatever your goal, you need to articulate the desired set of outcomes beforehand, or you won't know whether the marketing worked.

4. **Calculate your ROI.** Take the time to compare the cost of proposed marketing against the profit you expect from it–not sales, mind you, but actual profit.

    You want to monitor the range of customer response throughout the sales process so that you clearly understand what brought customers through the door or onto the Web site. Once you acquired the lead, how much did it cost in time and money to nail the sale? Can you make that more cost-effective? Did customers return or move on? What would help to make them more loyal?

    By setting up a table or grid that captures information about the campaign–whether in Microsoft Word, Excel, or Publisher–you can create a tool that lets you evaluate results. You need the following information:

Part Three:
Makes and
Models: How to
Stand Out from
the Crowd

Microsoft Small Business Kit

❑ The per-piece cost of your marketing material and distribution

❑ A score for the buying action respondents take, such as high, medium, or low

❑ Some tracking code to categorize customer response via phone, direct mail, e-mail, online, or in person

Now you have a way of figuring out how much it costs to get a customer's attention. You can also put a price tag on what it takes to drive a response and close the deal.

5. **Track results and adjust efforts.** By capturing data, updating results, and tracking your progress, you create increasingly integrated sales reports, financial analyses, and customer databases. That will tell you what's working—and what isn't. With such knowledge, you can customize the key marketing templates you use in Microsoft Publisher 2003.

Don't test once and stop. Keep refining your tactics and messages. Build up to larger, more expensive, and more proven marketing with low-cost, low-effort experiments.

Low-Cost, High-Impact Marketing Ideas

It's not easy being a baby. Raising the profile of a just-launched brand is always a challenge when cash is tight. Plus, customers usually lean toward tried-and-true products. Building buzz for a new business takes real smarts, creativity, and persistence. Here are some affordable and effective ways to build recognition and sales.

Creating Word of Mouth or Word of Mouse

Complimentary and consistent word-of-mouth turns customers and colleagues into brand missionaries. Over time, you build an all-volunteer sales force. No other marketing channel packs such power at so little cost. Typically, such support is sparked by glowing personal experiences. Maybe you earned customer loyalty with outstanding service. Or you gained vendor approval with 24-hour turnarounds. Whatever your standout specialty, word-of-mouth success means that everyone in the know can't wait to tell friends or associates about you.

One of the easiest word-of-mouth tactics is to swap business cards with firms that attract your target customers—now that you've learned who they are. For instance, if you own an auto body shop, you can partner with a car

Chapter Nine: Crafting Your Message

Part Three:
Makes and
Models: How to
Stand Out from
the Crowd

wash/detailing service. The car wash tucks your cards into envelopes with its mailed monthly statements or invoices and also places a stack of your cards on the counter for customers. You obviously do the same for them.

Get bigger bang for your buzz by offering a special discount available only to customers who show up with your cards from the partner firm—say, 5 to 20 percent off posted prices. You can print the special offer on the back of the cards. Similarly, business cards can be offered with variable discounts at strategic locations or businesses around town. In this case, you might put them at car dealerships or even at the local bank known for auto loans.

You can also customize designs and create slightly different versions of your card so that you can identify which customers came from which partner. That way, after some weeks, you'll discover which businesses are most effective for reeling in customers. Just don't make the designs too different from each other. You want to retain your company's consistent identity. Add a letter, some subtle text, or a symbol—perhaps a department number—that will be code for you alone.

If you think business cards might not be appropriate—say, if you're a discount retailer—you can also use postcards for these swap arrangements, with special offers printed on one side.

Raising Your Media Profile

Getting exposure and having more people aware of your products makes them easier to sell, and that grows the business. You can generate your own publicity—which is, essentially, free marketing. But first you need to come up with a compelling company story—a *media hook*. You'll also probably need a press kit to send out to the media and business contacts.

Media hooks come in all sizes and shapes. They don't need to advocate a cause or even make national news. Your hook can be local. It can build on the past—say, challenges overcome by the firm founder. Think about Orville Redenbacher's popcorn or Smucker's jam and how those two companies promote family history. You can also generate narrow-focus press within a business trade group, in an industry newsletter, or by becoming an expert in your field for trade shows and conferences. The key here is to be sincere. Don't promote anything you don't really believe in. The story must have authenticity.

Whatever your publicity goal, the first step is to create a media kit, which can be quickly done with Microsoft Publisher. The kit presents your company image, expertise, skills, background, and personality for the target

Part Three:
Makes and
Models: How to
Stand Out from
the Crowd

Microsoft Small Business Kit

audience. It must look crisp and professional, but it doesn't have to be fancy. A media kit usually contains:

- Your photo (professionally done, although it can be an informal pose)
- Your company mission and history
- The company brochure or other marketing materials
- Appropriate press releases about the latest news or triumphs
- Your bio with significant resumé details
- Your credentials or areas of expertise

Purchase some handsome folders at an office supply shop to collect the material. You can paste your company label on the front or create a special label that matches the company's design identity.

Next choose a targeted list of media prospects and send out the kits, along with a cover letter explaining your interest and appeal. Be patient but persistent and follow up with phone calls. After that, put your ear to the ground and respond to the queries that come your way.

Hiring a PR Agency

You can also raise your profile by hiring a PR agency to build media attention. Used strategically, PR agencies can do a lot more than manage media contacts or issue press releases, especially for small businesses that lack profile and reach. Just make sure your expectations are realistic. Lea Conner, at Conner Dudley Communications in Spokane, Washington, tells of a self-published author who wanted to appear on TV talk shows to publicize her book. But the author had never done any media interviews. "I learned what she really wanted was to sell her books," says Conner. So the two agreed to build up to major media over several months by creating marketing materials and having the author gain local media experience. A month later, the author grew impatient, wondering why she hadn't yet been booked on *The View* or *Oprah*.

Says Conner: "It's easy for clients to get so caught up in their own dreams that they fail to realize the amount of work it takes to achieve major results." In other words, be strategic and bold, but give it time. To hire PR pros that can boost your business, consider these issues:

- **Get a good fit.** Invest up-front time to determine whether the agency can add strategic value. Don't fall for fancy digs or impressive client lists, which might not be current. Instead, tap a pro who thoroughly

Chapter Nine: *Crafting Your Message*

Part Three:
**Makes and
Models: How to
Stand Out from
the Crowd**

gets what you do. Choose a publicist who not only has the right skills but also has some knowledge of your industry. Accreditation from the industry's largest association, the Public Relations Society of America (PRSA; *www.prsa.org*) carries weight. But the portfolio and experience count most. What successes has the agency had? Does it match your needs? Journalistic experience is helpful. It means that the PR person understands what makes a media story and how to approach editors and reporters. After that, you want to be a highly valued client who rates immediate attention. For smaller businesses, that usually translates into hiring a smaller agency or a sole practitioner. Once you sign a contract based on the star-studded pitch of a larger agency, your account is likely to be turned over to junior staffers. Always ask who at the agency will be working with you before signing on.

■ **Phase in the fees.**   Retainers for smaller agencies run $2,000 to $5,000 or so per month. But don't begin on retainer. Set up a specific project with a price tag attached to evaluate results. Paying for customized services is another option. For instance, hire a publicist to write press releases on an hourly basis for about $100 to $250. You can also contract with a PR pro to work in-house for you. Rates vary with experience, say, $50 to $200 per hour. Some PR companies provide a network of international independent agencies, so you can contract for services in any country or city.

■ **Define success, and measure results.**   Publicity and media coverage take time. When you're launching a product or service and want to build awareness, start talking to PR people at least six months beforehand. Some agencies promise a specific amount of media exposure within a month; others, within 100 days. Ask what you should expect. It will help enormously to figure out what you want to achieve, such as:

■ A certain amount of column inches, airtime, sound bites, or Web hits, or a feature in an influential journal

■ Greater customer awareness of your brand

■ A specific number of sales leads within a specific time frame

■ Invitations to speak at prestigious events or seminars

■ Specific industry awards

To track results, develop a survey before the publicist starts to set a benchmark. Then, after the work is done, resurvey to find if there's been any difference—whether more recognition, or more sales leads, or whatever your agreed-upon goal was.

Part Three:
Makes and
Models: How to
Stand Out from
the Crowd

Microsoft Small Business Kit

- **Plan ahead.** One of the most overlooked factors in public relations is that it's a *trailing indicator*. Press mentions or stories appear based on news and information that was sent out weeks or months earlier. As a result, when you sign on or discuss campaigns, talk about how you plan to grow and what the company will become, not what defines you today. That will certainly affect decisions about media kits and material or which influencers or analysts to target.

Adopting a Cause

American Express first used the term *cause-related marketing* in 1983 to describe its efforts to raise money to restore the Statue of Liberty. Each time a cardholder used his or her charge card, Amex donated a penny toward refurbishing the statue, eventually raising nearly $2 million. The number of new cardholders quickly bumped up 45 percent, according to The Foundation Center, a philanthropy research group. Card usage increased by double digits. Lately, American Express has resurrected this campaign.

And remember Ben & Jerry's ice cream? Founded with a scant $12,000 in Vermont back in 1978, the two owners created a national brand out of homespun roots, high-priced innovative flavors, and the good will of philanthropy. Before that, few firms took the risk of putting social responsibility front and center. Now dozens do.

Consider marketing with a cause

Cause marketing or cause branding is a partnership between a for-profit company and a nonprofit group or cause that's designed to benefit both. The nonprofit gets company dollars, resources, or reach. The company gets nonprofit credibility, good will, and, maybe, a donor database.

Cause-marketing alliances come in lots of flavors, and such campaigns definitely resonate with consumers. Cone, Inc., a Boston cause-marketing communications firm, has been tracking consumer sentiment about corporate citizenship for 15 years. In Cone's seventh annual Holiday Trend Tracker in 2003, the survey found that a majority of consumers (71 percent) were likely to consider a company's reputation for supporting causes when purchasing holiday gifts. That represented an 11 percent increase over 2002. Such customer motivation has a strong pull year-round, not only during holiday seasons.

Chapter Nine: Crafting Your Message

Part Three:
Makes and
Models: How to
Stand Out from
the Crowd

With cause marketing, the company gets a positive branding experience and appears thoughtful and caring. The nonprofit gets publicity and builds awareness for the cause. Everybody wins.

Doing good might be good for your business, too. It can lend emotional profile to the company and make customers feel good about buying your product. But before you partner with any group, thoroughly investigate the details. Search for issues that resonate with your target customers and vet the nonprofit organization to make sure it's legitimate. Your contributions don't have to be cash. They could also include employee time and skills, donated services or products, promotional activities, or short-term sales promotions, like the Amex model. Before you commit, get answers to these questions:

- **What do you want from the partnership?** You should have a passion for the cause you adopt, especially if you want your employees to participate. First, you want to support a cause. After that, you want to define the marketing goals. Nontangible benefits include credibility, enhanced reputation, brand differentiation, customer loyalty, and employee pride or retention. Tangibles might be increased sales and specific publicity, like walkathons, festivals, posters, Web sites, newsletters, or local press coverage.

- **What are the program objectives?** As a marketer, you want to publicize visible results, like pointing to the child-care center you helped build, or providing six months of meals to the homeless. Talk frankly to your nonprofit partners about what you want to see in the way of a return.

- **How will the program be evaluated?** You don't need to get carried away, but you do need to measure results. You might designate an employee who cares to be in charge of tracking sales or promotions.

Mounting a Direct Mail Campaign

For small businesses, where sales leads and customer contact information so often fall through the cracks, being able to market pinpointed prospects with postcards, flyers, catalogs, or personalized notes is a terrific opportunity.

A well-crafted, road-tested direct mail package represents a cost-effective sales cycle all on its own, including ad message, presentation, offer sweetener, call to action, and, ultimately, deal closer. If you take the time to do it right, direct marketing can generate gratifying and measurable results.

Part Three:
Makes and
Models: How to
Stand Out from
the Crowd

Microsoft Small Business Kit

The latest electronic tools are driving interest in commercial mail marketing. One consumer's throwaway is another prospect's prize, which puts value in the eye of your beholder. So the key to getting results from direct mail is a precisely targeted mailing list. Many experts say that 40 percent of direct mail's success will depend on the list. If you're a realtor, for example, think about a postcard campaign offering your services—and perhaps an invitation to a seminar about retirement communities—to home-owning parents whose youngest has just headed off to college. Or consider the effect of an insurance agency that specializes in business and property policies mailing personalized letters to companies that have just moved into new digs. That's the potential of electronic tools.

When hard-copy mailing lists are transformed into electronic databases, you can manipulate and mine the list for byte-sized nuggets. Whether it's an in-house list or one you rent from a trade group, a professional organization, or a list broker, a database lets you troll for customers as broadly or as narrowly as your prospect's profile. You can segment by age or income; by hobby or geography; by education, occupation, or gender; and by a dizzying array of special qualifiers, like car models or types of professional services or how many movies a consumer sees each month. Database marketing married to direct mail gives you tangible reach and power, not to mention lower costs. Precisely targeting consumers who are likely to want your wares hardly guarantees buyers, of course. Your list gives you higher odds. But parents who receive that realtor's postcard, for instance, might have no desire to move.

Perhaps the best part of direct mail is how quickly you discover whether it's working. Results are measurable and definite, with information you can act on. You learn exactly what hooks your

What Direct Mail Can Do

When mounting a direct mail (DM) effort, figure out what you want the campaign or mailing to accomplish. Focus your messaging and design on producing that result. A versatile and affordable marketing tool, DM can:

- Generate sales
- Bring in foot traffic
- Build recognition or brand awareness
- Acquire new customers or referrals
- Upgrade customer service
- Respond to competitors
- Support other marketing, such as newspaper or radio ads
- Reward top-tier customers
- Expand your market to a wider audience
- Test the appeal of new products or services
- Deliver news, say, of a sale or branch opening
- Act as a warm-up for later cold calls
- Stimulate higher purchases from existing customers

Chapter Nine: Crafting Your Message

Part Three:
Makes and
Models: How to
Stand Out from
the Crowd

customer—or doesn't. And direct mail is flexible. You can recalibrate or refine at any time. When you do invest in a winning list, you can rely on it to keep attracting business—as long as you keep that list updated, of course.

Here are the steps to take that will reel in results:

- **Define your objectives.**   Too many entrepreneurs dive into direct mail without a clear-cut strategy. Before drafting copy or evaluating lists, make sure you know what the mailer is expected to do. A recent survey from the U.S. Postal Service found that the top three reasons mailers increased the frequency of direct mailers were company growth or expansion (56 percent), change of strategy (55 percent), and introduction of a new product (39 percent).

- **Make sure you're clear about what spells success.**   Then make sure you don't muddy your chances by setting several goals at once.

- **Test your ROI.**   Industry averages for direct mail response rates are not particularly meaningful. Everything depends on your product and your price point. Conventional wisdom used to say that a 1 percent response rate was great. But that's not very sophisticated. What if, for instance, you get a 10 percent response, but you only break even at 20 percent? Or what if you sell $45,000 machines? One customer response in six months might be all you need to recoup your return on a direct mail investment. Make sure you've set goals that make sense for your business. You can't judge a direct mail campaign by how many sales you generate. Think about it. Ten purchases from a 1,000-piece mailing might add up to a 1 percent response, but what's your net cost? If you shell out $10,000 for the mailing, 10 orders cost you $1,000 each. Did you turn a profit? If not, time for Plan B. Recalculate your costs and package.

- **Figure out how much you must earn from a direct mail effort, not the number of sales.**   Test your assumptions with a smaller mailing to a select group of your overall list (sometimes called an *nth mailing*, because it goes to every *nth* fraction on the list). That will give you enough feedback to edit or refine the package and budget before committing.

Creating a Direct Mail Piece

Despite these positives, with direct mail marketing, you have only a moment to pique a customer's interest. To capture your prospect's attention, the design and wording of the mailer and package you produce is key.

Part Three:
Makes and
Models: How to
Stand Out from
the Crowd

Microsoft Small Business Kit

For instance, a financial planner or healthcare practice trying to build clientele must send mailers that convey trustworthiness.

Looks count. Using the right colors, typeface, and professional look and feel goes a long way toward attracting your target customer. There are four steps to creating your own distinctive direct mail piece:

- **Select your publication format.**   In Microsoft Office Publisher 2003, the New Publication task pane makes it easy to get started. Publication templates are organized into Publications For Print, Web Sites And E-mail, Design Sets, and Blank Publications. Under Publications For Print, you'll find a broad array of publication types appropriate for direct mail pieces, including postcards, catalogs, coupons, brochures, newsletters, gift certificates, and more.

- **Emphasize your brand.**   Although each piece should have its own look and message, you still need to make sure it's consistent with your company's other marketing materials and overall branding. Pay attention to color palette, fonts, design elements, and messaging tone. Using Publisher 2003, you might choose to start with one of the Master Sets' 45 customizable designs that carry the same consistent look across various types of marketing materials. Quickly apply a new color scheme or font scheme to get just the right look. You can also choose from among helpful templates that can be downloaded for free from the Office Online Template gallery into Publisher. These online templates include newsletters, ads, flyers, gift certificates, coupons and more. (Visit the Office Template gallery at: *http:// office.microsoft.com/templates.*)Polish the piece.

  Don't overlook the finishing touches and details. Publisher 2003 offers advanced layout features that quickly add gloss and interest. The improved Design Checker task pane identifies potential printing problems long before costly rework might be required.

- **Prepare for mailing.**   You can either print and send the piece yourself or package it to send to a printer and/or bulk mailing house. Use the File, Pack And Go, Take To A Commercial Printing Service feature in Publisher 2003 to bundle all your publications. If you need to find a local or an online printer familiar with Publisher files, search *mspublisher.saltmine.com/printersearch.aspx.*

Chapter Nine: Crafting Your Message

Part Three:
Makes and
Models: How to
Stand Out from
the Crowd

Getting Results from E-Mail Marketing

Got $100? That may be all you need to send 1,000 highly personalized e-mail messages to specially selected customers. And that's both the good news and the bad. When done right, e-mail marketing is not only breathtakingly affordable but also extremely effective. Depending on your metrics and your targets (whether new, existing, or best customers), e-mail marketing can yield response rates that range from a satisfying 5 percent to a heady 50 percent or more.

On the other hand, the cheap cost of entry has resulted in a sea of commercial e-mail messages. E-mail marketing in the U.S. is predicted to triple over the next few years, from $2 billion in 2003 to a whopping $6 billion in 2008, according to a recent report from JupiterResearch, an online researcher. The key market drivers are dramatic cost reductions in producing e-mail marketing, the growth of sponsored and acquisition campaigns, and the increasing challenges of spam— that is, the tide of unsolicited bulk mail messages. In 2003, for example, the average U.S. online consumer received 3,920 unwanted commercial e-mail messages. By 2008, that number is expected to reach a shocking 6,395. What's more, the majority of those messages, says the report, were from legitimate marketers who have previously done business with the recipients. That sort of message is not even defined as spam, which is a message sent by a marketer that has never before done business with a recipient.

How to Measure Success

E-mail marketing results can be measured in several ways, including:

- The number of opened messages

- The number of people who click on the link you embed in your message in order to visit a Web site, called "clickthroughs," or some other call to action

- The number of conversions or completed transactions or purchases

This tide of bulk e-mail has obviously made consumers wary and offended. As a result, Congress recently passed the "Controlling the Assault of Non-Solicited Pornography and Marketing Act of 2003," known as the CAN-SPAM Act of 2003. Many state and federal legislative initiatives are also pending. If you are considering unsolicited bulk e-mail marketing, make sure you're up-to-date on current laws, including those of the state in which you base your business.

Part Three:
Makes and
Models: How to
Stand Out from
the Crowd

Microsoft Small Business Kit

Gaining Permission

Concern about consumer resistance to e-mail marketing has led marketers to begin to shift gears in the ways they harness it. Increasingly, e-mail marketing is being used to reward or retain existing customers, rather than as a tool for customer acquisition. The reason is simple: Customers are more likely to accept offers or news from familiar marketers. Strange or unknown messages are ignored.

The smarter way to leverage e-mail marketing nowadays is to gain the recipient's permission before sending a message—that is, *opt-in* e-mail marketing. Before mounting an e-mail campaign, you want the customer to express some interest in receiving your messages. That can be done by having customers register online or via surface mail, by replying to your e-mail query, or by some prior contact, say, leaving a business card at your trade show booth.

With that in mind, here's how to launch an e-mail campaign:

- **Define your goals.**   No marketing can succeed with an unlimited or moving horizon. You must set goals that will define your success. When it comes to e-mail marketing, campaigns tend to get better results when there's a clear call to action, perhaps with the added urgency of a time-sensitive window. At the outset, carefully define what you want from the campaign. Then focus on the messaging and distribution that will achieve it. Typically, e-mail marketing can:

  - Announce special deals, sales, or discounts

  - Invite customers to events, VIP parties, or conferences

  - Offer news or information that drives performance or decisions

- **Connect with customers**.   Different designs and messages will yield different results. The idea is to customize batches of messages to emphasize benefits that speak to specific customer needs. The latest electronic tools make it much easier to segment customers and sales leads according to key characteristics. You can quickly group customers into byte-size market chunks of similar demographics, purchasing histories, or other qualifiers by using the new Business Contact Manager (BCM) for Microsoft Outlook 2003, available in the Small Business Edition. You'll find seven preformatted Account reports, such as Accounts By Rating or Neglected Accounts. Or you can use Modify

Chapter Nine: **Crafting Your Message**

Part Three:
**Makes and
Models: How to
Stand Out from
the Crowd**

Report to create customized reports with criteria you choose and then use Save As to store those tailor-made reports for further analysis in Excel.

Should you need additional, targeted e-mail addresses for your campaign, you can also use the fee-based Sales Leads service from Microsoft Small Business (at *www.microsoft.com/smallbusiness/products/online/cl/details.mspx*), which gives you access to comprehensive and up-to-date databases of more than 14 million businesses and more than 250 million consumers.

- **Manage the list.**   If you're developing your own campaign, first create your mailing list. Then select the style of your e-mail publication. You can avoid hassles by relying on the fee-based List Builder service from Microsoft Small Business Services (at *www.microsoft.com/smallbusiness/products/online/lb/details.mspx*), which creates and sends out your e-mail campaign and then automatically tracks both open and click-through rates for you. (See the section "Paid Search Engine Marketing," later in this chapter, to learn about tracking search engine submissions.) Don't forget to keep updating customer information. When a new customer contacts you, create an entry for the account in Microsoft Business Contact Manager. BCM enables you to consolidate all interactions with a given customer in the Business Contact History section, including e-mail messages, tasks, appointments, notes, and documents. If you send out your e-mail campaign from Outlook, this activity will be captured automatically in each recipient's Business Contact History.

- **Personalize, personalize, personalize.**   Recipients more readily sign up for e-mail marketing when offered a prize, entry in a sweepstakes, or the like. They're also more inclined to register and input personal data when they're already customers of the sponsoring company. So the more you reward customers for giving you access to personal information and the more familiar they are with your products or brand, the better your responses tend to be. To get customer buy-in, try using name-personalization messages. Make sure you test several subject lines, message copy, and landing pages before the launch.

That $100 mentioned above covers only the most basic campaigns, of course. If you want to use fancy attention-grabbers like video or animation or audio, your costs will rise. But you can still do quite a lot with straightforward text and links to a Web site or to special landing pages that offer premium sales or discounts only available to customers who receive your e-mailed marketing.

Part Three:
Makes and
Models: How to
Stand Out from
the Crowd

Microsoft Small Business Kit

- **Dos and don'ts.** Pay close attention to the details when communicating with your customers:

  - Do make messages short and compelling.

  - Don't include detailed product descriptions or windy stories about the company's history.

  - Do use lots of short titles and bulleted points or highlights so that customers can take in information at a glance. You might want to set up a summary at the top and jump-link to information that follows so that users can quickly access what interests them.

  - Do, always, set up a way for customers to easily update their information or unsubscribe.

  - Do check messages from time to time to make sure that the information is still timely and up-to-date. (Need we mention proofreading?)

  - Don't ever spam—not anyone, for any reason.

  - Do match your format and message to your customers. Try to include some point of difference or attitude or special service that makes you stand out.

Leveraging Online Advertising

Only a few years ago, online ads were dismissed as a waste of time and money. But in 2004, online ad revenue for the first quarter had rebounded to a record $2.3 billion, according to the Interactive Advertising Bureau (at *www.iab.net*).

Always Support Your Campaign

Don't simply send out messages and sit back. Be prepared for specific follow-ups. These might include:

- Sending automated bounceback replies

- Integrating the e-mail campaign with other channels

- Making phone sales calls

- Sending out direct mail that elaborates on the offer

The last thing you want is to generate customer interest and then be unprepared to act on it.

The previous peak of $1.7 billion had been way back in the exuberant days of 2001. Clearly, the industry is growing again and producing results. This change is being fueled by several factors, but the main cause is that the Internet medium has become accountable to marketers. That was not the case during the pioneering days of dot-coms and Web mania. Today, cost-effective electronic Web analytic tools and software can track results in real time. That means you find out, instantly, whether your ad is drawing visits, clickthroughs, customer queries, personal registration, or sales—whatever it is that you're targeting.

Chapter Nine: Crafting Your Message

Part Three:
Makes and
Models: How to
Stand Out from
the Crowd

In addition, better delivery and new technology are transforming the online ad experience. The rise of broadband across the country has accelerated Web usage and deepened its credibility among users and businesses. Rich media and faster, convenient access have also boosted growth. Made up of compressed data—audio and/or video—that is broadcast over the Internet, streaming media is stored on a server and continuously transmitted to the user. Streaming media is served live, in a steady stream of content, so you don't need to wait for access until it's totally downloaded. This significantly changes and enriches the options. You can now create ads that deliver content to your users, as opposed to making them jump from the page they were viewing every time they click on an ad.

Overall, an online ad can deliver a double whammy for marketers. The ad heightens brand recognition whenever users see it and, as an interactive tool, the ad also invites users to click on it for offers or calls to action. Each online ad then blurs the line between branding and direct-response marketing. Leveraged properly, it's got unbeatable power.

Paid Search Engine Marketing

Still evolving, paidsearch marketing is currently the most popular way to advertise online. As you probably know from your own reactions, people looking for something online tend to first visit one of the big search engines, like MSN (*search.msn.com/*) or Google. So marketing based on the power of online searches is increasingly targeted, cost-effective, and sophisticated.

The idea is that searches initiated by a consumer indicate a strong interest or intention, so having your product or Web site pop up at the top of response listings can lead to increased sales. You entice these searching potential customers and arrange for your site to show up at the top of search lists by figuring out which keywords your customers most frequently use to search for the products or services you market. You then submit those chosen keywords to search engines, whether smaller, targeted engines for niche audiences or large, general consumer engines like MSN, and then pay varying amounts to influence where on the lists your site appears in the results.

The more you bid per keyword, the higher on the results page the engine guarantees to place your site. Typically, engines bill on what's called a pay-per-click, or PPC, basis. That means you're charged only if and when a customer clicks on your link. Pricing will depend on the popularity of the keywords and categories. For instance, if you pay for the keyword "cashmere" because you sell cashmere sweaters, imagine how many other marketers

Part Three:
Makes and
Models: How to
Stand Out from
the Crowd

Microsoft Small Business Kit

will be bidding for the same keyword. Plus, you'd be bidding against every marketer of scarves and gloves, not simply companies that sell sweaters.

So the challenge is to choose and pay for only the keywords that your targeted customers will use and that make your company stand out. The more specific and targeted you can be, the better. When users input those keywords, your site comes up prominently displayed in the results page. The highest results go to the highest keyword bidder. When results conveniently top the search list, users are more likely to click.

Keyword power

Success in search engine marketing requires finding the right keywords, which then engage the user as he or she is ready to make a purchasing decision—for example, *Victorian-style brownstone* rather than *new home*.

The name of this game is the quality and kind of visitors you draw, not the volume of traffic. If you sell ski trips to Vermont slopes, and your keywords are *ski* or *ski package*, you'll attract hundreds of disappointed vacationers who were looking for Aspen or the Alps. You're trying to improve the odds of how your site is "seen" or scanned by the engines so that the audience you want can find you. Successful paidsearch ads require research, money, and the patience to plow through trials and errors. You can't afford hit-or-miss keywords. Your site must show up on most of the top 20 search engines–preferably placed high in the listings.

Spend some time and effort on learning how people look for you online. To get the phrases that work, you need to get inside the minds of your customers and learn how they see your business. Here are some tips to identify effective search and keyword phrases:

- Brainstorm with senior staff and salespeople to come up with words and phrases that are the DNA of your business.

- Visit competitor sites to get ideas–but don't use their exact phrases. Right-click on their pages, and select View Source to see keywords.

- Ask customers what words they use to talk about your products.

- Review Web logs and blogs to find phrases and search engines that delivered visitors who registered and/or purchased your products.

- Rely on services like Wordtracker (*www.wordtracker.com/*) to monitor popular phrases.

Chapter Nine: **Crafting Your Message**

Part Three:
Makes and
Models: How to
Stand Out from
the Crowd

■ Audition the small engines. Try testing your keywords and systems with second-tier, smaller engines first. When you know what works, you can draw on the reach of MSN and other large engines. It'll save you time and money.

This is an ongoing process. To keep directing the right traffic, you must continually update and refine keywords. And don't give up too soon. Make sure your expectations are realistic. Search engines can take up to eight weeks before listing your site. You'll need to fine-tune the right package of keywords, engines, and PPC or paid searches. Stay with it, and you'll be rewarded.

The power of paid search for small businesses is clearly growing. One recent study of small business advertisers found that they currently allocate 23 percent of their total ad budget to pay-per-click (PPC), with more than half planning increases in the subsequent year, according to market researchers The Kelsey Group and ConStat.

Optimize Your Site

For PPC ads to pull, engines must scan your site and find keywords you've bid on. Your listing is then included in the results page. But many businesses ignore online search needs. "The biggest mistakes are having all graphics or all the text as graphics," says Rosemary Brisco of ToTheWeb, a San Mateo Web marketer. "All Flash sites or sites with a Flash splash page means search engines don't go inside to scan for results." You don't have to start from scratch to improve. A refreshed home page or a quick text edit can do the trick.

You can also purchase affordable services for help. To manage and analyze your site, try Microsoft FastCounter Pro (*www.microsoft.com/ smallbusiness/products/online/fs/details.mspx*). To optimize your site for engine submission, check Microsoft Submit It! (*www. microsoft.com/ smallbusiness/products/online/si/details.mspx*).

More Online Options

Paid search marketing is not your only effective online advertising choice. Contrary to rumor, for instance, banner ads are alive and kicking. Yes, the banner ad was a near-death experience in the days of disintegrating click-through rates. (Translation: everyone simply ignored them.) But current measuring tools are also making banners effective, especially on niche sites, for narrow verticals or as small, call-to-action buttons. And there are always creative, new applications, depending on your customer research. A comprehensive online ad campaign blends search engine optimization, paid-search term listings, online ads, and integration with offline efforts.

Improvements in online ad efficiencies keep surfacing. Don't put a plan in place and then just walk away. Keep rejiggering, either by conducting your own research or by tapping the expertise of marketing consultants. Here are some other online ad options that are beginning to attract marketers:

Part Three:
Makes and
Models: How to
Stand Out from
the Crowd

Microsoft Small Business Kit

■ **Contextual search.** Companies are still experimenting with this tactic of marrying paid listings to relevant content. Contextual search moves the sponsored link off the results page and onto sites themselves. Instead of paying for placement on a results list, you pay engines to place your listing on pages of content related to your products. This online marketing will target customers at the very moment they're interested in learning about wares and services you market. For example, if a user is checking weather in Miami Beach, he or she might also see your listing for Miami hotels or car rentals. You might want to check in with Web marketing consultants before making decisions about contextual search marketing. Industry Brains, for example, is a young, business-to-business online marketer based in New York. Using Rich Site Summary (RSS) technology, an XML format that can aggregate Web content, Industry Brains syndicates your paid listing onto specifically targeted sites, mostly media companies. Costs or pay-per-click (PPC) average about $2, and can run a whopping $12 or so if you're targeting a very narrow group—say, government IT. That's a whole lot more than the 25-cent to 50-cent PPC of paid search. But so far, it looks as if advertisers can count on higher conversion rates with contextual search than with paidsearch results programs.

■ **Geographic targeting.** Other developing online technology is allowing marketers to find customers by region and locale. At CoolSavings, for example, a consumer marketer based in Chicago that provides services for e-mailed offers, coupons, and lead generation, chief executive Matt Moog says, "We have been geographically targeting down to the exact Zip Code for years." CoolSavings, according to Moog, spends about $10 million a year on online advertising for its clients, many of which are small businesses.

Once you've captured customer interest from a call to action or visit, don't lose it. If you have collected a potential customer's name and personal data—and if you have permission to contact him or her directly—you can measure responses and use online marketing as a way of prospecting for customers.

Generating Sales Leads

It's the job of marketing, of course, to evoke the interest that will transform cold clients into warm prospects. It's the sales team's responsibility to put the fire under those warm prospects that will nail the deal.

Chapter Nine: *Crafting Your Message*

Part Three:
Makes and
Models: How to
Stand Out from
the Crowd

As a result, more often than not, marketing managers and sales directors don't get along. When revenues drop or targets fall short, each gets busy blaming the other. Typically, tempers really flare over who drops the ball on sales leads. Meantime, the cost of generating leads gets more and more expensive. Here's how to resolve the argument and get marketing and sales people to speak each other's language.

What's a Lead?

When things go awry, marketing shows the impressive number of customer phone calls, e-mail queries, click-throughs, or Web impressions that were forwarded to sales and ignored. Salespeople then shake their heads about the effort they waste following up on marketing's trivial and tenuous queries. "All we get are window shoppers," say resentful sales directors. The reason neither side wins is because both are right.

The pipeline that fuels a sale typically begins with a query. It's a process that unfolds over time. As an example, check out the results of some sales follow-up surveys of more than 3,500 inquirers to blue chip advertisers conducted by Warne, a Toronto marketing company. Of some 3,500 queries, 19 percent purchased within six months (whether from the advertiser or from a competitor), and 29 percent purchased within a year. By 16 months, 43 percent had purchased, and by 25 months, 57 percent had made purchases.

Setting Goals for Search Marketing

A judicious combination of search marketing tactics can build business in a number of ways. You can:

- Boost brand profile or gain industry exposure
- Acquire new customers
- Increase traffic
- Generate leads for follow-up calls
- Advertise offers or sales
- Attract strategic partners
- Generate publicity
- Market offline products or events
- Increase or launch online sales

Translation: Two in 10 customers wanted to buy "now." Four others wanted to buy "later." There were a total of six prospects for every 10 queries—or 60 percent interest.

The kicker? The surveys found that sales reps followed up on less than 17 percent of all inquiries. Clearly, inquiries are key to sales. Just as clearly, most businesses are wasting marketing dollars by weak follow-up.

Part Three:
Makes and
Models: How to
Stand Out from
the Crowd

Microsoft Small Business Kit

That's because all queries look alike at the outset. You can't tell which will fade and which will turn into prospects. Because good follow-up requires at least three or four subsequent contacts, small businesses cannot afford to respond to every request for information or pricing with such attention. So the good gets tossed out with the bad. The solution is to set up a cost-efficient system that triggers appropriate responses at various points along the timeline. There are many affordable options. You just need to think ahead.

Responding to Customer Queries

Responses to customer and sales queries depend on your industry and sales cycle. Plan in advance what query triggers which response, such as:

- An automated e-mail program with preselected messages that respond to keywords in an electronic query

- A mailed media kit or annual report in response to phone call inquiries

- A series of increasingly detailed brochures to satisfy intensifying query interest—until you reach the moment for face-to-face sales

- Qualified invitations to events or Webcasts

- White papers given to anyone who stops by a trade show booth

- Free samples given to anyone who visits a store or showroom

Also decide whether marketing or sales will manage each response—and at which point sales takes over.

The Marketing and Sales Dialog

To get marketing and sales to cooperate, make sure each side understands the costs that count. Marketing must figure out how many customer contacts are needed, on average, to lead to a sale–and how much each one costs. The total number of clickthroughs or queries isn't particularly meaningful.

Sales must calculate how many deals are needed to hit company revenue targets or profitability. Setting a sales goal of a number of deals per month or quarter doesn't seriously matter. Each side must be clear about what's needed to drive inquiries into sales.

Here are nine practical ideas to find qualified leads:

- **Buy qualified leads.**   Scrubbed, reliable prospect lists can be rented from various sources, including trade groups, professional organizations, alumni associations, or list brokers, like Microsoft List Builder (*www.bcentral.com/products/lb/default.asp*). Such lists let you tailor messages to different customer segments. For instance, you can select highly qualified leads to receive discounted offers or rejigger your messages to appeal to different age groups.

Chapter Nine: Crafting Your Message

Part Three:
Makes and
Models: How to
Stand Out from
the Crowd

■ **Become the authority.**   Commission a survey or poll that offers pro-prietary market intelligence, and then publicize the results through the media or a Web site. The idea is to build recognition and demand. Turn the survey into an annual event, and you become an ongoing industry expert.

■ **Find a partner.**   Business professionals can work together to influence their contacts to open doors for each other.

■ **Create an industry profile.**   Develop expertise or an informative speech that's in demand for your industry. With a professionally pro-duced media kit and a few mailings, you can get on the lecture or sem-inar circuit. You'll also then be able to leverage media contacts to be quoted in news articles or broadcast features.

See the sections "Raising Your Media Profile" and "Hiring a PR Agency," earlier in this chapter, for more on creating media kits.

■ **Buy ads in electronic newsletters.**   Putting an ad in an industry or a professional e-mailed newsletter can direct a prospect right to your Web site, and that way you can also track the response.

■ **Read the newspaper.**   Your local daily paper is always filled with leads. A human resources consultancy, for example, can note mergers or expansions in the news.

■ **Check your database.**   Inactive customers who haven't bought any-thing for a while or infrequent buyers are ripe for sales pitches.

■ **Find a specialized show.**   Major trade shows tend to be expensive and might also overshadow your small business. Instead, you might find leads at smaller and more affordable regional or vertical shows—and the leads are likely to be better qualified, too.

■ **Join a networking organization.**   The idea is to share leads with mem-ber businesses that don't directly compete with yours. Annual dues vary, from a few hundred to several thousand dollars. Just make sure the group has a track record and that you can live with its rules about sharing contact information—some groups have rather onerous restrictions.

Successful Cold Calling

Last, there's the time-honored way of finding sales leads. You ring up total strangers to chat about your business. Cold calling is very hard to do. Sim-ply picking up the phone takes courage. But turning cold calls into actual sales calls—that's the true trick. It's got to rank first on the list of Top 10

Part Three:
Makes and
Models: How to
Stand Out from
the Crowd

Microsoft Small Business Kit

Things New Business Owners Find Terrifying. Prospects might react with hostility or courtesy, but that won't change the odds. You face a firestorm of rejection for every spark of interest you ignite. Even seasoned salespeople shudder at the thought of cold calling. But if you can't take rejection, you shouldn't get into business. Certainly, it's not a tactic for everyone or every kind of business. When it's done right, however, with smart research, scripts, presentation, and delivery, cold calls do land business.

Here are expert tips to get cold calls to yield some hot results:

- **Target your buyers.**   The more you can define your markets, the greater your chances of differentiating your business and gaining access to decision makers. Entrepreneurs often skip the up-front work of narrowly identifying markets appropriate for their services. As a result, sales efforts are all over the map. Until you know the companies or consumer markets that are ripe to buy your wares, don't pick up the phone.

Targeting Customer Prospects

Every owner should have a plan that explains:

- What you sell
- Who will buy it
- How you will find those buyers

See Chapter 2, "Developing a Business Plan," and Chapter 8, "Branding Basics," for more about defining your target markets.

- **Invest in research.**   Train your sales team to suggest solutions to client problems rather than to simply present demonstrations or describe the products. You need to research the company and know something of its business before you go cold calling.

See the section "Selling Benefits, Not Features," earlier in this chapter, for more about attracting customers.

- **Craft a script—and then use it.**   You can't wing it. Despite the fact that you're passionate about your business, communicating the benefits of your product takes distinct skills. With limited time on the phone, a written script lets you focus on points you want to make. You must provide, in a sentence or two, a description of your services and compelling reasons why the prospect should buy your product. You can then move on to secondary benefits or news. "The script shouldn't be

Chapter Nine: **Crafting Your Message**

Part Three:
**Makes and
Models: How to
Stand Out from
the Crowd**

word for word," says New York sales trainer Wendy Weiss, author of *Cold Calling for Women: Opening Doors and Closing Sales* (D. F. D. Publications, 2000). "It's a way to prepare yourself for the conversation. You decide ahead of time how you want to present yourself, what reaction you want to get, how to ask for what you want." Be ready to counter possible objections with specific explanations, statistics, or case studies. If an objection arises that you hadn't anticipated, react as best you can. Then write it down and prepare a detailed response before the next call.

- **Warm up every cold call.** It helps if you don't start on thin ice. Before calling, send the prospect a smart, useful, or introductory notice, such as a short, personal letter saying something like, "I'd like to introduce myself. I've developed a new product and I specialize in your industry. I'll be calling." Wait a few days—not too long—after they've gotten the letter, and then call. You can also precede the call with a direct mail or an e-mail campaign. Then when you call, you can say, "Hi. I'm following up on the brochure we sent to you. Did you receive it?" White papers or special reports are useful for consulting services. Introductory discounts might stand out for suppliers or retailers. Make sure you enclose a note describing your services and that you'll be calling in a few days to gauge interest. Then promptly follow up.

- **Be nice to gatekeepers.** A screener's job is to guard the inner sanctum. Becoming irritated, frustrated, or rude with such assistants will only hurt your business. Think through strategies to get gatekeepers to open doors. Create a friendly mood. Learn screeners' names and preferences. By making the gatekeeper an ally, you'll win access more easily.

- **Practice, practice, practice.** Like most skills, the more cold calling you do, the better you'll get. Rehearse your pitch out loud with friends or associates. Some experts suggest standing during calls to give your voice authority and energy. Everyone always says "smile while you talk," because that will also be conveyed in your voice. Some trainers advise facing a mirror when you call so that you can see when your energy or body language flags, and then adjust. All such strategies attempt to substitute for the usual visual clues of conversation, which some studies pinpoint as 80 percent of how people communicate. Whatever helps you infuse warmth and confidence in the calls, try it. You might also divide all your leads into A, B, and C lists. Practice on the Cs before calling the As.

Part Three:
Makes and
Models: How to
Stand Out from
the Crowd

Microsoft Small Business Kit

■ **Then customize.** Don't become too attached to any particular script or language. Once you have a framework, you must be able to fine-tune it to fit individual prospects. Every customer has specialized needs and preferences. Edit your calling script to hit nerves for each new audience. Make sure you're up-to-speed about your community and industry or market news. You want to sound plugged-in and connected whenever you call prospects.

In the end, all that entrepreneurial passion mentioned at the beginning of this chapter isn't enough to market your company. You do need thoughtful strategies and tactics. But the best marketing messages will harness both: a passion for what you do plus smart marketing.

For example, family owned and operated Showalter Flying Service, based at Orlando Executive Airport, is, says owner Kim Showalter succinctly, "a gas station for airplanes." Founded in 1945, the company services Fortune 500 jets as well as private planes. "Every time a customer arrives," says Kim, "we have an opportunity to make it a positive, memorable experience." Marketing at Showalter is done with the same opportunistic energy.

When Kim's daughter, Jenny, attended a meeting of company dispatchers, who are the prime decision makers about where corporate jets refuel, she met the Lands' End dispatcher. He noticed a T-shirt she wore that sported the Showalter logo. Jenny quickly showed off the Lands' End label. After that, the business relationship flourished. Soon enough, Bob Showalter, Jenny's dad, was showing off his shirt, logo, and smarts on the cover of the Lands' End corporate catalog—which went out to more than a million corporate buyers.

Slick marketing? Not for a moment. Says Kim Showalter: "If you work hard and believe in the liberal use of the *f* word—*fun*—then luck will follow."

For More Information

In addition to the resources mentioned in this chapter, you will find links and information on the companion CD. Some books and Web sites particularly useful as you market and advertise your new business include:

Books

■ Seth Godin, *Purple Cow: Transform Your Business by Being Remarkable* (Portfolio, 2003) (also consider Seth Godin's many other books)

- Gerald Zaltman, *How Customers Think: Essential Insights into the Mind of the Market* (Harvard Business School Press, 2003)

- Bob Burg, *Endless Referrals: Network Your Everyday Contacts Into Sales* (McGraw-Hill, 1998)

Web Sites

- Idea Site for Business—"useful ideas for creative business people": *http://www.ideasiteforbusiness.com/#*

- Templates, design ideas, advice, and more from ideabook.com: *http://ideabook.com/*

- Jay Conrad Levinson, the "father of guerilla marketing" has a Web site full of information: *http://www.gmarketing.com/*

Part Three
Makes and
Models: How to
Stand Out from
the Crowd

Microsoft Small Business Kit

If you put the sign on the back of an elephant and walk it into town, that's pro-motion. If the elephant walks through the mayor's flower bed, that's publicity. And if you get the mayor to laugh about it, that's public relations.

— *Anonymous*

Chapter Ten

Go to Market with Publisher, Make a Pitch with PowerPoint

You can't be shy about sales and marketing. But you can't go over-board, either. Producing glossy ads or brochures isn't the point. The point is to reach your audience and show them what you offer. The volume of sales isn't nearly as important as the profit you make on them. Your marketing goal is to increase profits, not simply sell a lot of stuff.

Chapter Ten: Go to Market with Publisher, Make a Pitch with PowerPoint

Part Three:
Makes and
Models: How to
Stand Out from
the Crowd

What you'll find:

❏ Business communications and Microsoft Publisher 2003

❏ The pitch and the presentation: using Microsoft PowerPoint 2003

Part Three:
Makes and
Models: How to
Stand Out from
the Crowd

Microsoft Small Business Kit

You've got a great idea for marketing your business—a relatively low-cost promotional opportunity that reaches a large segment of your untapped customer base. Now you need to create an advertisement (a brochure, a flyer, or a banner for your Web site) so that customers know where to find you. Reaching prospective customers is essential to staying in business, of course, and being able to design and produce marketing communication materials on your own makes that job easier.

Your business's identity is communicated and represented by individual graphic designs and words: logos, tag lines, letterhead, brochures, business cards, Web sites, posters, direct-mail fliers and postcards, press releases, word of mouth, TV or radio ads, CD promotions, highway billboards—the entire range, in short, of advertising and promotional options. The marketing publication templates included with Microsoft Publisher make it easy to produce high-quality and consistent messaging and design for every communication you create.

Producing materials that identify your business and promote its goods and services is one phase of your business's public face. You might also find yourself with the need or opportunity to talk with prospective clients and customers—or even a community business group—in a fairly formal setting. For these times, you'll benefit from having some background in the assembly and delivery of an interesting presentation—guidelines for condensing your ideas into digestible items in a list and then elaborating so that your points prove persuasive.

In this chapter, we'll first take a look at some of the work you can do to create business communications in Microsoft Publisher. After that, we'll review some tips for making presentations and cover a few of the fundamentals of creating a presentation in Microsoft PowerPoint.

Business Communications and Microsoft Publisher 2003

Almost any small business can effectively build a business identity and design materials to promote itself by making use of Microsoft Publisher. Publisher comes with a group of publication templates that you can turn into professional-looking marketing and communication materials that convey the identity, mission, and message of your business. The templates and wizards that Publisher provides facilitate the production of printed materials, e-mail marketing pieces, and Web pages. Also, by producing similar publications for print and online viewing—reusing text and images, for

Chapter Ten: Go to Market with Publisher, Make a Pitch with PowerPoint

Part Three:
Makes and
Models: How to
Stand Out from
the Crowd

example—you get better mileage from your marketing efforts. You'll reach more people and keep your message consistent.

A personal touch

Publisher also includes personal publication templates such as stationery, cards, and invitations.

The starting point for much of your work in Publisher is the New Publication task pane, shown in Figure 10-1.

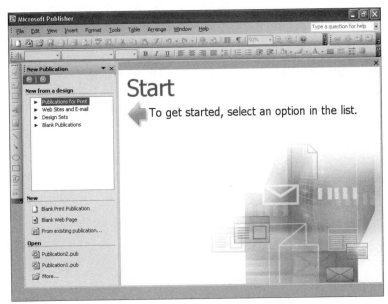

Figure 10-1 This is the window from which you start a new publication in Publisher.

From this task pane, you choose one of four options:

- Publications For Print
- Web Sites And E-Mail
- Design Sets
- Blank Publications

Publications For Print include brochures, calendars, catalogs, letters, and even menus if your business is a restaurant. The Easy Web Site Builder option under Web Sites And E-Mail leads you to a wizard that sets up a Web

Part Three:
Makes and
Models: How to
Stand Out from
the Crowd

Microsoft Small Business Kit

site in which you can display a product catalog, a list of services, and other features, as well as choices for producing publications (such as a newsletter) that you can distribute to customers through e-mail.

Design Sets incorporate color schemes and typographic formats into a coordinated group of publications that include items such as a business card, a catalog, a Web site, a brochure—even a fax cover sheet. Having a common look across a set of publications helps establish the identity of your business. You would choose Design Sets if you were initiating a group of publications and wanted a common look and feel for all the publications. If you're a do-it-yourselfer, the Blank Publications option gives you a choice of what kind of publication to create, and it's up to you to add the text and illustrations and choose which colors to apply and how to arrange and format the text.

In the sections that follow, we'll take a closer look at a few of the types of publications you can create in Publisher: a print advertisement, a Web site, and an e-mail marketing piece.

Online Training and Assistance for Publisher

Publisher provides a lot of assistance as you work with the application itself, but you might also want to develop and sharpen your skills with the program by viewing one or more of the online training courses on Microsoft Office Online. (To view Microsoft Office Online when you are working in Publisher, click Help, Microsoft Office Online.) At the time of writing this book, three of the training courses available were:

- "Get Started Designing Your Own Professional Publications"

- "Create Catalogs or Directories"

- "Prepare a Publication for Commercial Printing"

Office Online also provides assistance with particular tasks you'll need to perform when you're creating a publication in Publisher. Under the heading "Working with Text," for example, you'll find instructions for how to use text boxes—how to connect text boxes, how to align text within them, and how to handle text that overflows a text box. Other topics cover formatting and styles, printing, and working with graphics.

Producing a Print Advertisement

A single advertising format doesn't fit the needs of every business. The publication templates you can use to create a print ad in Publisher include (among others) one that emphasizes a piece of art in the ad, one that uses mostly text, and one that's designed with a coupon that customers return to you. These types of advertisements are generally designed for a single printed page. They're suitable for enclosing in a mass mailing, for submitting to a newspaper or other periodical, for distributing at point-of-purchase displays, and the like.

Chapter Ten: Go to Market with Publisher, Make a Pitch with PowerPoint

Part Three:
Makes and
Models: How to
Stand Out from
the Crowd

Here's an example of the steps you would take to create an advertisement with the works—text, an illustration, and an attention-getting burst.

Create a print publication in Publisher

1. Run Publisher from the Windows Start menu. In the Publisher window, click Publications For Print in the New Publication task pane (shown earlier in Figure 10-1), and then click Advertisements in the list of publications, as shown here:

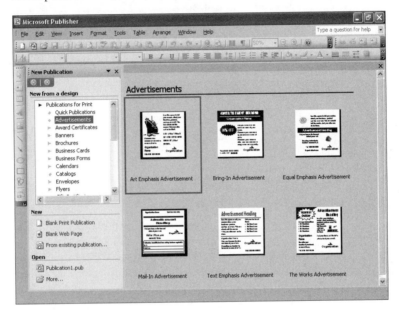

2. Click the publication template named The Works Advertisement. Publisher sets up the publication as you see here:

Part Three:
Makes and
Models: How to
Stand Out from
the Crowd

Microsoft Small Business Kit

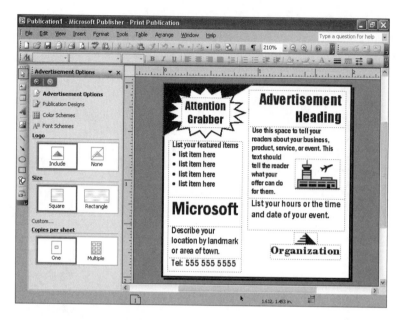

You have a few design decisions to make at this point, which you apply by choosing among the Advertisement Options in the task pane on the left side of the window. You can choose to include a logo or not (the publication is set up to include one; it appears at the bottom right of the publication), whether the shape of the ad should be square or rectangular (it's square by default), and whether to print one (the default setting) or more than one copy of the ad per sheet. If you include a logo, the logo image file should be stored on the computer you're using or on a disk you can insert. You'll see how to insert an image later in this section. The decision to create a square or a rectangular ad depends on factors such as the amount of space you're purchasing for the ad, assuming that the ad will be printed in a periodical of some kind. Often, periodicals sell advertising space in page increments—one-third of a page, one-fourth of a page, and so on. How you're using the ad will influence whether to print one or more copies on a single sheet. If you're enclosing the ad in a mailing, for example, printing more than one on a sheet will likely save printing costs.

In this example, we'll keep the default options and move on to add text and images to the advertisement.

3. Click in the Attention Grabber burst at the top left corner. You can use this section of the ad for notices such as *50% Off*, *Special Offer*, or *2 for 1 Sale*.

Chapter Ten: Go to Market with Publisher, Make a Pitch with PowerPoint

Part Three:
Makes and
Models: How to
Stand Out from
the Crowd

When you click in the Attention Grabber burst, notice that a button (which appears as a small magic wand) appears below the burst. Clicking this button displays a number of choices for how the Attention Grabber can be formatted—as a flag, an oval, or the corner starburst that Publisher provided at the start. Scroll through the options in the task pane to find the format that best fits the needs of the ad you're creating. To select a different format, simply click on your choice in the task pane. Once you've selected the burst format you want, enter the text for the burst. For this example, enter **50% Off Sale**. Publisher adjusts the font size as you type to accommodate the amount of text you add to the burst.

4. Keep building the publication by entering an advertisement heading— *Come to the Grand Opening*, for example, or *Spring Clearance Sale*. In the text box under the 50% Off burst, enter the names (and possibly prices) of products being featured in this ad. Below that text box, enter your business's name, directions to your business's location (or simply your address), and phone number. Again, Publisher adjusts the size of the text and other formatting as you enter information in each section. At this point, your ad might look something like the following. If you're creating the example yourself, use the sample text or information of your own.

Part Three:
Makes and
Models: How to
Stand Out from
the Crowd

Microsoft Small Business Kit

5. Under the advertisement's headline, click the placeholder for the ad's illustration. Publisher displays the Picture toolbar. Click the Insert Picture button (at the far left of the toolbar).

6. In the Insert Picture dialog box, shown here, select an image file you want to include in the ad. (We used the file named Blue Hills.jpg for this example, which is included in the Sample Pictures folder in Windows.) Click the Insert button in the dialog box to place the image in the ad.

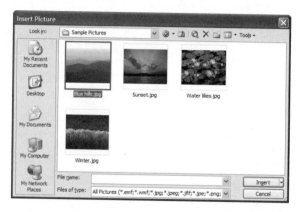

To insert a logo at the bottom right of the ad, you would repeat steps 5 and 6. We'll use the default pyramid in this example.

7. To finish adding the text to this sample advertisement, enter a short description under the headline, and then enter information about store hours or the time of the event. With all the copy entered, the ad looks like this:

Chapter Ten: Go to Market with Publisher, Make a Pitch with PowerPoint

Part Three:
Makes and
Models: How to
Stand Out from
the Crowd

8. Using the Color Schemes and Font Schemes links on the task pane, you can change the appearance of a publication. Font schemes include a major font, which is used mostly for display text (titles and headings), and a minor font, which is applied to the text in the body of the publication. After you apply a new font scheme to a publication, you might need to adjust the size of the font in some of the text boxes. Similarly, each publication is associated with a color scheme.

9. Because this advertisement was built using a template, you don't need to adjust the position of text boxes and images very much. In a publication you create yourself, you move an element by selecting it and then dragging it to a new position. If you need finer control in positioning, you can use commands on the Arrange menu, such as Align Or Distribute, Nudge, or Snap. You can arrange the elements of a publication so that their left or right sides are aligned or distribute shapes so that the vertical or horizontal space between them is equal. The Nudge command moves an object in fine increments of space, and the Snap command positions an object so that it's aligned to the ruler displayed in the Publisher window or to layout guides you define. You could use the Nudge command as shown here to reposition this ad's illustration so that it's closer to the text:

Part Three:
Makes and
Models: How to
Stand Out from
the Crowd

Microsoft Small Business Kit

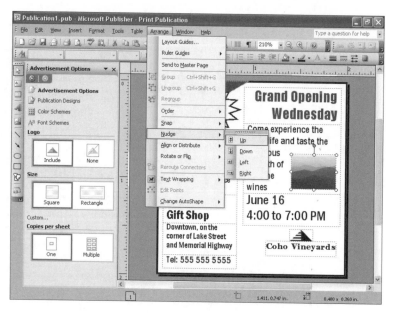

This example used only a few of the tools and features in Publisher. The template provided the basic layout and guidance about the content to display in the ad. You wouldn't need to do much more than complete the template to produce a very workable ad. You could, of course, do much more as you develop the skills for working with Publisher.

Putting Yourself Online: The Easy Web Site Builder

The widespread use of Web sites by businesses to advertise their goods and services, take and process orders, and connect with their customers in other ways has led software makers like Microsoft to develop programs that let people who don't know the ins and outs of creating Web pages to set up sites themselves. Publisher 2003 is one of these programs.

Don't forget your Web host

Remember that you need to have signed up with a Web hosting service (or have your own Web server software set up) to put the Web sites you create in Publisher on the Internet. For information about Web hosting services, see the section "Mastering Your Domains: Two Steps for Building a Presence on the Web," on page 192.

Chapter Ten: Go to Market with Publisher, Make a Pitch with PowerPoint

Part Three:
Makes and
Models: How to
Stand Out from
the Crowd

Printing Your Piece

If you're creating a marketing piece such as an in-store announcement—something you need five or six copies of to post on walls or on product shelves—using a desktop printer hooked up to your computer is probably the best choice. Most desktop printers provide adequate quality for materials like this, and the costs to you are the ink and the paper you use (once you've purchased the printer). For something like a brochure that describes your services—an item you want in regular supply—having a copy shop print the brochure might be the better choice. You'll pay for the services you secure, of course, but a copy shop will turn out lots of copies quickly and can also fold or bind a publication for you. The quality might also be a step up from your desktop printer. When you need a high-quality print job as well as a large number of copies and finish work such as folding, use a commercial printer. Working with a printer requires you to prepare the file you create in Publisher so that it's compatible with the equipment and technology commercial printers use. Consult with the printer you plan to hire (as part of getting a cost estimate) so that you know all the requirements in advance.

The online help for Publisher 2003 includes a checklist you can follow as you design and prepare a publication to be produced by a commercial printer. (See the topic "Checklist: Prepare a Publication for Commercial Printing.") You'll need to consider tasks such as who will scan photographs if any are included in the publication, the type and quality of the paper to use, how to set up the publication for color printing (whether spot colors are enough or whether you need to use process-color printing), and the format in which the printer wants files to be delivered—as a Microsoft Publisher file, a PostScript file, or as a PDF (Portable Document Format) file. If you need to provide a PDF file to the printer, you'll need to have a copy of the program Adobe Acrobat. (For information, see www.adobe.com.)

A good way to transport a Publisher file to an outside printer is to use the Pack And Go Wizard, which you run by choosing Pack And Go, Take To A Commercial Printing Service from the File menu. As you'll see when you run the wizard, the tasks the wizard performs are splitting large publications across multiple disks (if you are sending the publication on a series of floppy disks), embedding the fonts the publication uses, and so on.

Two other tools you should learn about are Graphics Manager and Design Checker. Graphics Manager updates links to images, repairs broken links, and performs other tasks related to the way images are set up in a publication. Design Checker is a troubleshooting tool that will alert you to potential problems in a publication. For example, it will indicate whether an element of a publication is positioned outside the margins of the page. You run both Graphics Manager and Design Checker by clicking the related command on the Tools menu.

You have four choices for the type of Web site you create in Publisher. Within each type, Publisher provides a group of design templates. You can step through the Easy Web Site Builder to create a Web site by defining the goals for your site—goals such as selling products or linking to other sites on the Internet. You can also start by choosing a three-page site (a Home page, a page that describes your business, and a page visitors use to contact you),

Part Three:
Makes and
Models: How to
Stand Out from
the Crowd

Microsoft Small Business Kit

a site that can be used for product sales, or a site designed for businesses that offer professional services.

If you are building a product catalog, you enter the product's name, a description, a stock-keeping unit (SKU) or an item number, additional details (colors, sizes, quantities, makes, models, and the like), and the price. The page that Publisher creates for a product catalog is set up initially for six products. You can add more by copying and pasting or by adding a duplicate page to the site (by choosing Insert, Duplicate Page). Figure 10-2 shows the template you use for the main product catalog page.

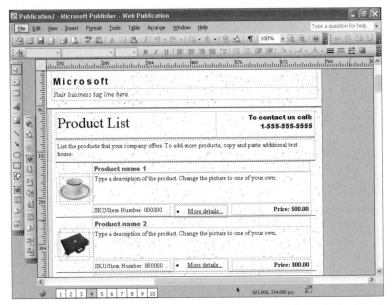

Figure 10-2 One of the Web sites you can build in Publisher is designed to display a product catalog.

The professional services templates (in addition to the standard Home page, About Us page, and Contact Us page), provide a Service List page, with room to describe and illustrate four services (you can add more or delete those you don't need), corresponding detail pages on which you can describe each service in greater depth, and a project list page that serves as a record of your and your company's professional activities.

Chapter Ten: Go to Market with Publisher, Make a Pitch with PowerPoint

Part Three:
Makes and
Models: How to
Stand Out from
the Crowd

Publisher doesn't provide a shopping cart

For businesses involved in selling goods and services over the Web, the product sales option in Publisher doesn't create a Web site that will process orders. It does, however, provide a means to create an online catalog.

Figure 10-3 shows the screen you see after you select Easy Web Site Builder in the New Publication task pane and select a design layout. You can check one or more of the listed Web site goals to identify how you want to use your Web site. Each item you select corresponds to a page or a section of a page on the site.

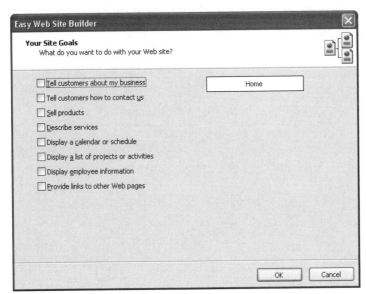

Figure 10-3   One of the ways to start building a Web site in Publisher is to define the goals for your site.

In the steps that follow, we'll walk through an example so that you can see the Easy Web Site Builder's work in more detail.

Use the Easy Web Site Builder

1. Run Publisher from the Windows Start menu. In the Publisher window, click Web Sites And E-Mail in the New Publication task pane, and then click Web Sites. The four Web site options mentioned earlier are listed.

2. Click Easy Web Site Builder, and then click the design template you want to use. For this example, we'll use the Arrows Easy Web Site tem-

Part Three:
Makes and
Models: How to
Stand Out from
the Crowd

Microsoft Small Business Kit

plate. You'll see the screen labeled Your Site Goals, shown earlier in Figure 10-3.

3. As the goals for our sample site, select the following options:

■ Tell Customers About My Business

■ Tell Customers How To Contact Us

■ Describe Services

■ Provide Links To Other Web Pages

Notice that Publisher builds an outline of the site as you select each option, as shown here:

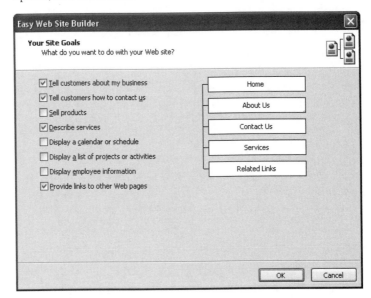

4. Click OK. Publisher builds the basic Web pages, as shown here, and displays a set of Web Site options in the task pane:

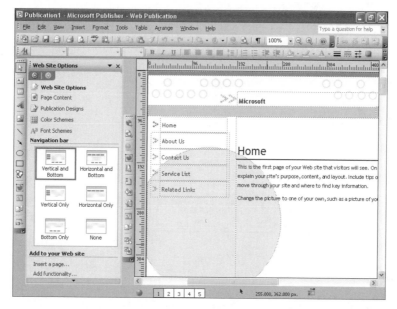

After the wizard builds the basic structure for the site based on the goals you select, you begin to add information such as the purpose of the site, a description of your business, a logo or other image, a business tag line, and so on. The templates for page layout and design that you choose from (Arrows, as well as designs with names such as Orbits, Perforation, Summer, Studio, and Spotlight) are starting points. You can change the page layout, design, color scheme, and fonts.

Near the bottom of the task pane is a link named Insert A Page. This link and the Add Functionality link offer a way to add pages with specific functions to your site. If you want your site to provide other features—a calendar or schedule, for example, or a list of products—you can return to the screen shown in Figure 10-3 by clicking Add Functionality. When you click Insert A Page, here's the dialog box you see:

Part Three:
Makes and
Models: How to
Stand Out from
the Crowd

Microsoft Small Business Kit

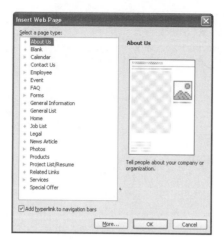

Form and content

Of special interest for some businesses are the forms you can add to your Web site—an order form, a response form, or a sign-up form. These forms can be used as the basis for an online customer survey, for example, or to take orders or register event participants. Remember, however, that these forms aren't fully functional online. The forms don't include a Submit or Check Out button that leads directly to a sale. You need to work with your Internet service provider (ISP), for example, to save the information collected on these forms, ask visitors to your site to print and mail the forms to you, or have the forms sent to you in e-mail. When you're working in Publisher, however, take a look at the level of detail these forms capture and how much of the design is already executed for you. For a business just getting under way, these forms provide a lot of value.

5. On the Home page, add your company name (where the *Microsoft* label appears), a description of the purpose of the site (or simply the nature of your business), a picture with a caption, and contact information (near the bottom of the page). The Home page would now look something like this:

Chapter Ten: Go to Market with Publisher, Make a Pitch with PowerPoint

Part Three:
Makes and
Models: How to
Stand Out from
the Crowd

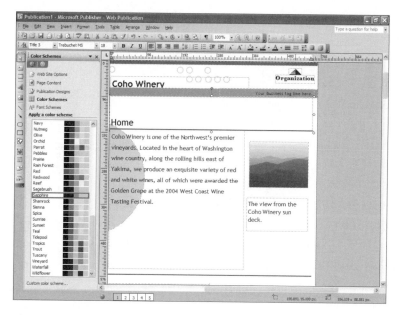

6. In the task pane (with Web Site Options displayed), you can change the number and location of the navigation bar (which by default appears vertically along the left side of each page and at the bottom). In this example, switch to the Vertical Only option.

7. At the bottom of the Publisher window, click 2 in the row of page numbers to display the About Us page. On this page, you can add text that describes your business and what you offer your customers, as well as other messaging. Especially for businesses such as consultants and professional services, this page provides space to expand on the summary offered on the Home page and tell the story of the services you offer. At the bottom of the About Us page, the contact information you enter on the Home page is repeated.

8. On page 3, the Contact Us page, you can add written directions to your place of business, add your address, and also insert a map.

9. Click 4 in the row of page numbers to display the Service List page, shown here:

Part Three:
Makes and
Models: How to
Stand Out from
the Crowd

Microsoft Small Business Kit

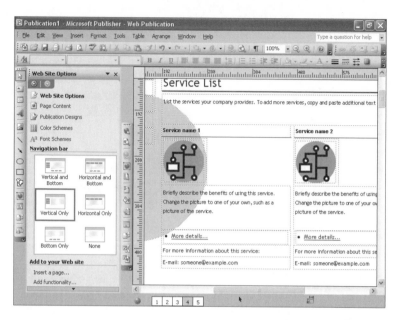

For each service you list (four service listings are provided when Publisher builds the site), you can add a name, an illustration, a description, and specific contact information. For example, you could direct customers to a salesperson who is in charge of a particular service or area. If you don't need to list different e-mail addresses for each service, select the text box and delete it.

10. Click 5 in the row of page numbers to display the last page in this publication, the Related Links page. This page lets you expand the scope of your site so that visitors can have quick access to other stops on the Internet. If your business is in or near an area frequented by tourists, for example, you might use this site to link to a site that advertises accommodations, recreational opportunities, or the local weather.

11. To add a link to this page, right-click the text that reads Web Site Or Page Name, and then click Hyperlink on the shortcut menu. You'll see a dialog box similar to the one shown here:

Chapter Ten: **Go to Market with Publisher, Make a Pitch with PowerPoint**

Part Three:
Makes and
Models: How to
Stand Out from
the Crowd

12. In the dialog box's Link To list, be sure that Existing File Or Web Page
is selected. Then insert the address for the Web site you want to link
to in the Address box. You can also insert links to other pages in your
site (by selecting Place In This Document in the Link To list) or to an
e-mail address.

13. After you've added the text and images you want on your site, you
need to save the publication by choosing the Save command from the
File menu. Like other Publisher documents, the Web site is saved with
the .pub extension so that you can open the file in Publisher to make
updates and changes. To publish the Web site on the Internet, you
need to work with an ISP or a Web hosting service. When you choose
Publish To The Web from the File menu, the dialog box that appears
includes a link to Microsoft Office Online, where you'll find a list of
Web hosting services.

14. If you want to see what your site looks like before publishing it on the
Web, choose Web Page Preview from the File menu. Here's the Home
page of the sample Web site opened in Internet Explorer:

Part Three:
Makes and
Models: How to
Stand Out from
the Crowd

Microsoft Small Business Kit

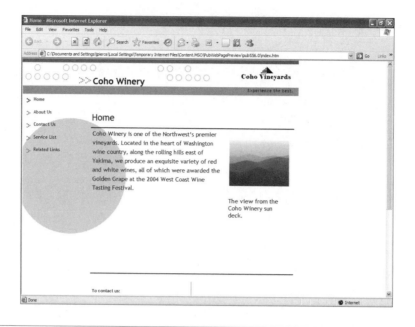

Stay on message

If you haven't yet read Chapter 9, "Crafting Your Message," now's the time. When you create a marketing brochure or Web site with Publisher, it is very easy—especially with all the design choices you have—to stray from the goals of the publication you're creating. You can't appeal to everyone in a single ad. As you'll learn in Chapter 9, advertising a wide range of services or product options can sometimes cause confusion. Make sure your brochures and other marketing pieces retain the focus the need.

Easy E-Mail Marketing

The last type of publication we'll introduce in this chapter is a newsletter you send via e-mail. Not all businesses use e-mail for marketing purposes, and not every customer wants to give out his or her e-mail address for the purpose of receiving what amounts to an ad. However, for some businesses—those with a regular base of customers they know fairly well, for example, or companies that do a lot of business on the Web—e-mail marketing, when it is focused and not sent indiscriminately, can be very effective.

You don't necessarily need to create a new publication for your e-mail marketing. You can send a single page of a publication you've already created, for example. When you send a publication through e-mail, you can send

Chapter Ten: Go to Market with Publisher, Make a Pitch with PowerPoint

Part Three:
Makes and
Models: How to
Stand Out from
the Crowd

either a single page of a publication as the body of an e-mail message or send a whole publication as an e-mail attachment.

People who receive a single page sent in the body of an e-mail message don't need to have Publisher installed on their computers to read the message. These messages can be read by e-mail programs such as Microsoft Outlook 2003 and Outlook Express (versions later than 5.0), Hotmail, Yahoo, AOL, and others that can read HTML-formatted messages. (HTML, which stands for Hypertext Markup Language, is the code used to create pages displayed on the Web.) On the other hand, if you send a publication as an attachment, anyone who doesn't have Publisher installed won't be able to view the attachment, which means you'll need to be selective about the customers you correspond with this way.

One Marketing Idea

When you get down to work in Publisher, here's one idea for how to use a publication you create. Produce a flyer that you mail to loyal customers announcing new products and services you offer. Add a detachable coupon to the flyer that can be redeemed for a discount. That coupon rewards special customers who are already doing with business with you. For new customers, set up a stack of in-store flyers at the cash register or by the reception desk to help word-of-mouth marketing. Be sure to save your flyer design as a template in Publisher so that you can print more whenever you need them. And don't forget that the flyer and coupon should be consistent with other publications you create in order to promote your company's identity.

Saving Publisher 2003 files for earlier versions of Publisher

If you know that customers or clients you send a publication to use an earlier version of Publisher (Publisher 2000 or Publisher 98, for example) you can save the publication in a format suitable for that version. You can also save Publisher publications in formats such as Rich Text Format or Post-Script files, but some of these formats won't support the graphics and layout in the publication. For more information about file formats you can work with in Publisher, see the online help topic "File formats that Publisher converts."

To start working on an e-mail newsletter, follow these steps.

Create an e-mail newsletter

1. Open Publisher, and then click Web Site And E-Mail in the New Publication task pane. Click E-Mail, and then click Newsletter. In the group of newsletter templates, click the one you want to use. (We'll use the Accent Box Newsletter template in this example.) Publisher sets up the publication, and you'll see a window similar to the one shown here:

Part Three:
Makes and
Models: How to
Stand Out from
the Crowd

Microsoft Small Business Kit

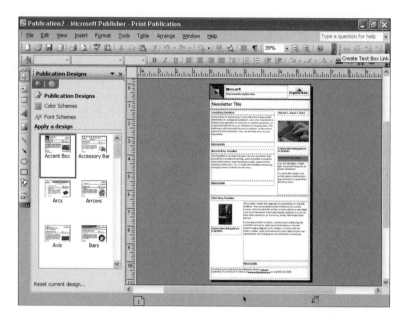

2. Publisher opens the newsletter at a scale that's hard to read (because
   the template includes space for a lot of information, which is good).
   To adjust the view of the publication, set the Zoom box on the toolbar
   to between 75 and 100 percent. You can also close the task pane to
   make more room.

   As you can see here, the template has details such as volume and issue
   number, the date of your newsletter, and also space for a title and a
   lead story. The newsletter includes areas for three stories overall, plus
   a spotlight article and some illustrations.

Chapter Ten: Go to Market with Publisher, Make a Pitch with PowerPoint

Part Three:
Makes and
Models: How to
Stand Out from
the Crowd

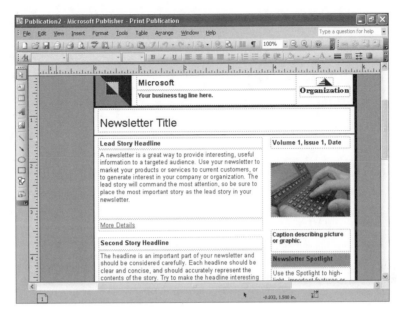

3. To complete the newsletter, enter a story headline and then write the story. If a story takes more space than what's provided in the text box, you can make use of the More Details link. First add a page to the publication by clicking Page on the Insert menu. Then right-click on the More Details link, and click Hyperlink on the shortcut menu. You'll see the Insert Hyperlink dialog box. In the dialog box's Link To list, select Place In This Document, and then choose the page of the publication you want to link to.

4. To add your own photograph or other image to the newsletter, right-click on the placeholder image, and then click Change Picture on the shortcut menu. You can then choose to insert a piece of Clip Art or insert an image file stored on your hard disk.

5. At the bottom of the publication, check out the notice that reads *To remove your name from our mailing list, please click here,* which is shown here. Using the Insert Hyperlink dialog box again, you can associate an e-mail address with this link so that customers can send you a message if they no longer want to receive the newsletter.

Part Three:
Makes and
Models: How to
Stand Out from
the Crowd

Microsoft Small Business Kit

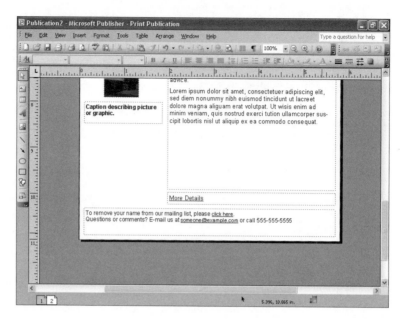

6. After you've entered all the news you want to report, you're ready to send the publication. If you are sending a complete publication as an attachment, save the publication, and then choose File, Send E-Mail, Send Publication As Attachment.

If you are sending a single page in an e-mail message, you can preview the page before you send it by choosing File, Send E-Mail, E-Mail Preview. Choosing this command opens the page in Internet Explorer so that you can review its appearance and format. To then send the page, choose File, Send E-Mail, Send This Page As Message. You might want to send the page to yourself before sending it to your customers. That way you can see what the page looks like in your e-mail program and you can check the size of the message. A page with a lot of graphics and color formatting will be fairly large, and it could take quite a while for a customer to download or open the message. You don't want to alienate trusted customers by clogging their e-mail programs.

Chapter Ten: Go to Market with Publisher, Make a Pitch with PowerPoint

Part Three:
Makes and
Models: How to
Stand Out from
the Crowd

Page preparedness

If you send a page of a publication you've set up for print in e-mail, you might want to change the width of the page so that it will be displayed more effectively in an e-mail program. You can change the page width by choosing Page Setup from the File menu. To decrease the width of the page, you might need to rearrange illustrations or text boxes so that all these elements are contained within the new dimensions. Also, some of the fonts you use in a printed publication might not be displayed correctly on a page you send through e-mail. The online help in Publisher has a list of fonts (called Web fonts) that are designed for viewing online. Arial, Impact, and Verdana are three of the fonts that are listed.

Most small business owners don't have the money to shoot a TV ad and then buy time during the Super Bowl to air it. For the majority, getting the word out about their business will take time. The marketing materials you can produce with Microsoft Publisher are designed with a professional look and can be created with little investment other than time. You'll have all your business publications and ads on hand to revise and reuse when you need them.

The Pitch and the Presentation: Using Microsoft PowerPoint 2003

Some people thrive when they're in front of an audience. They take to public speaking naturally and have an easy manner that's engaging and persuasive. For others, a public presentation isn't fun; it's just an experience they have to get through. Making an effective presentation—whether to a prospective financial backer, to your business partners, to employees, or to the local rotary—requires you to recite facts and figures as well as emphasize what's most important. You need to weave together a story that leads to the conclusion you want.

Microsoft PowerPoint is one of the most widely used software programs for creating presentations. Images and charts, tables documenting a company's financial performance, and lists of goals and objectives are all items that appear frequently in PowerPoint presentations. A successful presentation balances the information shown on the slides with the speaker's explanation and elaboration. If your business requires you to present information to others frequently—on sales calls, for example—it might be worth your while to read more about the best practices that we'll summarize here.

Part Three:
Makes and
Models: How to
Stand Out from
the Crowd

Microsoft Small Business Kit

Room for disagreement

PowerPoint is used by corporate executives and salespeople, by attorneys in courtrooms, and by classroom instructors. Not everyone, however, agrees that PowerPoint is the best communication tool. In an article from the *Chicago Tribune* titled "Is PowerPoint the Devil?" Julia Keller writes: "PowerPoint has a dark side. It squeezes ideas into a preconceived format, organizing and condensing not only your material but—inevitably, it seems—your way of thinking about and looking at that material." You can find similar critiques by people such as Edward Tufte, a well-known authority on visual presentation. What's the point of mentioning these perspectives? Just to say that PowerPoint is a tool you use. The persuasive and instructive quality of a presentation comes from the person making it.

Some Tips for Presenting Effectively

When you're on the Internet and search on the phrase *presentation tips*, you'll find a fair number of Web sites that list their take on the dos and don'ts of a good presentation. Here's a summary of some of the advice that's commonly given:

- Think of a presentation as a story you have to tell—a story that has a beginning, a middle, and an end. At the beginning, introduce the audience to the themes in the presentation. Throughout the body of the presentation, build on these themes and support them with facts, citations, diagrams, and the like. Finally, be sure the story has a conclusion—a summary of key points, a look ahead, a list of specific actions that result from decisions the presentation leads to.

- Remember that practice makes perfect. Rehearse your presentation ahead of time. Use family and friends for the dress rehearsal. If a live audience isn't available for rehearsal, tape-record the presentation, or rehearse in front of a video camera.

- As part of rehearsing, be sure to time the presentation. You don't want to run long. You can expect that you'll be asked a question that might throw off the timing of the presentation. You might need to skip a couple of slides to get back on track. If you do find yourself running long, be sure you still cover the most important points. Determine in advance which slides you can omit so that you don't need to rush through the critical ones. Even if you've given the presentation before—possibly a number of times—go over it again to be sure you smooth out the spots that have proved rough before.

- If you're making a presentation to potential clients or customers in a room you haven't used before, check the room ahead of time if you can so that you have a sense of the seating arrangement and can determine what equipment you might need. On the day of the presentation, give yourself time to set up or check the setup someone did for you. Make sure all equipment works the way you need it to.

- Come with printouts if necessary, and be prepared to deliver your presentation without the aid of a computer. You might have a sudden hard-disk crash, the room you're using might be ill equipped, or the presentation file might be corrupted. Be mindful of the old rule that whatever can go wrong, will go wrong.

- Know the needs of your audience and match your content to their needs. Modify the presentation so that you're not just repeating it but are delivering it for the specific audience assembled that day. During the presentation, keep your antenna up and change course if you need to. If you receive a lot of questions at some point, slow down and be sure you answer the questions carefully. If you have the sense that the audience is becoming impatient while you provide background, move ahead to the main points—those items where you interact with the audience about decisions or ask for their feedback.

- Avoid jargon, especially if you are speaking to an audience who doesn't share your expertise. Allow your personality to be displayed. Tell an appropriate joke or two or a personal anecdote.

- Remember that you are often trying to persuade someone in a presentation, so you need to speak confidently and you need to look your audience in the eye. Don't always look in the same direction, and make eye contact with different people in the audience. Look over the whole audience from time to time as well.

- Speak slowly and clearly, but don't speak in a monotone. Work to build a relationship with the audience. Your body language will convey your interest in the topic and will help establish rapport with the audience. Although looking down at your notes from time to time to check that you've covered all your points is fine, you'll quickly lose your audience if you simply read the notes. Move around the room a little if you can, and use gestures and expressions to emphasize the points you want to make.

- Use pointers, microphones, or other props as necessary. If a microphone is available, adjust and adapt your voice accordingly and be sure that even people in the back of the room can hear you.

Part Three:
Makes and
Models: How to
Stand Out from
the Crowd

Microsoft Small Business Kit

PowerPoint Training and Assistance from Microsoft Office Online

PowerPoint is an application that you can work with on your own fairly easily, given time to experiment and provided that you like to learn through trial and error. If you get stuck, want more formal training from the start, or want to learn how to accomplish a specific task, use the assistance and training available through Microsoft Office Online.

The Microsoft Office PowerPoint 2003 Assistance page provides links to topics that describe how to work with graphics and charts, how to set up printing options, and how to work with text and slide formatting. The online training modules provide specific instruction about animation techniques, how to work with organization charts and flowcharts, how to play sound and video files, and more.

■ Use illustrations or photographs where they're helpful in emphasizing or clarifying a point you want to make. Illustrations can often simplify a complex topic, and photographs add a realistic feel. If you use illustrations and charts, purchase a laser pointer. These pointers aren't very expensive and can draw attention to the parts of your presentation that you want to emphasize.

■ If you're presenting in a large room, be sure to repeat any questions you're asked so that everyone in the room can hear the questions.

■ Finish your presentation on a high note. Don't leave questions unanswered, and be sure that any next steps or decisions that need to be made are clearly identified and responsibilities assigned. Be sure to thank the audience for their time and interest.

A Brief PowerPoint Primer Using the Microsoft Office Online Marketing Plan Presentation

As a way of demonstrating a few of the basic features in PowerPoint, in this section we'll work with one of the PowerPoint templates available on Microsoft Office Online. This template is designed to be the basis of a marketing plan presentation. You might find this template helpful if you're building a marketing plan for your business or developing a presentation about one of the products or services you provide. The slides in the template can be edited to fit your own presentation, of course, but they also provide a framework for the topics you might cover in a presentation of this sort. One slide is titled Competition, another Positioning, and another Communication Strategies. The slides also contain descriptions of the kind of information you should add. For example, the Positioning slide prompts

Chapter Ten: Go to Market with Publisher, Make a Pitch with PowerPoint

Part Three:
Makes and
Models: How to
Stand Out from
the Crowd

you to add a statement that "distinctly defines the product in its market and against its competition over time" and a statement that highlights how consumers will benefit from the product or service.

The PowerPoint task pane

As you create and update presentations, you'll work frequently with the task pane in PowerPoint. From the task pane, you have access to presentation design templates, slide content layouts, and even a wizard (the Auto-Content Wizard) that sets up a multislide presentation, complete with color schemes and tailored for topics such as reviewing a new project, announcing a new strategy, and others.

If you want to work in PowerPoint as you read through this section (or just view the slides included in the template), you can open the copy of this template included on the companion CD or download the file from Microsoft Office Online.

A few PowerPoint basics

1. To locate the marketing plan presentation template online, open your Web browser, and go to *office.microsoft.com*, or open PowerPoint, and then click Microsoft Office Online on the Help menu.

2. On the Office Online site, click Templates in the navigation bar at the left, and then click Marketing under Browse Templates. On the Marketing Templates page, click Marketing Plans And Presentations, and then click on the template named Marketing Plan Presentation. Click Download Now.

   When you download the file to your computer, PowerPoint starts and you'll see the first slide in the presentation, shown here:

Part Three:
Makes and
Models: How to
Stand Out from
the Crowd

Microsoft Small Business Kit

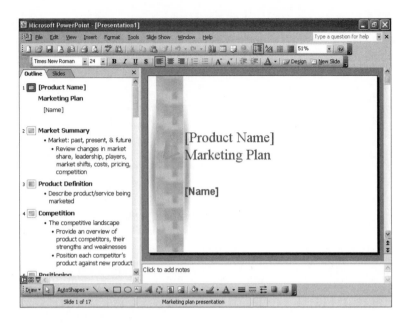

At the left of the PowerPoint window, notice the pane with the tabs Outline and Slides. Outline view, shown above, displays the text included on each slide. The Slides view shows thumbnail images of the slides, including any graphics the slides contain. Both views let you move from slide to slide in a presentation by clicking the slide you need. If you want to change the order of the slides in a presentation, you can select a slide in the pane and then drag it to a new position.

At the bottom of the PowerPoint window, you'll find the Drawing toolbar. The buttons on this toolbar let you select tools for drawing basic shapes, lines, and arrows; for adding a text box to a slide; for inserting diagrams and Clip Art; and for applying formatting such as line color, font color, and shadows to the text and graphics on a slide. Other formatting and editing tools you'll use in creating presentations appear on the Standard and Formatting toolbars, shown at the top of the PowerPoint window.

3. Click on the Product Name placeholder in slide 1, and then select and delete the placeholder text. Enter your business's name or the name of the product being presented. Triple-click the Name placeholder, and then enter your name or the name of the presenter. The first slide should look something like this:

Chapter Ten: Go to Market with Publisher, Make a Pitch with PowerPoint

Part Three:
Makes and
Models: How to
Stand Out from
the Crowd

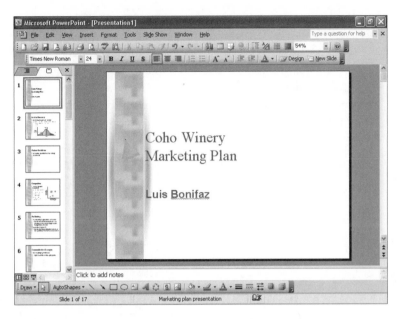

4. Click on slide 2 in the pane at the left to display the slide titled Market Summary, shown here:

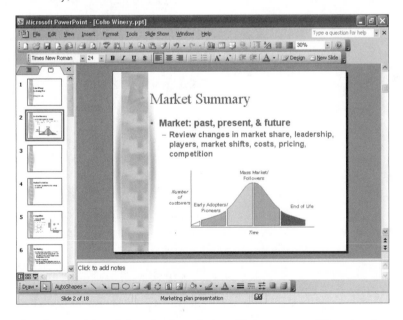

The chart on this slide is built with AutoShapes—a set of functional and decorative shapes that you can use to create a flowchart, for example, or a chart such as the one included on this slide. You insert an

Part Three:
Makes and
Models: How to
Stand Out from
the Crowd

Microsoft Small Business Kit

AutoShape by opening the AutoShapes menu that appears on the Drawing toolbar (usually at the bottom of the PowerPoint window), selecting the category and shape you want to use, and then clicking on the slide where you want to position the shape. The Action Buttons category, shown here, provides shapes that you can use for navigation. You can link an action button to the next or previous slide, to the first or last slide in a presentation, or to a site on the Internet–your company's Home page, for example.

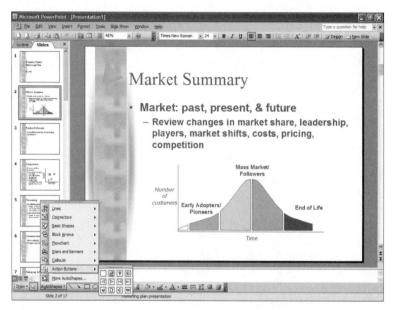

If you want to change the formatting of an AutoShape on a slide, double-click the shape, which opens the Format AutoShape dialog box. In that dialog box, you can adjust the size and position of the shape and modify formatting such as the shape's color, line width, and the like.

As you can see above, the purpose of slide 2 is to document the past, present, and future conditions of the market you are entering. If you needed more than one slide to present this information, you could add a slide to the presentation.

5. On the Insert menu, click New Slide (or click the New Slide button on the Formatting toolbar). You'll see the Slide Layout task pane at the right of the PowerPoint window, as shown here:

Chapter Ten: Go to Market with Publisher, Make a Pitch with PowerPoint

Part Three:
Makes and
Models: How to
Stand Out from
the Crowd

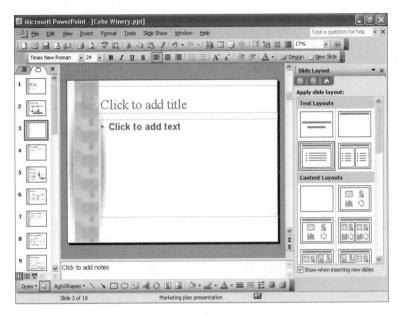

Notice that the new slide has placeholders for a title and text. On the Slide Layout task pane, you can select from a number of standard layouts. The one shown above is a text layout that includes a title and text. Content layouts provide areas for charts or other graphical elements. If you scroll down the Slide Layout task pane, you'll find layouts for combinations of text and content as well.

6. On the View menu, click Master, Slide Master. You'll see the slide shown here:

Part Three:
Makes and
Models: How to
Stand Out from
the Crowd

Microsoft Small Business Kit

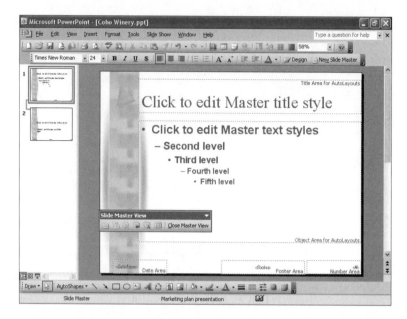

In a PowerPoint template, a *slide master* defines elements such as the font styles, the position and size of placeholders, and the background design. If you want to change the font used throughout a presentation, you can make that change to the slide master rather than change the font on each separate slide. You could use a slide master to store your company's logo if you wanted the logo to appear on each slide. Other information you add to a slide master might include a date that appears on the slides in a presentation.

7. Click on the decorative border along the left side of the slide master, and then press Delete. On the Format menu, click Background. In the Background dialog box, open the drop-down list box in the Background Fill area, as shown here:

Chapter Ten: Go to Market with Publisher, Make a Pitch with PowerPoint

Part Three:
**Makes and
Models: How to
Stand Out from
the Crowd**

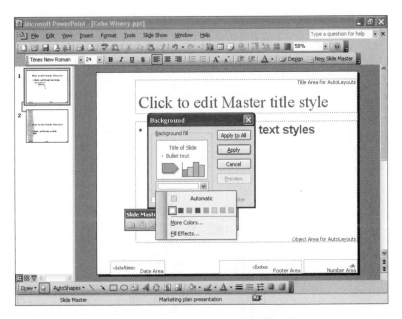

You can pick one of the colors displayed, click More Colors to widen the selection or create a custom color, or click Fill Effects to open a dialog box in which you build a background with shading styles, textures, patterns, or a picture. Here's the slide master again with the Blue Hills image used as a background:

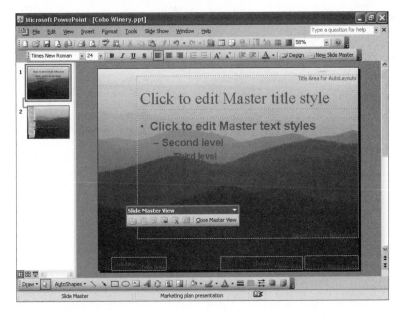

Part Three:
**Makes and
Models: How to
Stand Out from
the Crowd**

Microsoft Small Business Kit

8. Click Apply To All in the Background dialog box. Because we've updated the slide master, each slide in the presentation is updated to show the background image.

9. On the slide master, select the text in the master text styles placeholder, as shown here:

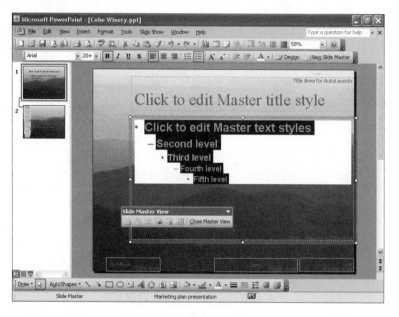

On the Formatting toolbar, click the drop-down arrow for the Font Color button, and then change the font color to white (or another light color) so that the text shows up against the darker blue of the background image. Click the Close Master View button on the Slide Master View toolbar after you've finished making changes.

10. In the slide pane, select slide 8, which is titled Packaging & Fulfillment. We'll use this slide to demonstrate a simple animation effect.

11. On the Slide Show menu, click Animation Schemes. In the task pane, you'll see a list of animation effects you can choose from. Under the Subtle effects, click Fade In One By One, and then watch the slide. It turns blank, and then the title followed by each of the two text blocks appear on the screen. If you want to try out other animation schemes, scroll down the task pane and try out one or more of the other items—spinning text, text that unfolds, a zoom effect, and more. Effects like these are useful to emphasize important points in a presentation and to set the mood.

Chapter Ten: Go to Market with Publisher, Make a Pitch with PowerPoint

Part Three:
Makes and
Models: How to
Stand Out from
the Crowd

12. Make any other changes you want to the text of other slides in this presentation. When you've finished, click View Show on the Slide Show menu to see how the presentation will appear when you show it.

Packaging a presentation

Sometimes you might need to run a presentation on a computer that doesn't have PowerPoint installed on it (provided the computer runs Microsoft Windows 98, Second Edition, or a later version of Windows). In a case like this, open the presentation file, and then click Package For CD on the File menu. In the dialog box that appears, you can choose to copy the presentation to a folder or to a CD. When you copy the files, you'll also copy the PowerPoint Viewer, a program that lets you view the presentation even when the full version of Power-Point isn't installed.

Tips for Slide Design and Formatting

Now that you've seen the basics of building a PowerPoint presentation, what are the important points to keep in mind when you go about creating presentations on your own? Just as body language and an animated voice are necessary ingredients for effectively engaging an audience, you can follow a number of best practices when designing and formatting the slides you use. Here's a list of some of the PowerPoint design wisdom that's been collected over the years:

- Don't crowd slides with too much information. Your audience won't be able to read a balance sheet or an income statement from across the room. Using roughly 40 words per slide is a good guideline. Try to include no more than six bullet points per slide. Compressing your ideas into short statements doesn't mean you can't get your point across. When you're giving your presentation, elaborate on the ideas behind the statements.

- Charts are useful for digesting detailed information, especially financial information. A bar chart or pie chart that shows the distribution of expenses over categories or highlights a six-month upward trend in sales is a far better format in a presentation than a table listing each detailed amount. Use line charts to show trends. If you need to provide lots of details in your presentation, include the material as a printed handout.

Part Three:
Makes and
Models: How to
Stand Out from
the Crowd

Microsoft Small Business Kit

- Use fonts and font sizes that are easy to read. A good minimum font size to use is 14 points, but even that size can be too small in larger rooms.

- Use a serif font (Times New Roman, for example) for larger blocks of text. For headings, use a sans serif font such as Arial or Verdana. (Verdana, Tahoma, and Bookman are three fonts designed for online viewing.) A serif font includes small lines (like tails) on many characters, whereas sans serif fonts have a plainer appearance.

- Keep in mind that the choice of font helps set the mood and tone of a presentation. Some fonts look more serious than others and are well suited to a presentation that's all about business. A font that has a more playful appearance might be effective if the occasion allows. Take a look at the slide shown in Figure 10-4. Is one font preferable for a presentation in which you're asking for someone's business?

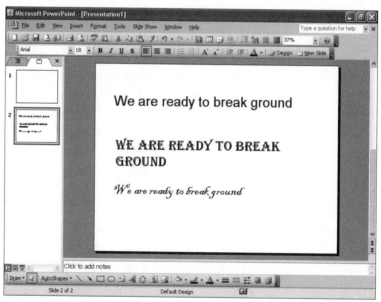

Figure 10-4   Select a font that's easy to read and conveys the seriousness of your presentation.

- Don't use more than a few different fonts.

- Instead of applying lots of boldface and italics to the text in your presentation, use your voice to emphasize important ideas.

- Add a title to each slide.

Chapter Ten: Go to Market with Publisher, Make a Pitch with PowerPoint

Part Three:
Makes and
Models: How to
Stand Out from
the Crowd

- List the items on a slide in the order of importance, with the most important point first.

Special effects

One of the pleasing parts of creating a PowerPoint presentation is the ease with which you can add special visual effects—slide transitions, spinning text, and the like. Use these effects in moderation. It's true that a jazzy presentation can catch the audience's attention, but approval of your PowerPoint skills isn't usually the approval you're after. You want your message to stand out more than the presentation itself.

- If at all possible, have someone in addition to you proofread your materials. A misspelled word can cause a sudden interruption or distraction if someone in the audience points it out during your presentation.

- The choice of colors you apply to text and other elements in a slide can affect the mood and response to a presentation. Red, for example, can signify an alert, and many people associate the color green with growth, black with the quality of strength, and gray with maturity. Avoid using red text. Red text is often hard to read.

- Use contrasting colors. A dark background with light text is easily readable.

- Use drop shadows to set off text and give it contrast. Adding drop shadows to text makes it more legible.

- Keep a background simple. A background that's too busy makes the text hard to read (as you saw earlier, when we had to change the color of the font to accommodate the range of colors in the Blue Hills image).

- Try to be consistent in how you capitalize the items in your list, but don't use all capital letters.

- Include a good combination of words, pictures, and graphics. Variety keeps the presentation interesting.

The art of effective presentations doesn't come in the box with PowerPoint, but you can use that program to help get your points across. Keep your presentations simple and brief. The audience, you hope, is more interested in what you have to say—in your products and business skills—than in dozens of special effects.

Part Three:
Makes and
Models: How to
Stand Out from
the Crowd

Microsoft Small Business Kit

For More Information

In addition to the resources mentioned in this chapter, you will find links and information on the companion CD. Some books and Web sites particularly useful as you develop ideas about how to develop sales and marketing materials include:

Books

- OTSI, *Microsoft Office PowerPoint 2003 Step by Step* (Microsoft Press, 2003)

- Jane Maas, *Better Brochures, Catalogs, and Mailing Pieces* (St. Martin's Press, 1984)

- Fred E. Hahn, *Do It Yourself Advertising and Promotion: How to Produce Great Ads, Brochures, Catalogs, Direct Mail, Web Sites, and More* (Wiley, 2003)

Web Sites

- The PowerPoint FAQ, an independent site with tutorials, tips, programming information, and more: *www.rdpslides.com/pptfaq/*

- Microsoft Publisher templates and ideas from desktoppublishing.com: *www.desktoppublishing.com/templ_mspub.html*

- The Direct Marketing Association has extensive resources available online: *www.the-dma.org/*

Part Four

Connect and Conquer: Building the Company

In this part

Chapter Eleven   **The Customer Comes First** 286

Chapter Twelve   **Managing Customer Contacts:**
Business Contact Manager 306

Part Four:
Connect and
Conquer:
Building the
Company

Microsoft Small Business Kit

There is only one boss. The customer. And he can fire everybody in the company from the chairman on down, simply by spending his money somewhere else.

— *Sam Walton (1918–1992), founder, Wal-Mart*

Chapter Eleven

The Customer Comes First

You build business by staying close to your best customer. Here's how to attract the customers that boost profits—and how to keep them coming back for more.

What you'll find:

❏ Identifying your best customers: the 80/20 rule

❏ Rewarding return customers

❏ Protecting customer trust and privacy

❏ Understanding when to expand

❏ Forging strategic alliances

Part Four:
Connect and
Conquer:
Building the
Company

Microsoft Small Business Kit

Identifying Your Best Customers: The 80/20 Rule

Quiz a business owner about the firm's best customers, and you'll get the reply in warp speed. "Ms. Major Buyer," announces the grateful CEO. "She accounts for 15 percent of our annual revenues all by herself." This is a no-brainer, right? Whoever buys the most units of whatever you sell deserves all the deep discounts, front-of-the-line attention, and expensive perks you can send her way.

Maybe. Assuming you really understand your bottom line.

Dig a bit into The Big One's habits. What if she returns a quarter of everything she buys and you make dough only on volume? What if the high-buying customer spends four hours a week lambasting your customer service team with unreasonable demands and complaints? What if, in short, the cost of servicing this mega-customer outweighs the high revenue she brings in? Until you have such information, you can't determine whether you have a customer worth all your fuss. Most business owners can't really define the characteristicsof their good customers. They haven't figured out what a good customer is.

No doubt you've heard something about the 80/20 rule. Originally devised by a nineteenth-century Italian economist named Vilfredo Pareto, the law grew out of his keen observations about "the trivial many and the critical few." Pareto noticed that 80 percent of the possible value of business activities tends to come from only 20 percent of the effort put into it.

Calculating Your 80/20 Customers

Once you've developed an established customer base, you'll find it easier to build the business if you spend time and money on targeting your best customers:

- Identify and characterize key customers.

- Target messages in suitable media to hit nerves among the important customer segments.

- Build in a payoff that rewards customers for giving you time and attention.

Given the 80/20 rule, if you can define your "critical few" customers and target marketing directly to their needs, your efforts are likely to pay off big time. The cost of acquiring new customers, according to many surveys, runs 8 to 10 times more than the cost of keeping existing ones. So you get a stronger return on marketing dollars and sales efforts by focusing on 20 percent or so of your top-tier prospects.

Even so, neither frequency nor volume defines a best customer. Instead, you want to identify customers who provide

Chapter Eleven: **The Customer Comes First**

Part Four:
Connect and
Conquer:
Building the
Company

the most profit. Only a thorough and ongoing analysis of customer buying habits and histories can yield such insights. The route to distinguishing between good customers and bad ones is to learn more about who they are and what they want—that is, *granular customer intelligence*. You need to know a wealth of details about your customers' habits, histories, and preferences. In tech terms, you need a way to capture all the customer data. (See the next section to learn more about how Business Contact Manager [BCM] can help.) In fact, you need a customer database.

Creating a Customer Database

To start assembling a seamless, accessible databank, you need ongoing answers to these three questions:

- Who are your customers—by age, gender, geographic location, and economic strata?

- Why do customers buy your product? Is it, for instance, because of price point or brand consciousness or convenience?

- What will your customers buy from you in the future?

See "How to Find Your Best Customer," page 25, for more about targeting customer segments. See also Chapter 12, "Managing Customer Contact: Business Contact Manager," for more information using this tool to manage your customer database.

Most up-and-going companies already have bits and bytes of such info. But most companies do not have a way to integrate such customer intelligence. Data is probably isolated and scattered on a dozen different hard drives, mobile laptops, PDAs (personal digital assistants), and hard-copy files. Your salesperson, for instance, might know how much customers buy, but not which products they prefer. The marketing consultant or director might be up to speed about the timing of customer purchases as well as their future needs but have no clue about inventory and whether the product is in stock or available in volume quantities. The billing clerk or accountant is crystal clear about who isn't paying on time, but not whether that long-time client rates some leeway. And your service desk might be all too familiar with the product installation procedure that provokes calls from every new customer, yet sales and the design staff remain blissfully unaware.

Imagine the benefits of having all those pieces of information integrated into a customer intelligence file so that each department can understand. Bingo! Trying to satisfy customer needs just got a whole lot easier, and that translates into better and bigger business.

Part Four:
Connect and
Conquer:
Building the
Company

Microsoft Small Business Kit

An easy way to collect and leverage customer information is to make the effort to create an in-house database. With each sale or customer contact, begin assembling the pieces of data that make up your customer's big picture—after first gaining the customer's permission, of course.

See the section "Protecting Customer Trust and Privacy," later in this chapter, for more about privacy issues.

The most helpful information to collect includes:

- Name, address, phone, and/or e-mail address, including all family members or company title and department, depending on the kind of business you have

- Date of birth, so that you can send out cards or e-mail messages with birthday discount offers or gifts

- Annual amount spent with your company

- Products purchased and past history

- Dates or schedule of purchases

- Special offers acted on

- Customer service history

- Special requests for products or service

- Participation in any promotional events and frequent-buyer or loyalty clubs

Business Contact Manager (BCM), a customer-contact application designed for small businesses of 1 to 25 or so employees, has been added to Microsoft Outlook in Microsoft Office Small Business Edition 2003. BCM is a useful electronic tool for collecting, storing, and manipulating customer information, and it has an easy Outlook interface. In all, BCM has 20 preformatted reports, including seven focused on current customers (Accounts) and five focused on sales leads (Opportunities) that can give you immediate information about who buys what, how well they pay, and more. The Accounts By Rating report, for example, serves up "great vs. marginal" customers. You can also find a Neglected Accounts report.

Within the Account History of BCM, you can go beyond collecting simple contact information to consolidating all interactions for a given customer, including e-mail messages, tasks, appointments or sales calls, notes, and other documents. Further, you can easily create customized reports with

Chapter Eleven: The Customer Comes First

Part Four:
Connect and
Conquer:
Building the
Company

criteria of your own choosing or, if needed, export those reports into Microsoft Excel for spreadsheet analysis.

Using such software, you should get into the habit of consistently updating customer information. At every customer touch point, try to learn a little more or verify what you have. For instance, ask why the customer is buying two instead of one. Why does he choose blue rather than gray? Has she been promoted, with a new title and responsibilities? Note the customer's responses to marketing efforts. Keep adding details and making sure the profile is up-to-date.

After a half-dozen interactions, you'll have insights into an individual account's purchasing history and proprietary profile. You'll have it captured in a centralized location—no more outdated sticky notes or multiple folders with conflicting information. Plus, all the actionable information will be accessible to the sales team or marketing or billing.

When you've formed some ideas, you might want to mail out a postcard survey to get more detailed answers, which is fast and affordable. Use one of these techniques to create a mailing list:

- Use the customer contact information in BCM, which can be exported into Microsoft Word or Microsoft Publisher, choosing only the address fields you need to establish your mailing list.

- Use the Mail Merge Wizard in either Microsoft Publisher 2003 or Word 2003 to seamlessly incorporate contacts from BCM or Excel 2003 directly into your survey.

Make sure you have enough responses to figure out what really moves customers to buy. You might need to send out a few mailings.

Leveraging Customer Intelligence

Once you've created the database, BCM or similar electronic tools give you terrific marketing power. Imagine, for instance:

- A financial services firm able to track the date that any of its clients plan to retire. You can then install a program that automatically sends a timely personalized note of congratulations along with an invitation to drop by for a financial tune-up.

- A "tween" fashion boutique that stores the brand of jeans its 12-year-old customers prefer. Whenever the latest line comes in, out goes a postcard.

Part Four:
Connect and
Conquer:
Building the
Company

Microsoft Small Business Kit

■ A tech consultancy that has instant access to all the software each client uses. When an update is released, an automated reminder pops up so that account managers can make a phone call to the grateful client.

Customer personalization has become the holy grail of modern marketing. When you can integrate business contact data across channels—such as sales, accounting, customer service, and customer contacts—clearly, marketing moves from shotgun uncertainty toward rifle-shot efficiency. If you're diligent about keeping the data current, contact management software can increase your revenue, improve customer satisfaction, cut costs per order, and pinpoint unexpected sales opportunities. With a seamless tool, you can track contacts and sales, quickly find every document or memo connected to an account, and automate the process of sending out customized e-mail marketing.

See "Getting Results from E-Mail Marketing," page 229, for more about customized marketing, and see the sidebar "Personalized E-Mail Services," later in this chapter, to learn about Microsoft List Builder electronic marketing services.

When you know the buying habits of your target customers, you won't waste dollars on marketing to the wrong audience. Armed with the results and the ongoing customer information, you can categorize customers into four target groups—from highest to lowest spenders. Then analyze which products and services grab the most attention or sales. You'll also know how to allocate your resources among the other groups and, perhaps, the profile or categories of new customers you can most easily tap for growth.

Here are five dos and don'ts to help achieve the cost-effective promises of contact management tools:

Don't be greedy. Every company relies on customer information to grow, of course. But how much customer data do you actually need to leverage opportunities? More importantly, in this age of heightened sensitivities, might customers balk or walk if you request too much personal data? Don't set up an overly complex or ambitious system that tries to capture every byte of info or data from customers. Start simply. You can always change the system later if you find a need for more details.

Don't expect magic. No one thinks expense-tracking software will solve the problem when staff travel and entertainment costs spike. You simply change practices and set new guidelines and rules. Yet when it comes to sales or contact software, somehow, businesses expect the

Chapter Eleven: **The Customer Comes First**

Part Four:
Connect and
Conquer:
Building the
Company

mere act of capturing customer data to boost sales revenue. It won't. The information and leverage offered by a business contact management software system won't help if your employees don't use it or don't talk to each other. Solve any communications problems before installing it, not afterward.

Do put customers first.   Dave Ratner, based in Agawam, Massachusetts, owns three retail shops called Soda & Pet City. He has been relying on contact management software for years. He says that small businesses can now quickly capture customer names, transactions, buying patterns, and just about everything else they might ever need to know about the customer. Soda & Pet City routinely uses that data to send out targeted promotions, including postcards that let customers know when their preferred brand of pet food is on sale, as well as special offers, discount coupons, and other deals that aren't offered to the general public. "We live by our database," says Ratner. But he warns that none of it will make a difference if the salespeople aren't good or if managers and clerks don't share the same goals.

Don't just collect data, manage it.   Capturing information and automating the process is just a beginning. You need to make sure the data is accessible and analyzed on an ongoing basis. A growing dilemma for businesses nowadays is what to do with all this data, including the issue of trying to integrate ever-proliferating new bytes with older information. Data quality and management is key to whether it's worthwhile to invest time and resources in business contact databases and software. Make sure you have policies in place that update and scrub your lists on a regular basis.

Do make allowances for sales staff.   A terrific salesperson is not likely to develop tidy IT habits. Yes, there are exceptions. But selling typically attracts a certain personality, and that's not the type that enjoys manipulating data on a computer screen. Organizations rarely acknowledge this truism. As a result, many business contact management programs quietly become dusty, outdated, and eventually ineffective. Prepare for this. You might need to set up some fail-safe procedures to keep the sales team on track.

By relying on smart, centralized customer information, you can send specialized offerings to selected customer segments. Here are some ways to tailor your offerings:

- Cross-sell or up-sell additional offers and products.
- Provide well-timed rewards or discounts.

Part Four:
Connect and
Conquer:
Building the
Company

Microsoft Small Business Kit

- Communicate with customers in the medium they prefer—be that direct mail, postcards, e-mail, phone, letters, flyers, or in some cases, simply an annual thank-you note.

- Create insider or time-sensitive deals.

- Launch frequent-buyer clubs or promotions.

- Package or bundle services that are a natural fit with your primary product.

- Expand into product lines your customer will definitely buy.

Just don't forget the payoff. Once you've focused on the right targets, make it worth your customer's time to listen to your message.

Rewarding Return Customers

Marketing programs that reward customers for their patronage are hardly new. Before airline frequent-flier clubs and credit card points, there was S&H Green Stamps. Sperry & Hutchison, the distributor of the stamps, launched that loyalty program back in 1896. At its height in the mid-1960s, with 80 percent of U.S. households collecting stamps and 800 redemption centers nationwide, S&H was overseeing an $825 million market.

There's no question consumers love to participate when the loyalty program is right. It's also clear that such programs can enhance profits. Recent research conducted across industries by consultant Bain & Company indicates that increasing a customer retention rate by only five percentage points can boost the average customer net present value (NPV) by an astonishing 35 to 95 percent. The strategy is simple enough. Give high-paying customers enough of an incentive, and they'll come back and buy more. That way, you boost sales, find new customers through referrals, and lower your costs for marketing and customer acquisition.

See "Creating Word of Mouth or Word of Mouse," page 220, for more on customer referral marketing.

But today, the challenge is how to engender that loyalty. Competition is fierce, price often drives decisions, and consumers can pick and choose among dozens of options and outlets, whether it's health care or hamburgers. Your edge becomes that database profile of best customers. Once you've characterized your key customers and prospects and identified what motivates them to buy, you can figure out what will entice them to buy more.

Chapter Eleven: **The Customer Comes First**

Part Four:
Connect and
Conquer:
Building the
Company

There are dozens of ways to reward customers, including the well-known frequent-buyer clubs, buy-several-get-one-free offers, and time-sensitive promotions and discounts made available only to loyal customers. Such ideas are tried and true. But you don't have to start big. Loyalty programs—and the marketing materials you create to promote them—can be very affordable.

Here are some ideas that let you start small and expand when you're ready:

Send personalized thank-you notes. Simple or immoderate, e-mailed or on expensive stationery, saying thank-you always works. After each visit or major purchase, send notes that thank the customer for his or her business. You might also enclose a discount or special offer that can be applied to the next purchase.

Send reminders. Set up a tracking system that automatically generates a postcard or note offering a 10 percent or greater discount after a certain interval of time during which the customer hasn't bought anything. (See the section "Creating a Customer Database," earlier in this chapter, for more about how to quickly set up a customer intelligence system.)

Send e-mail offers. Obviously, you'll need to capture e-mail addresses first—with the customers' permission. Plus, you must have safeguards in place to protect the information. A promise of upgrades or e-mail-only offers often motivates customers to register personal data.

Send holiday or personal offers. A freebie or treat on a customer's birthday means you've paid special attention. Sending news or sales dates for a customer's preferred brand or product will also net attention and loyalty.

Share proprietary information or intelligence. For professional services, a newsletter or special bulletin about industry news or events is a great value. You can also enclose discounts and offers.

Send value-added appreciation. "We maintain files of articles we have written or that are relevant to our business position," says Alex Ramsey, president of Lode Star Universal, a business consultancy in Dallas. "We mail these out to treasured clients or intriguing prospects." Whenever you come across a white paper, industry report, or competitive intelligence that you think a customer or supplier might find enlightening, clip it and send it along at the right moment. Of course, make sure these are timely. But even if your clients have already seen it, they'll appreciate that you're supporting their interests.

Offer steep discounts at off times. If your business has any specific downtime, let loyal customers in on a bargain.

Part Four:
Connect and
Conquer:
Building the
Company

Microsoft Small Business Kit

Personalized E-Mail Services

To target different customer segments with per-mission-based, personalized e-mail messages, consider Microsoft List Builder services, which allow you to:

- Use templates to send e-news, offers, or announcements

- Address customers by name

- Send targeted offers based on subscriber demographic information

- Track e-mail to find how many recipients received, opened, and clicked on links in your message

Visit List Builder, at *www.microsoft.com/ smallbusiness/products/online/lb.mspx.*

Give them VIP treatment. Jump best customers to the head of the line. Usher them into comfortable waiting areas. Give them cards or special tags that confer status.

Markets and customers both have a way of evolving. So don't simply set up a loyalty program and walk away. Keep track of any changes in customer or prospect information, and make sure your customer list and data are regularly updated. You can definitely build a better business by rewarding better customers.

Timing Your Marketing Message

How would you feel if your insurance broker phoned once a week to pitch a tad more coverage on your life insurance policy? Outrageous, right? He might be trying hard, but insurance isn't an everyday purchase. You'd decide that he thinks more about his commissions than he does about your needs. Or how about the ski resort that sends out monthly reminders in June, July, and August to "Reserve Now." Useless, no? You haven't even planned your summer getaway.

On the other hand, what if the local florist mailed you a discreet and timely preprinted postcard, inquiring whether you'd like to duplicate delivery of last year's order of a dozen roses on a certain day? That date—natch!—happens to be your wedding anniversary. Perfect, huh?

The point is that reaching out to customers with personalized messages is not only about focusing on loyal or high-volume buyers. Timing and frequency counts. You need to market customers at the time and on occasions when they're receptive to your message—that is, when they need or want what you're selling. How often and when you send out messages are key drivers of successful sales.

Generally, how frequently you contact a customer and the form you use to communicate are determined by the kind of business you have and, sometimes, by the personality or circumstances of your customers. Different businesses demand different timing and tactics. You want to be in touch often

Chapter Eleven: **The Customer Comes First**

Part Four:
Connect and
Conquer:
Building the
Company

enough that you develop recognition and trust, but not so much that you turn into a nuisance. A retailer with weekly specials, for instance, might send out flyers or discount coupons every week or two. A dry cleaner with just-opened doors might mail a few rounds of flyers to nearby homeowners, announcing the grand opening and the short-term deals created to persuade customers to switch services.

Health-care practices, law firms, or management consultants, of course, see clients on very different timetables than retailers do. Their customer contact, therefore, is both more formal and less frequent. Weekly communications from the dentist would probably irritate clients enough that they'd put off appointments altogether. Service firms benefit from sending out messages once or twice a year, such as "Time to Make an Appointment" reminder postcards. All of that communicates to clients that the firm is poised to serve their needs.

When you want to forge customer bonds over the long term, newsletters are the way to go. They're affordable and effective, and they set up an expected and anticipated benefit for customers. By sending out the newsletter on a regular basis, over time you become an authority in your field or the trusted source for advice. Good newsletters make people feel like insiders, putting them in the know or getting them up-to-speed ahead of their peers. Arriving at reliable intervals, the issues reward customer attention, while your payoff is the ongoing relationship and business. But newsletters will work only if customers value the information or features you deliver. You must offer articles or news they can't find as easily or at all anywhere else.

A wine shop owner, for instance, might create a wine-tasting club for top-tier customers, inviting them to special events. Once they join, customers get a monthly newsletter that provides news of tasting menus and schedules as well as features about the latest deals, harvests, imports, and expert ratings. The upshot is that customers feel like connoisseurs. Along with every bottle of wine they buy, club members get an ego boost, which is bound to help sales. Obviously, it takes a while to build momentum this way. That's why newsletters are best for long-term marketing goals.

What makes a worthwhile newsletter? Put yourself in your customers' shoes. Include stories that customers will find informative, educational, or entertaining. Don't emphasize articles about the state of your business, although an occasional item about some business success, such as an award or a big-deal contract is certainly appropriate. Some ideas:

Part Four:
Connect and
Conquer:
Building the
Company

Microsoft Small Business Kit

- Practical tips on getting more out of products or services, both ones that you sell and those your customers use in conjunction with yours

- Advice on achieving some goal or getting something done more conveniently, quickly, or efficiently

- News or views on your industry, field, product innovations, or services

- Statistics of the industry or field

- Reviews and announcements of relevant events and launches

- Resources that give customers deeper access to information or to free samples

- Interviews, profiles, or question-and-answer stories with key personalities or experts

Typically, newsletters are sent out once a month or every quarter because they require commitment, both for you to produce and for customers to read. When an issue is delivered, you're asking customers for considerable time and attention. You'd better make it worth their while.

Overall, when you target customers with the appropriate message at the right time, you'll build recognition and credibility, which converts to sales.

When Good Customers Go Bad

Is all this advice about serving the customer and luring return business just another way of saying the customer is always right? Yes and no. The customer is always right, except when you can't afford it.

When you've been worn out trying to please an impossible client, blame the received wisdom on Harry Gordon Selfridge (1864–1947). While working as a Chicago trader, the Wisconsin-born merchant visited London in 1906, and purchased an Oxford Street site upon which he built the famous store that bears his name and thrives today. Selfridges opened doors in 1909, when women were beginning to enjoy the fruits of emancipation by actually wandering unescorted around the City of London. A canny marketer, Selfridge promoted the then-radical notion of shopping for pleasure rather than necessity. His fashion-forward shop adopted the slogan now heard round the globe: "The customer is always right," declared Selfridge.

But today businesses run on real-time sales forecasts, preferred customer databases, time management applications, and activity-based costing software—all of which can calculate to the penny how much each transaction

Chapter Eleven: The Customer Comes First

Part Four:
Connect and
Conquer:
Building the
Company

costs you. Jettisoning customers must be a calibrated decision and a last resort, but it's an option to keep in mind, especially when you need to improve performance and profits.

Here are three categories of customers who often deserve a walk:

- Customers who expect the illegal or unethical
- Clients who are more trouble than they're worth
- Toxic customers, including someone you just don't like

However counterintuitive it might seem, firing customers can actually boost profits. Pruning your client base of low-margin, high-demand, and time-consuming customers lets sales and service staff totally focus on cost-effective customer acquisition and customers who matter: loyal, repeat buyers and worthy new customers.

Protecting Customer Trust and Privacy

Trust isn't something you can fake. You must sincerely mean what you say and do. If you make product claims or agree not to intrude on customers who share their personal data, you must keep those promises. Otherwise, you end up doing business on the consumer fault line. Then it's only a matter of time before your customers erupt and you squander your brand equity. Eventually, your best customers will cease to believe anything you have to say or offer.

See "Disciplined Messaging and the Seamless Sell," page 210, for more about creating a brand.

Even the appearance of misuse can lead to problems. If consumers perceive that their privacy is being violated, they will push back. Think that's an overstatement? One in six Americans say they have bought a privacy product to avoid identity theft, check their credit report, or surf or shop online anonymously, according to a June 2003 survey conducted by Harris Interactive and commissioned by Privacy & American Business (P&AB), a non-profit think tank. In overwhelming numbers, consumers now worry that companies they buy from will provide their personal data to other marketers without permission and that credit card transactions might not be secure and that thieves or hackers could steal their personal data.

If you want to attract and keep customers, you must take steps to allay consumer anxiety about security and privacy. Trust is not built overnight, of course. Nor will consumers be appeased by half-measures or gestures. First,

Part Four:
Connect and
Conquer:
Building the
Company

Microsoft Small Business Kit

tell consumers plainly and obviously what they need to know. To gain customer confidence, you need to provide appropriate assurances in the right way at the right time.

Some ways to bolster consumers' trust and reward them for sharing personal data:

Build your own marketing list. By creating your own database, you can be completely confident that everyone on your list wants to hear from you. Your best prospects are your current, happy customers and people who've already heard of you somehow. (See the section "Creating a Customer Database," earlier in this chapter, for more information.)

Deliver value. Customers are more receptive if you provide something of value in exchange for their time and opt-in permission. Include free samples, offers, product news, or discounts. For business clients, offer timely industry news, white papers, reports, surveys, market intelligence, or research. Good content still rules.

Prospect by phone. Do not blindly send out e-mail offers. First, prospect customer lists by phone. Once you've gained permission, you can follow up via e-mail offers and messages.

Rely on a privacy seal if you sell products online. Online consumer watchdogs, such as TRUSTe (*www.truste.org*) and BBBOnline (*www.bbbonline.com*) offer seals of reliability and privacy to businesses that apply and undergo inspection and evaluation. Fees for applications and seals are nominal, ranging from a few hundred to a few thousand dollars a year, depending on retail revenue. That might be cheap at the price. Consumers definitely notice seals and are more likely to purchase from companies that display them.

Watch your language. Your fab new widget will not "revolutionize" business or "totally change" life as we know it. Consumers are dead weary of howitzer marketing. They've seen and heard it all. Keep it straight and simple. Focus on authentic customer benefits.

Work the relationship. The best methods for forging connections with customers will vary with the industry. But technology has multiplied your options. With the latest CAN-SPAM legislation and all the filtering software, e-mail marketing is increasingly being used only to retain and reward valued customers—in other words, to build trust. (Customer acquisition is moving into direct mail and other channels.) Password-protected Web sites and premiums also provide possibilities that can satisfy best customers. Don't take any customer for granted.

Chapter Eleven: The Customer Comes First

Part Four:
Connect and
Conquer:
Building the
Company

Get customers to vouch for you. Include customer testimonials in your marketing with names, cities, and states that show real people are getting results by using your product. The cheapest and most effective marketing, of course, is one friend recommending your product to another. Whatever you do to build customer referrals and word of mouth will be worth it, including events, clubs, programs, prizes, or discounts.

Create missionaries. The same advice about how to treat customers applies to your staff. Treat employees the way you want them to interact with customers, and you'll be developing brand missionaries.

Learn more about privacy policies

To find guidelines about setting up company privacy policies, check the Platform for Privacy Preferences (P3P) Project, developed by the World Wide Web Consortium: *www.w3.org/P3P*. This evolving standard gives users some automated control over the use of personal information.

Understanding When to Expand

Eventually, if they're moving in the right direction, small businesses figure out what they want to be when they grow up. Then they face serious challenges. How do you boost sales when your cash flow can't carry a cracker-jack business developer? How do you attract more customers when your marketing looks like amateur hour? How do you plan next-stage innovation when every bit of juice is being squeezed to get your new product or service to market? How do you add staff at all? If you hire on the anticipation of work, you could get stung when a deal falls through. Wait until business booms, and you've lost opportunities. It's a challenge.

Business owners get accustomed to making do with less and still maintaining high productivity. They often dread the idea of getting bigger. Growth means significant investments in equipment, technology, staff, and marketing, just when owners are beginning to enjoy some cash flow and leisure time. Growth requires change and risk and loss of control. Rejiggering strategy or operations pushes everyone out of the comfort zone.

But you don't expand by standing still. Success breeds change, and vice versa. So how do you know when to expand? Here are some triggers that tell you it's a good time to grow:

Part Four:
Connect and
Conquer:
Building the
Company

Microsoft Small Business Kit

You reach the break-even point.   A key indicator of doing things right, the break-even point means that your total revenues equal the total of all your costs. The upshot: Congratulations! Your company is now generating a profit.

See Chapter 7, "By the Numbers: Analyzing Your Business with Excel," to learn how to run a breakeven analysis in Excel.

You raise prices with no resistance.   If customers keep flocking and demand stays high after you issue a price increase, you can expand services or volume.

You keep hiring temporary or contract help and consultants.   This says you've got more work than your current staff or in-house experts can handle.

See Chapter 14, "Managing Like a Coach," for more about working with free agents.

You've paid off all your debt.   Well, sure. Enjoy the moment for a week or so. But then, get ready to grow.

You've stopped being a jack-of-all-trades.   Most businesses lurch into growth, rather than expand incrementally. It's like leaping onto a plateau with a toehold and, after a while, pulling yourself up so that you can stand tall. When you are no longer answering the phone, mailing bills, stuffing envelopes, and sweeping the floor—in short, doing everything—you've likely tightened your focus. You're now concentrating on what you do best or what you really want the business to become. That's the moment to plan for growth.

Planning for Growing Pains

OK, so you've made the decision to expand. Now what? Just as in the beginning when you needed a business plan (which might or might not still be relevant at this point), you need a strategic plan for next-stage growth. You should consider these factors as you chart your goals:

Prepare best-case and worst-case scenarios.   Run all your numbers a few times. If revenues and/or profits fall off or—lucky day!—spike, how will you handle it?

Identify the expertise you'll need.   Growing usually demands a financial guru of some kind. Do you now need a Chief Financial Officer? Or perhaps an accountant who can describe the big picture? Will you need a better or bigger supplier? Or two? Evaluate the next level of

Chapter Eleven: **The Customer Comes First**

Part Four:
Connect and
Conquer:
Building the
Company

support you'll need. Can you outsource some of the services you need until you have enough cash flow to hire an expert?

Evaluate cash flow and liquidity.   Consider what kind of cash you'll need for the upcoming changes. Figure out whether you need to borrow or look for equity investors.

See Chapter 3, "How to Find Backing," for more about finding backers.

Get your marketing up-to-speed.   Don't imagine for a moment that if you build it bigger, they will just come. You need to get out the message in a new and, possibly, more sophisticated way.

Keep tabs on the strain.   Growing pains push everyone's buttons and limits. You need to stay attuned to both the staff and the technology to make sure nothing goes over the edge.

Forging Strategic Alliances

Some start-ups or companies take a while to shape their identities or chase enough customers. They're not quite ready to expand on their own, but some growth makes sense. In that case, consider finding a strategic partner. Building a special relationship with another company or service can boost your reach and profile while it minimizes the risks of all-or-nothing growth. Typically, partnerships work best after you've built some credibility, cash flow, reputation, and a sizable customer base. Both you and the partner need to bring something to the table to benefit from the relationship.

Strategic alliances or partnerships are close relationships with any number of other companies, including suppliers, customers, manufacturers, or a peer company that significantly adds to your volume or quality. Such alliances come in dozens of varieties but two basic shapes:

- A structured, legally binding alliance that's formalized in a contract or an agreement

- An outright acquisition, such as the following:
    - ❑ Acquisition by a direct competitor, which can cut costs and let you raise prices.
    - ❑ Vertical integration, whereby you acquire a firm along the supply or distribution chain, such as an auto company acquiring a parts manufacturer, giving you greater control over supply and pricing.

Part Four:
Connect and
Conquer:
Building the
Company

Microsoft Small Business Kit

❑ Acquisition of a company that has broad synergy with your own, such as your executive training company buying an executive recruiting service.

Small sister firms can partner, but that's likely a bootstrapping tactic, as in, "You do my Web site, and I'll do your mobile messaging." More typically, strategic partnerships are sealed between a large firm—sometimes *way* larger—and a small one. Frequently, potential partners begin with an alliance, and when everything clicks, an acquisition follows.

For small and mid-size firms, the benefits of a strategic alliance with a large partner include:

- Better entry into the market

- Industry-specific and dedicated sales support

- A larger customer base

- Access to key contacts

- Internal resources, such as financial planning, human resources, and support staff

- Image-building, high-profile marketing expertise

To get a real deal on paper and bank on a fruitful partnership, make sure that each partner has a strong, inside champion and that both sides identify and agree to focus on specific market events and targets. You'll need buy-in at all levels, including the most senior executives. Also make sure that the pieces really fit together. Sometimes small companies and larger ones experience an unbridgeable culture gap.

As you explore potential alliances for your business, remember to step quietly in the minefield that can be created by partnering. First, the trust required in such relationships can only be built over time and in small steps. For start-up tech companies in particular, if you move too quickly, you run the risk of losing your proprietary software to a larger company. There's always the temptation to show all your innovation and advantages to larger companies right away. But it might be smarter to present only the necessary components or advantages that get you to the next level.

Manage your expectations carefully. Be clear about what you want out of the relationship, and ask, specifically, what your partner is seeking. Writing down the goals and details before talking to the lawyers is a good way to work through the process. After that, you can shake hands and come out partners.

Chapter Eleven: **The Customer Comes First**

Part Four:
**Connect and
Conquer:
Building the
Company**

For More Information

In addition to the resources mentioned in this chapter, you will find links and information on the companion CD. Some books and Web sites particularly useful when you consider how to satisfy your customers include:

Books

- Jeffrey J. Fox, *How to Become a Rainmaker: The Rules for Getting and Keeping Customers and Clients* (Hyperion, 2000)

- Harry Beckwith, *What Clients Love: A Field Guide to Growing Your Business* (Warner Books, 2003)

- Jeffrey Gitomer, *Customer Satisfaction Is Worthless, Customer Loyalty Is Priceless: How to Make Customers Love You, Keep Them Coming Back and Tell Everyone They Know* (Bard Press, 1998)

Web Sites

Frankly, most Web sites that you might come across by searching on *marketing* or *customer relations* will be trying to sell you a particular methodology. That isn't necessarily a bad thing—some courses and seminars can be valuable—but it can be hard to winnow the nuggets of information that will truly guide your business. You might want to start with some of the broader resources, such as:

- *Black Enterprise* magazine: *www.blackenterprise.com/*

- *Inc.* magazine: *www.inc.com/home/*

- *Entrepreneur* magazine: *www.entrepreneur.com*

Part Four:
Connect and
Conquer:
Building the
Company

Microsoft Small Business Kit

Worry about being better; bigger will take care of itself. Think one customer at a time and take care of each one the best way you can.

— *Gary Comer, founder of Land's End*

Chapter Twelve

Managing Customer Contacts: Business Contact Manager

Engaging your customers is how you stay in business. You need a relationship with each one. You need to know when to approach a customer, when to follow up, and when it's better to let the customer have some space. A customer management system can be an indispensable part of the tools and tact you use when dealing with your customers.

Chapter Twelve: **Managing Customer Contacts: Business Contact Manager**

Part Four:
Connect and
Conquer:
Building the
Company

What you'll find:

- ❑ Understanding what Business Contact Manager (BCM) can do
- ❑ Installing and running BCM
- ❑ Working with business contacts
- ❑ Creating and using accounts
- ❑ Creating and using opportunities
- ❑ Tracking item history
- ❑ Attaching items
- ❑ Creating reports
- ❑ Importing and exporting information
- ❑ Managing your BCM data

Part Four:
Connect and
Conquer:
Building the
Company

Microsoft Small Business Kit

Is anything more important to a business than its customers? Probably not. Customers and clients are critical to almost every kind of enterprise, but what differs from business to business are the requirements for managing relationships with customers and other business contacts. A retail store might want to assemble a mailing list of customers who come in the door so that it can send out notices of special offers and sales. Businesses that sell their goods and services to other businesses probably want to know who the chief buyers at each customer and supplier are, what the typical sales cycle for a customer is, and which customers with pending orders need to be called this week.

Decisions about storing and managing business contact information should be evaluated in the context of factors such as budget, the time required to keep the information current and usable, the value the information has to the business (measured by how frequently the information is used, for example), the type of customers you come in contact with (are they regular,

Learn About Outlook Before Using BCM

To best understand the examples and other information in this chapter, you should know how to work with Microsoft Outlook—how to create items, for example, and how to manage the folder list. You should also know a little about how Outlook manages e-mail accounts.

When you set up a user account in Outlook, you establish what Outlook refers to as a *profile*. A profile essentially refers to a group of e-mail accounts and address books. You'll need only one profile in most cases, but you can create more than one and associate a set of e-mail accounts and address books with each profile. Multiple profiles are useful if more than one person uses a computer. You can view information about a profile by opening Windows Control Panel, double-clicking on Mail (click User Accounts first if Control Panel is displayed in Categories view), and then clicking Show Profiles.

If you're interested in teaching yourself how to use Outlook (and BCM), Microsoft Office Online offers a lot of useful training and assistance. To display Microsoft Office Online, open Outlook, and then choose Microsoft Office Online from the Help menu. On the Office Online home page, click Assistance in the navigation pane on the left, and then click Outlook 2003 under Browse Assistance.

For more information about Outlook profiles, click the assistance heading E-Mail, and then see the articles under the topic "Configuring E-Mail Accounts." You can also find assistance about using attachments, reading and replying to messages in Outlook, and other basic tasks in this section of the online assistance. Another of the main assistance sections is "Finding and Managing Items." Here you can find articles about how to search for items, how to filter items (a particularly useful feature when working with items in BCM), and how to use folders in Outlook.

You can also learn more about how to manage e-mail messages in Outlook later in this book, in Chapter 15, "The Outlook Is Bright: E-Mail and Your Business."

Chapter Twelve: **Managing Customer Contacts: Business Contact Manager**

Part Four:
Connect and
Conquery:
Building the
Company

infrequent, or one-time customers), and the dollar amount of most of your customer transactions.

In a small business setting, several different approaches can be used to store and manage customer information—everything from a handwritten address list to a complex database. One of the most economical and straightforward alternatives available to users of Microsoft Office 2003 is Business Contact Manager (BCM), a contact management and sales-support tool that you can add on to Microsoft Outlook 2003.

This chapter explores BCM in depth. You'll gain a lot of hands-on experience with the application as you follow the steps to install the software, create accounts and contacts, generate reports, and use its other features. By the end of this chapter, you'll have a solid background in using BCM and can begin taking advantage of it to manage your business contacts and accounts. If you're new to using Outlook, read the sidebar titled "Learn About Outlook Before Using BCM." This sidebar provides information about some of the training in Outlook that's available on Microsoft Office Online.

Note   This chapter is adapted from Chapter 15, "Using Microsoft Business Contact Manager," from the book *Microsoft Office Outlook 2003 Inside Out*, by Jim Boyce (Microsoft Press, 2003). On Jim Boyce's Web site, *www.boyce.us*, you can find a number of tips and tricks for using Outlook.

Understanding What Business Contact Manager (BCM) Can Do

BCM is a customer resource management (CRM) tool that integrates with Outlook 2003. By itself, Outlook lets you manage contacts, e-mail, a calendar, and tasks. BCM offers a system for managing clients, sales opportunities, and other business data by providing Outlook items for accounts, business contacts, and business opportunities. These items appear under the Business Contact Manager branch in the folder list, as shown in Figure 12-1.

Part Four:
Connect and
Conquer:
Building the
Company

Microsoft Small Business Kit

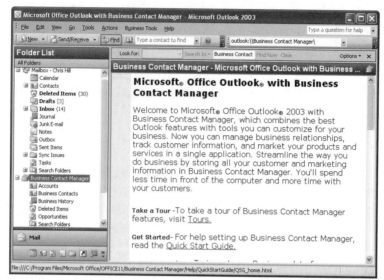

Figure 12-1   BCM adds folders and item types to Outlook.

BCM doesn't work with Exchange

BCM is designed for Outlook users whose e-mail accounts are set up with an Internet service provider (ISP). You cannot use BCM with an Outlook e-mail account that connects to Microsoft Exchange Server. If your e-mail system includes Exchange Server, you can create a separate Outlook profile that's not associated with Exchange Server and then use BCM with that profile. (A profile is a group of e-mail accounts and address books in Outlook. In most cases, you'll need only one profile, but you can create more than one, and each can have its own set of e-mail accounts and address books.) You can export contacts and other data from your Exchange Server account to an Outlook .pst file to import into BCM.

The main benefit of using BCM is that it gives you the means to easily integrate all information about a customer account in one place. (See Figure 12-2.) You can link e-mail, contacts, notes, documents, and other items related to an account and view and manage those items from a single point. Because all account data is organized in one location, you can quickly find information and improve customer response, which ultimately should mean both a cost savings and potentially more revenue.

Chapter Twelve: Managing Customer Contacts: Business Contact Manager

Part Four:
Connect and
Conquery:
Building the
Company

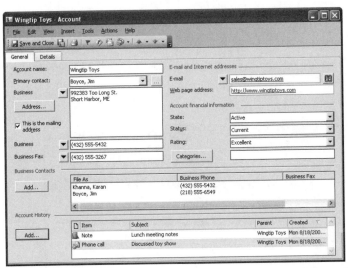

Figure 12-2 Account items give you a means to manage information about a customer account.

BCM also enables you to keep track of sales opportunities and the product information associated with those sales, from initial contact through after-sale customer support. The Opportunity item type, shown in Figure 12-3, stores information about a sales contact, potential or actual order, product items, and other details related to the potential sale.

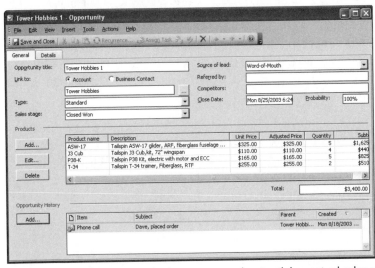

Figure 12-3 Use Opportunity items to record potential or actual sales and related information.

Part Four:
Connect and
Conquer:
Building the
Company

Microsoft Small Business Kit

The Business History folder, shown in Figure 12-4, keeps track of events associated with each contact, account, or opportunity, in much the same way that Outlook's Journal folder records which documents and other items you've worked on. By providing a record of your activity with these items, the Business History folder makes searching for and locating these items relatively easy.

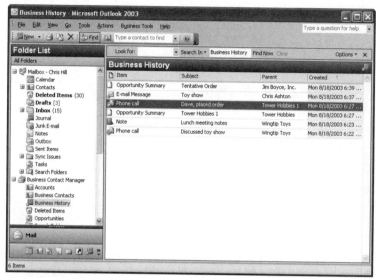

Figure 12-4   Use the Business History folder to quickly locate items.

In addition to these special-purpose folders, BCM adds reporting capabilities to Outlook to help you manage and analyze the information you've stored about your accounts, contacts, and sales. These include several predefined reports for each item type, which you can use as is or modify to suit your needs.

This section has provided a brief overview of what BCM can do. In a nutshell, the program adds new item types and folders to Outlook to give you a set of tools for managing your business accounts, contacts, and sales opportunities. As you experiment with BCM, you'll develop a better understanding of how the program can fit in with your business practices. Before you can start, however, you need to get BCM installed.

More assistance for using BCM

Microsoft Office Online assistance for Outlook 2003 includes several topics related to BCM. You can reinforce and learn more about the procedures presented in this chapter by using the online assistance.

Chapter Twelve: Managing Customer Contacts: Business Contact Manager

Part Four:
Connect and
Conquery:
Building the
Company

Installing and Running BCM

BCM is included with Microsoft Office Small Business Edition 2003 (as well as with Microsoft Office Professional Enterprise Edition 2003 and Microsoft Office Professional Edition 2003). The installation process for BCM is straightforward.

When you run Setup from the BCM CD, Setup first determines whether the Microsoft .NET Framework, which is required to run BCM, is installed on the computer. If not, Setup launches the .NET Framework installation. You'll see a handful of dialog boxes that track the .NET Framework installation progress. The only input you need to provide during this phase is to accept the .NET Framework license agreement, shown in Figure 12-5.

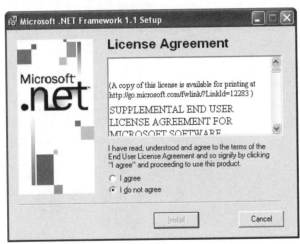

Figure 12-5 Accept the .NET Framework license agreement to complete its installation.

After the .NET Framework installation is finished, Setup starts the installation process for BCM, displaying the Setup Wizard For Business Contact Manager For Outlook 2003. After you accept the license agreement, the wizard prompts you for the location in which to install BCM, as shown in Figure 12-6. This is the only option you can configure for the installation. Select the installation location, click Next, and click Install to complete the installation.

Part Four:
Connect and
Conquer:
Building the
Company

Microsoft Small Business Kit

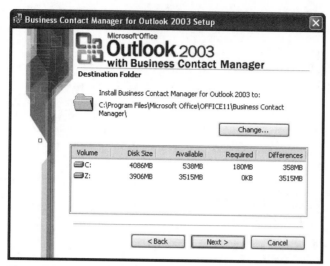

Figure 12-6 Select the location in which to install BCM.

BCM installation locations

You must install BCM on a local hard disk for this release. Installation on a network share is not supported.

The first time you run Outlook after installing BCM, you'll see the dialog box shown in Figure 12-7. Click Yes to begin using the software with your current Outlook profile. After you click Yes, BCM automatically creates a new database in which to store your BCM data if one does not already exist. If BCM detects a database, it gives you the option of selecting an existing database or creating a new one. (See Figure 12-8.) To create a new database, choose Create A New Database, and click Next. (To use an existing database, such as one you copied from another computer, choose Use An Existing Database, select the database from the drop-down list, and click Next.) For a new database, specify a unique name for the database (such as **MyBCMData**), and click Next. After the database is created, click Finish, and you're ready to start setting up your business items, as described in the section "Working with Business Contacts," later in this chapter. First, however, you might want to know more about how to control BCM.

Chapter Twelve: **Managing Customer Contacts: Business Contact Manager**

Part Four:
Connect and
Conquery:
Building the
Company

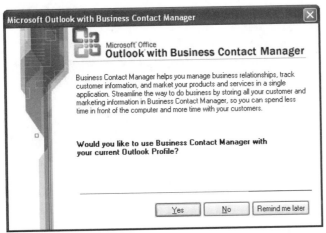

Figure 12-7   BCM asks whether you want to use the program with your current Outlook profile.

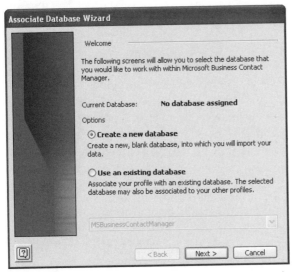

Figure 12-8   You have the option of creating a new database or using an existing one.

The BCM database

BCM uses a program called the Microsoft SQL Server Desktop Engine (MSDE) to store the databases it uses. MSDE is a database engine that provides the core features of its bigger sibling, Microsoft SQL Server, without the expense or installation of SQL Server. BCM's setup program installs its own copy of MSDE even if you have an existing installation already on your computer. If you remove BCM, Setup removes this copy of MSDE as well, but leaves any other versions installed on the computer.

Part Four:
Connect and
Conquer:
Building the
Company

Microsoft Small Business Kit

Where Is BCM?

As you first start to use BCM, you might not need to know where it's located on your computer, but as time goes on and you need to perform other tasks such as backing up your database, you'll want to know where its files are located.

Setup installs BCM by default in the folder \Program Files\Microsoft Office\Office11\Business Contact Manager. This main folder stores the files that run BCM as well as support files such as templates, scripts, icons, and documentation.

Adding and Removing BCM for a Profile

When BCM is installed on a computer, you receive a prompt (shown earlier in Figure 12-7) asking whether you want to enable it the first time you open Outlook with a profile that doesn't include BCM. Simply click Yes, and follow the prompts as explained in the section "Installing and Running BCM," earlier in this chapter.

If you decide you don't want to use BCM with a particular profile after it is enabled, you can close BCM easily enough. Open the folder list, right-click the Business Contact Manager branch, and choose Close Business Contact Manager. Outlook removes the folders from the folder list and removes the BCM-related commands from the Outlook menu. This method affects only the current profile; it does not remove BCM entirely from the computer, nor does it affect other profiles.

Perhaps you are creating a new Outlook profile and want to explicitly add a BCM database to the profile. Or, after you remove BCM from a profile, you might decide you want it back again.

You can add a BCM database to a new profile or to an existing one. If you choose the former approach, simply create an Outlook profile that contains your existing Outlook data. When you start Outlook with that profile, Outlook asks whether you want to use BCM. Click Yes to add it to the profile.

If you click No, Outlook will not add a database to the profile. However, you can add one manually. To add or restore a BCM database to an existing profile, follow these steps:

Add a BCM database to an Outlook profile

1. Open the Mail tool from Control Panel or right-click the Outlook icon on the Start menu, and choose Properties.

Chapter Twelve: **Managing Customer Contacts: Business Contact Manager**

Part Four:
Connect and
Conquery:
Building the
Company

2. Click Show Profiles, select the profile to which you want to add BCM, and then click Properties.

3. Click Data Files. In the Outlook Data Files dialog box, click Add.

4. Select Business Contact Manager Database, and then click OK.

5. To add an existing database, select Use An Existing Database, and then select the database previously used with the profile. Then click Next and Finish. To create a new database, choose the Create A New Database option, and then provide a name for the database. Click Next, and then click Finish.

6. Click Close, Close, OK to close the remaining dialog boxes, and then start Outlook and verify that your BCM data and folders are now available in Outlook.

Working with Business Contacts

One of the first tasks you will likely want to accomplish after installing BCM is to add business contacts. It makes sense to add contacts before you add accounts because each account will likely have at least one contact associated with it. If the contact is already created, you can simply assign it to an account when you create the account.

Importing contact data

BCM can import data from several different sources. If you currently use another contact management application and want to move its data to BCM, see the section "Importing and Exporting Information," later in this chapter, for details.

Copying Existing Contacts

You can copy existing contacts from Outlook's Contacts folder (or other contacts folders) to the Business Contacts folder. To do so, open the Contacts folder in Outlook, and then open the folder list. Scroll down in the folder list to locate the Business Contacts folder. Right-click a contact in the Contacts folder, drag it to the Business Contacts folder, and then choose Copy from the shortcut menu. To move the contact instead of copying it, choose Move from the menu or simply drag the contact to the Business Contacts folder.

Part Four:
Connect and
Conquer:
Building the
Company

Microsoft Small Business Kit

A Business Contact item includes fields not found in a standard Outlook Contact item. After you copy or move an item to the Business Contacts folder, you will likely want to edit the contact to include additional information. Double-click the contact to open it, and then add or edit information according to the descriptions provided in the following section.

Creating Business Contacts

You create a Business Contact item in much the same way you create a standard Outlook Contact item. Open the Business Contacts folder and, in the right-hand pane, double-click a blank area. (You can also click New on the toolbar or choose File, New, Business Contact.) Figure 12-9 shows a Business Contact item after many of its fields have been filled in.

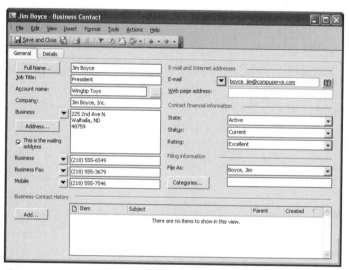

Figure 12-9   A Business Contact item includes several fields not found in a standard Contact item.

Most of the fields on the General tab are the same as those found in a standard Outlook Contact item. Two groups of fields on the General tab for a Business Contact item are new: Contact Financial Information and Business Contact History. The first of these two groups provides three drop-down lists that let you specify information about the contact's financial status:

State   Use this option to specify whether the contact is active or inactive. You can use this field in reports to separate active from inactive contacts.

Chapter Twelve: **Managing Customer Contacts: Business Contact Manager**

Part Four:
Connect and
Conquery:
Building the
Company

Status   Choose between Current and Overdue for the contact's account
   status.

Rating   Select an overall financial rating for the contact from this drop-
   down list.

The Business Contact History group shows all of the items that are linked
to the contact, including e-mail messages, notes, opportunities, tasks,
appointments, phone logs, and files. Some of these items you must link
yourself through the contact item, whereas others are linked automatically. For example, if you send an e-mail message to a business contact,
BCM automatically links the e-mail message to the contact and includes it
in the Business Contact History list.

*This section of the chapter focuses on creating and working with Busi-
ness Contact items. See the section "Attaching Items," later in this chapter, for details on linking items to your contacts.*

The Details tab for a Business Contact item, shown in Figure 12-10, provides several additional fields you can use to track various items of information about a business contact.

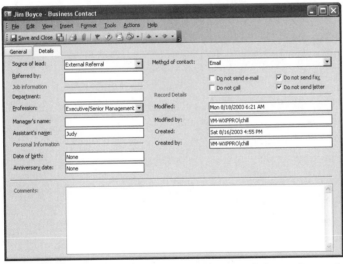

Figure 12-10   Use the Details tab to add more information to the contact.

The fields on the Details tab are generally self-explanatory. Note that the
four check boxes under the Method Of Contact field (Do Not Send E-
Mail, Do Not Call, Do Not Send Fax, and Do Not Send Letter) are infor-
mational fields only and do not actually prevent these actions. For example, if you select the Do Not Send E-Mail check box for the contact,

Part Four:
Connect and
Conquer:
Building the
Company

Microsoft Small Business Kit

Outlook does not honor that setting if you attempt to send an e-mail message. The message will go through without any prompts to the contrary. (See the sidebar "Use Views to Honor Contact Settings" for a way to make better use of these fields.)

Use Views to Honor Contact Settings

If you want to put the method of contact fields to use (for example, not calling someone if Do Not Call is selected for their contact item), you should make a habit of checking these fields before taking the actions specified by them. An alternative is to create a custom view that filters the items based on the pertinent field.

The following example shows how to create a view that shows only those contacts whose Do Not Send Email check box is cleared:

1. Open the Business Contacts folder, and choose View, Arrange By, Current View, Define Views.

2. In the Custom View Organizer dialog box, click New. Enter the name **OK To Email**, choose Table from the Type Of View list, and click OK.

3. In the Customize View dialog box, click Filter to display the Filter dialog box, and then click the Advanced tab, as shown in Figure 12-11.

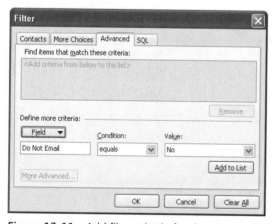

Figure 12-11 Add filter criteria for the view on the Advanced tab.

4. Click Field, choose User-Defined Fields In Folder, and choose Do Not Email. Choose a different field if you want to filter based on that field instead.

5. Verify that the Condition drop-down list is set to Equals, and choose No from the Value drop-down list. Then click Add To List.

6. Click OK, OK, Apply View to show the view you just created.

Currently, BCM does not properly initialize the values of these settings for imported contacts, so you should select and then clear the Value check boxes to set them to No. (Selected indicates Yes.) BCM does properly initialize these fields for newly created contacts.

Chapter Twelve: **Managing Customer Contacts: Business Contact Manager**

Part Four:
Connect and
Conquery:
Building the
Company

Using Contacts

There are several actions you might take with a business contact, including sending an e-mail message, calling, faxing, sending a letter, or adding a note. When you perform many of these tasks, BCM adds the item to the contact's history. For example, send an e-mail message to a contact, and BCM links that message to the contact. This linking happens automatically in most cases. In the case of an e-mail message, you don't even have to go through the Business Contacts folder to have the message linked to the contact. With the Inbox folder open, simply send the contact a message. Outlook checks the recipient; if it is one of your business contacts, Outlook links the e-mail message to that contact.

You can initiate actions for a business contact in different ways. For example, select a contact in the Business Contacts folder, and then choose Actions, followed by the action you want to perform, such as New Letter To Contact. You can also right-click a contact in the folder and choose an action that's displayed on the shortcut menu.

Creating and Using Accounts

BCM also adds *accounts* as a new type of Outlook item. An account is generally synonymous with a customer, but you might have different accounts for a single customer. To create a new account, open the Accounts folder and then double-click in an empty area of the right-hand pane. (You can also click New on the toolbar with the Accounts folder open or choose File, New, Account.)

As Figure 12-12 shows, the General tab for an account includes a name to identify the account, the name of the primary contact for the account, address, phone numbers, and several other items. An account also includes the same financial status information as a contact. It also enables you to associate multiple contacts with the account. At the bottom of the General tab, an Account History area lists all of the items (e-mail messages, tasks, notes, and so on) that are linked to the account.

Part Four:
Connect and
Conquer:
Building the
Company

Microsoft Small Business Kit

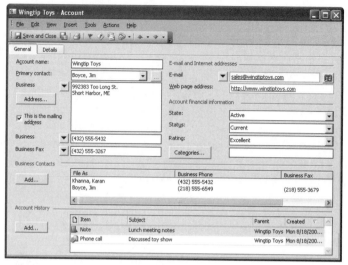

Figure 12-12   Use the General tab to set an account's name, the primary contact, and other general fields.

The useful Account History list

When you send an e-mail message to any contact associated with an account, BCM links the message to the contact. The Account History list shows all items linked to all of the account's contacts, not just for the primary contact. This automatic tracking is one of BCM's most useful features.

The Details tab, shown in Figure 12-13, provides fields to track other information about the account, such as Type Of Business and Territory, and provides a Comments area in which you can record comments about the account.

Many of the fields are the same for an account as they are for a contact. For example, contacts and accounts both have address fields, phone number fields, and financial status fields. However, the fields are unique. For example, the Phone Number field for an account can be different from the Phone Number field of the contact assigned as the primary contact for the account. Keep this in mind when creating accounts and contacts.

Chapter Twelve: **Managing Customer Contacts: Business Contact Manager**

Part Four:
Connect and
Conquery:
Building the
Company

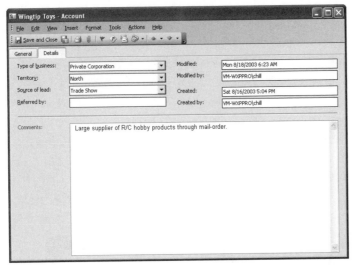

Figure 12-13   Specify additional information and comments on the Details tab.

Performing Actions with Accounts

You can also perform many of the same actions for an account as you can for a contact. For example, you can right-click an account and choose Call Contact from the shortcut menu to open the New Call dialog box with the account's phone number displayed. Or you might choose New Message To Contact to start an e-mail message to the address specified in the account's E-Mail field.

As with a contact, you can initiate an action from the Actions menu or by right-clicking an account and choosing an action from the shortcut menu. Keep in mind, however, that BCM performs the action using the information associated with the account, not with the contacts that are linked to the account. For example, if you right-click an account and choose Call Contact, BCM shows the account's phone number in the New Call dialog box, not the phone number assigned to the individual listed in the Primary Contact field. The same is true for an e-mail message—BCM addresses the message to the address specified in the account's E-mail field, not to the primary contact's e-mail address. If you need to work with a contact's information instead, either open the contact directly from the Business Contacts folder or double-click the contact in the Business Contacts area on the account's form and then use the Actions menu in the contact form that appears to perform the action.

Part Four:
Connect and
Conquer:
Building the
Company

Microsoft Small Business Kit

Creating and Using Opportunities

BCM is geared primarily to people in sales, and the inclusion of the Opportunity item-type illustrates that focus. You can use opportunities to track sales leads at various stages, from the initial inquiry through to the placement of the order.

To create an opportunity, open the Opportunities folder and click New on the toolbar (or choose File, New, Opportunity). As Figure 12-14 illustrates, the General tab for an Opportunity item includes a name for the opportunity, source for the lead, stage of the sale, and product list, among other sales-related fields. The Details tab includes a handful of additional fields and a place to add comments.

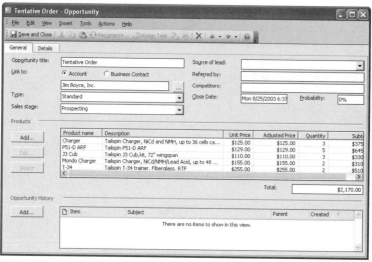

Figure 12-14   An Opportunity item defines a sale or a potential sale.

Each opportunity must be associated with an account or a business contact by the Link To options on the opportunity's General tab, just under the opportunity's title. Select either Account or Business Contact, click the ellipsis button beside the text box, and choose Add Existing Account (or Contact) or Create New Account (or Contact). If you choose to add an existing item, BCM displays either the Accounts or Business Contacts dialog box (see Figure 12-15), which you use to select the account or contact. Choose the item, and click OK to add it to the opportunity.

Chapter Twelve: Managing Customer Contacts: Business Contact Manager

Part Four:
Connect and
Conquery:
Building the
Company

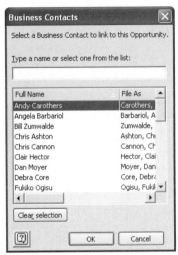

Figure 12-15 Use the Business Contacts dialog box to choose a contact to associate with the opportunity.

If you choose the command to create an account or contact, BCM prompts you to enter the name for the account or contact. After you enter the name and click OK, BCM creates a new item of the selected type and associates it with the opportunity. However, it does not prompt you to complete the other fields for the new account or contact. After you add the item to the opportunity and save the opportunity, you should open the account or business contact and enter any additional information for the new item.

Creating and Managing Products

In addition to the general information included in an opportunity, you can also track specific sales-related information, including products. BCM lets you create a product database in which you maintain your company's product line, and you can add items to the opportunity from this product database. You can add existing items to the opportunity or create new items in the database as you need to.

To manage the product list, choose Business Tools, Product List to open the Edit Product Master List dialog box, shown in Figure 12-16. This dialog box lists the existing product items in the database.

Part Four:
Connect and
Conquer:
Building the
Company

Microsoft Small Business Kit

Figure 12-16   Use the Edit Product Master List dialog box to add or modify products in the database.

To add a new item, click Add to display the Add/Edit Product Properties dialog box, shown in Figure 12-17. Enter information in the Product Name, Description, Unit Price, and Default Quantity fields, and click OK to add the information to the database. Repeat the process to add other items to the product database.

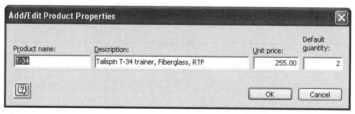

Figure 12-17   Enter a new product with the Add/Edit Product Properties dialog box.

Importing a product list

If you have already compiled a product database outside BCM, you can import the product information into BCM rather than re-create all of the entries, saving a lot of time and effort. See the section "Importing Products," later in this chapter, to learn how.

You can also manage products already listed in the database. In the Edit Product Master List dialog box, select a product, and click Edit to open the

Chapter Twelve: **Managing Customer Contacts: Business Contact Manager**

Part Four:
Connect and
Conquery:
Building the
Company

Add/Edit Product Properties dialog box for the item. To delete a product, select the product in the master list, and then click Delete.

Adding Products to an Opportunity

As you learned earlier in this section, an opportunity can include a list of products to be included in the sale. To add products, first open the Opportunity item. On the General tab, under the Products group, click Add. BCM displays an Add/Edit Product Entry dialog box that is similar to the Add/Edit Product Properties dialog box you use to create products in the database. However, as Figure 12-18 illustrates, you can enter additional information, including an adjusted price, an adjusted percentage, and a quantity. The dialog box also shows the subtotal for the item.

Figure 12-18   Add a product, and set an adjusted price, a quantity, and other items with the Add/Edit Product Entry dialog box.

You can create an item on the fly with this dialog box, but it's more likely you will want to select an existing item from the product database. Click the button between the Product Name and Description fields to display the Edit Product Master List dialog box. Select a product, and then click OK. BCM imports the product information from the database, and you can then set the adjusted price, percentage, or quantity as needed. Click OK to close the dialog box and return to the opportunity form, or click Add Next to save the current item, clear the form, and add another item.

Tracking Item History

The Business History folder provides a place for you to view all of the events and items that are linked to accounts, business contacts, and opportunities in your BCM database. The Business History folder is much like the Outlook Journal folder in that it automatically tracks events such as e-mail messages and meetings.

The Business History folder shows all linked items and is useful when you need a global view of all items. As with other folders, the Business History folder provides a handful of predefined views that you can use to change the

Part Four:
Connect and
Conquer:
Building the
Company

Microsoft Small Business Kit

way its information is displayed. For example, you can use the Messages view, shown in Figure 12-19, to see all of the messages linked to items in your BCM database.

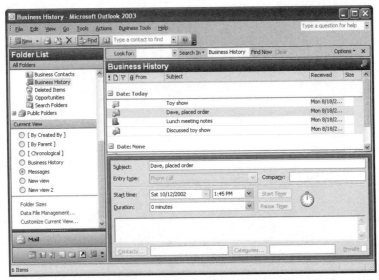

Figure 12-19   The Business History folder includes a handful of predefined views, including the Messages view.

You can also create your own views as needed to organize the folder's items in other ways. For example, you might create a custom view that shows messages from a specific sender or those associated with a particular account. The following steps illustrate an example of how to create a view of the Business History folder that shows all items for a specific account:

Show the business history for a specific account

1. Open the Business History folder, and choose View, Arrange By, Current View, Define Views.

2. In the Custom View Organizer dialog box, click New.

3. Enter the name **Wingtip Toys**, choose Table, and click OK.

4. Click Filter in the Customize View dialog box, and then click the Advanced tab, as shown in Figure 12-20.

Chapter Twelve: Managing Customer Contacts: Business Contact Manager

Part Four:
Connect and
Conquery:
Building the
Company

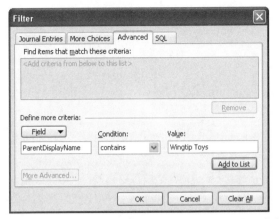

Figure 12-20 Use the Advanced tab in the Filter dialog box to create a filtered view of the Business History folder.

5. Click Field, User-Defined Fields In Folder, and ParentDisplayName.

6. Click in the Value field, and type **Wingtip Toys**. Click Add To List, and then click OK.

7. Click OK, and then click Apply View to view all items associated with the Wingtip Toys account.

View the history of an item

Because the Business History folder shows all items by default, it's not usually the best place to go to find items associated with a particular contact, account, or opportunity. Although you can create custom views that will locate these items for you, a better approach is to simply open the account, contact, or opportunity, and view the associated items there. Viewing the links from the item's form saves you the trouble of creating a view to locate the linked items.

Attaching Items

In most cases, BCM adds items to the Business History folder automatically. For example, send an e-mail message to a business contact, and BCM links the message to the contact and displays the message in the Business History folder. Or, create a Call Contact task for a contact, and BCM adds that to the contact.

You can also link items manually. For example, you might want to add a Phone Log item to an account when you receive a call from one of the

Part Four:
Connect and
Conquer:
Building the
Company

Microsoft Small Business Kit

account's contacts, attach a document to the account, or schedule an appointment for a contact. You can add the following to each of the BCM item types:

Business Note   A note containing a subject, comments, and information about who created the note and when it was created.

Task   A standard Outlook task.

Appointment   A standard Outlook appointment.

Phone Log   A phone log entry that includes the call's start time, duration, subject, and comments. The Business Phone Log form includes a timer that you can start and pause during the call to record the call's duration.

File   Any type of file. For example, you might add a Microsoft Word document, a Microsoft Excel worksheet, or a brochure in Portable Document Format (PDF) format.

You can also add the following to contacts and accounts:

Mail Message   Send an e-mail message to the business contact or to the e-mail address specified in the account's properties.

Opportunity   Add a new sales opportunity item to the business contact or account.

To add an item to an account, contact, or opportunity, first open that item from its folder. In the History area of the General tab, click Add, and then select the type of item to add. BCM opens a form that corresponds to the type of item selected. Enter information in the form, and click Save And Close to associate it with the selected item. The linked item will then show up in the History list as well as in the Business History folder.

Creating Reports

What would a CRM system be without reports? BCM includes several predefined reports that you can use as is or customize to suit specific needs. There are reports for business contacts, opportunities, and accounts, as well as two additional reports to display your business task list and sources of sales leads.

To create a report, click the Business Tools menu, choose Reports, and then choose the report category and specific report you want to view. A report window opens and displays the report, as shown in Figure 12-21.

Chapter Twelve: **Managing Customer Contacts: Business Contact Manager**

Part Four:
Connect and
Conquery:
Building the
Company

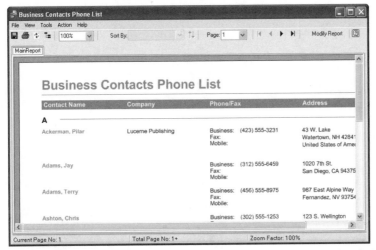

Figure 12-21 One of the reports BCM provides for analyzing information in your database.

The report window shows the first page of the report. You can page through the report using the arrow buttons at the top of the window or choose a page from the Page drop-down list. You can also zoom in or out to change the amount of information you can see. To go to a specific page, press Ctrl+G, enter the page number, and click OK.

Navigating Through a Report

If a report is lengthy, you can use its groupings to quickly move through the report to locate specific information. For example, in the Business Contacts Phone List report, you might want to view the entries that start with the letter R. You could page or scroll through the report until you find the Rs, but a better way is to click the Show/Hide Groupings button on the toolbar (or choose View, Show Group) to add a grouping pane to the left side of the report, as shown in Figure 12-22.

Part Four:
Connect and
Conquer:
Building the
Company

Microsoft Small Business Kit

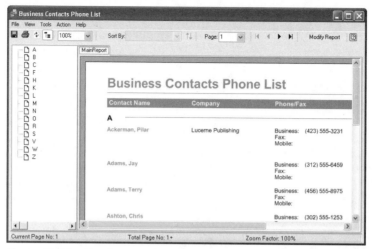

Figure 12-22   Use the grouping pane to quickly navigate through a long report.

Just click an item in the left pane to navigate to that location in the report. Click the Show/Hide Groupings button again to turn off the grouping pane.

Modifying Reports

You can modify the appearance or the information displayed in BCM reports. For example, you might want to make relatively minor changes, such as changing the report title, adding other information to the header, or turning off page numbers. Or you might want to make more extensive changes, such as filtering for only specific items—for example, including in a phone list only those contacts that begin with a certain letter.

Click the Modify Report button on the toolbar or choose Action, Modify Report to open the Modify Report dialog box, shown in Figure 12-23. The General tab contains several options that control the information that appears in the report. Options that don't pertain to the selected report are dimmed and unavailable. For example, for reports that don't include a date range, the Date Range group is dimmed.

Chapter Twelve: Managing Customer Contacts: Business Contact Manager

Part Four:
Connect and
Conquery:
Building the
Company

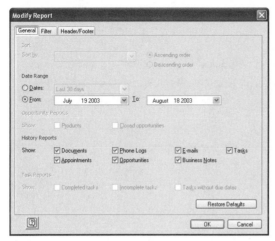

Figure 12-23   Use the General tab to control the information included on a report.

You can use the Filter tab, shown in Figure 12-24, to select which records are included in the report and to set up filters that include or exclude information. Under the Records group, click Select (the button name changes according to the report type) to explicitly choose the records you want included in the report. When you click Select, BCM displays a dialog box in which you select the items to include.

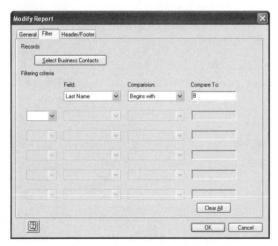

Figure 12-24   Use the Filter tab to include or exclude records in the report.

Part Four:
Connect and
Conquer:
Building the
Company

Microsoft Small Business Kit

The capability to filter the report is an important tool to tailor the information included in the report. You'll find that setting filters is easy, particularly if you have used the filter capabilities in Outlook's views, which are similar. The following example filters the Business Contacts Phone List to include only contacts with last names that start with *B* and a home state of *TX*.

Filter a report

1. Choose Business Tools, Reports, Business Contacts, Business Contacts Phone List to create a phone list report.

2. In the report window, click Modify Report on the toolbar, and then click the Filter tab.

3. In the first row in the Filtering Criteria area, select Last Name from the Field drop-down list. From the Comparison drop-down list, select Begins With, and then enter **B** in the Compare To box.

4. In the second row, select AND from the first drop-down list, select Home State/Province from the Field drop-down list, select Equals from the Comparison drop-down list, and then enter **TX** in the Compare To box.

5. Click OK to refresh the report based on the new filter criteria.

Use AND and OR logic

You can use AND or OR logic for a filter condition. Use AND when you want a condition to apply in addition to previous conditions—for example, to display contacts with names that start with *B and* who are located in Texas. Use OR to display contacts with names that start with *B or* who live in Texas. If you used OR logic in this example, a contact would appear in the report if his or her last name started with B, or he or she lived in Texas, or both.

The Header/Footer tab, shown in Figure 12-25, gives you a place to add other information to the report's header or footer. You can also specify the font used for specific items.

Chapter Twelve: **Managing Customer Contacts: Business Contact Manager**

Part Four:
Connect and
Conquery:
Building the
Company

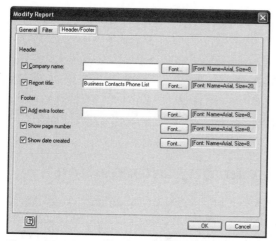

Figure 12-25 Use the Header/Footer tab to include other information in the report's header or footer or to change the fonts used in the header or footer.

Saving Reports

After you create a report, you can print it, but you might also want to save the report to disk so that you can edit it, send it to someone else, or post it on a Web site. BCM can save reports in four formats:

Word Document Choose this type to save the document in Microsoft Office Word 2003 format. You can then open the document in Word to edit it.

Rich-Text Format Choose this type to save the document in rich-text format (RTF), which is useful for sharing the report with others who do not have Microsoft Word. The WordPad application included with Windows can read and edit RTF files (as well as some Word files).

Excel Workbook Choose this type to save the report as a Microsoft Office Excel 2003 workbook. This type is particularly useful when you need to analyze numerical data included in a report.

Web Page Choose this type to save the report as an HTML file that you can post on a Web site.

To save a report, open the report and modify it as needed, and then choose File, Save As to open the Save As dialog box. Choose the file type, choose a path, enter a name for the report, and click Save. If you want to edit the report, simply locate the saved report and double-click it, and the appropriate application will open with the report loaded into it.

Part Four:
Connect and
Conquer:
Building the
Company

Microsoft Small Business Kit

Printing Reports

At some point, you will probably want to print a report. BCM gives you the capability to print reports, although the options are somewhat limited. To print a report, open the report, modify it as needed, and choose File, Print or click the Print button on the toolbar. BCM opens a standard Print dialog box that you can use to select a printer and indicate the number of copies to print. Just click OK to print the report.

Importing and Exporting Information

If you are starting to organize your business information in electronic format, you will likely have to enter most of it manually in BCM, creating contacts, accounts, and sales opportunities yourself. If you've been using other computer programs to keep track of this information and now want to move to BCM, you can import data from those applications to BCM and save quite a bit of time.

Importing Contacts or Accounts

BCM can import data from a handful of other applications. You can import data from Act!, Microsoft Excel, Microsoft List Builder, QuickBooks, or any application that can export data to a comma-separated value (.csv) file. (Importing from Act! requires that you have Act! installed on your computer.)

To import data, choose File, Import And Export, Business Contact Manager to open the Business Data Import/Export Wizard. Click Import A File, and click Next. Select the type of file to import (see Figure 12-26), and then click Next.

Chapter Twelve: Managing Customer Contacts: Business Contact Manager

Part Four:
Connect and
Conquery:
Building the
Company

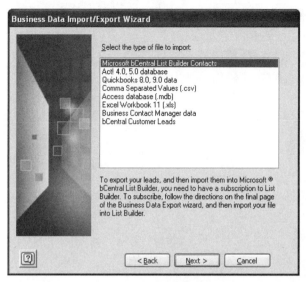

Figure 12-26   Choose the source for importing data to BCM.

The following example imports contacts from an Excel worksheet:

Import contact data from Excel

1. Choose File, Import And Export, Business Contact Manager to open the Business Data Import/Export Wizard. Select Import A File, and then click Next.

2. Choose Excel Workbook 11 (this item refers to Microsoft Office Excel 2003), and then click Next. Click Browse to locate and select the Excel file (with the extension .xls) containing your contact list. Specify how you want duplicates handled, and then click Next.

3. In the wizard screen shown in Figure 12-27, select the worksheet in the Excel file you want to import. As the destination, select either Business Contacts or Accounts.

Part Four:
Connect and
Conquer:
Building the
Company

Microsoft Small Business Kit

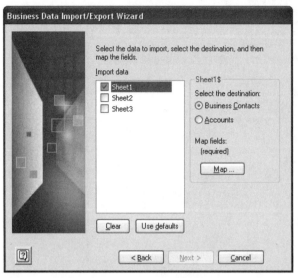

Figure 12-27 Select the destination for the incoming data.

4. Click the Map button to open the Map Fields dialog box, shown in Figure 12-28. Drag a field from the left pane to the right pane, dropping it on the field to which you want it to map. For example, drag the Last Name field in the left pane to the Last Name field in the right pane for a contact, or map the Company field to the Account Name field for an account. Repeat this step for each field you want to import. Ignore (do not map) those fields that you do not want to import into BCM.

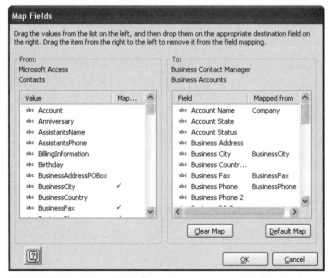

Figure 12-28 Map fields from the source to the destination.

Chapter Twelve: **Managing Customer Contacts: Business Contact Manager**

Part Four:
Connect and
Conquery:
Building the
Company

5. After you have mapped all of the fields you need, click OK in the Map Fields dialog box. Click Next, and then click Next again to start the import process.

Importing Products

In addition to importing contacts and accounts, you can also import a product list into BCM, although BCM will import products only from a .csv text file. This means that you must first export the data from its current location to a CSV file. It also means that you might need to tweak the existing database format before you export the data to be sure it's in the right format. BCM requires four fields, which must be in the following sequence: Product Name, Description, Unit Price, and Default Quantity. The database can include additional fields, but when you export the data, you must export it so that these four fields (or the ones that correspond to them in your existing product database) are exported as the first four fields and in the sequence specified.

What's the Default Quantity field?

The Edit Product Master List dialog box does not show the Default Quantity field, but it is included in the BCM Products database.

The following steps describe how to save an Excel worksheet as a CSV file and then import the product list into BCM. (For details on exporting from other applications, check the application's help documentation.)

Export product data from Excel

1. Open the Excel worksheet that contains the data you want to export. Rearrange the columns in the worksheet as necessary so that the data is in the order described earlier. Column A should contain the product name, Column B should contain the product description, and so on.

2. On the File menu, click Save As. In the Save As dialog box, shown in Figure 12-29, select CSV (Comma Delimited) from the Save As Type list, and then click Save. Save the CSV file in your My Documents folder or another location.

Part Four:
Connect and
Conquer:
Building the
Company

Microsoft Small Business Kit

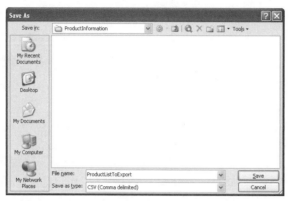

Figure 12-29   You can import product data saved in CSV format into BCM.

With the worksheet exported to a CSV file, you're ready to import the product list into BCM by following these steps:

Import product data into BCM

1. In Outlook, choose Business Tools, Product List to open the Edit Product Master List dialog box.

2. Click Import to open the Products Import dialog box, shown in Figure 12-30.

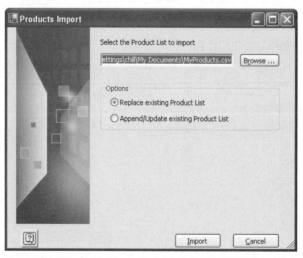

Figure 12-30   Import product items in the Products Import dialog box.

3. To replace any existing product list, choose the Replace Existing Product List option. To append the incoming data to your existing BCM product list, choose the Append/Update Existing Product List option.

Chapter Twelve: Managing Customer Contacts: Business Contact Manager

Part Four:
Connect and
Conquery:
Building the
Company

4. Click Browse, select the CSV file, and then click Import to import the data. The products should now appear in the Edit Product Master List dialog box. Click OK to close the dialog box.

With your product list now imported into BCM, you can begin associating products with opportunities as explained in the section "Adding Products to an Opportunity," earlier in this chapter.

Managing Your BCM Data

After you go through the time and trouble of setting up accounts, contacts, opportunities, and your product list, you certainly don't want to have to go through it all again if your system crashes. So, you should regularly back up your BCM database. If your system does crash or the database is lost for some other reason, you can recover the database from the backup copy.

BCM adds a handful of database management tasks to Outlook's File menu, as explained in the next few sections.

Cleaning Up the Database

One of the tasks you should perform regularly is to defragment the database to improve performance and check the database for errors. You can accomplish both of these tasks in one operation. Choose File, Business Database, Maintenance to open the Database Maintenance dialog box. Click Start to start the process. BCM displays the progress in the dialog box. Click Close when the process is finished.

Backing Up the Database

As a precaution against a lost or corrupted database, you should frequently back up your BCM databases. To back up a database, choose File, Business Database, Backup to display the Database Backup dialog box, shown in Figure 12-31. Click Browse, specify the location and file name for the database, and then click Save. Optionally, enter a password to protect the database, and then click OK. BCM creates a compressed backup of the database file. When BCM displays its completion message, click OK.

Part Four:
Connect and
Conquer:
Building the
Company

Microsoft Small Business Kit

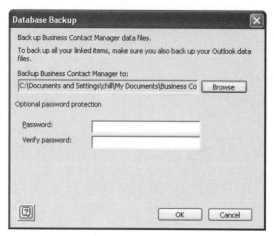

Figure 12-31 Click Browse to specify the backup location and file name.

Keep your backup copies in a safe place

For best recoverability, place backup copies of your database on a network server or copy them to a CD. This will enable you to recover the files if your local hard disk fails.

Restoring the Database

To restore a database, open Outlook, and choose File, Business Database, Restore to open the Database Restore dialog box. Click Browse to locate and select the backup file, and then click Open. Enter a password if the backup is password-protected, and then click OK to restore the database.

Deleting Databases

You can delete a BCM database if you no longer need it. A typical database can take up a lot of space, so deleting those you no longer need can help you conserve disk space.

To delete a database, first make sure that you don't need the database and that you know specifically which databases (by name) can be deleted. As a precaution, you should back up the database and copy it to a CD before deleting it. When you're ready to delete it, choose File, Business Database, Properties to open the Database Properties dialog box, shown in Figure 12-32. Select a database from the list, and click Delete.

Chapter Twelve: Managing Customer Contacts: Business Contact Manager

Part Four:
Connect and
Conquery:
Building the
Company

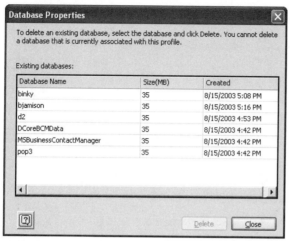

Figure 12-32 Delete a database in the Database Properties dialog box.

Remove a database associated with the current profile

You can't delete a database that is associated with the current profile. To remove it from the profile, right-click the Business Contact Manager branch in the folder list, and then click Close Business Contact Manager. You can also choose File, Data File Management to open the Outlook Data Files dialog box and remove the file. If you share your computer, be sure you aren't deleting someone else's BCM data.

Organizing customer and contact information in BCM is a great step forward, especially if your business relies on selling your products (or a portion of those you sell) to a group of customers fairly regularly. It lets you cull through sales opportunities, see which customers buy which products, and create reports on your recent sales activity. If you use the full capabilities of BCM and maintain the information you enter in it, the program can serve as a kind of control center from which you can correspond with and keep track of all your customer contact. But as much help as BCM (or a program like it) offers for managing your relationships with customers, this critical job can't be done with software alone. For many businesses, you'll greet customers when they enter your store or your office, or you'll meet with them periodically to initiate and then close a sale. Those encounters are how you take care of each customer the best way you can. They're the ones that put money in the bank.

Part Four:
Connect and
Conquer:
Building the
Company

Microsoft Small Business Kit

For More Information

In addition to the resources mentioned in this chapter, you will find links and information on the companion CD. Some books and Web sites particularly useful when managing customer contacts include:

Books

- Paul Greenberg, *CRM at the Speed of Light: Capturing and Keeping Customers in Internet Real Time* (Osborne/McGraw-Hill, 2002)

- C. K. Prahalad et al., *Harvard Business Review on Customer Relationship Management* (Harvard Business School Press, 2002)

- Jill Dyché, *The CRM Handbook: A Business Guide to Customer Relationship Management* (Addison-Wesley, 2001)

Web Sites

- Outlook Tips, a useful site for Outlook questions, answers, and add-ins: *www.outlook-tips.net/index.html*

- The CRM Knowledge Base from ITToolbox: *crm.ittoolbox.com/*

- The Microsoft Office Online Web site tutorial on Business Contact Manager: *www.microsoft.com/office/outlook/contactmanager/prodinfo/overview.mspx*

Part Five

Gurus, Guides, and Staff: Employment Dos and Don'ts

In this part

Chapter Thirteen **Hiring and Firing.** 346

Chapter Fourteen **Managing Like a Coach** 378

Part Five:
Gurus, Guides,
and Staff:
Employment
Dos and Don'ts

Microsoft Small Business Kit

You're only as good as the people you hire.

— Ray Kroc (1902–84), founder of McDonald's Corporation

Chapter Thirteen
Hiring and Firing

Hard-charging, fast-moving entrepreneurs have little time to spare when it comes to recruiting, hiring, and managing. Yet business success depends on being able to identify the right talent and then put needed skills to work in the right place at the right time.

Chapter Thirteen: **Hiring and Firing**

Part Five:
Gurus, Guides,
and Staff:
Employment
Dos and Don'ts

What you'll find:

- ❑ When to hire
- ❑ Where to find talent
- ❑ Conducting interviews and background checks
- ❑ Recruiting the 21st-century team
- ❑ Figuring out how much to pay
- ❑ Providing benefits you can afford
- ❑ Deciding when to call it quits

Part Five:
Gurus, Guides,
and Staff:
Employment
Dos and Don'ts

Microsoft Small Business Kit

When to Hire

As everyone always says, it pays to stay ahead of the curve. When your business is moving faster than you can, it might be time to think about getting help. Adding staff, however, is a significant decision for a small company. Among other changes, a new employee demands a serious kick up in cash flow. Every owner must evaluate the rhythm and pace of the business and come to this big decision in an individual way.

Still, there are some themes that consistently crop up when that time is nigh. If, for instance, you've been backing away from marketing because you have "all the business you can handle," think twice. Is that really a smart choice? Hiring help could mean the difference between growth and stagnation. If you've been expending lots of time, money, and angst on finding, interviewing, and training freelance, temporary, contract, or overtime help, there's your other tip-off. If you're so busy taking care of internal housekeeping jobs that you don't have time to talk to customers, well, then... Assuming you're not trying to scramble out of debt and your credit rating looks good, start thinking about what kind of staff makes sense.

See "Managing the New Work Force," page 395, to learn more about working with independent contractors.

See "Savings and Credit Cards", page 58, for details about checking your credit rating.

Your Very First Employee

There's nothing like the first time, of course. When you stop flying solo and bring on permanent help, it's like having an earthquake hit your operation. For starters, you take on responsibility for someone else's income and future. No small thing. Next, you have to keep tabs on this new someone, judging how he or she gets the job done. And vice versa—you're being measured as a boss. You'll also need to check in with someone every day. That alone is often enough to drive lone practitioners crazy. Many entrepreneurs start their own business expressly to get away from meetings and daily management chores.

Let's not overlook the positive, though. Business must be booming or you wouldn't need the help. Certainly, enjoy the moment. Go celebrate. But understand that, psychologically, a first-time hire is qualitatively different from all the others that might follow. When your baby business gets big enough to need more than one driver, be prepared to adjust. It's hard to

Chapter Thirteen: Hiring and Firing

Part Five:
Gurus, Guides,
and Staff:
Employment
Dos and Don'ts

trust a newcomer. It's hard to share confidential information and secret plans. It's hard to give up control.

It's especially difficult to remember to communicate all the details about strategies and operations that you're used to handling on your own. You must decide what to divulge and what to keep quiet. From the outside, everyone might be patting you on the back and congratulating you on the newfound support. That's swell, but things are definitely more complicated now.

When you're ready, here's how to take a lot of the worry out of hiring your first employee:

- **Grow up with your biz.** Start the hiring process by analyzing the level of help you need, the changes you must make to allow someone to enter the business, and the kind of manager you are. There's bound to be some anxiety about adding staff and growing. You're giving up a piece of the business that you're accustomed to controlling.

- **Don't just offload chores.** Hiring the first employee is not only about getting someone to help you with the overload. It's a decision about the path of company growth. To gain insights, tap the knowledge of other small business owners who have been through the process. Or consider paying a consultant to evaluate the business (before you choose a direction) and to offer some suggestions about strategies for the next few years and steps you can take.

- **Make a list of tasks.** List the company's critical jobs and responsibilities. Identify what only you can do, what you prefer to do, and what you can delegate. Decide on the title of this job you're creating. How much authority does it have? What is its scope and potential? You'll need to articulate that for candidates.

- **Set expectations for performance.** Make sure you're prepared to offer ongoing and constructive feedback.

- **Goldilocks rules.** Don't rush to hire when sales turn strong and cash is flush. All businesses fluctuate. The cost of adding an employee takes a sharp bite, including compensation, training time, bigger offices, and better technology. There are also employee tax and accounting costs. Presumably, such costs are outweighed by greater productivity, but you need to carefully balance the ledger. It's usually wise to go through the first year without hiring. Get a feel for the sales cycle and

Part Five:
Gurus, Guides,
and Staff:
Employment
Dos and Don'ts

Microsoft Small Business Kit

the downturns. Measure the "just right" temperature of income and outgo. Experts suggest squirreling away at least a year's worth of expenses and overhead before hiring in order to see you through any rough patches.

- **Hire attitude, not skills.**   You'll be working hard and spending lots of stressful time with your employee. Choose a simpatico go-getter rather than a collection of skills. Usually, if an applicant is smart, eager, and open-minded, skills and training will come easily, especially in a multitasking small business. Barbara Corcoran founded her well-known New York City residential real estate firm, The Corcoran Group, in 1973, with only $1,000. She now manages 1,100 employees in a company that racked up a mind-boggling $5.5 billion in revenues last year. Her formula for hiring? "Find an expander and a container and put them together. Hire opposites and lock them at the hip." That pairing works because they complement each other and they don't threaten the other's territory, says Corcoran. "There's mutual respect for each other because they realize they can't do what the other does. It's a mistake to put a container in the lead without an expander and it's a mistake to put an expander in the lead without a container."

- **Don't wait for perfection.**   Keep in mind that your first-time hire doesn't have to be the perfect solution. First, he or she must do several things pretty well—not one thing perfectly. Second, it's tough to find the right fit with a two-person team. Many entrepreneurs learn from an initial mismatch and use that knowledge to inform the next round of hiring. If your first-time choice turns memorable in all the wrong ways, chalk it up to experience. Then keep recruiting.

See "Delegating: Dos and Don'ts," pages 381, for more about loosening the reins.

Hiring for Next-Level Growth

It gets easier after one person is on board. Strange as it seems, going from 0 to 1 employee is a greater adjustment than going from 1 to 10 employees. For your future hires, much of the preceding advice applies. For instance, you'll need to figure out step-by-step strategies and what the smart next moves for growth ought to be. Yet it often gets trickier to determine what kind of help is actually needed. Let's say your two salespeople are swamped and customers are squawking. The reflex is to hire an additional salesperson. But that could result in yet another harried salesperson and more dissatisfied customers. What you really need is administrative support that will free up the salespeople you already employ. You might hire an assistant to

Chapter Thirteen: Hiring and Firing

Part Five:
Gurus, Guides,
and Staff:
Employment
Dos and Don'ts

keep track of sales and customer information. Or you could hire an IT consultant for a month or so to develop a customized inventory system. Maybe all you need is an intern for two days a week to handle schedules, confirm appointments, and send out appropriate follow-up materials.

When business gets overloaded, analyze the pain. Don't automatically hire more of what you already have. Think ahead to the skills you'll need over the upcoming several months. Once that's clear, write down an informal description of the job you're creating and your minimum requirements for qualifications. Include the following information:

- How the new hire will be managed and supervised
- Level of authority and responsibilities
- Specific skills you need, such as computer training or customer contact
- Educational requirements
- Performance expectations

Writing down the job description will help you to select the most efficient recruiting channel, winnow the candidate responses, and speed the interviewing process.

Where to Find Talent

Before recruiting outside the company, review your existing staff. It's a lot more efficient and cost-effective to hire from within. If you decide to recruit from the outside, you'll probably want to advertise for the job in appropriate journals or magazines. You might also post an ad on industry recruiting sites or on your own company Web site.

Here are additional ways to recruit the talent you need:

Recruiting Ads

You can quickly create a recruiting ad using Microsoft Publisher, the desktop publishing program included with Microsoft Office Small Business Edition 2003. Publisher offers convenient tools for creating distinctive and professional-looking print or digital ads (as well as marketing and other material, of course). You can design the ad in Publisher and then easily modify it for use across multiple recruiting channels and media, including the Web, print, or e-mail.

- **Word of mouth**   Share details of your job description with the staff, and ask for referrals. You might offer an incentive for any referral that leads to hiring. If cash is tight, promise a day off or a free lunch. Also put out the word with industry contacts and professional associations. Mention your opening when chatting with suppliers and vendors. Word spreads quickly.

Part Five:
Gurus, Guides,
and Staff:
Employment
Dos and Don'ts

Microsoft Small Business Kit

■ **Online recruiting**   Fast and affordable, online recruiting is increasingly sophisticated. There are now an estimated 40,000 Internet job sites, and a single ad can quickly pull hundreds of responses. The trick about online recruiting is that its virtues are also its flaws. A single online ad can now pull so many responses so quickly that it's fabulously cost-effective and efficient. Until, that is, you remember that time is money: you must sort through all those responses. Or until you remember that quantity isn't quality: you haven't attracted candidates with the right skills or experience.

For example, one marketing director looking for a sales rep bought an ad on Monster.com, the goliath that boasts a staggering 15 million or so resumés in its database and costs only a few hundred dollars for a 60-day ad. Within 15 minutes, she got three resumés. Wow. Then she got hundreds. Out of the deluge, she called in eight people to interview. Weeks later, she was still getting dozens of resumés and simply deleting them, unread. Overall, she's satisfied with the results, but it was enormously time consuming.

The three critical questions to answer for smart online recruiting are:

■ Which is the best recruiter site for your needs?

■ What's the definition and profile of your desired candidate?

■ Have you written a specific, appropriate, and accurate job description?

Before buying and posting an online ad, research the sites likely to turn up candidates qualified for your position. Then compare costs. Look for niche job boards that represent your targeted populations, geographic regions, or interest groups. Many industry association and professional organization sites have job-listing channels—often free to employers or members. To narrow the search for likely sites, canvas employees about where they log on. Quiz applicants you interview. And ask around at trade shows, conferences, or association events to get leads.

■ **Newspaper and trade magazine ads**   Classified ads in an appropriate publication will definitely pull candidates in your field. Run your ad a few times, and then check responses. Again, ask your staff and associates about which publications, newsletters, trade journals, or daily newspapers they read in order to reach the type of candidates you want. Keep the wording of your ad short and specific.

Chapter Thirteen: Hiring and Firing

Part Five:
Gurus, Guides,
and Staff:
Employment
Dos and Don'ts

Monitor which ads are effective

To check which publication pulls the best for you, insert a special department or code word (unique to each publication) in the ad. When applicants send responses, you'll know which publications turned up which candidates.

- **Search firms and recruiting agencies**   Usually, headhunters are hired for higher-level searches, including specialized talent or executive skills. They charge either contingency fees or retainers. The contingency fee is paid only after a successful hire, including some probationary time on the job, often 90 days. Recruiters on retainer get most of the fee up front and are paid to search until you choose a candidate or move on. Fees are typically 25 to 33 percent of the hire's first year of compensation, including salary, signing bonuses, or commissions. Such fees are always negotiable.

- **Colleges and universities**   A terrific source for full-time, temporary, part-time, or intern help, whether year-round or during summers, colleges are often overlooked as a recruiting channel. To learn about the level of skills and possible candidates offered by local schools, talk to directors of career centers or community outreach programs. Most schools are eager to form partnerships with businesses. Community colleges typically have entrepreneurship divisions with ties to local businesses or chambers of commerce. Chat with deans of departments that match your field and ask about internship programs and career days or fairs you can attend. Also consider placing ads in school newspapers. College Web sites are a good place to start to find contacts and information.

Conducting Interviews and Background Checks

After all the resumés and responses are in, make a preliminary cut. Eliminate any applicants who do not meet your minimum job requirements, which you defined in the job description. Next, prescreen the remaining applicants via phone, e-mail, or surface mail. Ask the applicants to respond to such questions as their availability, compensation expectations, and some specifics about experience. Based on those responses, eliminate the next round of applicants who don't fit your bill.

Part Five:
Gurus, Guides,
and Staff:
Employment
Dos and Don'ts

Microsoft Small Business Kit

Now you have a short, qualified list of applicants to invite in for personal interviews. Before the face-to-face meeting, ask applicants to fill out an application form so that you can later check their background and experience, including references, dates of employment, education, and previous positions. When appropriate, the application form can also include a section that gives you permission for pre-employment medical exams or drug screening. Legally, the form should inform the applicant that giving any false information could lead to termination of employment. Check with an employment lawyer or a human resources expert about the legal wording for such disclaimers before using the forms. Once an applicant signs the form, you've then covered the bases.

When interviewing applicants, don't monopolize the conversation. Be an active listener, which will encourage the applicant to open up. Experts suggest that applicants do 80 percent of the talking during interviews. Avoid questions about race, religion, age, sexual orientation, national origin, or mental or physical disabilities. These questions are illegal—again, talk to an employment attorney to learn more about what you can and cannot ask. You can make a rough comparison of applicant skills and presentations by keeping organized interview notes.

Here's a checklist of dos and don'ts for conducting interviews:

- **Don't wing it.**   Prepare by reading the applicant's resumé beforehand and developing key questions.

- **Do ask open-ended questions to give applicants an opportunity to interact.**   For instance, "What did you like most about your last job?" instead of, "Did you like your last job?"

- **Do explain the mission and the culture of your company as well as the job responsibilities.**   Hiring is not only about skills, it's also about the fit.

- **Do describe the job in detail.**   Ask the applicant if he or she is prepared to perform at the level you expect. Is there any hesitation?

- **Do set up 360-degree interviews.**   Have the applicants you like best undergo a round of interviews with your staff, including the potential hire's peer, subordinate, and supervisor, or what are known as *360-degree interviews*. Make sure you listen to staff reactions. That way, you get everybody's input as well as buy-in, and you learn more about the applicants.

Chapter Thirteen: Hiring and Firing

Part Five:
Gurus, Guides,
and Staff:
Employment
Dos and Don'ts

You might also consider a *situational interview*, which is becoming increasingly popular as a way to screen candidates. Given the challenge of making hard judgments based on a half-hour or so of chatting, many companies are now asking applicants to demonstrate their skills or abilities via a job "situation." Applicants are asked to meet some challenge or solve a problem that might arise on the job. For instance, an applicant could be asked to run a departmental meeting, make a sales presentation, or deal with an irate customer. Situational interviews give employers more insight into how applicants will cope with the demands of the position. Again, consider getting a lawyer's advice before creating any audition like this, just to make sure you stay within legal bounds.

Find Out Who You're Really Hiring

Hundreds of job seekers fudge facts or lie outright about their skills, experience, or education. That goes for seemingly inconsequential details and for executive candidates, too. Don't forget to check references before making an offer. Otherwise, you might land in a heap of legal, financial, or professional trouble. These days you can't afford not to check into an employee's background.

A few years back, for instance, two armed robbers caught ransacking an upscale California home wound up shooting the owner. The thieves hadn't expected anyone to be there. That's because they knew a lot about that house and its security. The pair had spent hours in the home, as carpet cleaners for a service that caters to wealthy homeowners. The cleaner-robbers had a clever scam. Most affluent owners don't hang around when workers arrive. Typically, one guy worked while the other roamed, casing the contents, alarm systems, doors, and windows. Then they left, only to return several months later to rob the place. Victims never made the connection to the carpet service—until the shooting.

When the robbers were found, the homeowner sued the service. It turned out that the men had criminal records and felony convictions before they were hired. The company was found guilty of "negligent hiring" and had to pay a crippling $11 million in damages.

When you tally the dollars and time it takes to recruit, interview, hire, and train an employee, it doesn't make sense to cheap out on verifying background details. That might be especially important for smaller businesses where staffers often have multiple responsibilities. Even tiny employee lies can hurt your firm's reputation or bank account. One bad hire can do enormous damage. You do the math.

Part Five:
Gurus, Guides,
and Staff:
Employment
Dos and Don'ts

Microsoft Small Business Kit

When you call personal and official references to ask about an applicant's prior employment, address these concerns:

- Verify all dates and statements on the resumé, including the social security number, all previous jobs, schools attended, and degrees attained.

- Look into criminal records or civil judgments against the applicant. You don't want a bookkeeper, for instance, who was sued for fraud.

- When appropriate, review professional licenses and certifications to ensure they're bona fide and up-to-date.

Consider Professional Screening

So much personal data is now computerized that you can hire professional pre-employment screeners to look into references for as little as $50 or so per request. That not only saves you time and wear and tear, but might also turn up information you wouldn't unearth. Third-party background checks are an especially good idea for certain positions, like security or law enforcement, healthcare, or childcare. More broadly, you ought to invest in deeper screening when employees will interact with the public or work in customers' homes or offices or if they will handle financial or other sensitive information.

To find reputable screeners, ask associates for referrals, check online, or check your local phone directory, and always ask for client references before signing on with a screening service. Background reports on job applicants can range from simply verifying social security numbers to full-dress investigations, much of it from public records, including:

- Education records
- Arrest, court, or criminal records
- Credit reports or bankruptcy filings
- Driving records and vehicle registrations
- Medical records and workers' compensation
- Military service records
- Property ownership
- State licensing records
- Character references or interviews with neighbors
- Employment verification

Chapter Thirteen: Hiring and Firing

Part Five:
Gurus, Guides,
and Staff:
Employment
Dos and Don'ts

State and federal laws police the kinds of information employers can use when making employment decisions, so consult an employment attorney, human resources expert, or the screener before proceeding. You don't need to invest in a criminal background check for every hire you make. But you should at least verify basic information on a resumé. The key to protecting yourself is to at least attempt to verify information provided by candidates. Keep some written document of your efforts, including the names of whomever you talk to and the dates and the questions you ask. Should trouble arise later, legal interpretations often hinge on whether you made every reasonable effort to check employee statements.

Here are some examples of online investigative services:

- Informus: *www.informus.com/*
- KnowX: *www.knowx.com/*
- PublicData.com: *www.publicdata.com/*

Recruiting the 21st-Century Team

While you're busy recruiting, think about the makeup of your staff. In the global economy, you can no longer afford a staff that looks, sounds, talks, and thinks all alike. In case you haven't noticed, every state in the United States now includes multicultural communities. Any or all of your customers, vendors, suppliers, or investors could well have a cultural background different from your own.

Whether you translate diversity into African American, Asian American, disabled, ethnic, female, gay, immigrant, Latino, minority, Native American, seniors, special needs, urban, or any other group besides so-called mainstream white male, you need to consider that rainbow demographics are now a fact of business life.

What does this mean to you? Any company that wants to stay competitive must come to terms with diversity, both inside

The Future of the American Work Force

The shift in demographics is dramatically spelled out in a recent U.S. Department of Labor report, titled "Futurework: Trends and Challenges for Work in the 21st Century":

> *By 2050, the U.S. population is expected to increase by 50 percent and minority groups will make up nearly half of the population. Immigration will account for almost two-thirds of the nation's population growth. The population of older Americans is expected to more than double. One-quarter of all Americans will be of Hispanic origin. Almost one in 10 Americans will be of Asian or Pacific Islander descent. And more women and people with disabilities will be on the job.*

Part Five:
Gurus, Guides,
and Staff:
Employment
Dos and Don'ts

Microsoft Small Business Kit

and outside the organization. Of course, the legal and moral arguments for diversity are unassailable. Discriminatory hiring practices not only demean the human spirit, they've been against the law for decades. Nonetheless, employers have been notoriously slow to change. No one thought much about making the business case for diverse employment until reports of the changing work force and consumer demographics added up to new math. At the same time, social and political policies like minority quotas and affirmative action turned controversial for advocates and critics alike—and even ran afoul of the law, as with university admissions polices.

Nowadays, global corporations are busy recruiting diversity because of profit motives. It's good for business. Small and mid-tier firms would be smart to follow that example. These five ways that diversity can boost business might persuade you to think about how your staff could benefit:

- **All business is now international.** With so much of business done online and via the Internet, there's no such thing as a local company anymore. Even mom-and-pop companies can't afford a localized or provincial attitude. Every business, whether small-town retailer or international marketer, must be savvy about the generation coming up, which speaks an international language and expects access to worldwide products and services.

- **Conflict is a good thing.** Small business owners may hesitate to hire qualified candidates different from themselves or the rest of the staff because of worries about resulting tension. But think about it. New ideas emerge only from friction and need. Innovation arises only out of conflict. Comfort zones are hardly the birthplace of creativity. Plus, a company's values and culture begin at the top. Diverse groups of people will have better antennae to sense opportunities that you might miss.

- **Small pools run dry.** With competition fierce and markets international, why narrow your search for skilled help to shallow areas of the talent pool? Business owners tend to hire people they "like," which usually means people who look and talk like they do. But if you focus on precise skills, competencies, and experience to do the job, you might find different talent. While you're at it, evaluate your preconceived notions.

For example, Joyce Bender has been running a technology consulting company for nearly 20 years. She partners with larger firms to provide employment for people with disabilities. Bender often faces the perception that workers with disabilities are "sick" or "absent" a lot. The

Chapter Thirteen: **Hiring and Firing**

Part Five:
Gurus, Guides,
and Staff:
Employment
Dos and Don'ts

reality? "I offer a $400 bonus to workers each year who don't miss a day of work. And I can' t tell you how many bonuses I've given to employees who haven't missed a day of work in five years. People with disabilities have to overcome obstacles and discrimination. They have to figure out how to get into and out of buildings. They've been in tough situations, and it's made them flexible problem solvers. They're really good workers for small businesses."

■ **Diversity drives sales.**   Nearly 80 percent of Fortune 500 companies now have some kind of diversity efforts in place, point out Fred Miller and Judith Katz in their book, *The Inclusion Breakthrough: Unleashing the Real Power of Diversity* (Berrett-Koehler Publishers, 2002). Increasingly, government and corporate vendors will contract only with suppliers that can demonstrate "cultural readiness," as Miller puts it. "The world is changing," says Miller, who runs the Kaleel Jamison Consulting Group, based in Troy, New York. "If it's not on your doorstep now, it will be soon. You can't wait. Reaction time must be instantaneous."

■ **Stable staffs are cost-effective.**   Suzanne and James Faustlin purchased their Tucson, Arizona, franchise for *The Maids Home Service* a half-dozen years ago. The business then had 13 employees and $250,000 in revenues, says Suzanne. By 2001, the couple had 34 staff members and $750,000 in revenues. Like many home-cleaning services, the staff is all female and more than 50 percent minority—in this case, Hopi Native American and Hispanic. But unlike many such services, the Faustlins play up the cultural differences. "We think it's fun," says Suzanne, "and the uniqueness of the traditions is an advantage."

Every workday starts with an early potluck breakfast. "We get tamales from different types of corn and Hopi blue marble bread," she says. "We encourage intermingling of the teams. It's a way to deal with the stresses." Suzanne says the staff also celebrates many different holidays. She credits those management policies with low staff turnover and easier recruitment. "We encourage employees to refer people, and we offer a finder's fee." The result: a very stable staff. "We have several family members working together."

Creating an inclusive company culture that values and respects individual difference is likely to yield tangible bottom-line results.

Part Five:
Gurus, Guides,
and Staff:
Employment
Dos and Don'ts

Microsoft Small Business Kit

Be Careful About Hiring Friends

The dream of starting a business often embraces a fantasy of getting all your best buddies to work alongside you—like a personal dream team. On the face of it, the arguments are understandable. Pals are trusted for support and honesty. Friends have values that mirror your own, so they're comfortable to be around. When friends hold down the fort, you figure you don't have to watch your back. Friends are also miraculously affordable. They'll work cheaper and longer than anyone else, which gives you more resources for the lunatic demands of a start-up.

It's at the founding phase that the temptation to hire friends is really appealing and most dangerous. Start-ups are free-for-alls. Everyone works full out at every task, from sweeping floors to making client presentations. Virtually every staffer has equal footing, with no one truly in charge. Accustomed to each other's moods and signals, friends will probably get teamwork and momentum going earlier and easier. Besides working cheap, a friend will invest the same huge gobs of time, sweat, and worry that you do. Pretty soon, that friend feels just like the owner, too. Then, sure as sunset, a day will arrive when the friend-employee decides to forge a path you'd rather not travel.

Those conflicts can easily get in the way of friendship, and the resulting differences can fester for any number of reasons. By and large, these are the basic problems that surface when you hire friends:

- **Friends are just like you.**   Who will challenge your strategies? Who will offer fresh perspective?

- **Friends are not usually qualified.**   You want to hire someone because he or she can do a terrific job, not because you went to high school together. You might be forced to tell a cherished friend that he or she simply isn't working out, which will certainly kill the friendship.

  The prime exception to this hiring rule is if the friendship originated when the two of you worked together. In that case, you're familiar with each other's work habits. There won't be rude surprises. Plus, if you're in a bind and must tap friends, give yourself an escape hatch. Explain that it's a short-term solution and he or she will be doing you a favor. Don't mention a time period or a budget until you know how it will work out.

Chapter Thirteen: **Hiring and Firing**

Part Five:
Gurus, Guides,
and Staff:
Employment
Dos and Don'ts

Why Drafting a Company Handbook Is a Smart Use of Precious Time

The way around accusations of favoritism, pleas of ignorance, or similar unrest is by citing the policies of a formal employee handbook or manual. Most small business owners can't be bothered to write one. But it's in their best interest. More often than not, small business owners are moving so fast that they can't remember what they tell everyone they hire. The result? Every employee works with different rules and guidelines. Writing an employee handbook—or even posting a page on the company intranet—is a convenient way of setting policies and guidelines for compensation, promotions, vacations, sick leave, legal compliance on family leave, discrimination, sex harassment (assuming the company has enough employees to be regulated by such laws), and more. Make sure you also check your state laws when you create the handbook. Many federal laws apply only to larger companies, while individual state laws have been passed to oversee small businesses. (See Table 13-1 for an overview of federal laws that govern employees.)

Your handbook or memo should include various legal disclaimers, such as that the policies contained in the handbook do not serve as an employee contract. (Otherwise, you might get into a legal wrangle if you must fire an employee.) Check with an employment attorney beforehand.

Table 13-1 describes major federal laws governing employers in the United States. Created by labor and employee relations expert Phillip B. Wilson (*www.lrims.com*), the table lists the major statutes and other laws or regulations that might apply in specific cases. These laws might be amended from time to time, of course, so you need to remain up-to-date. Additionally, state and local laws often cover smaller employers that

Secure Access and Management of Personnel Records

Microsoft Office Professional Edition 2003 has added a new feature called Information Rights Management (IRM), which can ease the steps for maintaining and managing personnel documents.

With IRM, you can:

- Set expiration dates for documents, such as performance reviews or benefits enrollment plans, so that they cannot be viewed after a certain period of time. This makes clear which information is most current.

- Protect documents so that files with confidential information cannot be forwarded, printed, faxed, edited, or e-mailed without authorization.

- Set rules and policies that control how e-mail communications are handled. A payroll manager, for example, can e-mail personal data and specify who can read the message and whether the contents can be copied, pasted, printed, forwarded, or edited.

Part Five:
Gurus, Guides,
and Staff:
Employment
Dos and Don'ts

Microsoft Small Business Kit

are exempt from federal law. These state and local laws might also supplement the federal requirements for larger companies. (Some states require employers to pay a higher minimum wage than the federal requirement, for example.) If you have any questions about whether your company is covered, you should talk to a lawyer who specializes in labor or employment law in your area. This table simply gives you an idea of which laws cover which situations.

Table 13-1 Overview of Federal Employment Laws

Law	Who Is Covered?	Summary
Age Discrimination in Employment Act	Employers with 20 or more employees	Bars discrimination against persons age 40 or older. Recordkeeping requirements of 1 to 3 years depending on record or until "final disposition" of claim.
Americans with Disabilities Act	Employers with 15 or more employees	Bars discrimination against individuals with disabilities and requires public areas to be usable and accessible to disabled persons. Recordkeeping requirements of 1 year or until "final disposition" of claim.
Civil Rights Act of 1866	All employers	Bars discrimination based on race in the making and enforcing of contracts.
Civil Rights Act of 1871	All employers	Bars individuals from violating the federal rights of others.
Civil Rights Act of 1964 (Title VII)	Employers with 15 or more employees	Bars employment discrimination based on race, color, religion, sex, pregnancy, or national origin. Recordkeeping requirements of 1 year or until "final disposition" of claim. Equal Opportunity report is required for all employers with 100 or more employees.

Table 13-1 Overview of Federal Employment Laws

Law	Who Is Covered?	Summary
Civil Rights Act of 1991	Employers with 15 or more employees	Allows plaintiffs to receive compensatory and punitive damages plus fees, subject to caps outlined in the statute. Also provides protection for U.S. citizens employed by U.S. companies overseas.
Consolidated Omnibus Budget Reconciliation Act (COBRA)	Employers with 20 or more employees	Requires employers to offer continued health insurance and provide notification of rights after certain legally specified "qualifying events," such as dates or reasons for termination.
Employee Retirement Income Security Act of 1974 (ERISA)	All employers who sponsor health insurance, pension, or retirement plans	Dictates rules regarding plan participation, contribution, funding, and reporting. ERISA records must be filed with the Pension Benefit Guaranty Corporation (PBGC), disclosed to participants, and kept for 6 years.
Employee Polygraph Protection Act	All employers	Regulates the use of lie detector tests. Polygraph records must be maintained for 3 years.
Equal Pay Act	All employers	Bars wage discrimination based on gender. Payroll records must be maintained for 3 years.

Part Five:
Gurus, Guides,
and Staff:
Employment
Dos and Don'ts

Microsoft Small Business Kit

Table 13-1   Overview of Federal Employment Laws

Law	Who Is Covered?	Summary
Executive Order 11246	Federal contracts exceeding $10,000	Requires affirmative action to prevent discrimination based on race, sex, religion, color, or national origin. Requires affirmative action plan to be developed and updated yearly. Related records must be maintained for 1 to 2 years.
Fair Labor Standards Act	All employers	Establishes minimum wage, overtime, and child labor laws. Specifies payroll records that must be maintained for a minimum of 3 years.
Family and Medical Leave Act	Employers with 50 or more employees	Requires unpaid, job-protected leave up to 12 weeks per year. Specifies payroll and leave-related records that must be maintained for a minimum of 3 years.
Federal Insurance Contribution Act, Federal Unemployment Tax Act, and Federal Income Tax Withholding	All employers	Require payment of payroll taxes on all wages paid. Payroll records must be kept for a minimum of 4 years.

Chapter Thirteen: Hiring and Firing

Part Five:
Gurus, Guides,
and Staff:
Employment
Dos and Don'ts

Table 13-1   Overview of Federal Employment Laws

Law	Who Is Covered?	Summary
Health Insurance Portability and Accountability Act of 1996 (HIPAA)	Companies that sponsor health plans or manage or receive information about individual medical or mental health conditions	Must comply with HIPAA privacy requirements (appoint an HIPAA privacy officer, train employees about requirements, obtain written permissions, and so on), secure protected health information (PHI), and maintain separate roles of employer and plan administrator (segregate and protect all PHI). Prohibits use of PHI or retaliation for failure to give written authorizations.
Immigration Reform and Control Act	Employers with 3 or more employees	Bars discrimination based on national origin or citizenship status. Prohibits employment of illegal aliens. Requires completion of specific form for all new hires; forms must be maintained for 3 years from date of hire or 1 year from date of termination, whichever is later.
National Labor Relations Act	All employers (2 employees required for legally defined union-related "concerted activity")	Governs union organizing and collective bargaining.
Occupational Safety and Health Act (OSHA)	All employers (employers with 10 or fewer employees exempt from recordkeeping requirements)	Requires safety and health standards to avoid illness, harm, or death. Must keep a log of work-related illness or injury, notify OSHA of certain injuries, and maintain medical records for an employee's job tenure plus 30 years.

Part Five:
Gurus, Guides,
and Staff:
Employment
Dos and Don'ts

Microsoft Small Business Kit

Table 13-1   Overview of Federal Employment Laws

Law	Who Is Covered?	Summary
Older Worker Benefit Protection Act	Employers with 15 or more employees	Regulates the circumstances under which an employee may validly waive rights under the Age Discrimination in Employment Act.
Rehabilitation Act of 1973 (Section 503)	Employers with federal contracts exceeding $10,000	Requires affirmative action to employ and promote qualified individuals with disabilities. Recordkeeping requirements of 1 to 2 years or until "final disposition," depending on employer size. The Affirmative Action Program (AAP) is updated annually.
Rehabilitation Act of 1973 (Section 504)	Programs or activities that receive federal funds	Prohibits discrimination against qualified individuals with disabilities. Recordkeeping requirements of 1 to 2 years or until "final disposition," depending on employer size.
Uniformed Services Employment and Reemployment Rights Act of 1994	All employers	Revision of the Veterans' Reemployment Rights Act of 1940, governs reemployment rights after military service and protects against discrimination based on military service or training.
Vietnam-Era Veterans' Readjustment Assistance Act (Section 4212)	Employers with federal contracts exceeding $25,000	Requires affirmative action in the hiring and promoting of veterans.
Worker Adjustment and Retraining Notification Act (WARN)	Employers with 100 or more employees	Requires a 60-day notice of plant closing or mass layoff.

Figuring Out How Much to Pay

Business owners tend to work harder and longer than anyone else—and for less money. That's the price of investing in your own destiny. Plus, of course, entrepreneurs believe in payoffs down the line. But you can't expect every staffer to act like an owner—nor, in fact, do you want that. Putting a price tag on a staff job can be harder than pricing the company's products and services themselves. Pay packages have so few rules. They go up and down depending on geography, industry conventions, seniority, and the job market, as well as a candidate's background. The salary you set must be high enough to attract top applicants but not so high that it eats into your profits or survival. Then too, salaries are a bet over time. You invest today in the training, loyalty, and productivity you hope to gain from the employee tomorrow. All in all, it can be a risky business.

How do you figure how much a job is worth? This five-step guide to benchmarking salaries can help you figure out how much to pay:

- **Review pay practices.** Don't wait until you find a candidate to come up with an offer. Do some homework beforehand. Business owners tend to wait to hear what individual candidates want before figuring out how much they will offer in compensation. Instead, get a handle on your past practices and precedents. Assuming you don't run afoul of employment or antidiscrimination law, the decision about salary comes down to assessing how you value the job and what your company can afford. You also need to keep the salary of new hires in line with what you pay current staffers. Check how much you spent on payroll for the past year or two. Decide how the position you're filling fits into that overall percentage. You want to balance company payroll against the marketplace.

- **Define the job.** You can't research a job's going rate unless you compare apples to apples—that is, you need a clear-cut job description. The job title isn't enough. Let's say you decide to hire a marketing director. Salaries for jobs with that title can run from $50,000 to $500,000 or more. So the title alone is a nonstarter. "The worst thing you can do is compare job titles because they can be totally out of whack with salaries," says Elena Bottos, compensation consultant at Salary.com, an online research and services company based in Needham, Massachusetts. Write a job description, and then use that as your point of comparison for the marketplace. Sure, staffers at every small business do a dozen different things, but there are always key responsibilities you can jot down and match.

Part Five:
Gurus, Guides,
and Staff:
Employment
Dos and Don'ts

Microsoft Small Business Kit

■ **Track the competition.** Uncovering the competitive rate for a job takes a bit of sleuthing. To find what competitors or similar-size companies are paying for the job you have in mind, research these sources:

❑ **Study classified ads.** Reading help wanted sections of newspapers, trade magazines, professional journals, or online job boards in your industry will give you an up-to-date overview of salaries. Look for jobs that are similar to the one you're offering. Depending on the position and periodical, ads sometimes list the salary or, just as helpfully, a salary range.

❑ **Quiz professional contacts.** Talking to officials at your local chamber of commerce, to expert panelists at a conference, or to other business owners will yield current salary data. Try joining a professional organization in your field. Many associations mount annual salary surveys designed to serve members. The data, funded by member fees, is collected just so companies have access to going pay rates. Also call staffing agencies, recruiters, and appropriate consultants or some of your vendors to learn more.

❑ **Search government and media sources.** The Web is a rich source for salary data. Your first stop should be the U.S. Bureau of Labor Statistics. This information, while deep and extensive, might be a few years old. For more current information, check business and trade magazine Web sites and over-the-counter issues. Many journals run annual salary surveys, both in print and online. Type salary surveys in MSN or another search engine, and you're likely to turn up several association or magazine surveys in the result.

Comparative salary data

On the home page of the U.S. Bureau of Labor Statistics (*www.bls.gov*), click Wages By Area And Occupation to find salary histories.

❑ **Pay for a customized survey.** Many compensation consultants and market researchers sell salary surveys for specific fields or certain-size companies. Ask around at industry conferences. Salary.com, for instance, has special packages of its Job Valuation Report that serve small businesses. The online service lets you

Chapter Thirteen: **Hiring and Firing**

Part Five:
**Gurus, Guides,
and Staff:
Employment
Dos and Don'ts**

search for market compensation data for specific jobs and geography and then issues a detailed report you can print out. Prices run under $100 to search for one job and up to a few hundred dollars for a 10-job package.

■ **Set the salary range.**   Once you have an idea of the competitive rate, experts suggest that you set parameters for the job—a floor and a ceiling. That will keep you focused. But everyone differs about the best time to mention the salary range to the candidate. Some recommend asking a candidate how much he or she earned at the last job as a way to begin. Others suggest mentioning the salary range as a screening device, during the first interview or even phone conversations. Still others think salary should be the last thing mentioned because you're better off getting to know the candidate's qualifications and skills first. With a good fit, money might not matter so much. Bottom line? It depends on what feels right for you.

■ **Bundle pay and perks.**   Jobs are rarely only about money, although that might be what applicants mention first. These days, benefits and "quality of life" perks go a long way toward attracting talent and enriching compensation offers. With employee contributions to healthcare insurance rising and employer funding for retirement and deferred-tax savings plans shrinking, it's less expensive to outbid competitors. (See the next section for more about how to afford company benefits.) Don't overlook flextime and other such options. Employees with two-career families, young children, and long commutes often choose more free time over more money. Consider offering:

❑   Work-at-home privileges

❑   Discretionary hours (earlier mornings or later nights)

❑   Paying for all or part of club memberships, association dues, or training courses

❑   Bonuses, time off, or other prizes pegged to performance goals

❑   Paying for all or part of home technology equipment and/or telecommuting expenses

❑   Paying part of transportation costs to and from work

❑   Picking up all or part of employee-assistance services, such as personal finances planning, tax or retirement planning, daycare, family counseling, and so on.

Part Five:
Gurus, Guides,
and Staff:
Employment
Dos and Don'ts

Microsoft Small Business Kit

However you structure the salary, don't forget to think ahead. Remember that you might need to raise the salary ceiling in six months or a year. If your candidate is hired at the top of your pay scale, you'll have nowhere to go but off the charts.

When you're ready, put the offer in writing in a job offer letter. Describe all the details and terms, including a job description, start date, pay package, benefits, vacations, and so on. You might also include the special perks, like telecommuting or flextime. That way, you avoid confusion or disagreements later on.

Providing Benefits You Can Afford

It's smart to step back and review whether your firm is known as a good place to work. It's not just job candidates who will notice. Every time the sales staff makes a presentation and a client must choose between you and a competitor, the image and skills of your company are on the line. Offering employee benefits, which helps retain trained, loyal staff and impresses stakeholders and customers, has a direct influence on company growth and success. Setting up benefits plans can be your best marketing strategy.

The down side, of course, is the very immediate costs. Many start-ups and small companies can't or don't want to commit the necessary cash to employee benefits. "About 75 percent of small firms already offer health insurance because that's usually the first concern of employees," says small business analyst Alice Magos at CCH, Inc., a business information group. Owners might be understandably reluctant to take on any other benefits. Plus, health insurance costs alone have been skyrocketing in the past few years.

Financial Advantages of Offering Employee Benefits

Many insurance carriers now sell healthcare and/or retirement packages specifically structured for cash-strapped small businesses. These offerings depend on employee contributions, so employers pick up only minimal tabs. There are financial advantages for employers in offering benefits, including:

- **Tax savings.** Plan contributions are tax deductible.

- **Personal savings.** Setting up plans for the staff might net you better benefits for less money than paying for your plan alone.

- **Payroll savings.** Some employees might accept certain benefits as a substitute for higher salaries or raises.

Chapter Thirteen: **Hiring and Firing**

Part Five:
Gurus, Guides,
and Staff:
Employment
Dos and Don'ts

If you're worried about costs or you already offer healthcare coverage and want to consider other, affordable benefits, there are other options. In addition to the tax deductions, you can offset costs by requiring employees to contribute to the costs and then deduct their share from paychecks.

Important   Remember: offering benefits has legal and tax implications. Check with your accountant, attorney, and perhaps a benefits specialist for more details.

These days, dozens of cost-efficient benefits consultants can customize and administrate plans for small and mid-size companies. There are also a growing number of small business alliances or purchasing consortiums that can give you the clout and buying power of large companies. Quiz your industry associations, local businesses, or chamber of commerce for referrals. Most important, canvas your employees to learn what they most want and what they feel they can afford to contribute. Then consider the following options:

- **Retirement plans.**   The recent tax law changes have revised some rules of retirement benefits, which took effect as of 2002. But the basics remain the same. Such savings plans, as you probably know, allow you and your employees to put away pretax income that grows tax-deferred until you withdraw the money at retirement age. As the employer, you can deduct any plan contributions. But while 8 out of every 10 (79 percent) full-time employees at larger firms are covered by employer plans, less than half (46 percent) of employees at smaller firms have such retirement coverage, according to the 2001 Small Employer Retirement Survey published by the Employee Benefit Research Institute (*www.ebri.org*), a nonprofit, nonpartisan policy and research organization. To attract top-flight talent, consider these plans—and check with your accountant for details:

  - ❏   Profit-sharing plans.

  - ❏   Savings Incentive Match Plan for Employees (SIMPLE).

  - ❏   Simplified Employee Pension (SEP) individual retirement accounts (IRAs).

  - ❏   401(k)s. Many large corporations combine an Employee Stock Option Plan (ESOP) with a 401(k) into a hybrid called a KSOP. That offers sizable tax deductions when the company matches employee contributions with company stock. If your firm is big enough for such options, check with your accountant.

Part Five:
Gurus, Guides,
and Staff:
Employment
Dos and Don'ts

Microsoft Small Business Kit

❑ Flexible Spending Accounts (FSAs). Also called *medical flex plans*, FSAs allow you and employees to use pretax dollars to pay certain expenses, such as medical, dental, vision, and childcare costs. Such accounts can reduce income taxes. Typically, employees earmark a predetermined amount for the year that's deducted from each paycheck, up to certain limits for different expenses. According to federal rules, all the money must be used that year for eligible expenses or forfeited.

■ **Time off.**   Giving employees some control over their schedules to spend time with family has become very popular—and won't cost you up-front dollars. Such personal days do not include holidays. Depending on seniority, the vacation days are typically set at an annual number that staff can take at their discretion (with advance notice, of course).

■ **Childcare.**   Starting in 2002, the new tax law allows employers to claim a 25 percent tax credit of qualified expenses for providing an employee daycare facility. The tax credit is capped at $150,000 worth of expenses for the year, which makes it more suited to small businesses than large corporations. You can also get a 10 percent tax break by subsidizing childcare resources or referral services—for example, a referral phone hotline.

■ **Disability benefits.**   Offered as both short-term and long-term plans, this insurance replaces lost income for an employee recovering from extended illness or injury. Usually, the employee's salary determines the amount of the benefit. Without group coverage and the volume discount that affords, disability insurance is very expensive. As a result, employees sometimes prefer disability insurance to retirement plans because they can save money in tax-deferred retirement accounts on their own.

■ **Life insurance.**   Group rates for insurance plans, like disability, can be cheaper than buying plans privately. Frequently, companies pay premiums for employees of one to one-and-a-half times each salary. Employees can buy additional coverage, and the cost is deducted from paychecks.

■ **Voluntary benefits.**   Last, don't forget the power of being a boss. You can invite experts or facilitators or consultants to come talk to employees about investing or retirement or insurance. Most experts will show up free for the chance to get some business. That way, employees get a vote in choosing benefits, and you can deduct costs from paychecks. Even better, everyone's rewarded by a group rate.

Chapter Thirteen: Hiring and Firing

Part Five:
Gurus, Guides,
and Staff:
Employment
Dos and Don'ts

As a small business, you can better compete in the big leagues if you treat employees to bigger benefits.

Healthcare Innovations

In the past few years, various programs have surfaced to combat the rising costs of healthcare insurance, which is especially burdensome for small businesses.

The recent Health Savings Account (HSA) law, for example, works like a Family Savings Account (FSA), permitting employers and staff to contribute pretax dollars into a savings account that can be tapped to cover medical expenses. Contributions from the HSA are permitted until the high deductible on a health insurance plan has been met. Plans with high deductibles are much more affordable for both employers and employees. Many small businesses are gravitating to this option.

In April 2004, new compliance requirements of the Health Insurance Portability and Accountability Act (HIPAA) of 1996 kicked in. The requirements strengthen privacy safeguards for employees and have some penalities for noncompliance. If your company has an HSA or a Medical Reimbursement Account handled by a third party or an outside administrator, you need to check whether the plan is up-to-speed.

Various other legislation stalled in Congress is designed to help small businesses set up or maintain increasingly expensive health benefits for employees. One such proposal, the Small Business Health Fairness Act, creates Association Health Plans (AHPs), which would permit small business owners to form a group with other businesses across state lines to purchase more affordable health coverage for their families and workers.

In the meantime, an innovation in healthcare coverage, variously called *self-directed* or *consumer choice*, is taking the HSA idea further. Much like the shift from pensions to 401(k) plans, which moved retirement savings from

> ## Some Self-Directed Healthcare Providers
>
> Definity Health (*www.definityhealth.com*), based in Minneapolis, was one of the earliest pioneers.
>
> Other providers include HealthMarket (*www.healthmarket.com/*), Lumenos (*www.lumenos.com/*), MyHealthbank (*www.myhealthbank.com/*), and Vivius (*www.vivius.com/*). Established insurers are also busy launching products, including Wellpoint (*www.wellpoint.com/*), based in California.

Part Five:
Gurus, Guides,
and Staff:
Employment
Dos and Don'ts

Microsoft Small Business Kit

an *employer-defined benefit* to an *employee-defined contribution* plan, the consumer-driven plans aim to make healthcare a worker's responsibility. Also like 401(k)s, this coverage has tradeoffs. Employees must become sophisticated consumers of healthcare services for consumer-centric healthcare to work. With workers making decisions and spending their own money, the thinking goes, they will have incentives to find value.

Many insurers now offer the option of consumer-driven plans. As you put plans in place for your employees—or when your contract comes up for renewal—you'd be smart to compare some new plans with your current coverage.

Deciding When to Call It Quits

The boss who doesn't lose sleep over having to fire someone is a rare breed indeed. It's every supervisor's nightmare. But there is a worse ordeal: being on the receiving end. Many entrepreneurs are so busy with their own discomfort that they overlook the pain they're inflicting with dismissals. But the moment, the meeting, the entire day sears into memory and burrows there. People remember every detail for the rest of their lives. To maintain perspective, picture yourself on the other side of the desk. Imagine how you'd want to be treated.

The reason for any termination is important, of course. Before making the decision, get advice from a human resources expert or an employment lawyer. You don't want to run afoul of state or federal laws or stray far from company policies, whether set by past precedent or formally laid out in a handbook. (See the section "Why Drafting a Company Handbook Is a Smart Use of Precious Time," earlier in this chapter, for more about creating a handbook.) Nevertheless, the cause for dismissal typically has little bearing on how to break the news. Whether it's because of staff reductions and you're truly sorry or it's owing to the employee's lousy performance and you can't wait to see the back of someone, there is still a respectful way to terminate an employee—and there are downright awful ways.

Here's a thumbnail guide to the basics, including tips about legal and pay issues. And here too are the five heartless things you must bite your tongue not to say. Every one of these comments is a mistake, and each is something bosses tend to fall back on.

Chapter Thirteen: **Hiring and Firing**

Part Five:
Gurus, Guides,
and Staff:
Employment
Dos and Don'ts

■ **"How's the family?"**   There should be no small talk at this meeting. Don't try to warm the mood or pretend it's an ordinary exchange. You're only delaying the blow. Later, when the employee relives the conversation (and he or she will), any gratuitous comments will provide ammunition for deeper resentment. Make it a short meeting, no more than 10 minutes or so. Get to the point, quickly. Also plan ahead. Figure out what you will say or prepare a script of talking points that is vetted by the human resources manager or an outside lawyer.

■ **"I'm sure you're surprised."**   If the company must cut staff, you ought to have prepared employees. If it's a performance concern, this meeting should certainly not blindside an employee. Dismissal is a last resort. Not only is it smart and cost-effective to first try to improve performance, but for legal protection, you also should have a paper trail documenting your efforts. Write summary reports of what's discussed at each meeting. Ask the employee to sign the memos, which shows that he or she understands and agrees to the action or behavior requested. Set deadlines for results and the next reviews. If you'd rather be informal, make sure another manager joins each meeting. That way, you have a witness in case it ends in dismissal and a legal hearing. No one else on staff should be surprised either. Let other employees know about the termination—especially quickly if there's more than one. Communicate the reasons without rancor or confidential details. People will want reassurance about their jobs and the status of the company.

■ **"I know how you feel."**   This is a doozy, isn't it? Any such patronizing remarks (another being "I'm sorry to have to do this") are only uttered to make a boss feel less guilty. You're hurting someone. This comment rubs salt in the wound. On the other hand, bosses frequently shut down their emotions at such times, presuming it's more "business-like." But that translates as cold and uncaring. There's a happy medium. You can candidly and carefully explain the reasons and still offer sympathy. If the employee wants to talk or argue, hear him or her out. Don't argue back. Firmly repeat your honest reasons, your final decision, your sincere sympathy—and then politely show him or her out.

■ **"Let me know how I can help."**   Owners actually sometimes mean this, at least momentarily. But even when the business is downsizing, it's usually a transparent sop. Some staffers are obviously staying. This one is getting axed. Unless you plan to be a solid reference or you're

Part Five:
Gurus, Guides,
and Staff:
Employment
Dos and Don'ts

Microsoft Small Business Kit

willing to make calls on the employee's behalf, don't offer help. It's a dangerous and false sentiment. You're belying the message you've just delivered, which might give the employee grounds for legal or other appeals.

■ **"Take all the time you need."**   Don't cloud the need for an exit with misplaced sympathy. Be clear about departure: "We've made the decision, and this is your last day"—or week, or whatever's appropriate. There's little consensus from experts about when to deliver such bad news. Some say Friday, because there's the weekend to recover. Others say Friday leads to two days of withdrawal and depression, or worse. Some gurus suggest midmorning so that the employee can head out to lunch and support from friends. Or there's the end of the business day so that he or she can leave quickly without causing undue gossip. Everyone agrees about only one thing. Firing someone first thing in the morning is never done for the sake of an employee. It's always so that the boss can get that burden off his or her chest. Usually, it's a good idea to anchor the news with money. Have the final paycheck ready. Hand it over at the end of the meeting or give the employee a business card or note with the name and contact information of whoever handles arrangements.

Clearly, there is no easy or right time to fire anyone. But that doesn't mean you must be harsh or unfeeling. Do not rush into a termination meeting just to get it over with. Think it through. Put yourself in the employee's shoes. The more candid and respectful you can be, the less pain you will cause. And the more respect you might get back.

For More Information

In addition to the resources mentioned in this chapter, you will find links and information on the companion CD. Some books and Web sites particularly useful for understanding how to find and, when necessary, remove employees include:

Books

Fred S. Steingold, *The Employer's Legal Handbook* (Nolo Press, 2004)

Del J. Still, *High Impact Hiring: How to Interview and Select Outstanding Employees* (Management Development Systems, 1997)

Chapter Thirteen:

Part Five:
**Gurus, Guides,
and Staff:
Employment
Dos and Don'ts**

Amy DelPo and Lisa Guerin, *Dealing with Problem Employees: A Legal Guide* (Nolo Press, 2003)

Web Sites

- The Nolo Legal Encyclopedia is an outstanding, free resource for small businesses: *www.nolo.com/lawcenter/ency/index.cfm.*

- You can find out about IRS rules and regulations at: *www.irs.gov/ businesses/small.*

- HR Zone includes information on many topics related to small businesses, including pointers on the hiring process: *www.hrzone.com/ topics/hiring.html.*

Part Five:
Gurus, Guides,
and Staff:
Employment
Dos and Don'ts

Microsoft Small Business Kit

When people walk in the door, they want to know: What do you expect out of me? What's in this deal for me? What do I have to do to get ahead? Where do I go in this organization to get justice if I'm not treated appropriately? They want to know how they're doing. They want some feedback. And they want to know that what they are doing is important. If you take the basic principles of leadership and answer those questions over and over again, you can be successful dealing with people.

— *Frederick Smith, founder, Federal Express*

Chapter Fourteen
Managing Like a Coach

As a business grows, you must hire others to do the work you'd probably rather do yourself. It's not easy to let go. Here's how to loosen control and motivate your staff.

What you'll find:

❑ The bossing thing

❑ Delegating: dos and don'ts

❑ Making employees feel valued

❑ Measuring performance

❑ Training staff pays off

❑ Managing the new work force

Part Five:
Gurus, Guides,
and Staff:
Employment
Dos and Don'ts

Microsoft Small Business Kit

The Bossing Thing

Managing people and performance is hardly the stuff of entrepreneurial dreams. Rather, the ambition to start a company typically begins with the love of doing something, whether that's programming, designing, investing, or helping people. When the business begins to grow, you must hire employees to accomplish the expanding work. In turn, your job becomes coordination and improvement. It's now up to you to take care of staff, operations, and delivery. You set benchmarks, oversee results, and consider future growth. Those are very different skills from designing, programming, or whatever. Such responsibilities are also a far cry from the energy, aggressiveness, and passion needed to drive a start-up.

How Do You Know When You Need Help?

These warning signs should tell you to think about expanding your staff.

- Staff turnover increases.

- Everyone starts hiding things from the boss.

- The mission is diluted—everyone's going in different directions.

- Key managers and employees keep saying, "We don't get any time with you."

So the irony of small business success is that it frequently translates into no longer being able to do the work you love. Good builders usually make bad bosses. Entrepreneurs tend to be controlling about the baby firm they birthed. They're perfectionists, preferring to do everything themselves. They like to micromanage. Entrepreneurs are also mavericks and risk-takers. They're impatient and won't bother waiting for consensus or listening to feedback. "The challenge is believing that anyone else can do it better," admits Emory Mulling, chairman of his own executive outplacement, coaching, and search firms in Atlanta. "For too long," he says, "I worked with every individual in our training program. It took four years for me to find someone else who I thought could take over the training."

Yet at some point—let's hope an opportune one—you must face the inevitable. If the company is to continue to succeed, founders must change the I-can-do-it-all approach into one that accepts and harnesses the expertise of others. How do you know when it's time?

Chapter Fourteen: Managing Like a Coach

Part Five:
Gurus, Guides,
and Staff:
Employment
Dos and Don'ts

Basically, the decision comes down to answering these two questions:

- Is the business continuing to generate increasing revenues?

- How well are your goods or services being delivered?

Delegating: Dos and Don'ts

When owners can't let go, companies become stunted. Employees and opportunities hit the wall when the chief executive insists on knowing every trivial thing, being at every routine meeting, calling each and every shot. If you want your business to grow, you'll need to evolve from the controlling passion of your start-up days into being able to hand over power and responsibility to trusted deputies.

Before loosening the reins, review your tasks and responsibilities, perhaps in a written list. Identify the tasks you do that can be done by someone else or eliminated entirely. Focus on the work only you can accomplish, and give responsibility for the rest to subordinates. When delegating, the first rule is empowerment. Don't keep second-guessing deputy decisions. Other advice:

- **Chuck your ego.** Resist self-flattery. Don't keep telling yourself that no one does anything as well as you do and nobody works harder or longer. You can't start letting go until you have a clear-eyed assessment of your own strengths and weaknesses. Then you need to review the additional talent, skills, or personalities required to drive growth. Hiring people just like you won't add up to the balance you need to grow the business. There really are people out there who know more than you do.

See "When to Hire," page 348, and "Where to Find Talent," page 351 for more advice on hiring.

- **Let go in stages.** Despite the entrepreneur's tendency to get everything done yesterday, don't rush into delegating. If you have staff ready to shoulder the load, suddenly shifting your responsibilities won't stick. It must be done gradually so that both you and they can grow into the unaccustomed roles. If you need to hire new help, move thoughtfully.

For instance, Katherine Rothman founded her New York public relations agency, KMR Communications, in 1999, at the age of 28. She specializes in healthcare and the beauty industry. Now grown to a staff of 15, the agency racks up multimillion-dollar annual revenues.

Part Five:
Gurus, Guides,
and Staff:
Employment
Dos and Don'ts

Microsoft Small Business Kit

Yet Rothman was still overseeing all day-to-day operations, including payroll, invoicing, and billing; ordering supplies; human resources; and employee benefits and orientation. She assigned chores to different employees, but no one tracked everything besides her. "It was all done piecemeal," she says.

Mostly, Rothman was afraid to trust anyone with the financial side of the business: "I've heard so many bad experiences. People being robbed by bookkeepers, turning over control and having that person leave, losing confidential records." Eventually, she was pushed to make changes. She recruited a director of operations and chose a candidate who had 20 years of experience, all at one company. That stability increased Rothman's comfort level. Still, Rothman says, "I did not turn every task over to her at once. It would have been hard for me and overwhelming for her." Instead, Rothman kept her own set of records and notations while letting the new director work alongside her, making an additional set.

In time, Rothman grew confident. "I have seen how accurate and meticulous she is and now have relinquished more and more to her jurisdiction. This was the smartest hiring move I ever made. My life is so much easier and efficient now."

■ **Get help from informed specialists.**   Tapping the objective insights of outsiders can help you figure out where to hold on and where to let go. But be selective about who you ask. The point is to find people you respect and will heed—advisors who have both the expertise and good will to help you grow. Some suggestions:

❑   Work with a professional business coach for a few months, but check references before signing on.

❑   Rely on close friends or professional associates.

❑   Get advice from the bank executive where the company does business.

❑   Work with a management consultant for a few sessions or hours.

❑   Talk to the local chamber of commerce officer.

❑   Talk to a local Small Business Administration (SBA) or Small Business Development Center (SBDC) officer.

❑   Check out your state government small business resources.

Chapter Fourteen: **Managing Like a Coach**

Part Five:
Gurus, Guides,
and Staff:
Employment
Dos and Don'ts

❑   Regular meetings with an informal board of advisors can help, whether they're paid or not, and whether you see them individually or as a group.

See "Forming an Advisory Board," page 95, for more about advisors.

■   **Don't play favorites.**   Select the deputy who has the skills to get the job done, not simply a friend or a favored protégé.

■   **Make your intentions clear.**   Communicate your expectations and goals to the deputy. Explain *what* needs to be accomplished, but don't tell him or her *how* to do it.

■   **Set up a procedure to review results.**   That can be an informal breakfast once a week or a formal monthly report.

■   **Ask for input.**   In getting to your desired goals, ask for your deputy's advice and ideas. You could learn something.

■   **Formally introduce the deputy.**   Explain to the staff that the deputy has a new or enhanced role. Clearly describe his or her authority. Everyone in the company—and, eventually, outside as well—should understand there's been a change. When employees make end runs around the deputy to report to you, don't fall for it.

■   **Don't give and then take away.**   Be consistent about the authority you delegate.

■   **Never criticize in a crowd.**   Don't tell the deputy what he or she is doing wrong in front of other staff. For that matter, don't do that with any employee. Always set up a one-to-one, private meeting for feedback. Then offer specific, positive ways to correct the problem rather than ticking off a list of disappointments.

■   **Don't dump, delegate.**   Don Dymer, a former Scotland Yard police inspector, started his preemployment screening business in Jacksonville Beach, Florida, in 1995. SingleSource Services now screens about a half-million people each year and has 12 employees. Dymer says he learned a lot about how to delegate by working within the military hierarchy of a police force. "You have to empower people and give them status. You can't just dump a job on people with the attitude that you can't be bothered to do it so you're asking them."

■   **Delegate, but set priorities.**   Fast-growing companies are often so intensely focused on moving to the next level that no one is actually in charge. Company leaders must set the mission and the agenda. A hands-off policy can only go so far.

Part Five:
Gurus, Guides,
and Staff:
Employment
Dos and Don'ts

Microsoft Small Business Kit

Generally, in the process of learning how to delegate, try not to point fingers. No company can flourish in an environment that penalizes experimentation or trust. While that sounds obvious, on a day-to-day basis, the nature of risk-taking inevitably means a great number of dead ends before any eureka breakthrough. Very few managers remain calm after hitting the wall. But how you handle those crashes, and how you encourage employees to pick up the pieces and start anew makes all the difference between a company that encourages innovation and one that stagnates. The remedy is to put your trust in the people you hire and give every employee sincere responsibility. Hands-on, my-way-or-the-highway entrepreneurs won't find this easy. But that's how the business gets better.

Making Employees Feel Valued

How you manage your staff and handle their conflicts and goals directly influences the company climate. That weather report—fair or foul—is endlessly broadcast to customers, vendors, suppliers, and everyone else in your industry. When companies recognize employees with tangible rewards, the business becomes more productive and better at retaining talent. In addition, setting policies that make employees want to stick around is cost-effective. Besides boosting profits, a stable staff cuts the costs of recruiting and training and avoids downtime and irate customers.

The route to making employees feel they matter takes some attention, which, of course, will pay off for you. Here are some proven strategies:

- **Recognize the individual.** Let each staff member know that he or she can make a difference.

- **Be responsive.** If you solicit ideas from employees on, say, teamwork or how to develop new business, follow through. Don't ask for feedback or suggestions and then simply ignore them.

- **Tap your top performers as teachers.** Have employees share their expertise by training or mentoring other staff members. You'll not only save your training budget, you'll also make the skilled employees feel more important.

- **Interact with employees.** Each workday, don't rush through the door and immediately head for your desk or office. Stop and chat with employees. No one likes to be taken for granted or feel interchangeable.

- **Help employees to achieve their dreams and goals.** Your company is also their company. If you want them invested in your success, you need to invest in theirs, as well. Periodically, meet with each employee

Chapter Fourteen: Managing Like a Coach

Part Five:
Gurus, Guides,
and Staff:
Employment
Dos and Don'ts

to set yearly goals and accomplishments and keep a written record so that you can benchmark progress. (See the section "Measuring Performance," later in this chapter, for advice about reviews.)

- **Create an atmosphere of trust.** Employees don't like secrets or surprises. Don't spring things on the staff or make changes without communicating why you're doing it.

- **Don't turn into Superowner.** Ask for help. Brainstorm with employees and ask for their input to solve problems or develop strategy. It might take a bit more time, but you'll end up with a happier, more productive staff—as well as some great ideas.

Saying Thanks with Low-Cost Rewards

New businesses, of course, can't afford to hand out hefty bonuses or expensive perks to ace performers. But you don't have to spend a lot to say, "Thank you." A spot bonus for performance can be a sharp, quick return. Or express appreciation without any cash. Typically, talented employees who run extra miles are not thinking about paychecks. For example, on the assembly line at the early Saturn factory, the carmaker that became synonymous with team spirit, the team reward was a Hostess Twinkie. Saturn broke all records for bulk orders of Twinkies.

Many studies have shown that recognition and time off are as effective rewards for workers as money. Never underestimate the power of individual attention and direct praise. You don't have to avoid rewards simply because cash is tight. Here are low-cost ideas to let employees know you appreciate their work:

Instill Faith

Motivation often boils down to giving employees straight answers to these three questions:

- **What's the plan?** If you don't explain your plan, there's no way employees will believe the new company will work.

- **Where are the tools?** OK, now that the staff has a plan, they want to see how it will actually happen.

- **How are the tools used?** Employees need training to best use the tools you provide within the plan's guidelines.

- Hold an award ceremony in the office or at a more formal evening venue to hand out plaques or certificates or funny T-shirts.

- Host award dinners at local restaurants, either for the entire team or as gifts for an employee and a partner.

- Give the employee a weekend getaway.

- Give a lottery ticket each week to an employee who performs well.

Part Five:
Gurus, Guides,
and Staff:
Employment
Dos and Don'ts

Microsoft Small Business Kit

- Buy the employee two tickets to a sports event, concert, movie, or play.

- Offer time off or flexible hours for a specified period of time.

- Take out an ad in the local newspaper or an industry trade journal that thanks the employee or the team.

- Donate money or time to a charity or organization designated by the employee.

- Send out a card or special announcement to the company's clients recognizing the employee's efforts.

- Give the employee a training course of his or her choice.

- Put the employee in charge of the company or a department for a day.

- Assign more high-quality and demanding work. Offering more challenging assignments tells employees you appreciate what they are doing and you trust them to handle more responsibility. Plus, it provides training and experience.

- When staffers bring in new employees, award $500 or dinner on the company if the applicants are hired.

- Find a company with excess inventory or some service downtime that your employees would enjoy, and set a swap. You can trade your product for theirs. For instance, your managers get a swell dinner at the local five-star restaurant and their senior staff receives free legal advice from your firm—or similar exchanges. Make sure to check with your accountant before sealing any deal. There are usually tax consequences from such bartering.

Measuring Performance

Most larger companies set aside a special week or month for the dreaded yearly ritual of employee performance appraisals. Smaller companies tend to schedule reviews on the anniversary of an employee's hire, a date that invariably slides for several weeks before actually happening. At a typical review, the manager might not even remember how Sam saved the day six months ago when the big-fish client was about to walk. What's top in the manager's mind is how Sam waltzed in late three days in the past few weeks. So most of the annual hour is devoted to coaching Sam on the virtues of punctuality.

More than likely, the manager is harassed and oblique, saying things like: "We really need you here for the *entire* day." Then with 15 minutes left, it's

Chapter Fourteen: **Managing Like a Coach**

Part Five:
Gurus, Guides,
and Staff:
Employment
Dos and Don'ts

time to catalog and critique Sam's skills, training, 12 months of contributions, job satisfaction, teamwork, communications ability, how he manages projects, prospects for growth, and—thank goodness!—it's over, punctuated by the meaningless closer: "Keep up the good work."

Bosses and employees both tend to postpone these encounters, which often turn tense and defensive. Still, everyone eventually does them. Why? Performance evaluations are used to justify compensation decisions and promotions or terminations. They help document personnel actions that might otherwise provoke legal claims. So they're just an annoying chore business owners gotta do, right? Yes and no.

Templates to help you manage employees

Microsoft Office Online provides a number of templates (most as Microsoft Word documents) related to employee management. To locate these templates, go to Office Online (click Microsoft Office Online on the Help menu in Word), and then click Templates in the first set of links in the navigation pane on the left side of the window. Under Browse Templates, click Human Resources. Among the templates, you'll find everything from a form in which you collect emergency information for an employee, to performance review forms, to time sheets and schedules, to an employee status report.

Reviewing the Review

The purpose of an appraisal, of course, is to measure an employee's job performance against a previously defined standard or benchmark that you or a manager has clearly communicated beforehand. In contrast to a dreaded annual summit, regular meetings that review expectations and performance help to build skills and loyalty. A company review guide can clarify expectations on both sides. You want to provide productive feedback to each staffer so that he or she can improve performance and better understand and support the company's direction. Appraisals are also intended to help employees grow and develop skills. Keep all that in mind when setting up reviews.

You can choose among several review options, depending on what makes you most comfortable. The traditional format is a scheduled meeting between a supervisor and an employee to talk about performance and job satisfaction. Usually, it's set up a few weeks in advance so that both of you have time to prepare and consider your goals. This is a dialog. Don't take over and simply catalog everything you want changed or improved. You should be listening as well as reviewing. Make the assumption that everyone tries to do his or her best. Also, don't discuss wage increases and job

Part Five:
Gurus, Guides,
and Staff:
Employment
Dos and Don'ts

Microsoft Small Business Kit

performance in the same meeting. The two issues should be unbundled so that you can honestly address each one at separate times.

You can skip some of the tension by scheduling more frequent, casual conversations, one-to-one coffee hours, or lunches that let you interact with the employee about goals, job pressures, strategy, and achievements throughout the year. That way, the meeting is likely to be a continuing dialog rather than a surprise announcement.

To be effective, feedback for employee performance ought to be provided often, objectively, and without disrupting everyone's peace of mind or budget. Reviews should be open and interactive. Given those demands of time and emotion, many businesses are now combining one-to-one meetings with a growing use of electronic formats. Increasingly, companies are moving away from the annual subjective review to continuous appraisals that look at the employee from all sides of the organization, not just a supervisor's view. This kind of appraisal gathers full-circle performance reviews of the employee from supervisors, subordinates, peers, and sometimes even customers or clients and is known as a "360-degree performance review." All comments are strictly anonymous, and reviews can be conducted on a regular basis or following special projects or tasks. Software programs that automate the process, allowing every part of the review to be electronically input and tracked, leverage the 360-degree concept. Dozens of solution providers and application service providers (ASPs) now offer convenient interactive applications with easy survey forms for such rounded performance reviews. Results can be archived, and companies can personalize the process and limit access. Nevertheless, when using electronic formats, you still should schedule one-to-one meetings to discuss the results.

As a company grows, 360-degree surveys help staff see interdependencies. Employees can then resolve any friction or misunderstandings. The sales team, for instance, might get feedback that says the tech staff thinks salespeople are intimidated about approaching the IT experts. Wouldn't that be helpful to know sooner rather than later?

With job performance more clearly and objectively tracked, you'll be able to make informed and cost-saving decisions about staff training, compensation, and promotions or growth. Over time, you'll likely improve staff performance as well as integrate review components with your other IT tools.

Chapter Fourteen: Managing Like a Coach

Part Five:
Gurus, Guides,
and Staff:
Employment
Dos and Don'ts

Tough Love and Accountability

Obviously, it's up to you to set on-the-job standards and direction. But that issue of the entrepreneurial personality might arise again. Start-up owners aren't known for patience or touchy-feely expertise. Pressed for time and stretched for profits, chief execs find excuses to avoid the discomfort of talking to employees who can't or won't perform. When staff trouble is ignored, however, everyone suffers, especially—and critically—the customers. Letting a staffer get away with poor or damaging work sends a signal that talented performers are neither valued nor rewarded. Why should anyone else go the distance if the guy who won't leave his chair is never called on it?

Employees screw up for all kinds of reasons. Maybe a promotion turns sour. Maybe an employee feels unappreciated. Some workers collect a stack of negative attitudes and hand out one a day. How exactly do you motivate an employee to perform at a higher level?

Barring a total mismatch, most workers want to do well. There might be valid reasons why the employee is not up to par. Frequently, a worker doesn't realize her work isn't satisfactory. The first step is to talk to the employee—an informal chat outside the office will do. You'll accomplish a lot more by identifying solutions rather than pointing out problems. Start by discovering answers to these questions:

- What value does the employee think he brings to the company?

- What are the employee's goals within the firm?

- If she does a better than average job, what rewards does the employee think she rates?

- How does the employee think he is doing?

- Where does the employee go when she needs help?

Tracking Job Performance

You can encourage and support top-level employee performance with these simple steps:

- Survey employee satisfaction and attitudes.

- Offer targeted or personalized business information or access.

- Provide tools for continuous employee evaluations and feedback.

- Create instant access to employee ratings tools for compensation decisions.

Part Five:
Gurus, Guides,
and Staff:
Employment
Dos and Don'ts

Microsoft Small Business Kit

Listen closely, and then respond with your own answers. This dialog will build a foundation for describing your job expectations. Be specific. Then, working together, draft a fair and realistic plan for improvement, including periodic reviews and time-sensitive benchmarks. To prevent legal trouble, keep a written record. Ask the employee to sign and date the agreement, including the deadlines and stages for improvement. One-time events don't change behavior over the long haul, of course. You must reinforce expectations.

You might also need to change your own behavior. Your praise should be directed to specific tasks. "Nice work" is not nearly as effective as "Nailing that sale with Acme was really smart." Handing out personal compliments about, say, a worker's new haircut won't boost morale or performance. You're trying to develop a worker, not chat up a pal. Make sure compensation or pay-for-performance policies are rewarding desired behavior. Do you, for instance, penalize the wrong workers? When employees who take time to train others or to develop teams don't make the same "numbers" as the workers they've helped, those people shouldn't be made to feel like suckers.

Don't become so invested in the employee's turnaround that you lose sight of business. If nothing changes, you might need to cut the employee loose.

See "Deciding When to Call It Quits," page 374, for more about terminating employees.

Why Employees Fail to Perform

Check out these typical reasons to explain why an employee isn't working up to speed. Then see if you can bolster communications or remedy the circumstances so the performance improves. Often enough, simply acknowledging the problem can help put performance on track.

- Do employees receive training? Do they get ample time and constructive feedback to build needed skills? Too often, new hires are left to figure out roles all by themselves.

- Are expectations clear? Frequently , business owners and employees disagree about the specific skills needed to get the job done.

- Are expectations realistic? Many business owners get angry when employees don't work at the same level they do.

Training Staff Pays Off

Your profits might be slim and your staff might be lean, but you must still keep employees sharp and honed. Dumb and dumber don't reel in juicy contracts. On-the-job learning is key to staying competitive and to retaining top-notch talent.

Chapter Fourteen: Managing Like a Coach

Part Five:
Gurus, Guides,
and Staff:
Employment
Dos and Don'ts

But training takes employees out of loop—sometimes for days on end just when you need them most. There's often a stiff price tag, too. Average costs for training consultants, according to the American Society for Training and Development (ASTD), run $55 to $150 an hour, or flat day rates of $250 to a staggering $10,000. Expenses don't stop with training either. There's the cost of lost work or business, transportation and accommodations, meals, not to mention possible overtime pay. All of it quickly mounts up.

The solution is to develop innovative and cost-effective ways to train. Maybe continuous learning is a necessary expense and can't be compromised, but pricey and traditional instructor-led classroom training isn't the only option.

Here are smart ways to set up low-cost training sessions, whether to develop leadership skills, compliance programs, sales or marketing skills, customer service, IT or technology tutoring, financial management, or accounting. In the following section, you'll also find a rundown of e-learning options—that is, training delivered via learning technologies and the Web.

- **Train the trainer.** Assign an appropriate staffer to attend training workshops or seminars. Then have that employee teach everyone else. Consider the person you select. You want the right person to attend specific programs and, upon his or her return, to be responsible for training others.

- **Call your community college.** The best-kept secret of business training is the country's network of community colleges. Supported by a range of public funding, including SBDCs (the SBA's Small Business Development Centers), and the Workforce Investment Act of 1998, as well as state and city grants, community colleges provide a rich and efficient resource for tutoring staff, from entry-level to executive. At Monroe Community College in Rochester, New York, for example, more than 5,000 people were trained in 2002, says Charles Caples, program director at the Office of Workforce Development. "Costs run 50 percent to 60 percent cheaper than for-profit training centers," he says.

- **Share the cost.** You can set up your own training sessions and invite a group of other small businesses to buy seats or register. Or recruit partner companies, and set up classes with open enrollment so that staffers from any participating company can attend. Obviously, this works only with noncompeting firms and nonproprietary skills.

- **Work the phones.** Cheap, effective, and reliable, audio or phone courses are often overlooked. Audiotapes and books are also useful.

Part Five:
Gurus, Guides,
and Staff:
Employment
Dos and Don'ts

Microsoft Small Business Kit

E-Learning Options

Lately, training delivered via learning technologies is gaining particular favor, according to the ASTD. Web-based learning options offer terrific flexibility and cost savings. Courses can be taken online in synchronous or real-time sessions. Or self-study modules can be accessed in asynchronous or just-in-time sessions via archive or download. That way, employees can study whenever they prefer, day or night, weekends or holidays.

You save significant dollars because you don't need to hire experts, trainers, or in-class instructors. You avoid the expense of employee travel and hotel stays, and you gain time previously lost from the job. In addition, unlike classroom settings, e-learning employees advance at their own pace, and they can update or refresh lessons whenever they choose.

Early versions of online training and education suffered serious dropout rates because pioneering courses emphasized technology over personal interaction, no matter the quality of content. E-learning formats had a passive, "just the facts" on-screen delivery—the electronic equivalent of a classroom teacher droning on in a monotone. It was hard to stay alert. Nowadays, students enjoy a rich range of interaction while still benefiting from e-learning's flexible schedules and user-directed pace. Educational institutions and online providers are harnessing sophisticated advances, such as off-the-shelf Flash and Java applications, instant messaging interactions, and audio and video enhancements. Plus, a host of smaller providers market tailor-made simulations and personalized instructor designs. Most providers also have online demonstrations so that you can evaluate the content and usability before you buy. Best of all, e-learning is still cheap compared to conventional training methods. New and improved Web-based models developed by large-volume providers run $100 to $300 per person for several sessions, depending on content and delivery.

Finding Offerings

You can now find Web-based training for everything from the practical ("Accounting & Cash Flow"), to primers ("Core Training for Microsoft PowerPoint"), to career development and human resources ("HIPAA Compliance Solutions") and the softer side of business skills ("Bridging Marketing and Sales"). Here are some better-known e-learning sources and how to find out more:

Chapter Fourteen: **Managing Like a Coach**

Part Five:
Gurus, Guides,
and Staff:
Employment
Dos and Don'ts

- The Microsoft E-Learning Library (MELL) offers browser-based interactive training that's self-directed on a wide range of skills and subjects. A search tool lets you access installed online references and components for answers to questions as they arise. Offerings cover using Microsoft systems or software, Web site building and training, as well as business solutions, such as competitive intelligence or project management.

- The free online courses in entrepreneurship from the SBA's Small Business Training Network (*http://www.sba.gov/training/ coursestake.html*) are offered in collaboration with nonprofit provider My Own Business. Presented in English or Spanish, courses are interactive, with audio bytes, quizzes, feedback, and online tools that cover such skills as creating or updating a business plan, borrowing money, setting up an exporting business, buying a franchise, developing communication tools, leasing equipment, and more.

- State and online colleges and universities across the country offer a wealth of e-learning options designed for business training. In New York, for example, Empire State University was founded in 1971 to offer self-directed study customized for business and working professionals. Empire has some 40 centers around the state and offers 400 online courses that cost $99 to $199 each for 12 or so sessions, including such topics as paralegal training, learning Web-based design or Java, management training, and more. "Five or six years ago, completion rates were only 45 to 50 percent, but now they're 75 to 80 percent," says Joe Boudreau, who heads the Corporate Education division at Empire. Check your state's university and community college offerings or register online for an out-of-state course.

An exclusively online facility, the accredited University of Phoenix Online relies on an asynchronous teaching model for professional development and continuing education, with such courses as call center training, human resources management, supply chain or project management, and more. Typically, a credit hour runs about $450. Groups of students also participate in asynchronous discussions with each other and the remote instructor.

- eLearners.com or WorldwideLearn.com are two independent online services that connect consumers and businesses to distance-learning resources. Each portal has a robust corporate training section that lists hundreds of e-learning courses and links to dozens of colleges and other providers.

Part Five:
Gurus, Guides,
and Staff:
Employment
Dos and Don'ts

Microsoft Small Business Kit

- SkillSoft, which mostly markets to large-volume providers like universities, has a subscription service more suitable for small business called Books24X7. This service provides access to unabridged books online. Pricing varies: for about $400 or less, you get 25 "seats" to one or more "collections" that include FinancePro, ITPro, BusinessPro, and OfficeEssentials.

Customized E-Training

Tailor-made e-learning solutions are also turning affordable. For example, one small shop called Punctuation Media, based in Boca Raton, Florida, has found that small companies with little or no IT resources are taking advantage of cost-effective online training that is both interactive and customized, according to Lenny Schloss, the company co-owner and developer. One Punctuation Media client, NursesSTAT, is a growing healthcare staffing agency in South Florida. The company was relying on in-class instructors to train new nurses to use its proprietary staffing technology system. That necessary training was slowing the operation, which meant the agency wasn't meeting staffing needs for its client hospitals. Punctuation Media implemented a customized multimedia course that trained new recruits via the Internet. Once NursesSTAT moved its course online, the delay evaporated. Administrators could track compliance more quickly, and nurses also could access ongoing support after the initial training.

Many businesses are blending online and traditional training to get the most out of each method. Great-West Healthcare, a health and life insurer based in Greenwood Village, Colorado, uses a desktop tool called Trainersoft from e-learning provider OutStart to develop product knowledge for its sales force. But for soft skills, salespeople are trained in instructor-led classrooms.

Shopping for a Provider

Today's e-learning and electronic corporate training is far more sophisticated than in the days of "Click True or False" and "Next screen." To find a suitable e-learning provider:

- Investigate the quality and depth of the training offerings. Check whether courses are interactive, are flexible, and won't bog down employees with details and unnecessary chores.

- Look for a provider with an established record and credentials. Get references. There are a lot of fly-by-night players out there.

Chapter Fourteen: Managing Like a Coach

Part Five:
Gurus, Guides,
and Staff:
Employment
Dos and Don'ts

■ Determine whether you want off-the-shelf courseware or a customized solution. Commissioning a course might cost more up-front, but in the long run, you might save by having training that precisely suits your business.

Microsoft's Skills Quiz

To sign up for an e-learning IT or software training course from Microsoft, first check out the free skills assessment quiz, at *www.microsoft.com/learning/assessment/default.asp*.

Managing the New Work Force

Increasingly, success hinges on the quality of work done outside the office by a new breed of independents for hire. Smaller businesses, in particular, reap benefits from teleworkers and free agents, such as contract workers, freelancers, self-employed experts, and independent consultants. Various studies show that telework programs can boost performance 10 to 15 percent and cut expenses, sometimes as much as 40 percent, on fixed costs like office space, furniture, and fixtures, as well as on parking facilities, utility bills, and copy machines and printers. Telecommuting also helps you save on recruiting and training costs and any relocation allowances. It gives you access to expert help wherever you can find it, whether for project, contract, or full-time work. Owners are able to recruit and retain better talent by outsourcing certain functions and letting experts work from home.

But management challenges change dramatically when dealing with either remote or contract workers. Here's what you need to know to swim in the free agent pool. And here's how to get the best performance out of the contemporary work force.

Getting Return on Investment (ROI) from On-Staff Telecommuters

Business owners have stubbornly resisted telecommuting. They don't like being unable to see an employee. If staffers are "home," by definition, they aren't "on the job." Human resources directors have nightmares about ceding special privileges to a couple of employees. What if everyone wants to work from home? And there have been many high-profile failures, usually

Part Five:
Gurus, Guides,
and Staff:
Employment
Dos and Don'ts

Microsoft Small Business Kit

because companies do not set benchmarks or procedures for getting it right. But interest in teleworking is picking up. With the cost and time and security worries of travel, remote and dispersed collaborations are attracting more attention.

On the employee side, telework deepens worker satisfaction. Almost 70 percent of teleworkers report being very satisfied with their jobs, according to a 2001 national survey from the International Telework Association & Council (ITAC). "For the employee, it's not just about saving time on commuting," says Bob Smith, ITAC's executive director. "Telework enables the employee to manage his life and work in a reasonable way." In Finland, where roughly 15 percent of the working population teleworks, government researchers point out that the challenges to even greater teleworking are not technical or economic, but psychological and cultural. The way to make such arrangements work is to think through decisions beforehand. You should:

- **Evaluate the workspace.** Remote offices ought to be set up to get the job done as well as protect you from liability. Spaces need proper lighting and workstations. Work out written agreements for IT, legal, and insurance issues. Who owns the equipment? How will you handle maintenance? Who's responsible for what sort of injuries? What about state worker compensation laws? Visits themselves might cause conflict. Can you drop in at an employee's home any time, just as you'd wander into an on-site office? Some companies limit liability by hours and others by defining the workspace. Get expert advice to ensure you're adequately protected.

Telecommuting Tip

When setting up any telecommuting or remote management, leverage the power of today's affordable technology.

Microsoft Office 2003 and Microsoft Windows SharePoint Services allow for easy collaborations of off-site or remote workers. SharePoint can set up a Web site for document storage and retrieval that gives every user check-in and checkout privileges. It maintains a document version history and offers other benefits as well. Users can find and share data while you're protected from losing any information or records. By integrating Microsoft Office 2003 with Microsoft Windows SharePoint Services, remote employees can collaborate and plan, schedule, and interact with one another in real time. Plus, teleworkers will be comfortable using familiar Office applications, including Word, Excel, Outlook, and PowerPoint.

For more information, visit *www.microsoft.com/sharepoint/*.

- **Stay in touch.** Communications and follow-up with isolated employees demand special and consistent effort. After all, on site, every staffer takes one look at the boss's face and instantly gets a company weather report. For remote workers, relying on e-mail will not cut it.

Chapter Fourteen: **Managing Like a Coach**

Part Five:
Gurus, Guides,
and Staff:
Employment
Dos and Don'ts

Pick up the phone, often. Bring in teleworkers for periodic updates to maintain ties with the rest of the staff.

- **Bridge HR and IT.** What happens when a teleworker calls in sick? Do you even believe it? If a teleworker doesn't need to get dressed and travel to work, surely he or she can put in at least a half-day, right? It's a tough call. And how can mobile workers take advantage of company benefits or training programs? HR forms, benefits, and policies must be as immediately accessible and clear to remote workers as they are to on-site employees.

- **Measure productivity, not activity.** Off-site staffers have a hard time proving themselves. Teleworkers might be slower to achieve promotions because they don't have face-to-face relationships with the boss or manager. Create clear remote-performance benchmarks.

- **Be selective about choosing off-site positions.** A coaching or management job, for example, is harder to handle from remote locations than, say, data entry.

- **Be equally choosy about choosing employees.** When given telecommuting privileges, employees with poor performance don't improve and might, indeed, worsen. Good telecommuters are self-motivated.

- **Create a written contract or agreement.** When an employee is working at a remote location, whether from home, on the road, or at a satellite office, it's tough to keep tabs on day-to-day operations. Discussing the objectives and then writing down every part of the agreement will help. Include such specifics as:

  - ❑ Expectations
  - ❑ How performance will be evaluated
  - ❑ What defines success
  - ❑ When and how reviews will occur

Harnessing the Power of Free Agents

Entrepreneurs have a lot of trouble figuring out when to add staff. If you hire on the anticipation of work, you could get stung when a deal falls through. Wait until business booms, and you've lost opportunities. It's a challenge. What's the solution?

The smart response to uncertain demand is to hedge your hiring bets. That is, hire contingency or free agent workers to build your business incrementally.

Part Five:
Gurus, Guides,
and Staff:
Employment
Dos and Don'ts

Microsoft Small Business Kit

Contingency workers are temporary or contract employees, freelancers, self-employed experts, and independent consultants. They can work onsite or from remote locations. You can outsource an entire project to a consultant who then hires and manages his or her own staff, or you can maintain hands-on direction of each player. You can contract with a staffing agency to recruit, evaluate, and hire workers you need, or you can canvas associates and associations to find them on your own. There are dozens of options. With specialized and short-term help, your staff becomes infinitely flexible. It can expand or shrink along with your work.

The pool of free-agent talent has also deepened and widened over the past several years. College-educated, technical, and managerial contract workers have been on the rise, while industrial and clerical contingency workers have been declining, according to the latest U.S. Bureau of Labor statistics. For better or worse—and that's another story—business owners are increasingly viewing employees as a variable cost rather than a fixed one. Companies today gain and shed workers along with business prospects. That shift is further fueled by the options offered by contract workers, some of whom don't want permanent positions.

You can now find contract workers in every field at every level, including lawyers, mail clerks, dentists, CFOs, nurses, IT gurus, marketing specialists, data processors, physical therapists, teachers, manufacturing workers, sales help, call center reps—you name it. But contingency workers and consultants require different handling than permanent staff does. Such workers also represent a new breed of management tradeoffs and challenges.

Here's what you need to know to get the most out of free agents and manage workers who come and go:

- **Explain the mission and job.** Often, contingency help is hurried into starting tasks and then left isolated. Some companies don't even bother to introduce the worker or to tell the staff why he or she was hired. This can cause trouble in both directions, with contract workers and with your standing staff. Instead, set up a formal orientation. Tell the incoming worker why you're hiring a contingency worker, what the company is all about, and perhaps as an incentive, what kind of training or learning he or she can gain while on the job.

- **Define your needs.** If a permanent position is an option down the line, say so. The more honest you are, the better the work you'll get. Make your expectations clear.

Chapter Fourteen: Managing Like a Coach

Part Five:
Gurus, Guides,
and Staff:
Employment
Dos and Don'ts

- **Review policies and benefits beforehand.**   Several government agencies take dim views of any company that hires "temporary" workers as a way to save on permanent worker benefits or taxes or to avoid laws and regulations. The IRS, for instance, can assess costly fines and penalties if it decides that you've avoided paying employment taxes. The Employee Retirement Income Security Act (ERISA) has a 12-factor test to check whether an employee deserves benefits. There are other federal compliance issues about worker status for immigration, employment discrimination and harassment, wage and hourly entitlements, and so on. Then there are state issues about worker compensation and injuries.

  This isn't, by the way, only a concern for low-level workers. Hiring an independent CEO or CFO can run afoul of SEC regulations or, for instance, the financial oversights for publicly traded companies now mandated by the recent Sarbanes-Oxley law. Have a lawyer review your policies. And make sure your benefits plan excludes temporary help. Or you could be facing legal claims and fines.

- **Understand who works for whom.**   When you rely on a temp or staffing agency, make sure everyone in your company who manages the contract worker is clear that the staffing company is the employer for what's called a *co-employment relationship*. The staffing company takes care of all employer-related responsibilities, including payroll taxes, wages, health insurance, and the rest. If there's a performance or management issue, you need to call the staffing company and discuss it with them before addressing the employee.

- **Protect yourself.**   Depending on the work and the worker, you might want to ask a contract employee to sign a release or a confidentiality agreement before beginning work. Ask the worker to sign a simple document that says he or she agrees not to use any competitive information learned on the job for a period of one year after leaving the company. Experts say this kind of agreement has good legal standing.

For More Information

In addition to the resources mentioned in this chapter, you will find links and information on the companion CD. Some books and Web sites particularly useful for understanding how to manage employees include:

Part Five:
Gurus, Guides,
and Staff:
Employment
Dos and Don'ts

Microsoft Small Business Kit

Books

- Stephen C. Lundin et al., *Fish! A Remarkable Way to Boost Morale and Improve Results*, (Hyperion, 2001) (and the other *Fish!* books)

- Warren Bennis, *On Becoming A Leader*, (Perseus Publishing, 2003)

- Max Depree, *Leadership Is an Art*, (Dell, 1990)

Web Sites

- Smart Biz—"How Small Businesses Get Big"—has a wide range of articles on management and other topics: *www.smartbiz.com/*

- HR.com has a variety of resources about managing employees: *hr.com*

- The Human Resources section at about.com offers articles and advice: *humanresources.about.com*

Part Six

The Electronic Desk,
The Digital Business

In this part

Chapter Fifteen   **The Outlook Is Bright:**
                   E-Mail and Your Business. **404**

Chapter Sixteen   **Small Business Networks and Servers** **442**

Chapter Seventeen **Computer Security Basics** **458**

We can lick gravity, but sometimes the paperwork is overwhelming.

— Werner von Braun (1912-1977), German-American rocket expert

Chapter Fifteen

The Outlook Is Bright: E-Mail and Your Business

E-mail speeds up the pace of business. It's an efficient and cost-effective way to stay in touch and transmit documents. But e-mail also has a way of getting ahead of us–both the sheer volume of messages we might need to handle and how quickly we're expected to reply. A few well-conceived strategies will keep you on top of your correspondence.

What you'll find:

❑ E-mail decisions: what do you and your business need?

❑ Online training and assistance for Outlook

❑ E-mail security and protecting e-mail data

❑ Taking care of the messages you need—and those you don't

❑ Simple e-mail marketing: adding a signature

❑ Scheduling appointments and tasks

Like the traffic in Mexico City, the rain in Seattle, or the trade winds that blow through the tropics, e-mail is part of the environment for many people. The widespread use of e-mail helps foster communication and increase the pace of business. A purchase order, lease, or contract that's sent through e-mail arrives at its destination far more quickly than do documents sent by regular mail and far more cheaply than documents sent by overnight express. Using a portable computer or a computer at an Internet café, businesspeople can read and respond to e-mail while commuting or traveling. We're rarely out of touch for long.

However, disadvantages come with the relative ease of using e-mail. Computer viruses often start and spread through malicious e-mail messages. Spam is a significant waste of time and a security risk, and spam messages often contain material that people find offensive. Even legitimate e-mail messages pose a problem when you receive too many. If you use e-mail for business and personal communication, the number of messages builds quickly and requires frequent, if not constant, attention to avoid falling behind. Your correspondents expect a quick, sometimes instantaneous, response.

In this chapter, we'll look at some of the steps you can take to manage e-mail more effectively when you're using Microsoft Outlook 2003, the e-mail program that comes with Microsoft Office, or Outlook Express, an e-mail program that's installed with Microsoft Internet Explorer. We'll provide some background information about the types of e-mail accounts available, describe the security measures provided in Outlook and Outlook Express, and review some of the other features of Outlook that let you use it as a full-fledged electronic personal assistant.

E-mail facts and figures

A Gartner research report titled "E-Mail Overload Reaches Crisis Levels" estimates that the compound annual growth of e-mail messages approaches 40 percent. At that rate, the convenience of e-mail as a communication tool might be its own worst enemy. More than 25 percent of employees surveyed for the report indicated that they spend more than one hour each day working on e-mail. Managers spend nearly two hours every day.

E-Mail Decisions: What Do You and Your Business Need?

The needs that a small business has for e-mail might be addressed through a single account set up for free on MSN's Hotmail. In a case such as this, e-mail clearly isn't the backbone of the business, but one account could be used effectively in a small retail enterprise, for example, to send and receive purchase orders, confirm receipt of shipments, and address (probably on a limited basis) concerns raised by customers. On the other hand, a business might choose to set up its own e-mail server as part of the business's computer network. Somewhere in between, many small businesses will opt to purchase a Web-hosting package that includes 10 or more e-mail accounts as part of the package.

Web-hosting options

For more information about Web-hosting packages, see the section "Mastering Your Domains," on page 192. For information about Web-hosting packages for small business available from Microsoft, see *www.microsoft.com/smallbusiness*.

To set up a basic e-mail account through a service such as Hotmail, for example, you don't need much more information than your name and address (and billing information, if you sign up for one of the packages that has a monthly charge). If you're setting up e-mail accounts with a Web-hosting company, you'll need to know the type of e-mail program you plan to use (Outlook or Outlook Express, for example), have a plan for how to name accounts (you might use something like *firstlast@yourcompany.com*), and know which kind of format (or *messaging protocol*) the Web-hosting company's e-mail server and your e-mail program will use to communicate and transfer messages.

A Quick Guide to E-Mail Protocols

E-mail programs come in twos: an *e-mail client* and an *e-mail server*. A client program such as Outlook or Outlook Express is installed on your computer, and you use your client program to send and receive messages. An e-mail server is the e-mail processing center, or post office. Servers might be managed by your Internet service provider (ISP), the Web-hosting company you use, or as part of your own network. Messages travel from your client to your server and are then routed to the server (or servers) on which the person (or persons) you're sending the message to has his or her account. That server sends the message on to the recipient's e-mail client.

When you set up an e-mail account, you have to designate the protocol with which your client will send messages and the protocol the server will use to send and receive messages. The protocol used by the server must be supported by the e-mail client you're using. Standard messaging protocols include Internet Message Access Protocol (IMAP), Post Office Protocol 3 (POP3), Hypertext Transfer Protocol (HTTP), and Simple Messaging Transfer Protocol (SMTP).

Most e-mail systems use SMTP to send e-mail messages across the Internet from a client to a server. When communicating with Internet-based e-mail servers, Outlook uses SMTP to connect to a server and send messages. Outlook uses POP3 to retrieve messages from an Internet-based mail server. When you set up an e-mail account, you'll often specify POP3 or IMAP for the incoming server (messages coming to you) and SMTP for the outgoing server (messages you send).

IMAP and POP3 are used widely by e-mail servers that transfer messages over the Internet. Both Outlook and Outlook Express will work with a server that supports IMAP or POP3. IMAP is designed primarily to store messages on the server, whereas POP3 is designed to download messages from the server and store them on your computer. With IMAP, you generally need to be connected to the server to read and work with your e-mail messages. With POP3, after you've downloaded messages, you can disconnect from the server, sort and answer messages, and then connect to the server again to send replies and new messages.

IMAP has advantages that make it a good choice for many users. Here are some of the reasons to set up an e-mail account based on IMAP:

- You don't need to download an entire message, which is helpful when someone sends you a message with a large attachment or as a means for avoiding spam. Instead, you can view only the *message headers* (headers indicate who sent you the message, the subject of the message, and whether the message includes an attachment) and decide whether you want to download the complete message.

- Because your e-mail is stored on the server and not on your local computer, your e-mail is available even when you're on the road, for example, and reading e-mail at an Internet café, in your hotel room, or when visiting family or friends.

When you use POP3, your e-mail is stored initially on the server. When you connect to the server and access your e-mail account, messages are downloaded to the e-mail client on the computer you're using. Messages are removed from the server (although you can configure a POP3 e-mail account to store a copy of messages on the server). POP3 is helpful if you use a dial-up connection to retrieve your e-mail messages, because connection times are shorter. (The connection time can become longer, however, if someone sends you a large attachment that's downloaded automatically or the number of spam messages you receive on a particular day is huge.) If your e-mail provider has a limit on the size of your mailbox, downloading messages to your own computer frees up space on the server.

A POP3 e-mail account is best suited for a person who uses only one computer to read and reply to e-mail. If, for example, you use one computer at work and another computer at home, the messages you download onto your home computer won't be available on your e-mail server when you get to the office the next workday. If you keep a copy of the messages on the server, you'll need to deal with those messages again at the office, even if that means only filing them. (Maybe setting up a POP3 account has the advantage of keeping you away from e-mail at night.)

HTTP is best known as the protocol that's used to display pages on the World Wide Web. HTTP is also used as an e-mail protocol over the Internet. Outlook uses HTTP as an e-mail protocol, for example, as does Hotmail. One advantage of HTTP is that you can read e-mail messages from any computer with an Internet connection and a Web browser.

In brief, consider how you're going to use e-mail in your business to determine what kind of account to set up. An e-mail account that uses IMAP probably fits the e-mail habits of most people, especially if you need access to e-mail from more than one computer.

What to Look for in a Microsoft E-Mail Program

Both Outlook and Outlook Express support the protocols that most e-mail servers provided by ISPs use—IMAP, POP3, and HTTP. In addition, Outlook includes a number of features that rely on its integration with Microsoft's e-mail server application, Microsoft Exchange Server (a little more about Exchange Server shortly). Both programs provide an address book and a contacts folder. (Outlook supports multiple address books.) With either program, you can use stationery as a background for an e-mail message (a background can add a distinctive look to your messages, but a background also increases the size of the message) or add a standard signature to the messages you send.

E-mail signatures as a simple marketing tool

Later in this chapter, in the section "Simple E-Mail Marketing: Adding a Signature," you'll learn how to set up a standard e-mail signature—a bit of text or an image that is appended to the end of each e-mail message you send. A signature that includes your contact information or a link to your Web site is a convenient way to generate a little notice for your business.

Both programs also come with built-in security measures, and both Outlook Express and Outlook provide rules for managing e-mail (for example, you can set up a rule that automatically forwards or deletes messages from a sender you specify). We'll describe security features and how to set up rules in more detail later in this chapter, in the sections "E-Mail Security and Protecting E-Mail Data" and "Taking Care of the Messages You Need—and Those You Don't." All in all, however, Outlook Express is a good choice for an e-mail client if you don't need much more than the basics. Outlook offers a greater range of features. For example, the Business Contact Manager add-on to Outlook, which is described in depth in Chapter 12, "Managing Customer Contacts: Business Contact Manager," can be set up as a customer relationship manager for a small business. Depending on how you implement and use e-mail in your business, here are some other considerations to keep in mind that would likely lead you to use Outlook rather than Outlook Express:

- Your business is going to run Microsoft Exchange Server.

- You want to use your e-mail program for scheduling meetings and appointments and for compiling and managing your to-do list.

- You want a junk-mail filter to help control spam.

- You want to archive e-mail messages (manually or automatically). Archiving messages helps keep your mailbox at a manageable size. You can set up Outlook's archiving mechanism so that it archives messages (or calendar or task items as well) at set intervals (all messages that are older than a certain date, for example), or you can archive messages yourself when you feel the need.

■ You receive a lot of documents through e-mail and want to apply additional security measures to ensure that the documents you receive don't carry a virus or worm to your computer.

Separate personal and business e-mail

If you use e-mail to stay in touch with friends and family and also to conduct business, consider using a different e-mail address for each purpose. Even with multiple e-mail addresses, you can set up Outlook or Outlook Express to manage both accounts. In Outlook, you can switch between accounts without opening a different window.

Does Your Business Need Its Own E-Mail Server?

The technology requirements for small businesses vary, of course, and it's wise to carefully assess the sort of software and hardware you need, especially at the start of things, because everything takes time and everything costs money. As you learn about bookkeeping, taxes, payroll, hiring, inventory management, leasing, advertising, and marketing, for example, you'll probably be pleased to find that you need only an e-mail address or two from Hotmail or can procure the e-mail services and support you need through a Web-hosting package.

On the other hand, some business owners might need or want to invest more deeply in technology from the start, setting up a network with one or more servers and multiple workstations. Again, depending on needs and interest, the network could include software that's used to set up an e-mail center for the business. Microsoft Windows Small Business Server 2003 includes Microsoft Exchange Server 2003, a product used to manage e-mail, as well as other server software.

To set up your own e-mail server, you need networking hardware (such as a router, a hub or switch, and a computer with memory and processing speed capable of running server software) and an account with an ISP. You also need to decide how you'll connect to the Internet: through a dial-up connection or through broadband technology such as ISDN (which stands for Integrated Services Digital Network), a digital subscriber line (DSL), or a cable modem. Budget and location play a part in this decision (not all types of broadband service are available everywhere), as do performance needs. A dial-up connection is fairly easy to configure and is less expensive than other options, but the connection speed is slow and transferring large documents or data rapidly is a hardship. DSL is much faster than a dial-up connection, but DSL isn't available everywhere. (Its availability is increasing, however.) A cable modem (especially for a business based in the home) is another alternative. Cable connections can be more expensive (in some locations more than others) than DSL. (ISDN isn't used as much as DSL or cable, but it is an alternative for areas in which DSL isn't available.)

For more information about computer networks and the hardware and software required to set one up for your business, see Chapter 16, "Small Business Networks and Servers."

One of the tools provided in Windows Small Business Server, the Configure E-Mail And Internet Connection Wizard, helps you configure a network, set up an Internet connection users can share (either a broadband connection or a dial-up connection), set up a firewall, and get Exchange Server ready to host e-mail accounts. A basic configuration in Exchange Server 2003 involves decisions such as the routing protocol for outgoing e-mail and the protocol by which e-mail is delivered to you. You can find a summary of these protocols earlier in this chapter, in the section "A Quick Guide to E-Mail Protocols." You'll need to know which messaging protocol your ISP prefers, so obtain that information before forging ahead with the wizard.

Implementing Small Business Server

Microsoft Windows Small Business Server 2003 Administrator's Companion by Charlie Russel, Sharon Crawford, and Jason Gerend (Microsoft Press, 2004), provides step-by-step instructions for setting up Windows Small Business Server, including the steps required to set up an Internet connection and configure Exchange Server. You can find more information about Windows Small Business Server at *www.microsoft.com/windowsserver2003/ sbs*. Documentation about Small Business Server is available at *www.microsoft.com/windowsserver2003/sbs/techinfo/productdoc/ default.mspx*.

Online Training and Assistance for Outlook

For some people, using *managing* and *e-mail* in the same sentence is like talking about a *working holiday* or *jumbo shrimp*—they're terms that don't go together. However, learning about your e-mail program and setting it up to help you deal with the messages you send and receive leads to a constructive middle ground.

If you aren't familiar with the basic features in Outlook (and the basic features are not difficult to master) or you want to deepen your understanding of how to use Outlook, you can find online training and assistance at Microsoft Office Online (*www.microsoft.com/office*). Online training modules cover tasks such as sharing calendars, archiving e-mail (a practice that helps manage the size of your inbox and other folders), and managing contact information. Microsoft Office Outlook 2003 online assistance includes articles that describe procedures such as how to create and send an e-mail message, how to format messages, and how to use Outlook to manage your schedule.

A number of books are also available. Two published by Microsoft Press are *Microsoft Office Outlook 2003 Step by Step*, by Online Training Solutions, Inc., a self-paced learning experience that guides you through managing e-mail, contacts, and scheduling in Outlook, and *Microsoft Office Outlook 2003 Inside Out*, by Jim Boyce, a comprehensive reference that describes Outlook features in detail.

E-Mail Security and Protecting E-Mail Data

The security of computer systems is among the most pressing business issues of the day. A company of any size loses valuable time when its systems are down, and as e-mail is used more often to conduct business and transfer documents, losing important messages that are stored on your computer can be very costly. Although sometimes backing up your data seems like the last thing you have time to do, taking the time to do it—and taking time to install security patches and keep your virus-protection software up to date—always pays off. You'll save time and money in the future by securing your system and setting up data-maintenance routines from the start.

For more information about securing your computer, including virus-protection software and backup procedures, see Chapter 17, "Computer Security Basics."

Backing Up and Exporting Outlook Data Files

In Chapter 17, "Computer Security Basics," you can read about the steps you take to develop and manage a plan for backing up your data. Among the files you should include in regular backups are Outlook personal folder files

(files with the extension .pst, which are often simply referred to as *PST files*). A PST file can be quite large—at least 30 or 40 megabytes (MB) of data and often twice that size—so you need to use a backup medium that can store large files. Usually, this means using a writeable CD, a Zip drive, or a folder on a computer you use as a network server. (Of course, files on the server will also need to be backed up regularly.)

You can also export data stored in Outlook as a way to create a backup copy. For example, you can export e-mail messages to a PST file you've created or export the Outlook Contact folder to a Microsoft Excel workbook or a Microsoft Access database. The Import And Export Wizard built into Outlook, shown in Figure 15-1, steps you through the process of transferring Outlook data to the new file.

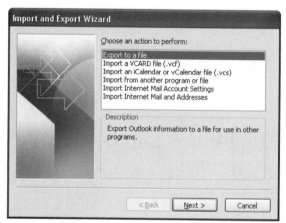

Figure 15-1 Export the information you store in Outlook as part of a backup plan so that you don't lose messages and contact information.

When you export a list of contacts to Excel or Access, you can select which information about the contacts you want to export—you don't need to export every field. For holiday greeting cards you send (all addressed by hand for a personal touch), you might want to create a spreadsheet with just names and mailing addresses, skipping phone numbers and e-mail addresses for your contacts. To tailor the information so that it fits your needs, after stepping through several screens in the wizard, click the Map Custom Fields button. In the Map Custom Fields dialog box, shown in Figure 15-2, click Clear Map to empty the list of default fields from the list on the right, and then follow the wizard's instructions to build the list of fields you want.

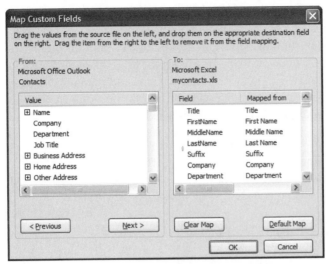

Figure 15-2 You can select which fields you want to export when you export contact information to Microsoft Excel or Microsoft Access.

Exporting data doesn't remove the data from Outlook. If you export messages to a PST file, for example, the messages will be stored in two places. After creating a copy of the messages by exporting them, go ahead and delete the messages if you don't need to refer to them regularly in Outlook.

Securing Outlook and Outlook Express

Because Microsoft software is used so extensively, the computers that run Windows and other Microsoft software applications are often the target of malicious attacks involving viruses and worms. Understanding the weak spots in your computer systems and the steps you need to take to secure them is important. Two areas you should know about are the security measures built into Outlook and Outlook Express and the sort of vulnerabilities these measures are designed to prevent.

Preventing Viruses from Spreading: Macro Security Settings

Computer viruses often spread through a macro that's included in a document, including documents attached to an e-mail message. A *macro*, if you aren't familiar with the term, is a small computer program used to automate common tasks. When a harmful macro runs, the instructions contained in the macro can damage your computer's system files and the data you've stored, so you need several lines of defense against this kind of attack. One method is to install a virus scanner that checks documents for macro viruses. Another method is to control when macros run.

Outlook itself can't determine whether a macro included in a particular attachment is infected, but you can set up Outlook to prevent macros that you don't trust from running. For example, in Outlook (and the other Office applications), when macro security is set to High (the setting that's in effect after you install Office), macros that aren't created by you or that are not digitally signed (authenticated, in other words) by a source that you trust can't be run. Macros that aren't signed are deleted.

The level of macro security, which is set in Outlook by choosing Tools, Macro, Security, can also be set to Very High, Medium, or Low. Figure 15-3 shows the dialog box you use to set the level of macro security. Each option includes a brief description of the level of security it provides.

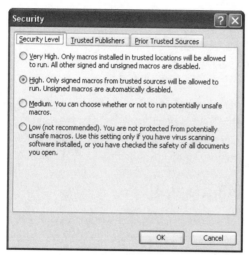

Figure 15-3 The setting you choose in the Security dialog box controls whether a macro runs when you open a document.

The Very High setting lets only those macros installed in a trusted location to run. All other signed and unsigned macros, even those you've created and those that are digitally signed, are not allowed to run. The Medium option is less secure than High, but it does provide you with the option to enable a macro or immobilize it. With macro security set to Medium, when you open a document by double-clicking the attachment in an e-mail message, you'll see a dialog box similar to the one shown in Figure 15-4.

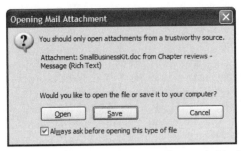

Figure 15-4   With macro security set to Medium, you can decide whether a macro is enabled when you open an attachment.

Microsoft does not recommend that you use the Low setting, which allows any macro to run without warning. Don't use this option except in a tightly controlled environment in which you know the status of every document you open and know that the computer or computers used for composing the document aren't connected to the Internet.

Attachment Types

Another way Outlook and Outlook Express help keep your computer secure is by blocking attachments that contain the types of files that run programs. By running those programs (simply by opening the file in some cases), you might damage your system. If an attachment is blocked, you'll still see the attachment icon in your inbox, but when you open the message, Outlook will indicate that it has blocked the attachment, as shown in Figure 15-5.

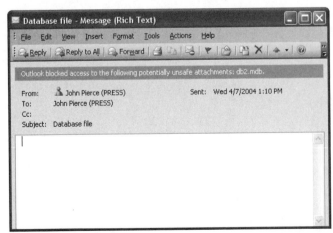

Figure 15-5   Outlook blocks attachments that are potentially harmful.

Highly Formatted Messages Can Pose a Danger

Plain text e-mail messages seem a little old hat, especially when you're using a program such as Outlook, which lets you format e-mail messages extensively. Unfortunately, the capabilities of HTML or Rich Text Format (RTF), two of the standard message types that you can use in Outlook, provide the means for virus writers to distribute their malicious wares. A script or program component that's embedded in an HTML-formatted message, for example, can let loose damage similar to a macro virus. Outlook won't let a script contained in a message run without the recipient's explicit say-so. This level of security is designed to protect computers against likely attacks.

If you need to run a script in an e-mail message, open the message, choose View In Internet Zone from the View menu, and then click Yes in the message box shown here:

And what's the Internet zone? It's a cousin of the Restricted Sites zone, one of the security zones set up in Internet Explorer. To prevent scripts in HTML-formatted e-mail messages from running, the messages are opened by default in the Restricted Sites zone, where scripts aren't allowed to run. Viewing HTML messages (or Web pages) in the Internet zone allows scripts to run.

Outlook and Outlook Express block files with the extensions .bat, .exe, .wsf, and others. (You can find a complete list of file types in the Outlook online help, under the topic "Attachment File Types Blocked by Outlook.") If you send a message to which you've attached a file whose type is included in the blocked list, Outlook warns you that some recipients of the message won't be able to receive or open the attachment. If you need to send one of the blocked file types through e-mail, use a program such as WinZip or the file compression tool that's provided in Windows XP to package the file before sending it.

Beware the messenger

Many e-mail viruses spread by infiltrating a system and then sending a message to, for example, the first 50 people in the address book of the person whose computer has been infected. Even if you receive an attachment in a message from someone you know, that's no guarantee that the message is safe.

Security Settings in Outlook Express

If you're using Outlook Express as your e-mail client, be sure that you understand the settings provided on the Security tab in the Options dialog box, shown in Figure 15-6. (To display the dialog box, click Tools, Options.)

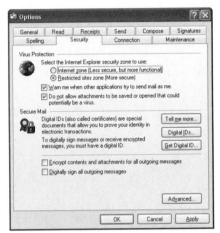

Figure 15-6   Security settings in Outlook Express are implemented through the Options dialog box.

The standard setting in Outlook Express is to not allow any attachment that might contain a virus to be saved or opened. This option provides good protection, but it might be too restrictive if you need to transfer files of these types frequently through e-mail. If you turn this option off, it's imperative that you include defenses such as virus-detection software and that you set macro security to High or Medium in the Office applications you use.

Notice that Outlook Express is set up to warn you when a computer application assumes your e-mail identity and tries to send a message to people in your address book or list of contacts, one of the mechanisms used to spread viruses. Keep this option turned on. If you know that another program is legitimately sending e-mail on your behalf, you'll be warned and can then say OK. Outlook provides a similar sort of warning as well.

Digital Signatures

Identify theft is a growing problem, especially with the amount of information that's transferred and stored online. If you use e-mail in your business to send and receive critical documents and information—materials for which you want proof of origin and validity—you should look into using a digital signature on the messages that require it.

When you digitally sign an e-mail message, you enclose a certificate of your identity with the message. You obtain a certificate from a certificate authority (CA); CAs include companies such as VeriSign (*www.verisign.com*) or Thawte (*www.thawte.com*). When you've obtained a certificate (instructions are included on the CA's Web site), you add the certificate to the certificate store in Windows. You can find a description of the steps you take to add a certificate (and other topics that describe the use of digital certificates) in the Windows XP Help And Support Center.

After the certificate is in place, you can add it to a message you send in Outlook by following these steps:

Add a digital signature to an e-mail message

1. Open a new message window in Outlook.

2. On the message window's toolbar, click the Options button. (Don't confuse the Options button on the message window's toolbar with the Options command on the Tools menu.)

3. Click Security Settings in the Message Options dialog box. In the dialog box shown here, select the option Add Digital Signature To This Message. Also select the option Request S/MIME Receipt For This Message if you want to verify that your signature is validated by the person or persons you've sent the message to and also to receive a confirmation that the message was received without being changed.

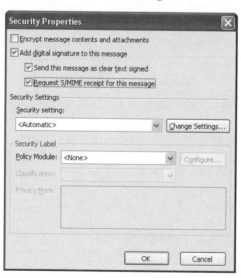

In Outlook Express, you can add a digital signature to a message by choosing Digitally Sign on the Tools menu in the message window. The Security tab in the Outlook Express Options dialog box, shown earlier in Figure 15-6, includes a link to an online help topic about sending secure messages, a link to the certificates installed on your computer, and a link to a page on the Microsoft Web site that lists some of the companies that will provide you with a digital ID.

Not everyone uses e-mail in a manner that requires a digital ID, but in businesses that handle a lot of confidential information, using one is a step you should take.

Taking Care of the Messages You Need— and Those You Don't

One old adage about managing your work and time is "Touch a piece of paper only once." When you receive a report, a memo, or something of the sort, extract the information you need, take the actions required (or delegate those tasks if that's your job), add any follow-up items to your to-do list, and be done with it. File it or shred it, but don't put it back in the pile, where you'll come upon it again. The same can be said about e-mail messages. Take the time to set up your e-mail program so that it can help you sort and prioritize messages and follow up on the work items that the messages entail.

Before You Send a Message

The pace at which correspondence takes place over e-mail is often at odds with best practices— everything from spelling to manners. A few simple steps provide balance and help foster good impressions:

- Some people say that e-mail cultivates bad behavior, exhibited in flame mail in which the sender vents and fumes, capitalizing all the words he or she doesn't want you to miss. Use eloquence and reason rather than brute force to get your points across.

- Make sure to correct spelling and grammar mistakes. Any written communication— even a short e-mail message—creates a better impression when it's presented well. At a minimum, use a spelling checker, and be sure to reread messages before you send them.

- Keep an eye on the size of attachments. Large files clog inboxes, and downloading time equals money—yours and your clients'. Some e-mail programs limit the size of the attachments they can send or receive. If you need to send a file that approaches 1 MB, compress the file and check with your intended recipients so that you know whether any size limitations are at play.

- People love to reply to e-mail messages— sometimes the same one over and over again. A message in which you started a discussion about next week's design review with a client in Toronto could morph into a discussion of company travel policy. Keep the subject lines of messages relevant to the subject being discussed. When necessary, send a new message or simply change the wording in the subject line.

E-Mail Message Folders

One of the best steps you can take to manage volumes of e-mail is to set up folders in which you store e-mail messages in an organized fashion—for example, all the messages you receive from a particular customer in one folder, and all the messages about your new marketing campaign in another. Sounds simple and practical, but even in the halls of Microsoft, you'll see employees with every message they've received for the past year in their inbox—sometimes thousands of messages. That's often not an efficient way to work.

To create a folder in either Outlook Express or Outlook, choose New, Folder from the File menu, select the folder in which you want the new folder to reside, enter a name for the folder, and then click OK. Once you've set up a folder you need, use the Move To Folder and Copy To Folder commands on the Edit menu to transfer a message from your inbox (or from another folder) to the folder where you want to store it. Figure 15-7 shows the Create Folder dialog box in Outlook Express. To see the list of folders in Outlook, be sure you have the navigation pane displayed. (Choose Navigation Pane from the View menu.)

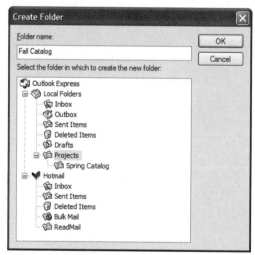

Figure 15-7   One easy step to help organize e-mail messages is to create a set of folders for storing messages about specific projects or from specific senders.

Setting up folders also puts you in a better position to archive messages if you're using Outlook. If all the messages about your current project are filed in their own folder, when you finish the project, you can archive the messages in that folder in just a few steps. If the messages are spread out, you need to sort and hunt to find them all before creating the archive file. You can learn more about archiving items in Outlook later in this section.

Follow-Up Flags

You can't drop everything you're doing the moment a new e-mail message arrives asking something of you. When a message requires you to perform some task in the future, flag the message for follow-up. When you want to provide a coworker or an employee with a gentle reminder that he or she needs to do something for you by a particular date, add a follow-up flag to a message you send.

On the Actions menu in Outlook, you'll find the Follow Up command. When you click this command, you'll see a series of colored flags, as shown in Figure 15-8. You might want to devise your own system for using the flags—blue for tasks that need follow-up this week, red for those that can wait until the end of the month, green for one employee, orange for another.

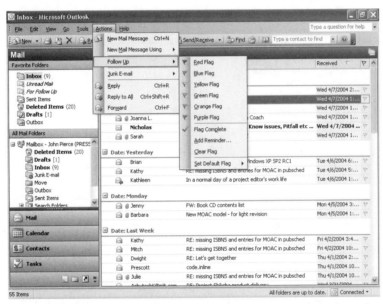

Figure 15-8 Use follow-up flags to indicate that you need to take action in response to an e-mail message.

In addition to attaching a flag, you can set a reminder (click Add Reminder) for when the follow-up activity needs to be completed. When the time comes, the message subject line is highlighted in your (or someone else's) inbox, making it hard to miss.

One of the standard folders in Outlook 2003 is named For Follow Up, shown in the Outlook folder list in Figure 15-9. When you flag a message for follow-up, Outlook adds a copy of the message to that folder. By opening the folder, you see only those messages that need follow-up attention.

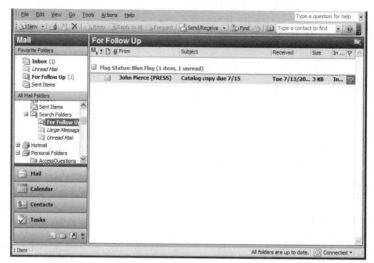

Figure 15-9   Outlook 2003 includes a built-in folder where it places a copy of a message if it's flagged for follow-up.

Flags in Outlook Express

Outlook Express lets you place a flag beside a message header in the inbox, but it doesn't include the rainbow of flags available in Outlook or the other options described above. Still, if you're using Outlook Express and want to mark a message as one you need to return to, adding a flag acts as a reminder. Another step you can take in Outlook Express is to follow the device Outlook 2003 uses: create a folder named For Follow Up, and then move messages that require future action to that folder.

Playing by the Rules

Instructing a computer program to do something for you and then having the program accomplish the task can be a very satisfying experience—it goes a long way toward dispelling the feeling that computers occasionally make more work for us. Setting up rules by which Outlook (or Outlook Express) handles e-mail in the ways you want is an effective means for managing messages.

First, what is an *e-mail rule*? Let's say you're working with a sales rep to purchase spring inventory at a discount. You don't want to miss any message from the sales rep that might get lost among the many that arrive in your inbox. You'd rather have all the messages from the rep in one folder by themselves. You could set up a rule in Outlook so that messages you receive from the sales rep are moved to a folder you've named Spring Inventory. As part of the rule, you can have Outlook also alert you that a new message from the sales rep has arrived.

Outlook's Rules Wizard guides you through the process of setting up a rule. Here are the steps you take as you step through the wizard:

Setting up an e-mail rule

1. From the Tools menu in Outlook, choose Rules And Alerts. You'll see the Rules And Alerts dialog box. Click New Rule, and you'll see the first page of the Rules Wizard, shown here:

Notice the two options at the top of the dialog box. You can generate a rule following one of the rule templates listed under Stay Organized or Stay Up To Date or begin defining a rule on your own. The first item listed among the templates designed to help you stay organized—Move Messages From Someone To A Folder—fits the example involving the sales rep.

2. Select this item, and then go to the area labeled Step 2, where you'll describe the details of the rule.

3. To identify the person whose messages you want Outlook to act on, click the People Or Distribution List link. In the Rule Address dialog box, enter the e-mail address you want Outlook to act on, and then click OK. Click on the Specified link to select the folder to which Outlook will move messages, and then click OK.

4. Click Next in the Rules Wizard, and you'll see the dialog box shown here:

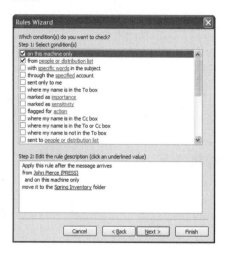

In this page, you refine the rule. Say, for example, that the sales rep happens to be in the same soccer league as you, and he's in charge of scheduling games this season. You could add the condition Sent Only To Me to the rule so that when the sales rep sends a message to league members, the message stays in your inbox (or gets moved to the Soccer folder by using another rule). When the message is sent just to you, Outlook moves the message to the folder you designated earlier.

5. Click Next after identifying the conditions you want to use in the rule, and you'll see the wizard's next page, shown here:

You can begin to see that you can build a fair degree of detail into the rules you define, and that's a good thing because it gives you control over how rules manage your e-mail. On this page, you indicate what to do with the message (in addition to moving it) when the message arrives. You can, for example, choose to play a sound. A bit of an interruption, perhaps, but during the week the inventory deal is supposed to close, you'll know right away that the sale rep needs something from you.

6. Click Next in the wizard again, and you'll see that the wizard allows (just as most of us do) every rule to have its exceptions:

You don't need to add conditions, actions, or exceptions to a rule. But here, let's say we want to take account of the possibility that the sales rep will slip up and send a soccer-related message just to you. To exclude those messages from being moved to the Spring Inventory folder, you could select the option Except If The Subject Contains Specific Words in Step 1, enter **soccer** as the operative word in Step 2, and add that level of refinement to the rule. Any message from the rep that includes *soccer* in the subject line, even if the message is sent only to you, stays in your inbox.

7. Click Next in the exceptions page, and you'll see the dialog box shown here. Enter a name for the rule, and choose to run the rule on messages you've already received as well as to activate the rule for future messages, and then click Finish.

If you'd rather start with a blank rule, you follow steps similar to those related to choosing a rules template. The first choice for a blank rule is whether the rule applies to messages you receive or messages you send, as you can see in Figure 15-10.

Figure 15-10 You can create a rule using a template or start with a blank rule. When you start with a blank rule, you choose to apply the rule to messages you send or those that you receive.

After you make this choice and start stepping through the wizard, you'll be presented with pages where you select the conditions to apply to the rule (Sent Only To Me, or Where My Name Is In The To Box, for example), the actions to take (deleting a message, moving a message, and the like), and exceptions such as when specific words appear in the subject line or when you're copied on a message (included in the CC line) rather than a primary recipient (included on the To line).

One trick to using rules is to know how one rule can affect another. Rules you apply to messages you receive are applied when the messages reach your inbox. Let's say you had two rules—one that moved messages from a particular sender to a folder and another that played a sound when you received a message from that sender. The rule designed to play a sound won't take effect if the message has been moved from the inbox. In this case, you want the rule that moves the messages to be processed after the rule that plays the sound. To set the order in which rules are processed, first click Rules And Alerts on the Tools menu. In the list of rules, select the rule you need to move, and then use the Move Up and Move Down buttons to position the rules as you need them.

You can also set up rules in Outlook Express, although you don't have as many options for adding specific conditions or exceptions to a rule. In Outlook Express, choose Tools, Message Rules, Mail, and then click New. In the New Mail Rule dialog box, shown in Figure 15-11, select the conditions for your rule (you can select more than one item in this list); select the actions for the rules; describe the rule by clicking the underlined links; and provide a name for the rule.

Figure 15-11 In Outlook Express, you can select more than one condition to define the actions the rule will take.

Throwing Out the Garbage: Filtering Junk E-Mail Messages

Spam is the word used to describe the unwelcome and (in some cases) offensive messages sent in bulk to e-mail addresses around the globe. Microsoft Outlook 2003 is set up with a folder named Junk E-Mail and contains several features that help you manage messages from senders who you don't want to deal with repeatedly.

On its own, using technology that scans information such as the time of day a message was sent and a message's content, Outlook moves the most obvious junk e-mail messages to the Junk E-Mail folder. You can bolster Outlook's junk mail filtering by building lists of senders whose messages you want to block and lists of senders and recipients who you know are safe.

If you receive a message from a source (an individual or a domain name) whose messages you want to block in the future, select the message in the Inbox, choose Junk E-Mail on the Actions menu in Outlook, and then click Add Sender To Blocked Senders List, as shown in Figure 15-12.

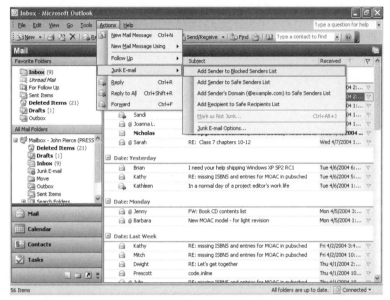

Figure 15-12 To help manage junk e-mail, add a sender's name to your Blocked Senders list.

You build a list of safe senders—individual addresses and domain names whose messages you always want to receive—in the same way, using the commands for the Safe Senders List on the Actions, Junk E-Mail menu. The people you've set up as contacts in Outlook are added to the Safe Senders list by default.

The Safe Recipients List, which you also build using a command on the Junk E-Mail menu, is a list of mailing lists or domain names you've subscribed to. (Perhaps you receive an e-mail newsletter, for example.) Messages sent to these addresses are not treated as junk e-mail.

Outlook also provides several junk e-mail filtering options. You can display the dialog box shown in Figure 15-13 and change or set the filtering you want by choosing Junk E-Mail Options from the Actions, Junk E-Mail menu.

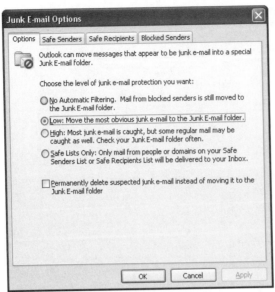

Figure 15-13   Use this dialog box to set options for filtering junk e-mail.

The choices here give you a range of control, from no automatic filtering (although messages from any sender included on the Blocked Senders list are still excluded) to allowing delivery of messages only from a select list of trusted senders and recipients. If you choose one of the more restrictive options, which could have the effect of moving legitimate messages to the Junk E-Mail folder, be sure you frequently check that folder to avoid missing any messages you actually wanted to receive, and add appropriate items to the Safe Senders List.

Building Your Business E-Mail Archives

When you install Outlook, it is set up to automatically archive e-mail messages (and its calendar and tasks items as well) after a certain period of time. Archiving items is another step in keeping your e-mail well organized. You can archive whole folders—messages about last quarter's sales or a particular project, for example—to keep the Outlook folder list showing only current work.

For messages in your inbox, as well as for calendar and task items, the default archiving interval is 6 months. For items retained in the Sent Items folder or the Deleted Items folder, the interval is every 2 months. So, any e-mail message you received 6 months ago that you haven't moved from your inbox is a candidate for Outlook's automatic archiving. When Outlook begins its archiving process, it displays the message shown in Figure 15-14.

As you can see in the dialog box, Outlook places the items it archives automatically in a PST file named Archive.pst, which is stored in one of the folders Windows creates as part of your user profile.

Figure 15-14　Outlook's built-in archiving feature helps keep your inbox and other folders up to date.

You can decide not to archive items when Outlook displays this dialog box by clicking No. By clicking AutoArchive Settings, you display the dialog box shown in Figure 15-15, which gives you the choice to turn off automatic archiving by clearing the check box labeled Run AutoArchive Every 14 (or some other number) Days, turn off the AutoArchive prompt, change the interval of time that passes before an item is archived, and choose to delete rather than store items when they reach that certain age.

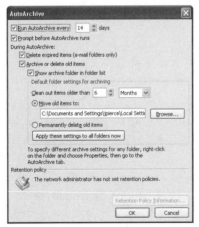

Figure 15-15　In the AutoArchive dialog box, you choose options such as the interval of time to retain an item, where to store archived items, and how often to run the automatic archiving feature.

Retaining records

If e-mail is used frequently in your business, especially if it's used to communicate important, possibly sensitive, information, set up a policy for how
long you should retain e-mail messages (and other documents) as part of
your business records. These policies might conflict with automatic
archiving settings in Outlook—especially if you choose to permanently
delete older items—so examine your retention policies in this context.

If automatic archiving isn't for you, turn off the feature, and use the Archive
command on the File menu to archive messages and other items by hand.
Figure 15-16 shows the dialog box you use.

Figure 15-16 If you archive manually, use this dialog box to select the folder
containing the items you want to archive and the cut-off date for items to be
archived. Use the Browse button to move to the folder where you want to store
the archive file.

Notice the option Include Items With "Do Not AutoArchive" Checked. For
any Outlook item that you don't want to include among those that are
archived automatically, open the item, click File, Properties, and then check
the option Do Not Archive This Item. When it comes time to manually
archive a folder, you can choose to include items marked Do Not Archive,
another example of the degree of control made available to you when you
dig a little deeper into Outlook.

Simple E-Mail Marketing: Adding a Signature

E-mail signatures are the wise or funny sayings and quotations, artwork, or animated GIFs that appear at the bottom of messages, following your name. You don't need to type in words or attach signature files for each outgoing message. You automate the process with a few simple selections in Outlook or Outlook Express. Business signatures can boost profits. Consider a signature consisting of your company's marketing tag line, or a special sales offer, or a direct link to your company's Web site or to a registration page so that customers can sign up to get news or offers. These simple marketing steps are very cost-effective ways to build business. Even sending signatures of quotations or sayings in business e-mail is a way to make you stand out from the crowd.

Well-crafted signatures are smart and to the point. They grab attention and reward reader interest. They evoke a chuckle, a sigh, a nod of agreement, a bond of understanding. If you create a signature that's boilerplate text—your contact information, for example, or a link to your Web site—it's fine to retain the same signature on all outgoing mail over time. But if you send witty or funny sayings or images, understand that you are making a commitment. You must change signatures like these frequently so that you don't bore or annoy your recipients.

Keep the following good practices in mind:

- Limit your signature to five or six lines.

- Don't use memory-hogging animation GIFs that fill up inboxes and take forever to load. Don't attach pictures or images that take up more space than the message itself. Illustrations created by keyboard characters (known as text art or ASCII art) are fun and load fast, but they tend to use a lot of screen space. To find appropriate examples, use an Internet search engine to search for *ASCII art*.

- Respect copyrights. If you quote someone, give credit. If you forward anything, say so.

- Always e-mail a test message to yourself before using a signature so that you can check the signature's shape and position.

- Create a stockpile of one or two dozen signatures you like before starting to send them out. Then keep adding to your collection.

To add a signature in Outlook, follow these steps:

Add an e-mail signature in Outlook

1. On the Tools menu, click Options, and then click the Mail Format tab.

2. At the bottom of the dialog box, click the Signatures button to display the Create Signatures dialog box. In the Create Signatures dialog box, click New. You'll see the Create New Signature dialog box, shown here:

At this point, enter a name for the signature you're creating. You can create several signatures, so you can use one signature on messages you send to customers and a different one on personal messages. If you want to create an electronic business card—also known as a *vCard*—or just use a text message as your signature, select Start With A Blank Signature, and then click Next. You'll see the dialog box shown here:

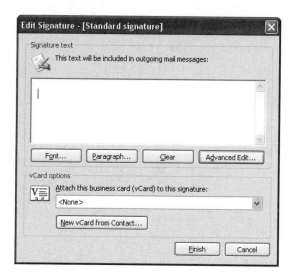

3. Enter the text you want to use, and then use the Font and Paragraph buttons to format the text—centering the text, for example, or selecting a particular size and color font. The Advanced Edit button opens Microsoft Word, where you can apply more formatting to the signature—including adding a hyperlink to a Web site.

4. To attach a vCard to a signature, click New vCard From Contact, and select the contact you want to use—most likely yourself.

To create your signature in Outlook Express 6, follow these three steps:

Add an e-mail signature in Outlook Express

1. On the Tools menu, click Options, and then click the Signatures tab, shown here:

2. Click New, and then enter the text you've chosen in the Edit Signature area. Or click File, and find the text or HTML file you want to use for your signature on your hard drive.

3. Select the Add Signatures To All Outgoing Messages check box if that's how you plan to use the signature you just created.

Scheduling Appointments and Tasks

Some years ago, a cartoon in *The New Yorker* magazine depicted a harried businessman, phone to his ear, exclaiming "No, Thursday's out. How about never—is never good for you?" Scheduling can be tricky, but it isn't impossible. Few people have the luxury of saying that "Never" is an option when it comes to meeting with a client or the warehouse staff or setting aside the time required to pay the invoices due this month.

Businesspeople use a mix of tools to keep track of their schedules and tasks—day books, picturesque calendars, scrap paper—and some of us are lucky enough to keep track in our head of all the things we need to do, all the places we have to go, and all the people we have to see. The Outlook calendar and tasks features provide still another approach. Keeping an online record of your time and task list has advantages. Making good use of these features in Outlook means regular attention to the data you enter, but the time you spend can pay off.

Blocking out time for an appointment is as simple as using the mouse to select the time when the appointment takes place, right-clicking, choosing New, Appointment, and then filling in the details you want in the Appointment window, shown in Figure 15-17.

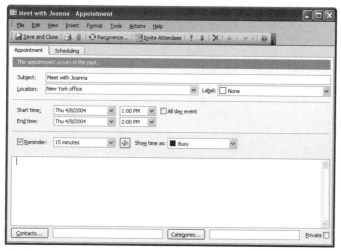

Figure 15-17　Keep track of appointments and meetings by keeping your calendar in Outlook. You can display appointments and meetings for a single day, for the work week, for the entire week, or for the month.

If you have a staff meeting or an appointment that occurs regularly—every week or every month, for example—set up a recurring meeting. In the Appointment window, click Recurrence. In the Appointment Recurrence dialog box, indicate whether the meeting happens daily, weekly, monthly at the same time, or in a pattern such as every two weeks on Wednesday.

Synchronizing Outlook and a PocketPC

A lot of people use a PocketPC or a Palm hand-held computer to store appointments, contact information, and other information. The information you keep in Outlook can be synchronized with your hand-held computer. If you're using a PocketPC, you can get Microsoft ActiveSync, and use ActiveSync to coordinate your PocketPC and the data stored in Outlook. If you are using a Palm hand-held computer, you can use third-party software. You can find more information on the Palm customer service Web site.

Keeping track of the tasks that you need to accomplish in Outlook is much like keeping your schedule. You can set up one-time tasks or recurring tasks. You can assign tasks to others. You can keep track of the date on which a task is due and indicate how much of a task is complete (useful for tasks that require a long time to finish). As you can see in Figure 15-18, you can also use an Outlook task to track information such as mileage, hours worked, and so on.

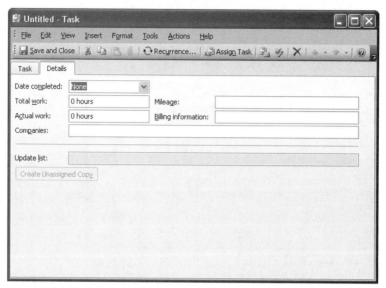

Figure 15-18   Build an online to-do list by entering tasks in Outlook.

E-mail has become a standard form of communication, in business especially, but also in our personal lives. The lower costs of sending documents and other information as attachments and the frequency with which you get an answer to a question you ask someone through e-mail right away are definite advantages. The computer security vulnerabilities often exploited through e-mail—and maybe the sense that you have to answer every message immediately and the frustration if you don't receive an immediate response from others—can be problems, one more serious than the others, of course. For some people, keeping on top of the e-mail messages they receive can be a challenge. Setting up folders and rules—and making sure that your e-mail system is as safe as it can be—are steps you can take to keep e-mail an effective business tool.

For More Information

In addition to the resources mentioned in this chapter, you will find links and information on the companion CD. Some books and Web sites particularly useful for understanding how to use Microsoft Office Outlook include:

Books

- OTSI, *Microsoft Office Outlook 2003 Step by Step* (Microsoft Press, 2003)

- Jim Boyce, *Microsoft Office Outlook 2003 Inside Out* (Microsoft Press, 2003)

- Michael J. Young and Jim Boyce, *Microsoft Outlook 2003 for Windows* (Visual QuickStart Guide) (Peachpit Press, 2003)

Web Sites

- *Outlook Power* magazine: *www.outlookpower.com/*

- Slipstick Systems Outlook resources, including tutorials, links, and development information: *www.slipstick.com/outlook/welcomefaq.htm*

- Outlook Tips, a useful site for Outlook questions, answers, and add-ins: *www.outlook-tips.net/index.html*

There are three kinds of death in this world. There's heart death, there's brain death, and there's being off the network.

— Guy Almes, Chief Engineer for Internet 2, and a leader and a pioneer in the development of the Internet

Chapter Sixteen

Small Business Networks and Servers

Just as the term small business covers a broad and diverse spectrum of activities, network can mean different things in different situations, from a shared printer to an interconnected, global, public, or private conglomeration of devices. In this chapter, we'll take a look at some common small business scenarios–local area networks (LANs)–focusing on where, what, and how. As with many of the topics discussed in this book, networking is a task you could turn over to a consultant. Even if you decide to bring in an expert, however, the information in this chapter should be valuable, because a basic understanding of the available technologies will help you to make better-informed decisions.

What you'll find:

❑ Determining needs and available choices

❑ Selecting network types

❑ Choosing networking equipment

❑ Enabling mobile computing

❑ Securing your network

Determining Needs and Available Choices

Not every type of network is appropriate for every business or location. In this section, we'll look at matching physical locations to the services available and mapping relationships among your devices. As you consider this information, keep in mind how your needs might change in the future, when the success of your business leads to new locations, new employees, or new services.

Assessing Your Location

The first thing to consider is your business location. If you've already made this decision, your location might impose restraints on the types of networking that are practical for your business. If you are still considering different premises (for more about site selection, see Chapter 4, "Self-Preservation"), existing network facilities or the physical setup of walls, doorways, and utility spaces such as dropped ceilings might affect your decision. We'll look at the different types of wired and wireless networking later in this chapter; first, let's consider how your location affects your choices.

Many modern buildings come with wired networking (usually known as Ethernet) in place. You might also find older buildings that have been retro-fitted with Ethernet. When wires are in place, you will often want to make use of them, although you might also decide to upgrade the cabling or mix wired and wireless.

If wires are not in place, you might be able to negotiate with the owner to have them added, since this will make the building more attractive to future tenants. This is a simple task if there are dropped ceilings with available conduits or raceways; it is somewhat more complex if wires will need to be routed through drywall. If the building's interior walls are brick or cinder-block, either wired or wireless networking will be a challenge, but not an impossibility. For a home-based business, an attic or an unfinished basement or crawlspace makes running Ethernet cable fairly easy.

Code requirements

The building owner—that is, you or your landlord—must check with building code officials before running any type of wire through interior or exterior walls, especially in a commercial building. Penetration, even by a thin wire, changes the fire resistance of the wall. You don't want to get yourself set up for business only to be shut down by building-code inspectors!

Ethernet cable can also be run along baseboards, with or without plastic conduit covering it. Office supply stores sell various lengths of cables and covering, including pieces designed to allow the cables to stretch across a traveled floor (although this is not desirable in a high-traffic area).

The most common alternative to Ethernet is wireless networking, often called *Wi-Fi* or *802.11*. When choosing a location, keep in mind that most current-generation wireless networks have a functional range of up to 150 feet and that this figure can be reduced by interior walls, floors, ceilings, bookcases, and other physical objects. Wireless is ideal within a single room or in a single-floor office with drywall partitions, or in most homes. It is more challenging, but certainly possible, in other physical locations where the building materials include steel and concrete.

Before we get to running wires or broadcasting Wi-Fi signals, however, you need to think about how to connect your LAN to the outside world.

Determining Service Types and Availability

While some businesses might set up a network that is entirely self-contained, most will want to connect to the Internet. So, the other basic consideration when planning your network is the availability of Internet service. Many locations will offer your new business a choice of providers and technologies. In this section, we'll go over the likely possibilities.

For the latest ratings of broadband service providers and equipment, plus current news about technologies, tutorials, and frequently asked questions (FAQs), visit Broadband Reports, at www.dslreports.com.

Telephone-Line Service

Internet connectivity can be delivered over existing telephone lines. Costs and speeds vary widely depending on your location. If your business will do only casual e-mail and Web browsing, you might be able to use a simple dial-up connection. Heavier use and the need for faster connectivity speeds call for a Digital Subscriber Line (DSL) or even dedicated lines.

Dial-up   Basic dial-up Internet service can be obtained in many locations for as little as $6 per month. The only equipment needed is a modem (probably already built into your computer) and a telephone line. The telephone line can be shared with a fax machine or even your regular telephone, but remember that only one device at a time can use the line. Often, you can share the dial-up connection over your business network—but check your terms of service to be sure. And bear in mind that sharing a dial-up connection further reduces the speed of each connection. Because this is an unlikely business scenario, we won't go into detail about sharing a dial-up connection. You can find more information about sharing connections in the Microsoft Windows XP Help And Support Center.

DSL Comes in a variety of types and speeds. DSL is not available in all areas, but when it is, there is often a choice of Internet service providers (ISPs), ranging from the local telephone company to national networks such as MSN and EarthLink. In some areas, you might be offered a choice of speeds, ranging from about 8 times the speed of dial-up to 50 times or more. DSL is ideal for many businesses and in some areas might be packaged with business telephone service at an attractive price. Unlike dial-up connections, DSL can be used for voice calls and data (Internet connection) at the same time, often simplifying wiring requirements. DSL requires a separate modem, generally offered by the ISP.

Dedicated or leased lines While few small businesses require the speed and capacity of T1, Integrated Services Digital Network (ISDN), or other dedicated lines (also known as *leased lines*), these are available in many areas, from both telephone companies and ISPs. If your business has significant data-transmission needs, consult with a provider to learn more about these options.

Cable Service

You're probably aware that cable television service providers also offer Internet connectivity in many areas. If you are in a strictly commercial zone, this might not be an option; also, in some places, basic cable television service is required by the cable company in order to provide you with Internet service. As with DSL, a special modem is required and generally is provided with the service. Connectivity via cable modem is often faster than DSL, but unlike DSL, you are sharing a "pipe" with your neighbors. Like water pipes in an old apartment building, cable modem speeds can vary based on the actions of others.

Choosing Between DSL and Cable

For most businesses, the differences between DSL and cable will not be apparent from the standpoint of using the Internet (or your local network). It's fine to decide between them based on past experience, price, availability, or other considerations.

Compare business services

Bear in mind that telephone and cable companies, depending on local regulations, often charge different fees for residential and commercial services, including home-based businesses. Make sure that you price the appropriate service.

Other Options

For most business locations, the choice will be between telephone and cable service, but there are other possibilities:

Satellite   Especially in rural areas, satellite-provided Internet connectivity might be the only choice for faster-than-dial-up service. Satellite is more expensive than DSL or cable, but if speed is required and the other services are not available, satellite service offers high speeds. For more information, contact your satellite television dealer. (Also, be sure zoning regulations permit a "dish" on your premises and that installing a dish does not constitute a leasehold improvement that your landlord will expect you to leave behind.)

Power companies   In some areas, the local electric utility delivers Internet connectivity via the power line that already reaches your location. These services are generally still "trials," but they might soon become more widespread.

Wireless   For most businesses, wireless Internet connectivity to the workplace is prohibitively expensive and slow—cell phone providers are still working to bring new equipment online to boost speeds. In a few areas, wireless wide area networks (WWANs) are being tested, and some start-ups are predicting widespread, fast, and affordable service within a few years. If such a service is available, it's worth considering, although you should be careful to assess its reliability for business use.

Planning Your Local Area Network (LAN)

A business network, often called a LAN, can be as simple as a cable connection (or an infrared connection) between one computer and one printer. In fact, if you have a computer, a printer, and a modem at home, you are already familiar with the same basic elements that you will use for your business LAN. Figure 16-1 shows a very basic network.

Figure 16-1   A very simple network.

A more typical scenario is two or more computers sharing a printer or printers and an Internet connection, as shown in Figure 16-2. You could draw a map of the connections among these devices, or you could plot them on an architectural drawing of your workspace. Such a drawing represents what network engineers call the *topology* of your network.

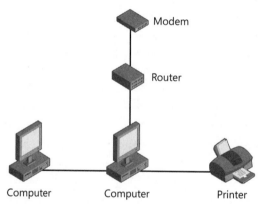

Figure 16-2   A two-computer small business LAN.

With a wireless network, the physical layout is constrained by distance and, sometimes, by walls or other physical structures. If your network will be wired, it is simpler to locate devices near the wired access points (*jacks*) in the walls or floor. How many connections will you make? Count computers and printers; also consider scanners, cash registers, and other devices needed in your business. You might think that it would be convenient to have the printer close at hand—that might be, but you might also find it too noisy to be a good neighbor. Locating it on the other side of the room or in another room entirely might be preferable. Figure 16-3 shows one possible small business LAN.

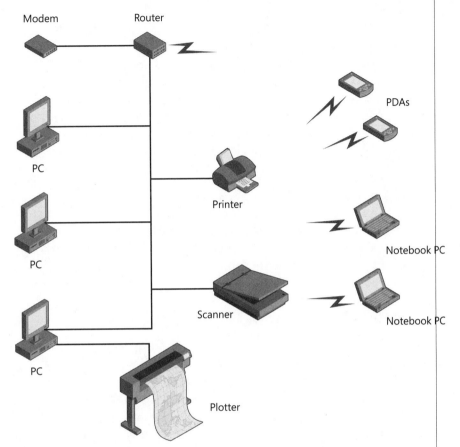

Figure 16-3 A more complex small business LAN.

As you learn more about how to connect devices, think about how the physical location of your business will affect your networking choices.

Selecting Network Types

As you've seen, your LAN can be wired or wireless. You can also mix these types—and mixing them isn't as hard as you might expect. In fact, it's easy to do and quite common. This section provides an overview of each type of network; we'll consider your equipment needs a bit later.

Wired Networks: Ethernet

There are three common types of Ethernet devices and cables; happily, they get along with each other. The differences are the speed at which they communicate. For many years, the standard was 10 megabits per second (Mbps), often called *10Base-T*. This cabling can still be found in older installations. Most computers made in the past five years or so, however, can handle Ethernet communications at 10 times that speed, or 100 Mbps. This is known as *100Base-T* or *Fast Ethernet*. Cabling to support this is what you would hope to find on your business premises, or what you would probably install. As you might expect, the latest and greatest Ethernet is *Gigabit Ethernet* (1000 Mbps), which is still relatively expensive and uncommon as of this writing. Soon, the cutting edge will be 10-Gigabit Ethernet.

Office supply and computer stores carry a wide range of Ethernet cabling (Category 5, or Cat 5, cable), in various lengths and colors. If you will be installing a new system or upgrading older wiring, you will also find jacks, splicing tools, and necessary bits and pieces. Many electricians, as well as computer technicians, can install a simple Ethernet network in a matter of an hour or so, although it's easy to find instructions to do it yourself, and the skills needed are well within the experience range of many homeowners.

Wireless Networks: Wi-Fi

Wireless networking is now common, but it is also still changing quite rapidly. There are a number of related technical standards, collectively known as *802.11*. Popular names for these devices include Wi-Fi and, in the Macintosh world, AirPort. The older widely used standard is 802.11b; devices for *b* connections are commonly available, and many public access points use this standard. The newer standard is 802.11g; it is faster and more secure, but equipment is slightly more expensive. Devices made for 802.11b can be used with 802.11g systems, at the lower *b* speed. Either technology will serve you well for your business, although if the $20 or so per device is not too much of a hurdle, the newer 802.11g will probably serve you better, for longer. (There is also 802.11a, but it has not achieved wide acceptance. Further variations are being announced and tested. It is likely that most will be "backward compatible" with the current *g* and *b* standards, allowing continued use of those devices.)

Your computer dealer or office supply store probably carries a variety of Wi-Fi devices. (We'll describe what you need in the next section.) You can mix brands, but if you're starting a new network, you'll probably find it easier to stick with one brand and a familiar set of instructions. One potentially serious drawback with Wi-Fi is that you really can't anticipate how well the network will work through walls or floors or partitions until you buy the equipment and bring it to your workplace. For this reason, check the store's return policy beforehand—or consider having the dealer install the system. You can also start small: setting up a wireless base station and just one Wi-Fi-enabled notebook computer allows you to assess signal strength throughout your location by carrying the notebook from room to room.

Mixed Network Types

As mentioned, you can mix Ethernet and Wi-Fi. Often, it might be easiest to cable together desktop computers and peripherals such as networked printers, while allowing notebook computers and PDAs to access the network wirelessly. Many wireless routers are designed to support both types of connections. (For more information about routers, see the section "Choosing Networking Equipment," below.)

Mixing operating systems

The other mixed network type that you might consider could include Macintosh or UNIX computers. As a general rule, you can share an Internet connection via Ethernet or Wi-Fi with any properly equipped computer. Sharing peripherals, such as printers, is also possible in this situation, but it requires setup work that is beyond the scope of this book.

Other Networking Methods

It is possible to network your devices using standard telephone lines. This arrangement is often slower than Ethernet or Wi-Fi connections, but it might be the best choice in older buildings where stout interior walls deter cabling and wireless. For more information, you can contact a computer dealer or networking consultant.

It is also feasible to set up a LAN using the electrical lines that already serve your building. This sort of network can be challenging to secure in a building with other tenants and sometimes might be subject to interference from other electrical devices, but improvements are being made in the technology. Again, see a dealer or consultant for more-detailed information.

Choosing Networking Equipment

Depending on your choice of ISP, you will have a coaxial cable or telephone wire somewhere on your premises, connecting to some type of modem. How do you share that modem with your network? You need another device to share that connection. This device can be a number of different things but will most commonly be a computer (server) or a stand-alone device–a *router* or *hub* or *switch*. Each of your networked devices will also need a way to connect to your new network. This section describes these pieces of equipment.

Routers and Hubs and Servers, Oh My!

Here's where network design can get complicated. To keep it simple, we'll focus on the most common networking device: the router. Routers can be found at computer dealers, office supply stores, and a number of other retailers or online merchants. They are fairly inexpensive, they come with good setup instructions and support, and they are reliable. If a friend assures you that you need a switch or a hub, that's fine too–they'll also do the job. (And the friend will set up your network, right?) In this section, we'll discuss routers and how to connect your devices to them to form a network, and we'll take a quick look at servers.

Routers

A router, not surprisingly, *routes* data from one device to another. This routing includes your Internet connectivity, as well as routing files to the printer or from computer to computer. A router is about the size of an average paperback book. It requires a power source and, for Internet use, a connecting Cat 5 cable from your DSL or cable modem. Routers are available for Ethernet use only, for Wi-Fi use only, or for mixed use. They commonly include a basic hardware firewall, to help protect your network. (For more information about firewalls, see Chapter 17, "Computer Security Basics.")

Ethernet routers are commonly positioned near the modem. They can be placed in closets or cabinets, out of sight. Once installed, they seldom require further attention until the time comes to add a new connection. If necessary, Ethernet cabling can run up to a hundred meters or even farther with *repeaters* along the line.

Wi-Fi routers, on the other hand, are most effective when they are out in the open, ideally on a high shelf. Their effective range depends on your individual situation, but their signal is strongest within 100 to 150 feet. (Yes, this does mean that your neighbors could use it, too. This is not necessarily a security risk, but it *is* prohibited by most service contracts, so routers should always be configured to require passwords.) Once configured, Wi-Fi routers too need little further attention.

Most wireless routers also accept Ethernet connections. There are some differences in speed, but few users will notice any significant disparities in performance. As mentioned, mixing Wi-Fi and Ethernet is often the best way to handle a LAN in the workplace. For example, it is somewhat difficult and relatively pointless to connect a network printer to the LAN with a wireless antenna device; an Ethernet cable will do the job well. On the other hand, freedom of movement throughout the office might be one of the attractions of using a notebook computer, so wireless connectivity is great when you have notebooks (or PDAs).

Routers, DSL modems, and cable modems generally come with excellent step-by-step instructions. Be sure you get a router with enough capacity (jacks or ports) for the wired portion of your planned network! Configuring the router and the modem to work together is not difficult, but working through the numerous possible combinations can be frustrating and might require time spent with a call center to find an answer.

Keeping the network up

Whether you set up your own network or have someone else do it, take these two additional steps:

1. Write down the configuration steps that achieve a successful connection. There might be a dozen or more in a specific sequence, and you will *not* remember them later!

2. Consider getting an uninterruptible power supply (UPS) for your modem and router so that brief power fluctuations don't require you to find the list you created in step 1 and then spend tedious time getting the network "up" again.

Ethernet Connections

Not all computers come with the network cards needed to support Ethernet connections. You can check yours, if you don't know, by referring to your owner's manual or sales documents, or by looking for a phone jack that looks a bit wide. This is known as an *RJ-45 connection.* (Your telephone uses the smaller size, RJ-11.) A network interface card (NIC) can be easily added to most recent computers to support Ethernet; the cost is nominal.

Wi-Fi Connections

The computers on your LAN will need Wi-Fi antennas and software to access the wireless network. The antenna devices can be on cards installed in a desktop computer, cards placed in a notebook computer's slot or built-in, or external boxes connected to a computer's USB port. For computers that are some distance from the router, a USB device might be the best choice: these include a cable about 3 feet long that allows you to position the box and antenna (about the size of a deck of playing cards) for best reception.

More about USB

USB devices and ports come in two speeds. Older and newer devices can be mixed, although they will always work at the slower speed. If your desktop computer does not have a USB port, you can add one with an expansion card, in the same manner as adding an Ethernet card.

Printers and Other Peripherals

Printers deserve special mention because there are two basic ways to add them to your network. If you have a computer and an inkjet or inexpensive laser printer, that printer can be made available to others on the network through the host computer, which runs the printer's driver and to which the printer is connected by a traditional printer cable. This is easy to do in Windows XP. Unless you have configured the printer not to be shared, it will appear in the Printers And Faxes window (accessed from the Start menu) of the other networked computers, and print jobs can be sent to it as if it were directly connected—provided that the host computer is turned on.

To add a printer directly to your LAN requires a *network printer*. Basically, this is a printer (usually a midrange to high-range laser printer) that has its own processor and memory, allowing it to accept and process print jobs from all the other devices on the network. It also monitors its supplies and status, reporting these either to a designated computer or on its own LCD screen.

Some businesses use a networked, black-and-white laser printer for most jobs and complement that with a color inkjet or color laser printer that is reserved for those print jobs where color is necessary. In that situation, the color device can easily be connected directly to just one of the computers in the office.

Similar arrangements can be made for plotters, scanners, and other peripheral devices: networked versions are available, or they can be attached directly to a specific computer and shared over the network (as long as that computer is running).

Servers

A *server* is a computer on your LAN that runs administrative software, which provides and controls access to resources such as printers, drives, and files. The server can be used for day-to-day business activities, such as word processing—or it can be a stand-alone device. For Ethernet LANs, when properly equipped, a server can take the place of a router; for wireless networks, you still need a wireless router even if you have a server.

A server can also maintain a Web site for your business, making it a Web server. Unlike a file server, print server, or networking server, a Web server can be provided by a third party and located off-site.

For more information about developing a Web site for your business, see the companion CD.

Servers can often be older computers with slower processors, although they commonly have large-capacity disk drives (so that they can hold and "serve" files for multiple users).

Many small businesses will find that their need for a server is determined by their database rather than their networking requirements. Businesses with two or three or up to five or more computers might have no needs that require a server. If the computers usually work independently, occasionally sharing files, the LAN will suffice. However, if there is

Microsoft Small Business Server 2003

For many firms needing a server solution, there is an excellent value package available called Microsoft Small Business Server. The Standard Edition includes server software based on Microsoft Windows Server 2003 and a range of other valuable software including:

- Microsoft Windows SharePoint Services, for internal communication and collaboration, including an intranet

- Microsoft Exchange Server 2003 technology, including Microsoft Outlook Web Access for e-mail access via the Web

- Microsoft Office Outlook 2003

- Microsoft Shared Fax Service

- Routing And Remote Access Services for secure Internet connections

The Premium Edition includes all this, plus Microsoft SQL Server 2000 for relational database tasks, Microsoft Office FrontPage 2003 for developing Web pages and SharePoint services, and additional firewall and security software.

Microsoft Small Business Server 2003 simplifies file and printer sharing, backups, collaboration, and mobile computing solutions. For more information about these products, including pricing and system requirements, visit *www.microsoft.com/windowsserver2003/sbs/evaluation/default.mspx*.

information that all or most users in the business must access frequently, such as a database of inventory, then a server is called for, even in a two-person or three-person office.

Designing and building a database is a task very specific to your individual business. You might decide to do the job yourself, with Microsoft Office Access or another database program; you might purchase a database designed by a value-added reseller, tailored to your type of business; or you might hire a consultant to customize a solution for you. In the latter two scenarios, you will need a server and should follow the recommendations of your vendor. With the first approach, you might be able to "grow into" a server as your business expands.

A more complete discussion of servers would require another book. When your needs include a server and its software, talk with your computer dealer or a consultant.

Enabling Mobile Computing

In today's world, many businesspeople are expected to be connected all the time, everywhere they travel. Pagers and cell phones have added Web features, enabling e-mail access from handheld devices. Pocket PCs and Palm Pilots, in turn, have added cell phone capabilities. SmartPhones and other new devices encompass all these technologies and more. Public Wi-Fi networks allow notebook computer users to access data from the Web or from their own private networks while in hotels, airports, and coffee shops.

What do you need for your business? Just a cell phone? Or do you need real-time access to the data on your network?

Describing mobility solutions in detail is beyond the scope of this book, but as you set up your LAN and plan for the future, you should be aware of changing technologies that might impact your business. Not so many years ago, a business needed just a telephone, a listing in the yellow pages, and perhaps some other advertising in order to be found by customers—parameters that were fairly unchanged for a century. Today, more than half of all businesses have at least a basic Web site. As a small business, you might not have the need or interest to manage your customers, products, and services 24 hours a day and seven days a week, but you might want to check stock or sales from home, for example, or finish a letter you left on a computer at the office. There are a number of mobility solutions that enable you to do this.

You can configure your LAN to allow remote access to files. For a fully mobile solution, this is most easily accomplished with a Web site: this could be an intranet site, with no public access, or it could be a private site linked from your public Web pages. You can also configure a dial-up connection to your server or use a software solution, such as PCAnywhere. For more information, consult your computer or office supply dealer.

Securing Your Network

Finally, don't neglect security. We'll describe some specifics in the next chapter, but remember as you set up your LAN that both physical networks and data are inherently insecure—you need to *plan* for security and *enable* security each time you introduce new devices to your network.

For More Information

In addition to the resources mentioned in this chapter, you will find links and information on the companion CD. Depending on the size of your new enterprise, you might find that the many resources available for home networking are adequate for your business needs. On the other hand, your new network might be sufficiently complex to require a network administrator. Some books and Web sites particularly useful for understanding how to set up and use a small business network include:

Books

- Ray Ramon, *Technology Solutions for Growing Businesses* (American Management Association, 2003)

- John Ross, *Computer Networking for the Small Business and Home Office* (Sams, 2001)

- Nathan J. Muller, *Wi-Fi for the Enterprise: Maximizing 802.11 for Business* (McGraw-Hill, 2003)

Web Sites

- "How Home Networking Works," from How Stuff Works: *computer.howstuffworks.com/home-network.htm*

- SmallBizPipeline, from TechWeb: *www.smallbizpipeline.com/*

- Wi-Fi Planet—The Source for Wi-Fi Business & Technology: *www.wifi-planet.com/*

Dealing with computer security is like changing the oil in your car or getting your teeth cleaned. You know you should do it but you just don't want to. It takes time, costs money and you see no benefit whatsoever when you're done. But this is one issue you simply cannot afford to ignore.

— *Dr. Robert Jones, president Craic Computing LLC*

Chapter Seventeen

Computer Security Basics

You could turn over the task of planning for computer security to a consultant (or perhaps a high school student), but we recommend that you yourself understand some basic guidelines for businesses. Planning how to secure computers and data–whether data means customer names, inventory and accounting records, or ideas–is essential to ensure that your company can operate day-to-day and recover from a disaster. In this chapter, we offer some ideas to get you started with your plans: who should be able to see what, how to keep systems and data safe, and how to prevent infections, intrusions, and malicious code.

What you'll find:

❑ Considering access requirements

❑ Planning physical security

❑ Backing up your data

❑ Protecting against viruses

❑ Choosing and using firewalls

❑ Dealing with spyware and adware

Considering Access Requirements

Unless your business model is an Internet café, customers will probably not interact directly with your systems at your place of business, although you might well plan to develop an interactive Web site. The logistics and mechanics of developing a Web site are beyond the scope of this book, but there are a great many tools and books available to help you with that task.

For our simple business model, let's say that there are usually two groups of people who interact with computer systems and data at your business: your permanent staff or employees, and any consultants, contractors, or vendors you engage. Each of these has different needs and expectations. Of course, each business also has its own distinct uses for data, and you should be sure to adopt policies that will suit your operation.

Planning to Share Data

If you have a two-person partnership, you could probably share all files and data, just as you would other business details. However, when you hire employees or vendors (for more about this, see Chapter 13, "Hiring and Firing"), you introduce a new level of complexity. Your bookkeeper will need access to your financial data, including purchases and sales, but probably has no reason to see employee background checks or your three-year plans. The front-office person you bring in to answer the phone would need to access customer records, inventory data, and perhaps your Microsoft Office Outlook calendar, but you would ordinarily arrange things so that he or she is not able to see your cash flow statements or tax information.

You should make a list of each type of data on your business network and cross-match it with everyone who has network access. Consider the results to be a *live document*, changing as your business develops. As your business grows, you will want to develop categories of employees and grant access to systems or data according to job function. Of course, this also means that you should categorize your data and place related files on the same system or drive.

In the early days, as you set up your network and files, always ask the question "Who should be able to access this information?" Remember too that you can grant permission to view data but not modify it, should that fit your need-to-know model.

Controlling Data

You can secure data from unauthorized access by creating individual files or folders; by creating logical partitions (on drives or *shares*—that is, shared portions of drives) on one or more computers; by keeping certain systems isolated from your network; and by a number of other means. The best method for your business depends on the structure of your organization, but we'll offer some general suggestions in this section.

File-Level and Folder-Level Security

If you want users on your network to be able to see but not change files, the simplest way, in the Microsoft Office products and many other applications, is to make the file *read-only*. You can even select some users who will have read-only access, others who will be able to fill in forms (but not change them), and others who can comment on the files without changing the originals.

To protect a file created in Word 2003, choose Formatting Restrictions from the Protect Document task pane (accessed from the Tools menu), or—for any file—select the file in a folder view, right-click it, and click Properties on the shortcut menu. You'll be able to allow or deny different levels of access for the users who have access to the file.

With Microsoft Office Professional Edition 2003, a more robust document-management system was introduced: Information Rights Management (IRM). IRM enables you to restrict access to Word 2003, Excel 2003, and PowerPoint 2003 files; prevent certain Outlook e-mail messages from being forwarded, printed, or copied; and otherwise protect sensitive information from being accessed without authorization. IRM is a free download, accessible from within Word, Excel, and PowerPoint; you might find it useful for information security at your business.

Information you store in a document can be private and confidential—information such as salaries and hourly wages, next year's budget, or plans for a new product. One step you can take to help protect information of this kind—especially when it's stored on a computer that you share with others at the office or at home—is to create a password for a document. You can define a password that's required to open a document or one that must be entered before someone can modify the information a document contains. You create a document password on the Security tab of the Options dialog box. (Click Tools, Options to open the dialog box.) Figure 17-1 shows the Security tab of the Options dialog box for Microsoft Word. (Microsoft Excel and PowerPoint have similar password options.)

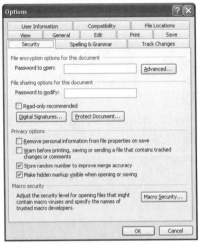

Figure 17-1   Use a password to help secure your Office documents, controlling who can open or modify a document.

Personal information saved with documents

When you save a document you've created in Word or Excel, for example, your name and company name (information provided during the installation of Microsoft Office) is saved as part of the file's properties. (File properties, which you can view by choosing Properties from the File menu, include the document's title, author, company name, and similar information.) If you don't want this information to be saved with a document, choose Tools, Options, and on the Security tab, select the option Remove Personal Information From File Properties On Save.

Protecting Word Documents   As mentioned earlier, when you want to prevent a Word document from being modified, open the document, and then click Protect Document on the Tools menu. You'll see the Protect Document task pane, shown in Figure 17-2.

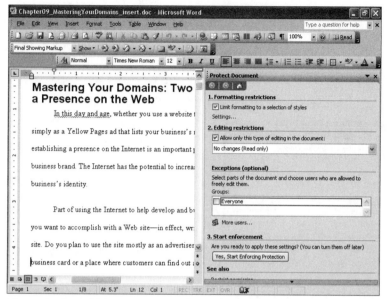

Figure 17-2 Add formatting and editing restrictions to a document to manage who can modify a document and how it can be modified.

Formatting restrictions are more about preserving how a document looks than they are about protecting a document's content. By setting up formatting restrictions, you prohibit users from applying styles to the document except for those styles you choose to include in the Styles list on the Formatting Restrictions dialog box. Formatting restrictions also prevent people working with the document from applying boldface, italic, or other formatting to the document's text.

Under Editing Restrictions in the Protect Document task pane, the options in the drop-down list let you manage how a document can be edited. Select No Changes (Read Only) to essentially lock the document's content. The other options you can select include tracking changes with Word's revision marks so that you can see any modifications someone makes or limiting editing to the insertion of comments—other users can offer suggestions and opinions about the document's content, but they can't actually change the text.

Sections of a document can be protected from changes by designating only those users who are allowed to edit a section. In a document you are working on with others, this level of protection gives you a substantial degree of control. In the Protect Document task pane, after you've selected the level of editing restrictions (No Changes or Comments), use the Exceptions area to designate the users who can edit, without restriction, those sections of the document you select. You can allow some sections to be edited by Everyone. For sections you want more control over, select the section, and then click More Users. You'll see the dialog box shown in Figure 17-3. The user names you enter in the Add Users dialog box can reflect the user accounts (groups or individual accounts) set up on the computer or e-mail addresses.

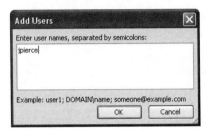

Figure 17-3 When you protect a document in Microsoft Word, you can make exceptions and designate users who can edit sections of a document you define.

After you've set up the protection scheme you want, click Yes, Start Enforcing Protection in the Protect Document task pane. In the dialog box that's displayed, you can enter a password that's required to remove document protection or choose to allow only an authenticated user to work with the document.

Protecting Worksheets in Excel   Excel worksheets often contain sensitive financial data that you don't want just anyone to revise or read. As you can with Word documents, you can protect a selection of rows and columns (a *cell range*) in Excel or entire worksheets or workbooks. Figure 17-4 shows the menu commands you use to protect the work you do in Excel.

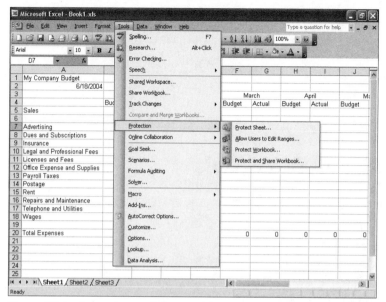

Figure 17-4   Protecting worksheets and workbooks in Excel can help keep sensitive financial information secure.

When you select Tools, Protection, Protect Sheet, you'll see the dialog box shown in Figure 17-5. In the Protect Sheet dialog box, you create a password that must be entered to remove protection from the worksheet and then select the actions that are protected—from formatting cells to deleting columns and rows. (Protecting a workbook also requires the creation of a password.)

Figure 17-5   Protecting a worksheet involves selecting the actions that users can and cannot perform.

Identifying a cell range that you want to protect involves a few additional steps. Here's the procedure to identify a worksheet section that you want to protect.

Protect a worksheet

1. On the Tools menu, click Protection, Allow Users To Edit Ranges.

2. In the Allow Users To Edit Ranges dialog box, click New. You'll see the dialog box shown here:

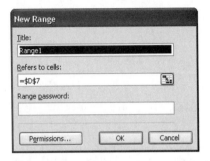

3. Enter a title for the range, and then enter the cell range (something like C3:D12) in the Refers To Cells text box. (You can also click in the Refers To Cells text box and then define the range by selecting it with the mouse in the worksheet.)

4. Enter a password in the Range Password text box, and then click OK. You'll be asked to enter the password again. After you do, click OK, and you'll see the Allow Users To Edit Ranges dialog box again.

5. In the dialog box, click Protect Sheet. In the Protect Sheet dialog box, make sure that the option at the top of the dialog box (Protect Worksheet And Contents Of Locked Cells) is selected, enter a password, and then click OK. Enter the password again to confirm it when Excel prompts you to.

6. When you need to make changes to information in any of the cells in the range you defined, click in the cell, and you'll see the dialog box shown here:

The dialog box appears after you attempt to enter data into a blank cell or edit data in a non-blank cell.

7. Enter the password you defined for the protected range (not the password that protects the worksheet); the cell range will be unlocked and can then be revised.

Microsoft Office files, and those of most other common applications, can also be encrypted or hidden. To hide an Office file, right-click the file in a folder view, click Properties on the shortcut menu, and select the Hidden check box on the General tab. To encrypt a file, click Advanced on the General tab, and select the Encrypt Contents To Secure Data check box. There are also a number of third-party tools that you can use to encrypt files. Note that neither of these methods can be completely successful at preventing unauthorized access—there are few guarantees in computer security, just best practices and degrees of protection. Most of the options described here can also be applied to folders through their Properties dialog box.

The difficulty with all of these methods, however, is that *each time* you create a file or folder, you must remember to restrict access, or if you have set standard restrictions, you must remember to enable access to files and folders that must be shared. A much more effective technique is sequestering valuable data on shares or drives that you isolate from the general community of users with network access.

Shares and Drives

Whether you have a peer-to-peer, an ad hoc, or a server-based network, you should plan to segregate your business data based on the need-to-know guidelines presented earlier in this chapter. With both new and established networks, you can then extend or restrict users' access to data (and applications) based on their need to know.

Planning Physical Security

Once you have given thought to how people will interact with your computer systems, you should also plan for the physical security of your systems. Both hardware and data require protection. The specifics will depend on your actual location, but this section gives you some places to start.

Avoiding Hardware Theft

Very soon, perhaps by the time you read this, the balance between desktop and notebook computer systems will have shifted in favor of the notebook, including Tablet PCs. More and more people, whether for business or personal use, are opting for notebook computers. They are portable, quieter, easier to set up, require less space, and compare well feature for feature with all but the highest-end, multiprocessor desktop systems. But their portability can be a significant liability if your workplace is open to the public—it takes just a moment to steal a notebook computer.

Most notebook computers come with a slot where a cable lock can be attached to make a temporary but theft-deterring link with a piece of furniture (preferably large and heavy). You give up instant portability, but you also eliminate an undesirable risk. In addition, you can attach a proximity alarm, which will sound if your notebook computer is moved. Some docking stations also effectively lock down notebooks. Ask your computer dealer or office supply retailer for more information.

For both notebooks and desktops, as well as other significant physical assets, you should consider identification tags. These permanent tags will identify your equipment, often preventing resale and aiding in recovery. You can find these tags for sale on the Web, often with associated insurance; your own insurance agent might be able to provide tags or make other recommendations that could save you money on premiums while helping to safeguard your business property.

Guarding Against Data Loss

For many businesses, the data on the computer is much more critical and valuable than the hardware itself. In the remainder of this chapter, we'll offer suggestions about how to develop a backup plan to safeguard your data from accidents and crashes, as well as how to keep intruders and malicious code away from your network.

Bear in mind that any of your systems can be easily compromised if you leave it unattended while logged on. Microsoft Windows can be set to lock the computer after a period of inactivity, requiring a password to resume. It should be your policy to set up all systems with sensitive data to require passwords to begin or resume sessions.

You should also consider an uninterruptible power supply (UPS) for your most critical systems, particularly if your business operates in an area prone to power outages. Your computer retailer or office supply dealer has a range of choices available, and most are quite inexpensive. (If you use notebook computers exclusively, of course, you effectively have a UPS on each system.)

Backing Up Your Data

In the early days of the personal computer, the commonly offered advice was "Save often!"—as often as every two or three minutes, back in the days when data was saved to floppy disks. Happily, those days are gone. Background saves, reliable hard disks, and more robust operating systems have greatly reduced accidental data loss.

But hard disks do crash. Things happen. When you have a business and you rely on your data, you must have a backup plan, and you must be sure to use it.

Developing a Backup Strategy

The most important thing to plan for in your backup strategy is how to make it simple, reliable, and as automatic as possible. Do you rotate the tires on your car every 5,000 miles? Isn't it a good idea? Well, the good idea of a backup plan doesn't work either, unless you make it work. Fortunately, creating and implementing a backup plan is less arduous than tire rotation.

There are many different physical means to achieve this end, and we will consider each later in this section. First you should give some thought to what data supports your business and how to design and execute a well-thought-out backup plan.

A service business will have different backup requirements than a retail store. Customer data has different value to an interior decorator than it does to a rental business; for an interior decorator, a weekly backup might suffice, whereas for a rental business, much more frequent backups will be needed (in addition to the paper trail of transaction receipts). Financial data can often be reconstructed from bank records, but sometimes at a significant cost of time. Just as you did when planning data access, think about what data is stored on your system. What would be the consequences to your business if you were without it for an hour (a few minutes, a few days)?

Different strategies have different costs, in time and resources. If you can't afford to have your data offline for an hour, your strategy will be different than if an interruption would be merely annoying. Setting up parallel systems to ensure 24/7 availability is beyond the scope of this book, but a computer dealer or consultant would be happy to develop a plan to fit your needs.

Implementing a Backup Plan

After you have thought about your business data and developed a strategy, you are ready to consider the specific means and methods.

Backup Types and Frequency

Data can be backed up in different ways, but backups are generally created in two types: *full backups* and *incremental backups*. As the name implies, a full backup makes a copy of *all* the data you designate. An incremental backup copies just the changes since the last backup (either a full backup or a previous incremental backup). A good plan includes a schedule for both types.

A full backup takes longer to create. Incremental backups take less time, but if they are made on a daily basis, they can become numerous and unwieldy in a relatively brief time. For many businesses, a weekly full backup with daily incremental backups will suffice, but you should consider carefully your own circumstances.

Planning Backups

The first thing you need to understand is that most "fully automated backups" are still, in important ways, *attended* backups. Any on-site backup device requires attention, either to change media or to remove the backup for safekeeping. (See the sidebar "Have That Data Leave the Building," later in this section, for more information.) The keys to successful automation are setting a schedule in software and making sure that the media is swapped as required.

You might already be familiar with backups: Windows has a built-in backup program that can be set in Task Manager to perform at specified intervals. But you probably *don't* back up on a schedule, do you? Most people don't, largely because you need a plan and some hands-on attention to make it happen.

Choosing Backup Media

Any computer media that will hold data can be used as a backup device, but here are the main varieties of backup media:

- **Tape** Backups to tape are the classic method of ensuring that you have copied and can restore your critical data. Tape drives are not inexpensive, nor are the tapes, but they are still the method of choice at most large enterprises because they are robust and simple to operate, they require little attention, and—because they are not multipurpose devices—they aren't being used for something else when the time for the scheduled backup rolls around.

- **CD or DVD** If you have a CD or DVD burner on any of your networked computers, you have all you need to perform regular backups to removable media. You must ensure, however, that a disc with enough available space to store the backup is in the drive, ready to go, at the scheduled time. Be sure to label those discs!

- **A designated hard drive** You can back up data to any drive networked into your system. This can be a full computer system or simply a stand-alone external drive. The disadvantage of using a computer is that the data will not be easily transportable unless you back up to a notebook computer. A wide variety of inexpensive external drives that plug into a USB port are available; some of these are remarkably small. These external drives can be excellent and cost-effective backup devices, but just as with CD or DVD media, you must have them plugged in and available at the scheduled backup time, or your plan will fail.

- **Online storage** A number of commercial enterprises will allow you to back up your data onto their servers. You are, in effect, renting space from them on a monthly or an annual basis. The best of them are reliable and fully secure, offering the advantage of simple off-site storage. This is the only true fully automated method available; for this reason, it might be the best choice if your data is critical but your schedule is erratic. Unless your network or systems are down, online backups will always take place as scheduled.

Scheduling and Performing Backups

You can use Task Manager and Windows Backup to accomplish backups to any of the physical media. Tape drives often come with backup software, and there are a number of software products that offer a variety of data-replication techniques that you might prefer to the basics in Windows. If you use an online service, software to automate the process is usually included.

Making Your Backup Plan Work

You should periodically test your backup plan by performing a data restore from the backup files. Perform this restore immediately after completing a backup, being sure to use that backup's files, so that you have no opportunity to lose any data gathered since the time of the backup. For smaller businesses, you probably need to do this only a couple of times a year, to ensure that the method works and that you know how to perform a restore. For larger amounts of critical data, you should double-check your backups more frequently.

It is also a good idea to rotate your backup media. For example, designate two tapes or discs for full backups and alternate between them. Incremental backups can often be made to the same media for the week's data, but use a different tape or disc the following week.

Have That Data Leave the Building

However you decide to back up your data, the backup file will not do you a bit of good if it succumbs to the fire or another calamity that affects your business premises. At least once a week, make a full backup to tape, CD, DVD, or external hard drive, and remove it from your place of business. Take it home. (Don't leave it in your car.) If your business is in your home, give the backup to a trusted neighbor or put it in a safe-deposit box. Periodically, leave a copy with your accountant or attorney. Even if you use an online backup service, make a physical copy of your key data periodically and have it leave the building.

Protecting Against Viruses

Protecting your network and your business data from the threat of viruses, worms, Trojan Horses, and other malicious code is *never* optional. For simplicity, you should choose a single vendor and install that antivirus protection on every system in your business. The best antivirus software automatically updates itself with no user intervention; a further level of security is added if you configure the program to scan the system's drives on a regular basis (such as weekly, after the close of business).

Choosing an Antivirus Program

There are a great many reputable and highly capable antivirus programs available. If you have acquired new computer systems for your business, some form of basic protection was probably included. If you are happy with that program, don't let it expire unless you determine that a better option is available. If you don't already have a preference, comparative reviews are frequently published.

For more about antivirus programs, check these links for reviews and ratings:

- *www.scotsnewsletter.com*

- *www.cnet.com*

- *techupdate.zdnet.com*

- *www.pcworld.com*

- *www.pcmagazine.com*

Some further suggestions:

- Don't install more than one form of antivirus program on a single computer; they seldom play well together.

- If you decide to change vendors, remove your old antivirus program before you install the new one. Be aware too that some antivirus programs must be shut down before you can install new software or updates to your operating system.

- Configure the options for automatic updates. Many programs, in addition to checking for new versions at predetermined times, can be activated by the vendor in cases where new and fast-spreading code represents a danger. Other vendors will e-mail you with notifications that updates are ready—don't ignore these messages.

- It is not necessary to choose an antivirus program and a firewall from the same vendor, but you should not install parts of different *security suites*. These too tend to interfere with each other. For more about firewalls, see the section "Choosing and Using Firewalls," later in this chapter.

Maintaining Virus Protection

As mentioned, you should use the automatic-update feature of your antivirus program to ensure that it always has the latest threat information. Periodically, scan all the systems on your network for viruses; this task is time-consuming and generally needs to be done outside of working hours because you might need to leave systems running overnight. If cleaning personnel or others have access to your premises during non-business hours, be sure to lock down the running systems before you leave.

Choosing and Using Firewalls

Firewalls are software programs or hardware devices that help to prevent intrusions from outside your network. The miscreants who stage these attacks are often not looking for data on your intranet—they would rather hijack a portion of your system (and occasionally your good name) to spread spam or viruses. But whatever the reason for the intrusion, you need to have a firewall keep them out of your network and your data.

Internet Connection Firewall and Windows Firewall

Windows XP includes Internet Connection Firewall (ICF), a basic software tool that can often prevent intrusions. In early versions of Windows XP, ICF was not enabled by default; by mid-2004 (Service Pack 2), the operating system is installed with a more advanced version of ICF, known as Windows Firewall, enabled. To learn more about ICF and Windows Firewall, including how to enable or disable them, search the Windows XP Help And Support Center for *firewall*, or visit *http://www.microsoft.com/windowsxp/downloads/updates/default.mspx.*

You might decide that this is all the protection you need. If you use another solution, be sure to check the documentation to determine whether you need to disable ICF or Windows Firewall.

Windows Service Packs

Windows XP Service Pack 2 also includes important enhancements to e-mail and instant-messaging security, changes to Microsoft Internet Explorer that can help prevent malicious downloads, and other features. Service packs can occasionally cause problems with third-party applications, so first check with the vendors of any such programs on which you depend. Then download and install the service pack to keep your systems up-to-date.

As with antivirus software, many firewall programs are available. Most update themselves automatically and come with initial settings that are an attempt at one-size-fits-all rules for your network. The best of them watch your behavior; they ask you questions as needed about programs that attempt to access the Internet, remember your answers, and thereby develop custom settings for your situation. Hardware firewalls are often supplied with routers and hubs (for more about these devices, see Chapter 16, "Small Business Networks and Servers"); many security experts recommend a software firewall in addition to any hardware firewall supplied with your network devices.

For more information about blocking intrusions to your network, visit the Web sites listed in the section "Protecting Against Viruses," earlier in this chapter—all of these sites also review and rate firewalls.

Dealing with Spyware and Adware

You might be aware, from your personal use of the Web, that many software programs have been developed to track Internet use and report information back to their masters. In fact, if you operate a Web-based business, you might be considering using one of these programs yourself. Most are small, harmless bits of code that track whether an e-mail has been opened or which areas on a Web page have attracted a browser's interest. More obviously, many sites place cookies on your machine to track your usage. Again, these are often harmless and they allow the site to customize your experi-

Preventing Internet Abuse

- **E-mail** Simply dealing with work-related e-mail can be time-consuming. Personal e-mail should be kept to a minimum: from school and family as needed, for example, but no "Words of the Day" or extensive correspondence that is not work-related. Most large corporations notify their employees that e-mail might be monitored. You probably don't want to take the time to do this, but when you provide the system and the software, doing so is within your rights.

- **Web access** Every employee is going to check sports scores, weather forecasts, news and traffic reports, or other sites while at work. A reasonable policy for a small business would be something like: for non-work-related sites, visit them on break, during lunch, or just before you leave in the afternoon. No offensive sites are allowed, and *never* download games or other applications. You could configure and manage a Web-filtering program, if you discover a need, but that's time and money away from other business tasks, so a minimalist approach is probably best unless you discover an issue.

- **Subterfuge** Your policy should make it clear that soliciting your business customers for an employee's personal endeavors is not allowed. Additionally, be aware that a few unscrupulous individuals might try to use their access to your Internet connection to e-mail spam, spread viruses, deface Web sites, or otherwise exploit your trust. Needless to say, such behavior should be defined in your policy as resulting in immediate termination.

ence (such as by setting the page to show local weather conditions, or the like).

You can customize your security settings to manage cookies by choosing Internet Options on the Tools menu in Internet Explorer. To learn more, review the information available in the Windows XP Help And Support Center.

Unfortunately, not all hidden code is benign: *spyware*, including *keystroke loggers*, is proliferating. A keystroke logger can track highly sensitive activities—such as entering a credit card number—and deliver that information to someone who will attempt to use it illegally. Some *adware* not only reports on your browsing habits, it also attempts to actively redirect your browsing (known as *hijacking*). Many of these malicious programs are tucked away inside something else—something with perceived value that you decide to download. Others are viral, installing themselves without your knowledge.

For your business (and for your home computers), it is a best practice not just to try to avoid malicious code, but also to take steps to ensure that your computers are periodically swept for infections. A number of excellent tools are available for this purpose. Overall, they tend not to be as automatic as antivirus and firewall programs, but their regular use is essential to maintain a secure computing environment and to safeguard your business's and your customers' data.

For more information about blocking spyware and adware, visit the Web sites listed in the section "Protecting Against Viruses," earlier in this chapter—all of these sites also review and rate spyware and adware eradication tools.

For More Information

In addition to the resources mentioned in this chapter, you will find links and information on the companion CD. Some books and Web sites particularly useful for understanding computer security include:

Books

- Thomas C. Greene, *Computer Security for the Home and Small Office* (APress, 2004)

- Debby Russell and Sr. G. T. Gangemi, *Computer Security Basics* (O'Reilly, 1991)

- Chey Cobb, *Network Security for Dummies* (Wiley, 2002)

Web Sites

- The Computer Security Resource Center from the National Institute of Standards and Technology (NIST): *csrc.nist.gov/*. See, particularly, the Small Business Corner.

- A vast amount of information is available at the CERT Coordination Center from the Software Engineering Institute (SEI) at Carnegie Mellon Institute: *www.cert.org/nav/index_main.html*. Much of this information is quite technical, but browse the Articles & Reports links for good, readable advice.

- The ITsecurity.com Dictionary+ of Information Security: *www.itsecurity.com/*.

Index

Symbols & Numerics

© (copyright symbol), 203
P (copyright symbol), 203
® (federal registration symbol), 201
SM (service mark symbol), 201
™ (trademark symbol), 201
10Base-T, 450
12 Month Cash Flow Statement template, 122
50+ customers, 7, 13
80/20 rule, 288
100Base-T, 450
360-degree interviews, 354
401(k), borrowing from, 58
802.11 standards, 450

A

abbreviations, domain name, 194
absolute cell references, 151
Access, e-mail transfers, 414
access rights. *See* security
Access to Capital Electronic Network
    (ACE-Net), 66
Account History report, 290
accountability, employee, 389, 395–397
accounting
    budgets, 11, 116–123
    cash flow, 121–123
    chart of accounts, 108–114
    closing books, 115
    depreciation, 111
    discounts, 113
    double-entry, 105
    financial statements, 106–108
    IRS publications, 105
    methods, 103
    net worth, 114
    overview, 102–103
    paychecks, 114
    periods, 105
    software, 102
    tax years, 105
accounts
    contact management, 321–328
    numbering, 108
    payable, 113, 121
    receivable, 109–110, 121
reports, 290
Accounts By Rating report, 290
Accounts Ledger Database, 102

Accounts Receivable Aging Workbook, 110
accrual accounting, 103
accrued expenses, 113
acquisitions, business, 303
actions, contact management, 321, 323
actual cost mileage deductions, 137
actual cost travel deductions, 138
addresses
    domain names, 193–195
    e-mail databases, 231
    Web sites, 193
administration plans, 39
administrative software, 455
Advanced Filter, 168
adventure industry, ideas targeting, 9
advertising. *See also* advertising ideas;
      branding; presentations
    benefits vs. features, 213–216
    business plans, 38, 44
    crossing markets, 216–217
    customer personalization, 292–294, 296
    flexibility, 213
    goals, 211
    job openings, 351–353
    market research, 24–29
    marketing, defined, 212
    multiple targets, 212
    myths, 215
    networking, 213
    overview, 210–211
    return on investment, 217–220
    sales leads, 236–242
    strategies, 212–213
    target marketing, 217
advertising ideas
    low-cost
      cause-related, 224–225
      direct mail, 225–228
      e-mail, 229–232
      media hooks, 221
      online advertising, 232–236
      overview, 220
      PR agencies, 222–224
      word-of-mouth, 220
    Publisher
      e-mail newsletters, 264–269
      help, 248
      overview, 246–248
      print ads, 248–254
      printing, 255
      Web sites, 254–264

advisory boards, 22–24, 95–97
adware, 475
affirmative action, 358
African-American customers, 14
age
    discrimination, 362, 366
    entrepreneurs, 6
    senior customers, 7, 13
    teen customers, 12
Age Discrimination in Employment Act,
    362
aging reports, 110
agreements, legal, 81, 88–89
AHPs (Association Health Plans), 373
AIO (customer activities, interests, and
    opinions), 25
alerts, e-mail message, 425
All Excel option, 167
alliances, strategic, 303–304
American FactFinder, 24
American Society for Training and
    Development (ASTD), 391
Americans with Disabilities Act, 362
amortization, 104, 111, 129, 137, 140
analyzing data, Excel
    charting, 171–172
    data collection, 147
    filtering, 167–171
    future values, 179
    overview, 146
    PivotTables, 173–177
    present values, 178
    sorting, 166
    training, 146
    trends, 106, 165–172
    what-if scenarios, 148–165
AND, 334
and criteria, 170
Angel Capital Electronic Network
    (ACE-Net), 66
angels, financial, 64–67
animal market, ideas targeting, 7
animation, 280
annual income statistics, 15
antenna devices, 454
antivirus software, 415–417, 472–474
appearance, public speaking, 93–94
applicants, job. See hiring
appointment management, 438–440
architectural copyrights, 202
archived
    computer records, 469–472
    databases, 341
    e-mail files, 413–415

e-mail messages, 432–434
    training sessions, 392
art, 190–192, 252
Asian-American customers, 14
asset-based lenders, 70
assets. See also intellectual property (IP)
    balance sheets, 106
    current, 70, 111
    depreciation, 111
    fixed, 111
    intangible, 55, 112
    tangible, 55, 70
Association Health Plans (AHPs), 373
assumptions. See what-if analysis
asynchronous training, 392–395
ATF (Bureau of Alcohol Tobacco and
    Firearms), 79
attachments, 329–330, 417
attended backups, 470
attention grabbers, advertising, 250
attorneys, when to hire, 200–201, 205, 354
attracting customers. See marketing
audio, 200, 202
author copyright protections, 202–203
AutoArchive, 433
AutoFilter, 167
automated backups, 470
automatic e-mail archiving, 432–434
automobile insurance, 83
automobile tax deductions, 129, 137
AutoShapes, 275

B
b connections, 450
baby boomers, 7, 13
background checks, employee, 355–357
backgrounds, PowerPoint, 279
backing, financial. See financing
backups
    computer records, 469–472
    databases, 341
    e-mail files, 413–415
balance sheets, 39, 106, 115
balancing account books, 115
bank cards, financing with, 59
banks, borrowing from, 67–69
banner ads, 235
bar charts, 171
barriers to entry, 38
bartering, 64
BBBOnline, 300
BCM (Business Contact Manager). See
    Business Contact Manager (BCM)

beginning a business. *See also* business
    plans; financing
  advisory boards, 22–24, 95–97
  how to begin
    customers, identifying, 11–15
    market trends, 6–9, 11–15
    mistakes, 9–11
    overview, 4
    resources, 18
    small business criteria, 5–6
    success stories, 15–17
  image, 93–94
  insurance, 81–85
  legal agreements, 88–89
  licenses, 78–80
  location renting or leasing, 86–88
  recordkeeping, 89–90
  statistics, 6
benchmarks, employee performance,
    386–388
benefits, employee, 92, 370–373, 399
bids, search engine rankings, 233
bilingual customers, 15
biotech industry, ideas targeting, 8
.biz, 194
blocked attachments, e-mail, 417
Blocked Senders List, e-mail, 430
boards, advisory, 22–24, 95–97
body language, 93
boilerplate text, 88
bonus depreciation, 129
bonuses, paying, 92, 385–386
bookkeeping. *See also* computer security
  accounting methods, 103
  budgets, 11, 116–123
  cash flow, 121–123
  chart of accounts, 108–114
  closing books, 115
  double-entry accounting, 105
  equipment documentation, 140
  financial statements, 106–108
  IRS publications, 105
  mistakes, 136–138
  net worth, 114
  overview, 89–90, 102–103
  paychecks, 114
  periods, 105
  software, 102
  tax years, 105
Books24X7, 394
boomers, baby, 7, 13
bootstrapping, 62–64

borrowing money
  commercial banks, 67–69
  commercial finance companies, 70
  government, 70–72
  how much, calculating, 152–154, 161
  overview, 67
  retirement accounts, 58
  venture capital, 73
  from your business, 92
boss, being the
  accountability, 389–390
  contingency workers, 395–399
  delegating, 381–384
  expanding staff, 380–381
  mistakes, 10
  overview, 380–381
  performance reviews, 386–388
  poor performance, reasons for, 390
  rewarding staff, 384–386
  telecommuting, 395–397
  training, 390–395
brain trusts, 23
branding
  credibility, 198
  direct mail, 228
  intellectual property, 199–205
  logos, 190–192
  mission statements, 186–188
  overview, 184–186
  point of difference, 188–190
  policies, 192
  pricing, 28
  Web presence, 192–197
breakeven points, 28, 150
broadband service providers, 445
brochures. *See* Publisher
budgets. *See also* data analysis; financing
  cash flow, 121–123
  expenses, 116
  goals, 116
  mistakes, 11
  preparing, 116–121
bulk direct mail campaigns, 225–228
bulk e-mail campaigns, 229–236
bundle pay, 369
Bureau of Alcohol, Tobacco, and Firearms
    (ATF), 79
Bureau of Industry and Security, 79
business angel investors, 65
business cards, 190, 220, 436
Business Contact History group, 319

Business Contact Manager (BCM)
   accounts, 321–323
   adding contacts, 317–320
   attachments, 329–330
   copying contacts, 317
   creating contacts, 318–320
   data management, 341–343
   e-mail marketing, 230
   Exchange, 310
   exporting, 339
   financial status, 318
   history tracking, 327–329
   importing, 336–341
   installing, 313
   location, 316
   options, 321
   Outlook basics, 308
   overview, 290, 309–312
   profiles, 316–317
   reports, 330–336
   running, 314
   sales opportunities, 324–327
   views, 320
Business Contacts Phone List report, 331
business expansion, 301–303
Business History folder, 327–330
business insurance, 81–85
business licenses, 78–80
business locations, 86–88
business mistakes, 9–11
business models, 6–9, 15–17, 56
business owner's policy (BOP), 82
business plans
   advisory boards, 22–24
   business growth, 302
   formats, 41–49
   guidelines, 36–41
   layouts, 36–41
   loan applications, 68
   market research, 24–29
   overview, 22
   ownership structures, 29–36
   revising later, 56
   templates, 41–49
business records, 89–90
business signatures, e-mail, 435–438
business statistics, 5–6, 8, 12, 15
business taxes
   expenses
      computer equipment, 140–142
      meals, 138–140
      overview, 128–130
      property, 140
      travel, 138–140

   expert secrets, 131–136
   extensions, 135
   IRS resources, 138
   managing yourself, 132–134
   mistakes, 136–138
   overview, 128
   resources, 128
business types
   accounting methods, 104
   C Corporations, 32
   customers, identifying, 11–15
   DBAs, 31
   EINs, 80
   general partnerships, 34
   ideas, 6–9
   Limited Liability Corporations, 36
   overview, 29–30
   sole proprietorships, 30
   Subchapter S Corporations, 33
BusinessLaw online resource, 79
buying habits, customer, 290
buy-sell agreements, 39

C
C (copyright symbol), 203
C Corporations, 32, 104
cable modems, 446
cables, networking, 450
calculating. *See also* data analysis
   breakeven points, 150
   future values, 179
   loan amounts, 152–154, 161
   net present values, 218
   present values, 178
   prices, 27–29
calendar tax years, 105
calendars, appointment management,
   438–440
calling, cold, 239–242
CAN-SPAM Act of 2003, 229
capital. *See* financing
car insurance, 83
car tax deductions, 129, 137
cash accounting, 103
cash flow. *See also* data analysis; financing
   business plans, 39
   loan applications, 68
   managing, 121–123
   mistakes, 11
   statistics, 15
   templates, 122
catalogs, 225–228, 256
cause-related marketing, 224–225
CD backups, 471

cell references, 151
census research, 24
CEO Club, 97
certificate authorities (CAs), 420
Certificate of Doing Business Under an
    Assumed Name (DBAs), 31
certificates, e-mail sender, 419–421
certified public accountants (CPAs), 131
challenges, market, 38
chamber of commerce, 71
channels, crossing market, 216–217
charities, cause-related marketing,
    224–225
chart of accounts, 108–114
charts, 171–172, 281
childcare benefits, 372
children, purchasing power, 12
citizenship discrimination, 365
Civil Rights Act of 1866, 362
Civil Rights Act of 1871, 362
Civil Rights Act of 1964, 362
Civil Rights Act of 1991, 363
closing account books, 115
COBRA (Consolidated Omnibus Budget
    Reconciliation Act), 363
co-employment relationships, 399
cold calling, 239–242
collateral, 67, 71
collecting business data, 147
collective bargaining, 365
colleges
    online training at, 393
    recruiting at, 353
    savings, borrowing from, 58
color discrimination, 362
colors
    company image, 191
    PowerPoint, 279, 283
    Publisher, 253
    publishing software, 191
    trademarking, 200
.com, 194
comma-separated value (.csv) files, 336
commercial banks, 67–69
commercial finance companies, 70
commercial space, renting or leasing,
    86–88
commissioned work copyrights, 203
communications. See advertising;
    branding; e-mail; presentations
community colleges, 353, 391
company descriptions, business plans, 37
company expansion, 301–303, 380–381
company handbooks, 361–366

company identity
    credibility, 198
    intellectual property, 199–205
    logos, 190–192, 250
    mission statements, 186–188
    overview, 184–186
    point of difference, 188–190
    policies, 192
    Web presence, 192–197
company logos, 190–192, 250
company mission statements
    business plans, 37
    graphical representations, 191
    overview, 186–188
    public speaking, 93
    Web sites, 193
compensation
    consultants, 368–369
    employees, 367–370, 384–386
    paying yourself, 91–92
    taxes, 115
competition, industry, 8, 28, 190
comprehensive marketing plans, 213
compressing files, 418
computer industry, ideas targeting, 8
computer networks. See also computer
    security
    business locations, 444
    e-mail servers, 411
    equipment options, 451–456
    Ethernet, 449, 453
    Internet services, 445–447
    LANs, 447
    mixed types, 451
    mobile users, 456
    options, 444–449
    peripherals, 454
    printers, 454
    routers, 452
    servers, 455
    types, 449–451
    Wi-Fi, 450, 454
computer security
    adware, 475
    backups, 469–472
    data sharing, 460
    firewalls, 474
    options, 461–467
    overview, 460
    physical, 467–469
    spyware, 475
    viruses, 472–474
computer software programs, 202
computer tax deductions, 140–142

computer usage logs, 142
computerized accounting systems, 102
computerized training options, 392–395
conditional formatting, 122
conferences, networking at, 213
confidential e-mails, 419–421
connectivity. *See* computer networks
Consolidated Omnibus Budget
    Reconciliation Act (COBRA), 363
constructive receipts, 104
consultants
    advisory boards, 22–24, 95–97
    freelancers, 397–399
    intellectual property, 200
    PR agencies, 222–224
    staff management, 382
    tax, 131–136
consumer choice healthcare plans, 373
consumer opinions, asking, 25
consumer watchdogs, 300
contact management
    Business Contact Manager
        accounts, 321–323
        adding contacts, 317–320
        attachments, 329–330
        copying contacts, 317
        creating contacts, 318–320
        data management, 341–343
        exporting, 339, 414
        financial status, 318
        history tracking, 327–329
        importing, 336–341
        installing, 313
        location, 316
        options, 321
        overview, 309–312
        profiles, 316–317
        reports, 330–336
        running, 314
        sales opportunities, 324–327
        views, 320
    overview, 308–309
    personalized marketing, 291–294
contextual searches, 236
contingency plans, financial backing, 58
contingency workers, 203, 395–399
contingent liabilities, 114
contract workers, 203, 395–399
contracts, legal, 81, 88–89
contractual alliances, 303
contributions, cause-related marketing,
    224–225
controlled spending techniques, 62–64
cookies, 476

copr., 203
copying
    contacts, 317
    databases, 341
    e-mail files, 413–415
    e-mail messages, 422, 432–434
    Publisher documents, 255
copyrights, 202–203
corporations
    C Corporations, 32
    Limited Liability Corporations, 36
    Subchapter S Corporations, 33
costs. *See also* data analysis; marketing
        ideas
    accounting methods, 104
    breakeven points, 150
    depreciation, 111
    employee benefits, 370
    employee training, 390–395
    PR agencies, 223
    product pricing, 27–29
    search engine rankings, 233
    space renting or leasing, 86–88
    telecommuting, 395–397
    unexpected, 56–58
    value over time, 218
counseling
    advisory boards, 22–24, 95–97
    SBDC program, 71
    SCORE, 68
CPAs (certified public accountants), 131
credentials
    job applicants, 355–357
    professional, 79
    tax experts, 131
credibility, brand, 198
credit accounts, 105
credit bureaus, 60
credit cards, financing with, 59
credit rating checks, 60
credits, customer, 105, 121
crossing markets, 216–217
crossing state lines, 78
cryptography, 467
Cs, five lending criteria, 70
csv files, 336
cultures, employee diversity, 357–359
current assets, 70, 111
current liabilities, 112
current values, calculating, 178
Custom Excel option, 168
customer resource management (CRM),
    309

customers. *See also* branding; contact
    management; data analysis
  buying habits, 290
  characteristics, 26
  data collection, 147
  databanks, 26
  databases, 289–291
  demographics, 24
  ending relationships, 298–299
  expanding to support, 301–303
  identifying, 11–15, 24–29, 288–289
  intelligence, granular, 289, 291–294
  marketing timetables, 296–298
  perceptions, 187, 299
  personalization, 292–294, 296
  privacy, 299–301
  referrals, 294, 301
  relationships, 188
  researching, 218
  retention rates, 294
  rewarding, 294–296
  touch points, 184
  trust, 299–301

D
data analysis
  charting, 171–172
  data collection, 147
  filtering, 167–171
  future values, 179
  overview, 146
  PivotTables, 173–177
  present values, 178
  sorting, 166
  training, 146
  trends, 165–172
  what-if scenarios, 148–165
data collection options, 147
data security. *See* security
data tables, 154–161
databases
  accounting, 102
  backing up, 341
  Business Contact Manager, 315
  cleaning up, 341
  contact information, 341–343
  customer information, 26, 289–294
  deleting, 342
  e-mail addresses, 231
  product, 325–327
  restoring, 342
DBAs (Certificate of Doing Business Under
  an Assumed Name), 31
debit accounts, 105

debits, double-entry accounting, 105
debts
  C Corporations, 32
  credit cards, 59
  financing, 54
  Limited Liability Corporations, 36
  partnerships, 34
  sole proprietorships, 30
  Subchapter S Corporations, 33
dedicated lines, 446
deductions. *See* taxes
defaulting, loan, 67, 70
defragmentation, 341
delayed compensation, 92
delegating tasks, 381–384
demographics, 24, 357–359
Department of Transportation (DOT), 79
depreciation, 104, 111, 129, 137, 140
deputy, delegating to, 381–383
Design Checker, 255
design patents, 204
design sets, Publisher, 191, 248
designated hard drive backups, 471
designs. *See also* Publisher
  direct mail, 227
  PowerPoint presentations, 273–283
  trademarking, 200
desktop publishing software, 191
devices
  computer backups, 471
  Ethernet, 449
  handheld, 439, 456
  LANs, 447
  routers, 452
  Wi-Fi, 450
dial-up connections, 445
diet industry, ideas targeting, 8
differentiating products
  credibility, 198
  intellectual property, 199–205
  logos, 190–192
  mission statements, 186–188
  overview, 184–186
  point of difference, 188–190
  policies, 192
  Web presence, 192–197
difficulties, market, 38
digital IDs, 421
digital signatures, 419–421
Digital Subscriber Line (DSL), 446
direct expenses, 109
Direct Marketing Association, 25
direct-mail (DM), 25, 190, 225–228
disability benefits, 372

disabled persons, employing, 359, 362
disc backups, 471
discounts, 113, 121, 221, 296
discrimination, employment, 362
dismissing employees, 374–376
diversity, 6, 14, 357–359
dividend distribution, 92
Do Not Call option, 319
Do Not Send E-mail option, 319
Do Not Send Fax option, 319
Do Not Send Letter option, 319
documentation. *See also* business plans;
 security
 loan applications, 68, 72
 personnel, 361
 recordkeeping, 89–90
 remote management options, 396
Doing Business Under an Assumed Name
 (DBAs), 31
domain names, registering, 193–195
domestic travel per diem rates, 139
donations, cause-related marketing,
 224–225
DOT (Department of Transportation), 79
double taxation, 33
double-declining depreciation, 112
double-entry accounting, 105
downloading. *See* Web sites
drive partitions, 461
drop shadows, 283
DSL (Digital Subscriber Line), 446
DVD backups, 471

E
EAs (enrolled agents), 131
Easy Web Site Builder, 254–264
echo boomers, 13
education
 business plans, 22
 e-learning options, 392–395
 e-mail management, 412
 employee training, 390–395
 Excel training, 146
 savings, borrowing from, 58
 SBDC program, 71
 SCORE, 68
 tax preparers, 131
EIN (Employer Identification Number), 80
e-learning options, 392–395
electric utility Internet connectivity, 447
electronic business cards, 436
e-mail. *See also* computer security; contact
 management
 access restrictions, 461
 archives, 432–434

attachments, 417
BCM attachments, 329–330
clients, 407
 customer retention, 295
 digital signatures, 419–421
 domain names, 193
 flags, 423
 folders, 422
 help, 412
 junk messages, 229, 430–432
 macros, 415–417
 marketing, 229–236, 264–269
 need assessments, 407–412
 overview, 406
 protocols, 407–409
 receiving rules, 424–430
 security, 413–421
 sending best practices, 421
 servers, 407, 411–412
 signatures, 419–421, 435–440
 software options, 409–411
 surveys, 25
 tasks, 439
 viruses, 415–417
Employee Polygraph Protection Act, 363
Employee Retirement Income Security Act
 of 1974 (ERISA), 363, 399
Employee Stock Option Plan (ESOP), 371
employee-defined contribution plans, 374
employees
 accountability, 389–390
 background checks, 355–357
 benefits, 370–374
 company handbooks, 361–366
 compensation, 367–370
 computer tax deductions, 142
 contingency workers, 395–399
 delegating, 381–384
 diversity, 357–359
 federal laws, 361
 firing, 374–376
 first hire, 348–350
 friends, 360
 growth, company, 350, 380–381
 interviewing, 353–355
 marketing strategies, 212
 performance reviews, 386–388
 recognition programs, 384–386
 records management, 361
 recruiting, 351–353
 relatives, 360
 telecommuting, 395–397
 training, 390–395
 when to hire, 348

Employer Identification Number (EIN), 80
employer taxes, 114
employer-defined benefits, 374
employment trends, 5
Encarta, 44
encryption, 467
ending customer relationships, 298–299
ending employment, 374–376
enrolled agents (EAs), 131
entertainment use vs. business use, 141
entrepreneurs. *See also* business plans;
    financing
  advisory boards, 22–24, 95–97
  how to begin
    customers, identifying, 11–15
    market trends, 6–9, 11–15
    mistakes, 9–11
    overview, 4
    resources, 18
    small business criteria, 5–6
    success stories, 15–17
  image, 93–94
  insurance, 81–85
  legal agreements, 88–89
  licenses, 78–80
  location renting or leasing, 86–88
  recordkeeping, 89–90
  statistics, 6
environment, ideas targeting, 8
environmental protection regulations, 78
Equal Pay Act, 363
Equifax, 60
equipment, 83, 136, 140, 451–456
equity, owner's, 108, 114
equity financing, 54
ERISA (Employee Retirement Income
    Security Act of 1974), 363
Errors and Omissions insurance, 83
ESOP (Employee Stock Option Plan), 371
estimating
  breakeven points, 150
  cash flow, 122
  future values, 179
  loan amounts, 152–154, 161
  net present values, 218
  present values, 178
Ethernet, 449, 452–453
ethnic groups, 6, 14, 357–359
evaluating performance. *See* performance
    reviews, employee
Excel. *See also* data analysis
  access restrictions, 461
  accounting, 102
  aging reports, 110
  balance sheets, 107

budgets, 117
business plan templates, 42
cell references, 151
conditional formatting, 122
contact management, 337, 339
e-mail transfers, 414
Exchange Server, 310, 409
exclusive rights, 199–205
Executive Order 11246, 364
executive summary, 37
exercise industry, ideas targeting, 8
existing contacts, copying, 317
exit strategies, 39, 55
expansion, business, 301–303, 380–381
expectations, employee, 386–390
expenses. *See also* data analysis; marketing
    ideas
  accounting methods, 104
  accrued, 113
  breakeven points, 150
  budgets, 11, 116–123
  cars, 129, 137
  cash flow, 121
  computer equipment, 140–142
  deducting, 92
  direct, 109
  discounts, 113
  employees, 370, 384–386
  gifts, 138
  indirect, 109
  insurance, 83
  liabilities, 112–114
  miscellaneous, 109
  pricing products and services, 27
  receipts, 136
  reimbursable, 137
  space renting or leasing, 86–88
  tax impact, 128–130, 140–142
  travel, 138–140
  types, 116
  value over time, 218
Experian, 60
experts
  advisory boards, 95–97
  freelancers, 395–399
  intellectual property, 200
  PR agencies, 222–224
  staff management, 382
  tax preparers, 131–136
expirations
  copyrights, 204
  domain name registrations, 195
  patents, 205
  trademarks, 201

exporting contact information, 339
exporting e-mail files, 413–415
extensions, tax, 135
eye contact, 93

F
Factiva News service, 45
factoring lenders, 70
Fair Labor Standards Act, 364
family
    borrowing from, 60–62
    hiring, 92, 360
    purchasing power, 12
Family and Medical Leave Act, 364
Family Savings Accounts (FSAs), 373
Fast Ethernet, 450
FastCounter Pro, 235
FCC (Federal Communications
    Commission), 79
FDA (Food and Drug Administration), 79
federal government loans, 70–72
federal government venture capital
    programs, 66, 73
Federal Income Tax Withholding, 364
Federal Insurance Contribution Act, 364
federal licensing, 78
federal per diem rates, 139
federal registration symbols, 201
federal resources, 18
federal taxes. *See* taxes
Federal Unemployment Tax Act (FUTA),
    115, 364
FedStat, 24
female customers, 12
FICA (Federal Insurance Contributions
    Act), 114
files
    attachments, 329–330, 417
    bookkeeping mistakes, 136–138
    encrypting, 467
    hiding, 467
    security
        adware, 475
        backups, 469–472
        data sharing, 460
        file-level, 461
        firewalls, 474
        options, 461–467
        overview, 460
        physical, 467–469
        spyware, 475
        viruses, 472–474
    filing tax returns. *See* taxes
Filter command, 167

filtering
    BCM reports, 333
    e-mail, 424–432
    Excel, 167–171
finance companies, commercial, 70
finances. *See also* data analysis; employees;
        financing; taxes
    accounting
        chart of accounts, 108–114
        closing books, 115
        depreciation, 111
        double-entry, 105
        financial statements, 106–108
        fixed assets, 111
        inventory, 110
        IRS publications, 105
        liabilities, 112–114
        methods, 103
        net worth, 114
        overview, 102–103
        paychecks, 114
        periods, 105
        software, 102
        tax years, 105
    budgets, 11, 116–123
    business plans, 39
    cash flow, 121–123
    client financial health, 318
    paying yourself, 91–92
financial statements, 106–108
financing. *See also* business plans; money
    angels, 64–67
    bootstrapping, 62–64
    categories, 54
        commercial banks, 67–69
    commercial finance companies, 70
    credit cards, 59
    friends or relatives, 60–62
    government, 70–72
    loans, 67–72
    overview, 54
    savings, 58
    stages, 54–55
    unexpected costs, 56–58
    venture capital, 73
finding sales leads, 238–239
firewalls, 474
firing customers, 298–299
firing employees, 374–376
first employee, hiring, 348–350
first impressions, importance of, 93–94
first-stage financing, 55
fiscal tax years, 105
fitness industry, ideas targeting, 8

five Cs lending criteria, 70
fixed assets, 111
fixed expenses, 116
fixed-declining depreciation, 112
flags, e-mail, 423
Flash sites, 235
flex plans, medical, 372
Flexible Spending Accounts (FSAs), 372
floating expenses, 59
flowcharts, PowerPoint, 275
flyers, 225–228, 248–255, 265
focus groups, 25
folder-level security, 461
folders, e-mail, 422
follow-up flags, e-mail, 423
fonts, 191, 253, 278, 282
Food and Drug Administration (FDA), 79
food deductions, 138–140
food industry, ideas targeting, 8
footers, Word, 48
For Follow Up folders, 424
forecasting. *See* estimating
foreign travel per diem rates, 140
for-hire workers, 397–399
Form SS-4 (EIN applications), 80
formal agreements, financial, 61
formats. *See also* Publisher
    business plans, 41–49
    conditional formatting, 122
    direct mail, 228
    e-mail messages, 418
    PowerPoint presentations, 273–283
    publishing software, 191, 265
    Word documents, 45–47
forms, Web site, 260
formulas, Excel
    data tables, 156
    Goal Seek command, 151
    loan payments, 153
    Scenario Manager, 162
forwarding, Web site, 196
free
    marketing, 212, 221
    research sources, 24
    Web site hosting, 196
freelance workers, 64, 397–399
frequency, marketing communication,
    296–298
friends
    borrowing from, 60–62
    hiring, 360
frugal spending, 62–64
FSAs (Family Savings Accounts), 373
FSAs (Flexible Spending Accounts), 372

full backups, 470
full-circle performance reviews, 388
full-service marketing plans, 213
fully automated backups, 470
fund of funds, 66, 73
FUTA (Federal Unemployment Tax Act),
    115, 364
future plans, documenting, 39
future value calculations, 179
future value over time, 218
FV function, 179

G
gender, 6, 12
general partnerships, 34
Generation Y, 13
geographical targeting, 236
gifts, tax deductions, 138
Gigabit Ethernet, 450
global issues, 357–359
Goal Seek command, 149–154
goals, financial, 116
government. *See also* taxes
    census, 24
    licenses, 78–80
    loans, 70–72
    resources, 18
    venture capital programs, 73
grants, applying for, 71
granular customer intelligence, 289,
    291–294
graphics, 190–192, 252, 281
Graphics Manager, 255
graphing data, 171–172
green products, ideas targeting, 8
gross income, 15
grouping customers, 25
grouping data, Excel, 166
grouping pane, BCM, 331
groups, healthcare coverage, 373
growth, business, 301–303, 380–381
guarantees, loan, 67
guidelines, business. *See* business plans

H
handbooks, company, 361–366
handheld devices, 439, 456
hard copy direct mail campaigns, 225–228
hard drive backups, 471
hardware, 411, 468
harvesting, 39
headers, document, 48, 408
headhunters, 353

headings
  Excel columns, 171
  Publisher ad creation, 251
health codes, 79
health food, ideas targeting, 8
Health Savings Accounts (HSAs), 373
health standards, work place, 365
healthcare benefits, 373
healthcare laws, 363
hiding files, 467
high school customers, 12
high-low method, 139
hijacking computers, 476
HIPAA (Health Insurance Portability and
    Accountability Act of 1996), 365, 373
hiring. *See also* employees
  contingency workers, 395–397
  freelancers, 397-399
  PR agencies, 222–224
  tax consultants, 131–136
Hispanic customers, 14
historical information, client, 290, 321,
    327–330
holiday specials, 295
home
  business insurance, 85
  computer tax deductions, 141
  equity loans, 59
  telecommuting from, 395–397
hooks, media, 221
hosting Web sites, 195–197
hotel deductions, 138–140
HTML messages, 418
HTTP (Hypertext Transfer Protocol), 408
human resources. *See* employees

I
icons, company, 190–192, 198
ideas, business, 6–9, 11–15, 22
identifying customers
  contact management, 291–294
  market research, 24–29
  overview, 11–15, 288–289
identity, product. *See* branding
identity theft, 419
IDs, digital, 421
illegal aliens, 365
image
  credibility, 198
  intellectual property, 199–205
  logos, 190–192
  mission statements, 186–188
  overview, 184–186
  point of difference, 188–190

policies, 192
public speaking tips, 93–94
Web presence, 192–197
Immigration Reform and Control Act, 365
importing contact information, 336–341
importing product data, 339–341
impressions, presenting appropriate,
    93–94
incentive programs, customer, 294–296
incentives to pay early, 113, 121
income. *See also* taxes
  accounting methods, 104
  breakeven points, 150
  business interruption insurance, 82
  business plans, 39
  cash flow, 121
  past due, 110
  paying yourself, 91–92
  prices, 27–29
  statements, 106
  statistics, 15
  tax withholdings, 114
incremental backups, 470
independent finance companies, 70
independent for-hire workers, 397–399
indirect expenses, 109
industry branding. *See* branding
industry competition, 8, 28, 190
industry licenses, 79
Information Rights Management (IRM),
    361, 461
in-house customer databases, 290
initial public offerings (IPOs), 55
injuries, on the job, 365
inkjet printers, 454
in-person surveys, 25
insurance, 81–85
intangible assets, 55, 112
integrated marketing, 213
intellectual property (IP)
  copyrights, 202–203
  legal options, 200
  overview, 199–200
  patents, 204–205
  trademarks, 200
intelligence, customer, 289, 291–294
Interactive Advertising Bureau, 232
interest
  accounting, 113
  rates, 70–71
  loan calculations, 152–154, 161
international issues, 357–359, 363
International Telework Association &
    Council (ITAC), 396

international travel per diem rates, 140
Internet. *See also* computer networks
  backup storage, 471
  business presence on, 192–197
  e-mail servers, 411
  employee recruiting, 352
  information resources, 18
  marketing campaigns, 229–236
  mobile users accessing, 456
  Publisher, site creation with, 254–263
  routers, 452
  service options, 195, 445–447
  training via, 392–395
  zones, 418
Internet Connection Firewall (ICF), 474
Internet Corporation for Assigned Names
  and Numbers (ICANN), 193
Internet Message Access Protocol (IMAP),
  408
Internet service providers (ISPs), 195, 446
Internet-based industries, ideas targeting,
  8
InterNIC, 194
internships, 353
intervals, e-mail archiving, 432
interviewing employees, 353–355
interviewing tax experts, 131–132
inventor patent protections, 204–205
inventory, 110, 121
investigative services, 356
investment value calculations, 178–179
investors. *See* financing
invoices, 121
IP (intellectual property). *See* intellectual
  property (IP)
IRAs, borrowing from, 58
IRS (Internal Revenue Service). *See also*
  taxes
  accounting, 105
  EINs, 80
  online resources, 138
  per diem rates, 139
item-by-item transaction reports, 115

J
jacks, wired access points, 448
jobs. *See* employees
joint venture partnerships, 35
junior high customers, 12
junk e-mail, 229, 430–432
just-in-time training sessions, 392–395

K
Keep Lines Together option, 49
Keep With Next option, 49
key man insurance, 84
keystroke loggers, 476
keywords, search engine, 233
KSOP (401(k) Employee Stock Option
  Plan hybrid), 371

L
labor. *See* employees
laptop computers, 142, 456, 468
laser printers, 454
lawyers, when to hire, 200–201, 205, 354
layouts. *See also* Publisher
  brand visual development, 191
  business plans, 36–41
  PowerPoint, 272–283
leads, sales, 236–242
leased lines, 446
leasing space, 86–88
leave of absences, 364
legal
  agreements, 81, 88–89
  employee terminations, 374
  employment disclaimers, 354
  employment laws, 361
  intellectual property, 199–205
legal ownership structures
  C Corporations, 32
  DBAs, 31
  general partnerships, 34
  Limited Liability Corporations, 36
  overview, 29–30
  sole proprietorships, 30
  Subchapter S Corporations, 33
lenders. *See* loans
letterheads, 190
liabilities
  accounts payable, 113
  balance sheets, 106
  C Corporations, 32
  contingent, 114
  discounts, 113
  insurance, 82
  Limited Liability Corporations, 36
  long-term, 113–114
  overview, 112
  partnerships, 34
  short-term, 113
  sole proprietorships, 30
  Subchapter S Corporations, 33

licenses, 78–80
lie detector tests, 363
life insurance, 59, 84, 372
life cycles
 assets, 112
 product, 29
lifestyles, customer, 25
Limited Liability Corporations (LLCs), 36
limited partnerships, 34
line breaks, 49
line charts, 171
lines of credit, 59
linking BCM items in messages, 329–330
List Builder, 231, 238, 296
listed property, 140
lists. *See also* Business Contact Manager
 (BCM); sales leads
 direct mail marketing, 226
 e-mail marketing, 231
 qualified prospects, 238
 search engine rankings, 233
literary copyrights, 202
live documents, 460
loans
 commercial banks, 67–69
 commercial finance companies, 70
 cover letters, 69
 government, 70–72
 long-term, 114
 overview, 67
 quantity, calculating, 152–154, 161
 short-term, 113
 venture capital, 73
 from your business, 92
local area networks (LANs), 447, 453
local business licenses, 78–80
local employment laws, 361
local government loans, 70–72
locations
 marketing strategies, 212
 networking options, 444
 space renting or leasing, 86–88
lodging deductions, 138–140
logical partitions, 461
logos, 190–192, 198, 250
logs, 141–142, 476
long-term liabilities, 113–114
love money, 60–62
low interest rates, 71
Low-Doc program, 72
loyalty programs, customer, 294–296
lump-sum bonuses, 92

M
MACRS (modified accelerated cost
 recovery system), 137
magazine employment ads, 352
mail. *See also* computer security; contact
 management
 access restrictions, 461
 customer retention options, 295
 direct mail campaigns, 25, 225–228, 291
 domain names, 193
 e-mail management
  appointments, 438–440
  archives, 432–434
  attachments, 417
  digital signatures, 419–421
  flags, 423
  folders, 422
  help, 412
  junk messages, 430–432
  macros, 415–417
  marketing signatures, 435–438
  need assessments, 407–412
  overview, 406
  protocols, 407–409
  receiving rules, 424–430
  security, 413–421
  sending best practices, 421
  servers, 411–412
  software options, 409–411
  tasks, 439
  viruses, 415–417
 e-mail marketing, 229–232, 264–269
 e-mail servers, 407
 lists, 25, 291
Mail Merge Wizard, 291
malicious code, protecting against, 472
mall customer surveys, 25
management mistakes, 10
management plans, 39
managing employees. *See* employees
margins, pricing, 27
market branding. *See* branding
market competition, 8, 28, 190
market research, 24–29, 44
market segments, 24
market trends, 6–9, 11–18, 24–29
marketing. *See also* branding; marketing
 ideas; presentations
 benefits vs. features, 213–216
 crossing markets, 216–217
 customer personalization, 292–294, 296
 flexibility, 213
 integrated, 213

job openings, 351–353
mistakes, 9
myths, 215
networking, 213
overview, 210–212
return on investment, 217–220
sales leads, 238–242
SBA online guides, 26
strategies, 212–213
tag lines, 188–189
target, 217
timetables, 296–298
marketing ideas
low-cost
cause-related, 224–225
direct mail, 225–228
e-mail, 229–232, 435–438
media hooks, 221
online advertising, 232–236
overview, 220
PR agencies, 222–224
word-of-mouth, 220
Publisher
e-mail newsletters, 264–269
help, 248
overview, 246–248
print ads, 248–254
printing, 255
Web sites, 254–264
marks (trademarks), 200
Master Sets designs, Publisher, 191
meal deductions, 138–140
media. *See also* branding
company image, 190
computer backups, 471
hooks, 221
kits, 221
public speaking tips, 93–94
medical benefits, 373
medical flex plans, 372
medical industry, ideas targeting, 8
medical insurance laws, 363
Medicare taxes, 115
memory-producing industries, ideas
targeting, 9
messages. *See* e-mail; marketing;
presentations
Microsoft E-Learning Library (MELL), 393
mileage tax deductions, 137
military service, 366
millennials, 13
minimum wage, 364
minorities, 6, 14, 357–358
miscellaneous expenses, 109

mission statements
business plans, 37
graphical representations, 191
overview, 186–188
public speaking, 93
Web sites, 193
mistakes, common start-up, 9–11
mixed network connections, 451–452
mixed operating systems, 451
mixed references, 151
mobile computer users, 142, 456, 468
models, business. *See* business models
modem connection options, 451
modified accelerated cost recovery system
(MACRS), 137
money. *See also* accounting; data analysis;
financing; taxes
borrowing from business, 92
budgets, 11, 116–123
business plans, 39
cash flow, 121–123
employee benefits, 370–373
employee compensation, 367–370
managing, 11, 15
Money software, 102
monitoring employees. *See* employees
monthly loan payment amounts, 152, 161
motivation programs, employee, 384–386,
389–390
motivations, self employment, 10
moving e-mail files, 413–415
moving e-mail messages, 422, 429
MSDE (Microsoft SQL Server Desktop
Engine), 315
MSN search engine, 44
multicultural demographics, 14, 357–359
multiple target markets, 212
multiple-variable scenarios, 161–165
music copyrights, 202
myths, marketing, 215

N
.name, 194
names
domains, 193–195
exclusive rights, 199–205
National Labor Relations Act, 365
national licensing, 78
national origin discrimination, 365
nationally regulated transactions, 78
Neglected Accounts report, 290
negligent hiring, 355
neighborhood zoning regulations, 78, 85
.net, 194

.NET Framework, 313
net present value (NPV), 218, 294
net worth, 106, 108, 114
network security. *See also* networks
 adware, 475
 backups, 469–472
 data sharing, 460
 firewalls, 474
 options, 461–467
 overview, 460
 physical, 467–469
 spyware, 475
 viruses, 472–474
networking, increasing sales with, 213,
 239
networks. *See also* network security
 business locations, 444
 e-mail servers, 411
 equipment options, 451–456
 Ethernet, 449, 453
 Internet services, 445–447
 LANs, 447
 mixed types, 451
 mobile users, 456
 options, 444–449
 peripherals, 454
 printers, 454
 routers, 452
 servers, 455
 types, 449–451
 Wi-Fi, 450, 454
newsletters, 225–228, 264–269, 297
newspaper job ads, 352
next-stage growth, 301–303
noncurrent liabilities, 113–114
nonprofit organizations, 18, 224–225
nonresidential real estate, 129
nonverbal communication, 93
notebook computers, 142, 456, 468
notes payable, 113
notifications, e-mail messages, 425
nth mailing, 227
Nudge command, 253
number crunching. *See* data analysis
numbered accounts, 108

O
Occupational Safety and Health Act
 (OSHA), 365
Occupational Safety and Health
 Administration (OSHA), 78
Office Online
 accounting databases, 102
 budgets, 117

templates
 accounts receivable, 110
 balance sheets, 107
 business plans, 41–49
 cash flow tracking, 122
 employee management, 387
 fixed assets, 111
 training, 42, 146
older consumers, 7, 13
Older Worker Benefit Protection Act, 366
one-variable data tables, 159
online
 advertising, 232–236
 backup storage, 471
 compensation consultants, 368–369
 consumer watchdogs, 300
 marketing campaigns, 229–236
 startup resources, 18
 surveys, 26
 training options, 392–395
on-the-job learning, 390–395
Opening Day Balance Sheet template, 107
operating money statistics, 15
operating systems, 451
operational plans. *See* business plans
opinions, customer, 25
opportunities
 business, 23
 contact management, 324–327
 sales lead reports, 290
opt-in e-mail option, 230
opt-out e-mail option, 267
OR, 334
or criteria, 170
.org, 194
ornamental design patents, 204
OSHA (Occupational Safety and Health
 Act), 365
OSHA (Occupational Safety and Health
 Administration), 78
out of balance entries, 115
outlines. *See* business plans
Outlook. *See also* Business Contact
 Manager (BCM)
 appointment management, 438–440
 archiving, 432–434
 attachments, 417
 basic information, 308
 digital signatures, 420
 folders, 422
 help, 413
 junk e-mail, 229, 430–432
 macros, 416
 marketing signatures, 435–437

vs. Outlook Express, 409–411
rules, 424–430
security, 415–421
Outlook Express
attachments, 417
digital signatures, 421
flags, 424
folders, 422
marketing signatures, 437
vs. Outlook, 409–411
rules, 429
security, 415–421
outsourcing jobs, 395–399
overhead, 27, 86–88, 395–397
overseas employment laws, 363
overseas travel per diem rates, 140
overspending money, 11, 56
overtime pay, 364
owed money, 109
owner's equity, 108, 114
ownership structures
C Corporations, 32
DBAs, 31
general partnerships, 34
Limited Liability Corporations, 36
overview, 29–30
sole proprietorships, 30
Subchapter S Corporations, 33

P
P (copyright symbol), 203
P&AB (Privacy & American Business),
    299
Page Break Before option, 49
page formats, business plans, 41–49
page layouts, business plans, 36–41
paid search engine marketing, 233–235
paper direct mail campaigns, 225–228
paperwork recordkeeping, 89–90
partitions, computer, 461
partnerships, 34, 239, 303–304
past due money, 110
patents, 204–205
patronage reward programs, 294–296
patterns, data analysis, 165–172
pay in trade, 64
payables, account, 113, 121
payments. See also expenses
    accounting methods, 104
    cash flow, 121
    liabilities, 112–114
    loan calculations, 152–154, 161
pay-per-click (PPC), 233

payroll
    employee benefits, 370–373
    employee reward programs, 384–386
    employee wages, 363, 367–370
paying yourself, 91–92
paycheck preparation, 114
taxes, 364
Pension Benefit Guaranty Corporation
    (PBGC), 363
pension plans, 371
per diem allowances, 139
perceptions. See public perceptions
performance reviews, employee, 386–388
periodic expenses, 116
periods, accounting, 105
peripherals, network, 454
perks, owner and employee, 92, 369,
    384–386
permissions, e-mail recipient, 230
permits, 78
personal compensation, 91–92
personal credit cards, financing with, 59
personal days, employee, 372
personal job interviews, 354
personal property write offs, 128–130,
    140–142
personal use vs. business use, 141
personalization, customer, 292–294, 296
personnel. See employees
pet market, ideas targeting, 7
PHI (protected health information), 365
philanthropy, cause-related marketing,
    224–225
phones. See also contact management
    cold calling, 239–242
    network connections, 445–446
    surveys, 25
phonorecord copyrights, 203
physical computer security, 467–469
physical inventory, 110
pictures, company art, 190–192, 252
pie charts, 171
PivotCharts, 173–177
PivotTables, 173–177
placement, marketing, 212
placeholders, document, 252, 277
planning a business. See beginning a
    business; business plans; financing
Platform for Privacy Preferences (P3P)
    Project, scheduling with, 301
PMT function, 153
Pocket PCs, 439, 456
point of difference (POD), 188–190

polls, marketing with, 239
polygraph tests, 363
POP3 (Post Office Protocol 3), 408
POP3 e-mail accounts, 409
positioning ad elements, 253
positions, product. *See* branding
postcards, 25, 190, 225–228, 295
posters, 190
potential sales. *See* sales leads
power company Internet connectivity, 447
power supplies, uninterruptible, 469
PowerPoint
    access restrictions, 461
    business plan templates, 42
    help, 272
    overview, 272–281
    running without software, 281
    slide design, 281–283
    task pane, 273
PPC (pay-per-click), 233
PR agencies, 222–224
predicting
    breakeven points, 150
    future values, 179
    loan amounts, 152–154, 161
    present values, 178
preemployment screeners, 356
present values, calculating, 178
presentations
    PowerPoint
        help, 272
        overview, 272–281
        running without software, 281
    slide design, 281–283
    tips, 93–94, 269–272
presents, tax deductions, 138
President's Resource Organization (PRO),
    97
press releases, 190
prices, product or service, 27–29, 212
primary research, 44
principals, loan, 152–154, 161
print advertising, 248–254
printers, 454
printing BCM reports, 336
printing Publisher documents, 255
privacy, customers, 299–301
Privacy & American Business (P&AB),
    299
private finance companies, 70
private investors, 64–67
process patents, 204
products. *See also* branding; contact
    management; marketing

databases, 325–327, 339–341
    lifecycles, 29
    pricing, 27–29, 212
professional
    liability insurance, 83
    licenses, 79
    PR agents, 222–224
    tax consultants, 131–136
professional services template, 256
profiles
    Business Contact Manager, 310, 316–317,
        343
    customers, 11
    industry, 239
    market trends, 12–15
    psychographic, 25
profit-and-loss statements, 106
profits, 27–29
projections, business, 39
promoting employees, 351
promotion ideas. *See also* promotional
        strategies
    low-cost ideas
        cause-related, 224–225
        direct mail, 225–228
        e-mail, 229–232
        media hooks, 221
        online advertising, 232–236
        overview, 220
        PR agencies, 222–224
        word-of-mouth, 220
    Publisher
        e-mail newsletters, 264–269
        help, 248
        overview, 246–248
        print ads, 248–254
        printing, 255
        Web sites, 254–264
promotional strategies. *See also* branding
    benefits vs. features, 213–216
    crossing markets, 216–217
    flexibility, 213
    goals, 211
    multiple targets, 212
    myths, 215
    networking, 213
    options, 212–213
    overview, 210–212
    return on investment, 217–220
    sales leads, 236–242
    target marketing, 217
property insurance, 82
property deductions, 140–141
proprietary information, 24, 295, 304

protected health information (PHI), 365
protections. *See* exclusive rights; security
protocols, e-mail, 407–409
prototypes, 191
PST files, 413–415, 433
psychographics, 25
public perceptions
    credibility, 198
    intellectual property, 199–205
    logos, 190–192
    mission statements, 186–188
    overview, 184–186
    point of difference, 188–190
    Web presence, 192–197
public relation agents, 222–224
public relation strategies, 212
Public Relations Society of America
    (PRSA), 223
public speaking
    PowerPoint
        help, 272
        options, 272–281
        running without software, 281
        slide design, 281–283
        tips, 93–94, 269–272
public stock offerings, 55
Public Wi-Fi connections, 450, 452, 454,
    456
publications, Publisher
    e-mail newsletters, 264–269
    print ads, 248–254
    printing, 255
    Web sites, 254–264
publicity. *See also* branding; publicity ideas
    benefits vs. features, 213–216
    crossing markets, 216–217
    customer personalization, 292–294, 296
    flexibility, 213
    goals, 211
    job openings, advertising, 351–353
    multiple targets, 212
    myths, 215
    networking, 213
    overview, 210–212
    return on investment, 217–220
    sales leads, 236–242
    strategies, 212–213
    target marketing, 217
publicity ideas
    low-cost
        cause-related, 224–225
        direct mail, 225–228
        e-mail, 229–232
        media hooks, 221

online advertising, 232–236
        overview, 220
        PR agencies, 222–224
        word-of-mouth, 220
    Publisher
        e-mail newsletters, 264–269
        help, 248
        overview, 246–248
        print ads, 248–254
        printing, 255
        Web sites, 254–264
public-private partnerships, 66, 73
published copyrights, 202–203
Publisher
    brand visual development, 191
    e-mail newsletters, 264–269
    file format options, 265
    help, 248
    overview, 246–248
    print ads, 248–254
    printing, 255
    Web site creation, 254–264
publishing software options, 191
purchases. *See also* data analysis
    cars, 129, 137
    cash flow, 121
    computer equipment, 140–142
    depreciation, 104, 111
    gifts, 138
    receipts, 136
    tax impact, 128–130, 140–142
purchasing power, demographic, 12–14
PV function, 178

Q
qualified sales leads, 238
quality, product, 10
queries, marketing, 237
questions
    customer surveys, 25, 27
    job applicants, 353–357
    self assessments, 4
    what-if analysis
        data tables, 154–161
        Goal Seek command, 149–154
        overview, 148
        Scenario Manager, 161–165
quotas, minority, 358

R
R (federal registration symbol), 201
race discrimination, 362
radio marketing, 190

raising funds. *See* financing

rankings, search engine, 233

ratings, credit, 60

read-only access, 461

real estate tax deductions, 129

real-time training sessions, 392

receipts, 89–90, 136

receivables, account, 109–110, 121

receiving e-mail, rules, 424–430

recognition, brand. *See* branding

recognizing employees, 384–386

recordkeeping. *See also* computer security
   bookkeeping mistakes, 136–138
   equipment documentation, 140
   overview, 89–90
   personnel documents, 361

recruiting employees, 351–353

redirecting, Web site, 196, 476

references, checking applicant, 355–357

referrals, customer, 294, 301

regional targeting, 236

registering
   businesses, 78
   copyrights, 202–203
   domain names, 193–195
   patents, 204–205
   trademarks, 201

regulated transactions, 78

Rehabilitation Act of 1973, 366

reimbursable expenses, 137

relationships
   building, 17
   customer emotional connections, 188
   ending, 298
   loved ones, 11
   partnerships, 303–304

relatives
   borrowing from, 60–62
   hiring, 92, 360

religious discrimination, 362

reminders, e-mail, 423

reminding customers, 295

remote employee management, 395–397

removable backup media, 471

removing databases, 342

removing Excel filters, 167

renewing licenses, 79

renting prospect lists, 238

renting space, 86–88

repayment terms, loan, 71

repeat customers, 294–296

repeaters, 452

reports
   Business Contact Manager, 290,
      330–336
   credit, 60
   Excel Summary Manager, 165

research
   entrepreneurs, 18
   market, 24–29, 44
   target customers, 218

residential real estate, 129

residential zoning regulations, 78, 85

restoring databases, 342

results
   marketing, 219, 223, 229
   search engine, 233

retention rates, customer, 294

retired customers, 7, 13

retirement accounts, borrowing from, 58

retirement plans, 371

retraining employees, 366

return customers, 294–296

return on investment (ROI), 217–220, 227,
      395–397

revenue, 27–29, 39

reviews, employee performance, 386–388

rewarding customers, 294–296

rewarding employees, 384–386

Rich Site Summary (RSS), 236

right impressions, creating, 93–94

RJ-45 connections, 453

routers, 452

RTF messages, 418

S

S Corp, 33

Safe Recipients List, e-mail, 431

Safe Senders List, e-mail, 431

safety, ideas targeting, 8

safety standards, work place, 365

salaries
   discrimination, 363
   how much to pay, 367–370
   paychecks, cutting, 114
   paying yourself, 91

sales force, when to hire, 10

sales goals. *See* contact management; data
      analysis

sales leads
   cold calling, 239–242
   contact management, 324–327
   finding, 238–239
   overview, 236–238
   reports, 290

salvage values, 112
satellite Internet connectivity, 447
saving
  BCM reports, 335
  computer backups, 469–472
  e-mail files, 413–415
  e-mail messages, 432–434
  PowerPoint files, 265
  for retirement, 371
savings, financing with, 58
Savings Incentive Match Plan for
    Employees (SIMPLE), 371
SBA (Small Business Administration)
  ACE-Net, 66
  awards, 54
  contact information, 18
  licensing, 80
  loans, 71
  marketing strategies guide, 26
  SBDC program, 71, 189
  SBIC program, 66, 73
  SCORE, 68
  small business criteria, 5
  training courses, 393
SBA Express loans, 72
SBDC (Small Business Development
    Centers), 71, 189
SBIC (Small Business Investment
    Companies), 66, 73
SBIR (Small Business Innovation and
    Research) grants, 71
scanners, 255, 455
Scenario Manager, 161–165
scheduling
  appointment management, 438–440
  computer backups, 469–472
  employee reviews, 386–388
school age customers, 12
schools, recruiting at, 353
SCORE (Service Corps of Retired
    Executives), 68, 107
screening companies, preemployment,
    356
scripts
  e-mail messages, 418
  marketing with, 240
search engine marketing, 233–235
searching
  domain name registrations, 194
  federally registered marks, 201
  patent libraries, 205
second mortgages, 59
secondary research, 44
second-stage financing, 55

Section 179 elections, 128
Securities and Exchange Commission
    (SEC), 79
security
  computer
    adware, 475
    attachments, 417
    backups, 469–472
    data sharing, 460
    e-mail, 413–421
    firewalls, 474
    macros, 415–417
    options, 461–467
    overview, 460
    physical, 467–469
    spyware, 475
    viruses, 415–417, 472–474
  customer privacy, 299–301
  employee background checks, 355–357
  intellectual property, 199–205
seed capital, 55
segmenting customers, 25
self assessments, business owner, 4
self employment planning. See also
    business plans; financing
  advisory boards, 22–24, 95–97
  how to begin
    customers, identifying, 11, 15
    market trends, 6–9, 11–15
    mistakes, 9–11
    overview, 4
    resources, 18
    small business criteria, 5–6
    success stories, 15, 17
  image, appropriate, 93–94
  insurance, 81–85
  legal agreements, 88–89
  licenses, 78–80
  location renting or leasing, 86–88
  recordkeeping, 89–90
self employment statistics, 5–6, 8, 12, 15
self-directed healthcare plans, 373
self-financing. See financing
self-hosting Web sites, 195
selling prices, determining, 27–29
selling public shares, 55
senders blocked list, e-mail, 430
senior customers, 7, 13
sensitivity analysis, 154–161
servers
  e-mail, 407, 411–412
  Small Business Server, 455
Service Corps of Retired Executives
    (SCORE), 68, 107

service marks, 200
sex discrimination, 362
shapes, PowerPoint, 275
share partitions, 461
SharePoint Services, 396
sharing data, 460
shopping carts, 257
short-term loans, 113
Show All, 167
side-by-side alternatives, 63
signatures, 419–421, 435–438
SIMPLE (Savings Incentive Match Plan for
    Employees), 371
Simplified Employee Pension (SEP), 371
single-owner operations, 30
sites. See Web sites
situational interviews, 355
slides, PowerPoint presentations, 272–283
SM (service mark symbol), 201
Small Business Administration (SBA)
    ACE-Net, 66
    awards, 54
    contact information, 18
    licensing, 80
    loans, 71
    marketing strategies guide, 26
    SBDC program, 71, 189
    SBIC program, 66, 73
    SCORE, 68
    small business criteria, 5
    training courses, 393
Small Business Cash Flow Projection
    template, 122
Small Business Development Centers
    (SBDC), 71, 189
Small Business Innovation and Research
    (SBIR) grants, 71
Small Business Investment Companies
    (SBIC), 66, 73
Small Business Person of the Year awards,
    54
Small Business Server, 412, 455
small businesses. See also business plans;
    financing
    advisory boards, 22–24, 95–97
    how to begin
        customers, identifying, 11–15
        defining, 5–6
        market trends, 6–9, 11–15
        mistakes, 9–11
        overview, 4
        resources, 18
        success stories, 15–17
    image, appropriate, 93–94

insurance, 81–85
legal agreements, 88–89
licenses, 78–80
location renting or leasing, 86–88
paying yourself, 91–92
recordkeeping, 89–90
statistics, 5–6, 8, 12, 15
SMTP (Simple Messaging Transfer
    Protocol), 408
Snap command, 253
Social Security, 80, 114
software. See also Publisher
    accounting, 102
    customer contact database, 290
    defined, 202
    e-mail programs, 409–411
    e-mail servers, 411
    employee reviews, 388
    PowerPoint, 272–283
    publishing, 191
    remote employees, 396
sole proprietors, 30, 139
Sort command, 166
sorting data, 166
sorting e-mail messages, 422
sound, 200, 202
space, commercial, 86–88
spam, 229, 430–432
special effects, PowerPoint, 283
special event industries, ideas targeting, 9
specials, marketing, 221
speeches
    PowerPoint
        help, 272
        overview, 272–281
        running without software, 281
        slide design, 281–283
    tips, 93–94, 269–272
spending. See expenses; finances
spreadsheets. See also data analysis
    accounting, 102
    aging reports, 110
    balance sheets, 107
    budgets, 117
    conditional formatting, 122
    contact management, 337, 339
spyware, 475
SQL Server Desktop Engine (MSDE), 315
staff. See employees; hiring
staffing agencies, 398
standard mileage deductions, 137
Start-Up Expenses template, 107
start-ups. See small businesses
state business licenses, 78–80

state employment laws, 361
state government loans, 70–72
state lines, operating across, 78
state taxes. *See* taxes
statements
  financial, 106–108
  mission, 37, 93, 186–188, 191, 193
  recordkeeping, 89–90
statistics
  angel financing, 65
  competition, 8
  credit card financing, 59
  entrepreneurs, 6
  government, 24
  money management, 15
  salary comparisons, 368
  small businesses nationally, 5–6, 12, 15
  women customers, 12
  work force demographics, 357
status, client financial, 318
stock offerings, 55
straight-line depreciation, 112, 137
strategic alliances, 303–304
strategic plans
  advisory boards, 22–24
  expansion, 302
  formats, 41–49
  guidelines, 36–41
  layouts, 36–41
  loan applications, 68
  market research, 24–29
  overview, 22
  ownership structure, 29–36
  revising later, 56
  templates, 41–49
strengths, business, 23
structure. *See* ownership structures
styles. *See also* Publisher
  business plans, 40
  direct mail marketing, 227
  e-mail marketing, 231
  PowerPoint presentations, 273–283
  publishing software, 191
  Word documents, 45–47
Subchapter S Corporations, 33
successes, marketing, 219, 223, 229
summary reports
  Excel Scenario Manager, 165
  executive, business plans, 37
supervising employees. *See* employees
supplies, tax mistakes, 136
surveys, 24–25, 27, 239, 368, 388
SWOT analysis, 23

symbols, trademarking, 200
synchronizing handheld devices, 439
synchronous training sessions, 392

T
table of contents, business plan, 37, 48
tables, 154–161, 173–177
tactical information, 38
tag lines, 188–189
talent, recruiting, 351–353
tangible assets, 55, 70
tape backups, 471
target customers, 11–15, 25
target marketing, 212, 217
tax election, 33
tax years, 105
tax-deferred savings plans, 371
taxes
  accounting methods, 105
  business types, 31, 33–35
  EINs, 80
  expenses
    computer equipment, 140–142
    meals, 138–140
    overview, 128–130
    property, 140
    travel, 138–140
  expert information, 131–136
  extensions, 135
  licensing and, 79
  managing yourself, 132–134
  mistakes, 136–138
  overview, 128
  payroll, 114, 364
  recordkeeping, 89
  resources, 128, 138
  unemployment, 115
taxpayer IDs, 80
technical assistance, 71
technical patents, 204
technology, ideas targeting, 8
teen customers, 12
telecommuting, 395–397
telephones. *See also* contact management
  cold calling, 239–242
  connections, 445–446
  surveys, 25
television cable modems, 446
television marketing, 190
temp agencies, 393
templates
  accounts receivable, 110
  balance sheets, 107

templates, *continued*
  bank loan requests, 69
  brand visual development, 191
  business plans, 41–49
  cash flow tracking, 122
  e-mail newsletters, 264–269
  e-mail rules, 428
  employee management, 387
  fixed assets, 111
  PowerPoint presentations, 272–281
  print ads, 248–254
  Web sites, 254–264
temporary workers, 64, 395–399
terminating employees, 374–376
testimonials, customer, 301
testing backup plans, 472
thanking customers, 295
thanking employees, 383–386
third-party background checks, 356
third-stage financing, 55
threats, business, 23
time
  business plan creation, 36
  e-mail archiving, 432
  employee time off benefits, 372, 385
  marketing timetables, 296–298
timing marketing communication,
    296–298
TM (trademark symbol), 201
Toastmasters, 94
TOC (table of contents), business plans,
    37, 48
tone, business plans, 40
Top 10 Excel option, 167
top end market, ideas targeting, 7
top-level domains, 194
topology, network, 448
trade licenses, 79
trade magazine job ads, 352
trade names
  credibility, 198
  intellectual property, 199–205
  logos, 190–192
  mission statements, 186–188
  overview, 184–186
  point of difference, 188–190
  policies, 192
  Web presence, 192–197
trademarks, 200
trailing indicators, 224
training
  business ideas targeting, 8

  e-mail management, 412
  employees, 392–395
  Excel, 146
  Office Online, 42
  SBDC, 71
  SCORE, 68
Transunion, 60
travel expenses, 138–140
travel mobile computing, 456
trends, market
  analysis, 106, 165–172
  customers, identifying, 11–15
  market research, 24–29
trial balances, 115
trip expense deductions, 138–140
trip mobile computing, 456
Trojans, protecting against, 472
trust, customer, 299–301
TRUSTe, 300
trusted advisors. *See* advisory boards;
    consultants
  TV cable modems, 446
TV marketing, 190
two-variable data tables, 159
types, business, 6–9, 11–15

U
umbrella insurance, 83
unauthorized access. *See* security
underestimating finances, 56
underpricing products and services, 27
unemployment taxes, 115
unenrolled tax preparers, 131
unexpected costs, 56–58
Uniformed Services Employment and
    Reemployment Rights Act of 1994,
    366
uninterruptible power supply (UPS), 469
unions, 365
unique selling proposition (USP),
    188–190
university online training, 393
university student recruiting, 353
university surveys, 24
unpublished copyrights, 202–203
untapped markets, 11–15
upscale market, ideas targeting, 7
URLs. *See* Web sites
U.S. Chamber of Commerce Small
    Business Center, 71
U.S. Copyright Office, 200, 203
U.S. government census, 24

U.S. Patent & Trademark Office (USPTO),
    200, 201
U.S. Social Security, 114
usage logs, equipment, 141
USB devices, 454
utility patents, 204

V
value
    customer appreciation, 295
    money over time, 218
    product or service, defining, 27
variable expenses, 116
vCards, 436
vegetation patents, 204
vehicle insurance, 83
vehicle tax deductions, 129, 137
venture capital, 73
VeriSign, 420
veteran employment laws, 366
Vietnam-Era Veterans' Readjustment
    Assistance Act, 366
VIP treatment, customer, 296
virus protection, 415–417, 472–474
visual aids, presentations, 272–283
visual appearance. *See* company identity
volunteer benefits, 372

W
wages
    discrimination, 363
    how much to pay, 367–370
    paychecks, cutting, 114
    paying yourself, 91–92
WARN (Worker Adjustment and
    Retraining Notification Act), 366
weaknesses, business, 23
wealthy investors, 64–67
Web hosting, 407
Web market research, 26
Web servers, 455
Web sites. *See also* computer security
    antivirus programs, 473
    business presence on, 192–197
    catalog pages, 256
    company image, 190
    consumer watchdogs, 300
    copyrights, 202
    creating, 254–263
    domain name registrars, 195

    forms, 260
    hosting companies, 197
    keywords, 235
    mobile users accessing, 456
    professional services pages, 256
    Public Relations Society of America, 223
    remote employees, 395–397
    salary research, 368
    self-directed healthcare, 373
    startup resources, 18
    U.S. Copyright Office, 200
    U.S. Patent & Trademark Office,
        200–201
Web-based backup storage, 471
Web-based employee recruiting, 352
Web-based industries, ideas targeting, 8
Web-based marketing campaigns,
    229–236
Web-based training options, 392–395
weight loss industry, ideas targeting, 8
what-if analysis
    data tables, 154–161
    Goal Seek command, 149–154
    overview, 148
    Scenario Manager, 161–165
Widow/Orphan option, 49
Wi-Fi connections, 450, 452, 454, 456
Windows Firewall, 474
Windows SharePoint Services, 396
Windows Small Business Server, 412
WinZip, 418
wired access points, 448
wired networking, 444, 449, 452–453
wireless connections, 445, 447, 454
wireless routers, 453
wireless wide area networks (WWANs),
    447
withholding taxes, 114, 364
woman-owned business, 6
women customers, 12
Word
    business plan templates, 41-49
    employee management templates, 387
    file security options, 462
word of mouth, 220, 351
word trademarking, 200
Wordtracker, 234
work copyrights, 203
work for hire copyrights, 203
work force. *See* employees; hiring
workbooks. *See* Excel

Worker
Adjustment
and
Retraining
Notification
Act

Index

Worker Adjustment and Retraining
   Notification Act (WARN), 366
worker compensation taxes, 115
workers. *See* employees; hiring
working from home, 395–397
worksheets. *See* Excel
workstation security. *See* computer
   security
worms, protecting against, 472
writing business plans. *See* business plans

writing mission statements. *See* mission
   statements
writing off expenses, 128–130, 140–142

Y
years, tax, 105
youth customers, 12

Z
zoning regulations, 78, 85

About the Authors

Joanna L. Krotz is a multimedia journalist and an experienced editorial manager. In 1998, she founded Muse2Muse Productions, a custom publishing company that creates magazines, newsletters, and digital communications for consumer and business-to-business imprints. As president and editorial director of Muse2Muse, Krotz launched MoneyMinded.com, a Web site dedicated to women's money management; *Lightspeed*, a quarterly publication about life in the networked world; *Gateway*, a digital lifestyle magazine; *Sirius,* an annual for Sirius Satellite Radio; and *Citibank PB*, a personal finances magazine for affluent families. Previously, she has been Executive editor at Hearst New Media, deputy editor at Time Inc.'s small business magazine *Your Company*, senior editor at *Money* magazine, features editor at Hearst Corp., the founding articles editor at *Metropolitan Home*, and author of *Renovation Style*, published by Random House. Her work has appeared in such publications as *Better Homes & Gardens, Food & Wine, New York, The New York Times, Playboy, Reader's Digest,* and *Town & Country.* Krotz is currently the weekly online marketing intelligence columnist for the Microsoft Small Business Center. Often featured at industry events and in national media, Krotz is a lecturer at New York University Center for Publishing and a member of the Online News Association, the Journalism and Women's Symposium, and the National Association of Women Business Owners.

John Pierce is currently a technical writer at Microsoft Corporation, and for nine years was an editor at Microsoft Press. He cowrote *Microsoft Office Access 2003 Inside Track* (Microsoft Press, 2004) and has edited numerous books about Microsoft Office applications. He is also a partner in a small real estate management business based in Mt. Shasta, California.

Ben Ryan is a program manager at Microsoft. He has been, at various times, a bookstore manager and buyer; a publisher's sales representative and field sales manager; a copy editor; and an acquisitions editor. He has run a number of small businesses, most of which were at least moderately successful. Some of his authors will be pleased to know that he now has firsthand experience with their tasks—others will be astounded to learn that he occasionally writes something other than e-mails asking when to expect the next chapter or proposal. He lives in the woods in Kitsap County, Washington, with an assortment of wildlife that includes his daughter and son.

What do you think of this book?
We want to hear from you!

Do you have a few minutes to participate in a brief online survey? Microsoft is interested in hearing your feedback about this publication so that we can continually improve our books and learning resources for you.

To participate in our survey, please visit:
www.microsoft.com/learning/booksurvey

And enter this book's ISBN, 0-7356-2054-7. As a thank-you to survey participants in the United States and Canada, each month we'll randomly select five respondents to win one of five $100 gift certificates from a leading online merchant.* At the conclusion of the survey, you can enter the drawing by providing your e-mail address, which will be used for prize notification *only*.

Thanks in advance for your input. Your opinion counts!

Sincerely,

Microsoft® Learning

Learn More. Go Further.

To see special offers on Microsoft Learning products for developers, IT professionals, and home and office users, visit: *www.microsoft.com/learning/booksurvey*